*Between Worlds*

JEWISH CULTURE AND CONTEXTS

Published in association with the Center for Advanced Judaic Studies of the University of Pennsylvania

David B. Ruderman, Series Editor



A complete list of books in the series is available from the publisher.

# *Between Worlds*

## Dybbuks, Exorcists, and Early Modern Judaism

J. H. Chajes

PENN

University of Pennsylvania Press
Philadelphia

*Publication of this volume was assisted by a grant from the Koret Jewish Studies Publication Program.*



*10 9 8 7 6 5 4 3 2 1*

*Published by*
*University of Pennsylvania Press*
*Philadelphia, Pennsylvania 19104-4011*

*Library of Congress Cataloging-in-Publication Data*
*Chajes, J.H.*
*Between worlds : dybbuks, exorcists, and early modern Judaism / J.H. Chajes.*
*p. cm. — (Jewish culture and contexts)*
*Includes bibliographical references and index.*
*ISBN 0-8122-3724-2 (cloth : alk. paper)*
*1. Dybbuk. 2. Spirit possession. 3. Exorcism. 4. Mysticism—Judaism. 5. Spiritual life—Judaism. 6. Future life—Judaism. I. Title. II. Series.*

*BM729.D92C53 2003*
*296.3'16—dc21*

*2003044763*

To my mother and mother-in-law, Annette Chajes and Karin Fenz, and in memory of my father and father-in-law, Julius Chajes *z"l* and Professor Emanuel Fenz

# *Contents*

*Reb Nachman laughed and said, "If scholars let one dead man step foot into their studies, all their work would be null and void!"*

—*Siḥot ha-Ran*, §226

# *Introduction*

*What therefore is the locus that authorizes me, today, to suppose that I can speak the other better than all of them? Lodged like them in knowledge that attempts to understand, with respect to the possessed I am reiterating the position—now with a few variants which must be evaluated—that formerly belonged to the demonologist or the doctor.*
*—Michel de Certeau*[1]

In the early 1540s, a Jewish boy in the Galilean—and, for nearly a generation, Ottoman—village of Safed, was possessed by the soul of a sinner, a *dybbuk*.[2] Furious that the boy's father had killed the dog in which he had formerly been lodged, the soul sought vengeance by killing the man's son. The eminent sage who was called upon to exorcise the spirit, having forced it to speak with threats of excommunication, discovered that there was little he could do but rescue the boy by removing the intruder and banishing him to the wilderness. This he accomplished by intoning a classic Hebrew liturgical formula, though with a magical twist: the rabbi recited the words both forward and backward. More cases were to follow. Safed would again be the locus of possession episodes in the early 1570s, as would, to a less dramatic extent, cities in both Christian and Muslim worlds: Ferrara, Ancona, Pesaro, Venice, Damascus, Prague, Cairo, Tituán, and Turin.

The possessed Jews of the sixteenth and seventeenth centuries were not alone. Convulsing, tearing off their veils, bleating like sheep, and climbing trees like cats, the nuns of Wertet, in the country of Hoorn, Brabant, were possessed in large numbers in 1550. So too the nuns of Xante, Spain, in 1560. Communities of nuns were overwhelmed by devils in Milan in 1590, in Aix-en-Provence in 1611, in Lille in 1613, in Madrid in 1628, and, famously, in

Loudun in 1634. Hundreds of accounts report the possession of individuals beyond these monastic communities as well.

The dramas of spirit possession episodes, macabre and in many cases sexually charged, have long been of interest to historians and lay readers. The fascination of the latter hardly requires explanation; by the sixteenth century, authors of the surviving accounts had realized that their tales would tantalize the reading public. Sharing this affection for colorful narratives, historians have made frequent use of possession accounts, recognizing the extent to which they communicate significant features of early modern culture. Exorcism rituals have also been subjected to a fascinating array of exegetical strategies and probed for their suggestive encryption of patterns of *mentalité* and theological suppositions. Whether used as indicators of shifts in the political and ecclesiastical realm or as signs of sexual and religious anxiety among the folk, materials related to the proliferation of spirit possession have been analyzed in various innovative ways by the conspicuously creative historians of early modern Europe.

Any attempt to treat spirit possession historically is challenged by the fact that it is a near-universal phenomenon of human culture.[3] One need only take a cursory glance at the anthropological literature on the subject: a recent review article by Janice Boddy cites no less than 221 studies on spirit possession amid peoples on every continent.[4] Yet this universalism must not obscure the distinctive place of spirit possession in different cultural settings. Its valence may vary diachronically, and at times it may occupy a more central or peripheral location in a given socioreligious group. A shift in the valuation or incidence of spirit possession may also be an indicator of broader cultural developments. And even when no such shift is evident, an analysis of the meaning and function of spirit possession may reveal deep structures of the religious culture under examination.

This study of spirit possession in early modern Jewish culture began with my realization that in the mid-sixteenth century, in the very period often referred to as "the golden age of the demoniac,"[5] accounts of spirit possession among Jews suddenly begin to appear—this following a millennium during which no such sources were produced or from which none are extant. Although accounts of possession and exorcism are to be found in ancient rabbinic literature—and, of course, figure prominently in the Gospels—they are exceedingly rare in medieval Jewish literature.[6] Might the apparent flourishing of this phenomenon be no more than the reflection of a new interest in the literary treatment of possession among Jews?[7] This reasonable hypothesis can be tested, albeit impressionistically, by an inspection of the Jewish documentation for signs of shock at a sudden proliferation in spirit possession, as has been found among Christians in this period.[8]

Early Jewish possession accounts do, in fact, indicate in a variety of ways that a new phenomenon was confronting the rabbinic exorcists of the mid-sixteenth century. The deaths of the early victims, as well as the obvious confusion and lack of experience that Jewish exorcists showed in early accounts, is telling. So, too, is R. Gedalia ibn Yaḥia's expression of wonder and bewilderment in his introduction to the 1575 Ferrara case—"The truth is, it [spirit possession by a disembodied soul] would seem to appear to be one of the wonders of our time and exceedingly strange."[9] Similar remarks were made by R. Eliezer Ashkenazi (1513–86) in his work of 1583, *Ma'asei ha-Shem* (Deeds of the Lord).[10] Ashkenazi wrote that he had heard "in this, our own time" of such cases of possession and that only "this year, in 5340 (1579–80)" had he become familiar with the phenomenon upon receiving a broadsheet from Safed, which may have reached him via Venice, describing such a case. Ashkenazi's testimony seems to signal both the appearance of a new phenomenon in Jewish culture as well as an effort to publicize it. The significance of such a campaign emanating from Safed before 1579 cannot be underestimated, because the circulation of possession accounts may have been a significant factor in the diffusion of the phenomenon.[11]

Although no narrative reports of spirit possession among Jews have been discovered from before the 1540s,[12] medieval manuscripts do preserve Jewish exorcism techniques from earlier centuries. This literary discrepancy is tantalizing and, although possibly deceptive, would seem to support the thesis that the sudden appearance of possession narratives in the sixteenth and, particularly, seventeenth centuries stemmed from a shift in literary conventions—for whatever reasons—rather than from the appearance of the phenomenon ex nihilo. We may imagine a situation in which exorcisms were carried out routinely for centuries, leaving traces only in the magical manuscripts that preserved and transmitted techniques over generations, the cases themselves left unrecorded. With a new interest in documenting cases of spirit possession emerging among sixteenth-century hagiographers, moralists, and other sundry rabbinic writers, the narrative possibilities of this genre are fully explored and exploited.

Such a scenario is not without medieval Christian parallels, though the order of literary progression is almost exactly the reverse. Although possession figured prominently in medieval saints' vitae, by the fifteenth century demonologists had taken over the field. One looking exclusively at the vitae would thus wrongly assume that exorcism died out in the late Middle Ages.[13]

Although this imagined scenario has much to recommend it, we must also bear in mind that the presence of a magical technique in manuscript says little about contemporary practice. Magical manuscripts are notoriously conservative and preserve material that may long since have been out of use and even unintelligible to adepts. This in addition to the fact that as prescriptive rather than descriptive texts, they must not be assumed to reflect the historical realia of their period.

And something *was* new. The construction of spirit possession in Jewish culture had changed radically since antiquity. *Gilgul*, or reincarnation, had become a central concern of Jewish thinkers by the sixteenth century, and deeply penetrated the communal psyche. In keeping with this obsession with transmigration, Jews reconceptualized the phenomenon of spirit possession.[14] The possessor was no longer a demon (which earlier techniques and ancient accounts suggest it had been for Jews and which it largely remained for Christians and Muslims), but a ghost, the soul of a deceased human being. Possession had become a subspecies of transmigration. The expressions of wonderment at the novelty of the noted phenomenon may well constitute responses to this etiologic development, for as we shall see, the ramifications of identifying the possessor as a disembodied soul were significant.

As an avid reader of the historiography of the early modern European witch-hunt, I could not help but wonder what all of this had to do with the golden age of the demoniac in Christian Europe. What sort of relationship could be reconstructed between Jewish and Christian cultures on this demonic ground? Did the cognate Jewish phenomena support or challenge the regnant interpretations of European historiography?[15]

European historians have long debated the reasons for the proliferation of witchcraft accusations and cases of spirit possession from the mid-sixteenth to the mid-seventeenth centuries.[16] Although the two phenomena ought not to be conflated, they were not unrelated.[17] Witch trials were typically initiated or exacerbated by accusations of the possessed, and demoniacs customarily ran the risk of being regarded as culpable witches. Indeed, major witch-hunts were triggered and perpetuated by demoniacs who blamed witches in their midst for their affliction.[18] Jews entertained such a possibility, though the early modern accounts do not preserve a case in which such an accusation was actually leveled.[19]

Belief in witches and witchcraft was widespread, however, and Jews often shared the magical beliefs of their Gentile neighbors.[20] German-Jewish pietists from the High Middle Ages had a pronounced fear of witches, at least some of whom were apparently Jewish.[21] The most heinous accusation leveled against these women was that they ate children and, even in death, continued to devour the living.[22] Pietistic sources relate that at the moment of their vigilante-style executions, such cannibalistic witches might be offered the opportunity for atonement in exchange for knowledge of techniques that would render them harmless in the grave. One "witch" suggested driving a stake through their mouths, clear through to the ground beneath, whereas another suggested filling the mouths of her dead cohorts with gravel.[23] Notwithstanding these beliefs and the apparent willingness to pass on these distasteful suggestions, if not implement them, there could be no witch-hunt within Jewish society. Jews simply lacked the judicial autonomy necessary to carry one out.[24]

Subtler relations between witchcraft and possession have been traced by historians who have correlated the development of the concept of the malevolent witch in the late Middle Ages with the gradual retreat from notions of positively valued embodied female spirituality attested to in many medieval vitae. This retreat left most embodied spirituality—especially where females were concerned—at best suspect and at worst demonic.[25] Thus rather than be lauded as prophets and healers, many women were accused of witchcraft or diagnosed as victims of possession. Although contemporaries thought it only natural that women be in league with the devil, historians and anthropologists offer various competing theories to account for the disproportionate number of women possessed by the spirits, that is, participating in the cultural construct of spirit possession.[26] The oft-cited 2:1 ratio of women victims of possession has been said to reflect a protofeminist attempt to take advantage of the license possession offered women to preach in public.[27] Young women have been seen as struggling with sexual anxieties expressed through the idiom of possession, often construed as a rapelike penetration of their bodies by the lascivious spirit.[28] Devout women, under the pressures of extreme religious demands and wrenching sectarian conflicts, are understood as having expressed their religious disturbance somatically.[29] At the heart of this historiographical debate is the question of the volition of the possessed. To what extent could victims use the phenomenon to advance their interests?[30]

Although the shocking rise of witch-hunting in early modern Europe has been well documented, there is less evidence to demonstrate a similarly exponential rise in contemporary cases of spirit possession. Unlike witchcraft, being possessed was not a criminal offense, so it was not subject to serialized documentation.[31] The absence of legal sources makes it impossible to chart the incidence of possession statistically—as has been done with so much success with the witch trials. Nevertheless, a marked increase in the incidence of possession beginning in the mid-sixteenth century is evident. According to H. C. Erik Midelfort, spirit possession, part and parcel of the "growing demonization of the world" in the sixteenth century, "became epidemic . . . only after about 1560."[32] D. P. Walker also claimed that there was a rise in the incidence of possession in this period. In addition to expressions in the sources attesting to the novelty of these events, exorcisms became more common as they came to be used, according to Walker, first as a form of religious propaganda—most commonly by Catholics against Protestants—and later as an intrinsic element of witch-hunts.[33] Indeed, Walker stressed that exorcism became one of the most powerful weapons in the arsenal of the early modern Catholic Church for demonstrating in a public, theatrical, and tangible manner that its doctrines and sacraments were true and that its priests were empowered by God to work miracles.[34] Of course, it may be an exaggeration to refer to a *proliferation* of spirit possession in the early modern period, though such a description is not lacking in the historiography. Perhaps Stuart Clark put it best in remarking that "the known examples suggest that [spirit possession] was a general phenomenon that intensified as demonism and witchcraft themselves grew to be major preoccupations."[35]

What influence could this new Christian preoccupation with demonism and witchcraft have had upon the reemergence of spirit possession in early modern Jewish culture? The temporal correspondence between "the demonization of the world" that historians have discerned in sixteenth-century Europe, with its attendant witch-hunts and possession epidemics, and the sudden reappearance of Jewish possession accounts is suggestive. So, too, are the many similarities between the Jewish and Christian idioms of spirit possession, from the symptomatic behaviors of the possessed to the rituals of exorcism designed to expel the spirits.

But we should not be too quick to jump to the conclusion that before us is a case of clear Christian influence on an occult facet of Jewish culture. Safed, the clear epicenter of the Jewish reemergence, was far from the centers of the European phenomena. Yet the cultural location of Safed was anything but simple. Safed's population had been in a state of flux, its communal composition changing rapidly in the wake of the Ottoman conquest of 1517. Jews were arriving in significant numbers from around the world, and the economic, political, and religious advantages of Safed were manifold. It became the proverbial melting pot, with a multicultural population estimated by scholars to have reached up to ten thousand Jews, including Spanish and

Portuguese exiles, Maghrebi and Ashkenazi immigrants, and a good number of the indigenous Mustaribs. By the mid-sixteenth century, Iberian Jews had become the large majority.[36]

Might Spain have served as the common denominator between the proliferation of possession in European Christendom and the Jewish Galilee? We know that the Spain left behind by the exiles was a hotbed of paranormal phenomena, from ecstatic forms of prophecy to esoteric techniques of binding the souls of the dead to the souls of grave-prostrating mystics. New Christians, Old Christians, and Jews could be found among the prophets and Illuminati of the period.[37] In mid-sixteenth-century Safed, the Sefardic rabbis Moses Cordovero,[38] Elazar Azikri,[39] and Judah Ḥallewa[40] recalled Iberian precedents for what was going on around them. Indeed, Yosef Kaplan has noted that "the deeper one delves into the literary sources of the Spanish-Portuguese Jewish Diaspora, the stronger one's impression becomes that many of the keys for the understanding of their views and concepts are found in the Iberian Peninsula."[41] A European background of the reemergence is also suggested by the Italian Jewish cases of the last quarter of the sixteenth century.

Nevertheless, Jews and Christians were not the only ones to suffer from spirit possession in this period, and in Safed no less than in Damascus and Cairo, they could witness Muslims falling victim to incursions by the spirits they called *jinn*.[42] Muslims too employed complex magical rituals to expel them, and as we shall see, Jewish exorcists were ready to turn to sheikhs for their diagnostic expertise and powerful magic when the need arose. Our assessment of cultural influences will therefore have to be awake to various possibilities, including the recognition of this phenomenon as a particularly vivid case of cultural hybridity borne of the confluence of Christian, Islamic, and ancient Jewish traditions. The multivocal complexity of this cultural situation and the dearth of sufficient secondary literature, particularly on the early modern Islamic context, will inevitably render my own attempts at comparative analysis provisional and speculative.

By pointing out the significance of the European background, I do not intend to argue for Christian influence on the construction of the Jewish idiom. The influence model is largely predicated upon a view of Jewish culture as foreign to its local environment. From this perspective, any parallels are a result of influence of the majority community upon the minority. My own view is more in keeping with the cosmopolitan conception of Jewish culture advocated by the late Professor Shlomo Pines and exemplified in any number of recent studies of Jewish acculturation in medieval and early modern

Europe.[43] Seeing Jews as integral to their local environment allows us to see them as full participants in broad cultural movements and *mentalités* that were no more owned by Christians than by Jews. The preoccupation with death, the ecstatic-prophetic modes of religiosity, and the attitudes toward the body, language, and illness were all undercurrents of a culture shared by all, the deep structures of the reality map that contemporaries held. The differences that existed might cast certain features of the map into relief, drop others into obscurity, magnify, or contour, but no single group owned the map. Of course, a good deal of the fascination of the early modern period derives from its constituting a transitional era from one "classical" reality map to another, distinctly modern one. The cultural historian of early modern Jewish culture thus has the task of elucidating the particular hues of the lenses through which Jews gazed upon the common map as it underwent profound transformation.

The cosmology of the early modern period drew the boundaries between the natural and the supernatural very differently from the way its successors would. Although our postmodern reality map is perhaps more forgiving and less triumphalist in its celebration of reason's vanquishing of superstition, it remains difficult to assess phenomena long since classified as supernatural without projecting the anachronistic boundaries of modernity's map upon our subjects.[44] Moreover, modern professional history is predicated upon the removal of God—or any other supernatural force or forces—as a causal factor. What we are left with, then, is a situation in which phenomena regarded in their time as natural are recast as supernatural; the supernatural is then dismissed or displaced in favor of a "scientific" explanation acceptable in the modern context. Needless to say, analytic reductionism, anachronism, and distortion are almost inevitable. In our case, what sorts of scientific-historical explanations of spirit possession are possible? Diane Purkiss summed up the situation neatly in her recent *The Witch in History*, noting, "History can say nothing about angels or demons or witches until they are psychoanalytic symptoms, chemicals, illnesses, political tools, or social categories."[45] Here is her sobering challenge to one who would attempt to do professional history while avoiding reductionism:

> The supernatural must be transformed into something else so that it can be discussed. For instance, the following ways to displace possession are on offer: the possessed are physically ill; they are mentally ill, in a thousand ways; they are poisoned; they are in an altered state induced by drugs; they are acting; they are taking a culturally sanctioned opportunity to express "bad" feelings about the family, the church

and sex; they are reducible to a textual sign. All these possibilities, even the last, were available to an educated early modern observer of the contorted and wildly writhing body of a victim of possession. However, most early modern observers had one more possibility in mind: that the person in question was inhabited by a demon, a demon who had moved into the body as one might invade a country or occupy a house, a demon automatically hostile to his host because at war with his whole race, a demon who had usurped the place of the soul of his victim.[46]

Purkiss, while recognizing the inherent impossibility of producing an academically acceptable history of the supernatural that is not, to use Michel de Certeau's phrase, "exiled from its subject matter,"[47] can offer no compelling alternative to the historian who wishes to overcome this conundrum.[48] From the standpoint of academia, no evidence of spirit possession could ever be adduced, because spirit possession could never have occurred.[49] At the same time, historians and anthropologists know only too well how ubiquitous spirit possession has been in human culture from time immemorial. And although not without methodological crises of its own, anthropological theory holds the most promise for the historian seeking to avoid reductionist analysis. Through descriptive analysis of ideas and behaviors, we aim to understand the meaning of the possession idiom to the possessed and their exorcists within their broader cultural environment. By keeping our conceptual conversions to a minimum, our goal is to avoid reductionist and anachronistic readings of unfamiliar worlds.[50]

The chapters that follow thus constitute something of a historical anthropology of spirit possession cases from the late sixteenth and early seventeenth centuries. Rather than be doctrinaire, however, my approach has been shaped by the literature at my disposal: mystical, magical, ethical, and legal. I have attempted to avail myself of a wide variety of sources and approaches, and have striven to provide thick description as well as sustained comparative-historical analysis. To assess the meaning of spirit possession in early modern Jewish culture, it was necessary to understand its relation to a constellation of related issues: mystical theory, magical practice, and afterlife beliefs, as well as notions of gender, illness, and the body. These are a few of the subjects that come in and out of focus throughout the following chapters.

In Chapter 1, I provide a genealogy of spirit possession, tracing the mystical theories and magical practices that provided the phenomenon with coherence in traditional Jewish society. A close reading of the Lurianic-era narratives of spirit possession follows in Chapter 2, in which I focus upon the role of the phenomenon in the peculiar spiritual economy of sixteenth-century Safed. Chapter 3 surveys the rituals employed by Jews to treat the possessed, from the classical techniques of antiquity preserved in medieval magical manuscripts, to the novel technique advocated by the preeminent Jewish mystic of the sixteenth century, R. Isaac Luria (1534–72).[51] I then examine the afterlife of Luria's exorcistic innovations and show how ancient magical procedures proved to be too hardy—or effective—to supplant with Luria's meditations. In this context, I also consider exorcism as a magical healing technique and show how licit exorcism exemplified the latitude provided by Jewish religious authorities to employ counter-magical magical techniques, even when the practices involved were clearly demonic or the practitioners gentile. Chapter 4 constitutes my exploration of gender and spirit possession among early modern Jews. Although scholars have noted the preponderance of female victims of *dybbukim* (pl.), none have analyzed cases of positively valued or sacred spirit possession among Jewish women, nor considered the whole problem of the "discernment of spirits"—that is, deciding whether the spirit was divine or demonic.[52] At the heart of this chapter is the account of a possessed girl who, after being exorcised, mastered her spirits and functioned as an oracle in her community. This young woman seems to have been a protégée of the leader of a circle of clairvoyant, visionary women active in late sixteenth- and early seventeenth-century centers of Safed, Jerusalem, and Damascus. A challenge to the regnant notion that women were absent from the Jewish mystical tradition, Chapter 4 represents the first examination of this circle of Jewish women mystical adepts. Having analyzed the extant sixteenth- and early seventeenth-century accounts of spirit possession, I devote Chapter 5 to a case study in their reception history: an analysis of the use of possession narratives in a work that sought to combat the metaphysical heresies that shook Amsterdam Jewry in the mid-seventeenth century. Finally, the major early modern Hebrew accounts of *dybbuk* possession are provided in my translation in the Appendix.

## *Chapter 1*

# *The Emergence of* Dybbuk *Possession*

How did sixteenth-century Jews make sense of spirit possession? To what affliction did they bear witness when someone in their midst began displaying the characteristic signs of the possessed? What sort of spirit was doing the possessing? Why and how did the possession take place? How distinctive was the Jewish construction of spirit possession in this period? These are the central questions we shall take up in this chapter.

Here it would be apposite to say something regarding the identity of ghosts of the evil dead and demonic spirits in Jewish sources. This view could be found in Greco-Roman antiquity, whether in Plato's general claim that the demons were souls of the dead or in the more specific belief that Josephus articulated, according to which they were ghosts of the wicked.[1] *Pirkei de-Rabbi Eliezer*, an eighth-century midrashic work likely composed in the Land of Israel, asserts that the generation of the biblical Flood would not rise at the Resurrection, having been transformed into *ruḥot* (spirits) and *mazzikim* (destructive spirits).[2] Jewish mystical sources occasionally enlarged upon this view, construing that all *mazzikim* were the metamorphosed souls of the wicked dead, as in the zoharic passage "in the name of R. Judah, that the souls of the wicked are the demons of this world."[3] Some decades later, the fourteenth-century Spanish Kabbalist R. Joseph ben Shalom Ashkenazi would cite *Pirkei de-Rabbi Eliezer* as proof that *shedim* were souls of the wicked dead.[4] In Ashkenazi's mystical transmigratory vision, however, anything could very well turn into anything else.[5] R. Eliezer Ashkenazi, the earliest recorded recipient of the broadsheet from Safed detailing a dramatic possession case from the early 1570s, adduced the account in the context of discussing his assertion that it is the fate of the wicked to turn into demons. "It has been explained that [to become] demons [*shedim*] is the punishment and ultimate destiny of evil people," wrote Ashkenazi in his 1583 work, *Maʿasei ha-Shem*.[6] In a philosophically informed discussion, Ashkenazi explains that their bodies "are from the hylic element that receives the forms . . . [enabling them to] appear at times in animal form, and at other times in the form of people. Moreover, what people have said of them—that they roam in flight—should not be cause for bewilderment, since their bodies are from a fine, simple substance." Idolaters of old used to animate their idols with impure spirits so that they might speak. Their punishment was to become like the very impure spirits they used to animate these idols. Ashkenazi adduces Psalm 135, verse 18, "they who make them become like them," in support of this thesis. Ashkenazi then continues to extend his structural analogy to the workings of wind instruments. Understanding their principle of amplification enables one to understand why the wicked dead demons enter a human to commandeer his or her organs of speech.

[B]odies that are from that same fine element are so highly refined that "their voices are unheard" (Psalms 19,4). Just as we see that when a sound comes to the hollow of instruments such as trumpets, rams' horns, or the like, it will amplify and sound. So too the voice from that body, due to its delicacy, is inaudible. But when it comes to the hollow of the throat of that fallen person [*ha-nofel*], the throat is an apt vessel to make the voice audible, notwithstanding its fineness. Thus the body will make its voice and its speech heard in that throat, without moving the lips at all. And people commonly say[7] of the fallen that an evil spirit [*ruaḥ ra'ah*] has entered them, for they too call them a wind/spirit [*ruaḥ*].

Ashkenazi largely conflates demons (*shedim*) and spirits (*ruḥot*) in his attempt to provide a cogent "natural" explanation for the phenomenon of spirit possession.[8] His analysis attempts to conform to contemporary natural philosophical notions of the nature of occult bodies, while referring repeatedly to biblical texts and contemporary *dybbuk* accounts to demonstrate the correctness of his thesis. His concerns were exclusively theoretical and metaphysical, and the consequences of his terminological conflation on the practice of exorcism were of no concern to him.

Yet even before such conflation, confusion reigned. The terms *ruḥot, mazzikim*, and *shedim* were used interchangeably in Jewish literature from the rabbinic era to the early modern period. This terminological fluidity was noticed by commentators such as R. Moshe bar Naḥman ("Ramban," 1194–1270), according to whom "the *shedim* [were] called *mazzikin* in the language of our rabbis, and *se'irim* in the language of scripture."[9] This imprecision notwithstanding, occasional attempts were made to impose order on these classifications. Thus the most eminent of medieval Jewish commentators, R. Solomon Yiẓḥaki ("Rashi," 1040–1105), distinguished in his talmudic commentary between "*shedim*—they have human shape and eat and drink like people; *ruḥin*—without body or form; and *lilin*—human form but they have wings."[10] No term was taken to refer to a human ghost, though all partook of familiar human characteristics.

Although the identification of a possessing spirit as a ghost seems to have been common among late medieval and early modern Christians, clerical authorities generally suppressed such notions as soon as they were summoned to perform an exorcism, though they did not eliminate belief in possession by the dead entirely.[11] In so doing, they were following theological traditions going back to Augustine that denied this possibility.[12] Islam similarly disallowed for the possibility of possession by souls of the deceased. As a recent orthodox scholar of Islamic demonology has written, "Since the human soul enters the *barzakh* upon the death of the body and the state of the *barzakh* prevents any contact with this world, it would not be possible for disembodied human spirits to possess living beings or to communicate with them."[13] Although Christian clerics attempted to suppress the notion that the dead could possess the bodies of the living and Islamic theorists dismissed the very possibility, Jewish religious authorities came to regard spirit possession as typically resulting from just such an etiology. An exceptional position could still be found among Jewish scholars: the sixteenth-century Italian physician-rabbi Abraham Yagel rejected altogether the notion that the possessing agents were disembodied souls and argued that they were in fact demons impersonating humans. Yagel's view was thus congruent with the one held by the religious authority of his broader cultural environment, the Catholic Church.[14]

Yagel's atypical view should not obscure the fact that early modern rabbis generally believed that ghosts as well as demons could possess the living. Sometimes they were thought to do so together. Whatever the case, the exorcist had to know whom he was up against in order to work effectively. R. Ḥayyim Vital (1542–1620), the most prominent disciple of R. Isaac Luria and a major figure in what follows,[15] described how one was to distinguish between possession by a ghost and by a demon:

> Demons [*Shedim*] and a ghost [*ruaḥ ra'ah*] are two distinct types. For the ghost is the spirit of a person, which after his death enters the body of a living person, as is known. First one must recognize their signs: the demon compels the person, and he moves spasmodically with his arms and legs, and emits white saliva from his mouth like horse-froth. With a ghost, he feels pain and distress in his heart to the point of

collapse. However, the primary clarification is when he speaks, for then he will tell what he is, particularly if he speaks after having been compelled by you with adjurations and decrees.[16]

In *Sefer ha-Goralot* (Book of Lots), a work attributed to Vital, a bibliomantic divination procedure promises to discern whether the spirit afflicting someone is a ghost or a demon.[17] In this source, the demon may be a Jew, a Muslim, or a Christian. This should be no great surprise, given the traditions noted above regarding the various human qualities and appetites of these creatures, sexual among them. It is also strikingly similar to Islamic demonological views according to which demons are either Muslims or *kuffars* (disbelievers).[18] Nevertheless, techniques designed to remove a demon were regarded as ineffective for removal of a ghost. In his unpublished work on practical kabbalah, Vital therefore provided a technique to exorcise such spirits, which, he wrote, would not work against a disembodied soul.[19] Although it therefore remained possible to view demons as potential possessing agents in early modern Judaism, most sources at our disposal clearly indicate that the primary agent in nearly every case was taken to be a ghost. Even where a demonic spirit was present, its role was as guardian and tormentor of the disembodied soul. Ghosts had become the clear stars of the show.

The doctrine of *gilgul* provided the ideational basis for this development and lent it cultural coherence. Rather than viewing *gilgul* in conceptual terms alone, and in isolation from other factors, in what follows I sketch a genealogy of *dybbuk* possession that traverses the historical terrain vertically as well as laterally. The vertical view emphasizes *gilgul* and kabbalistic practice; the lateral, cognate idioms and speculative contextualizations. The resulting image is one that narrows the phenomenological gap between *dybbuk* possession and spirit possession in early modern non-Jewish settings without effacing their distinctiveness.

Magico-mystical techniques employed by Spanish Kabbalists to bind disembodied spirits of the dead to the souls of the practitioners were decisive in first translating doctrine into practice; indeed, no a priori reason exists to assume that the techniques did not precede the doctrine. Although such techniques may have been indebted to ancient (and contemporary) magical necromancy, their inscription in kabbalistic sources affiliates them most directly to the concept of *'ibbur* (a masculine noun, literally meaning "conception"; v. *le-hit'abber*, to become pregnant; n. *'ubar*, fetus).[20] Before considering such techniques, however, we must briefly survey the development of this notion.[21]

Although it first appeared in Jewish mystical sources as a general term for reincarnation, synonymous with *gilgul*, *'ibbur* appears to have been imbued with a distinct meaning of its own for the first time in Ramban's commentary on Ecclesiastes.[22] Little is known of Ramban's views on reincarnation; the Geronese and Castilian schools of kabbalah treated *gilgul* as a profound mystery, referring to it only through hints and allusions.[23] The secrecy surrounding the subject among these kabbalists may stem from their belief that the secret of the messianic redemption was to be found in the mystery of *gilgul*. Ramban, an active disputant with Christians over matters of messianic belief, may have thought it indiscreet to treat the subject of reincarnation openly, given the sensitivity of the issue.[24] No less plausible a reason for the secrecy shrouding discussions of reincarnation in early kabbalistic literature is the simple fact that so much earlier Jewish literature implicitly or explicitly denied it as heretical, figuring nowhere in biblical or rabbinic literature, and complicating if not contradicting classical Jewish eschatological beliefs such as resurrection.[25] As reincarnation gradually came to be viewed as a punishment rather than as a soteriological mystery, however, exoteric treatment became increasingly possible.[26] *Gilgul* had become the carrot and the stick of mystical literature.

Not all kabbalists shared a common understanding of the term *'ibbur*, nor did they agree on the conditions and extent of reincarnation in general. By the end of the thirteenth century, however, Spanish Kabbalists had taken the term *'ibbur* to denote the temporary introduction of a foreign soul into a living body some time after birth. *Gilgul* was then taken to refer specifically to reincarnation coincident with conception or birth. The difference in timing was fraught with psychospiritual ramifications. Foremost was the fact that one who returned to the world by means of *gilgul* did not recall any former identity; the conscious continuity between the embodiments of past and present lives was severed. Moreover, the identity between the soul and its new bodily home was complete; the new body was its own. One returning as an *'ibbur*, however, remembered the former life and regarded the new bodily home as temporary. Its customary resident, or "host," was generally unaware of the presence, let alone personality, of the *'ibburic* guest.

The idea that two souls might even temporarily coexist in one body was consonant with early thirteenth-century assumptions that souls transmigrated in fragments, felicitously referred to by Joshua Trachtenberg as "the prevailing polypsychism of the Middle Ages."[27] According to such conceptions, the soul—itself a composite of the strata *nefesh* (vital soul), *ruaḥ* (*anima*, spirit), and *neshamah* (*spiritus*, rational soul), differently conceived depending upon one's metaphysical affiliations—need not transmigrate as a collective, integrated whole.[28] Thus, individuals might be born with "composite" souls, each stratum carrying an independent transmigratory history. The notion that multiple strata of souls might incarnate in a given body was not, however, invoked to explain bizarre personality disorders.[29] The "normal" individual was a composite of these multiple strata, which collaborated in a manner that obscured their multiplicity in the consciousness of the subject. Paranormal diagnostic skills were required to expose these layers and to guide the individual on a path of rectification that took into account his innate complexity. "Schizoid manifestations of the soul," as Gershom Scholem called the stranger disorders, were understood in terms of *'ibbur*—particularly when the *'ibburic* guest became known, through speech or other action, as a concomitant occupant of a person's body. In early kabbalistic literature, it was assumed that an *'ibbur* would most commonly impregnate a host's body when both the transmigrating soul and the soul of its temporary host stood to benefit from the association.

The Zohar, the greatest work of medieval Spanish Kabbalah, invokes this notion of *'ibbur* in linking Nadab and Abihu, the sons of Aaron whose mysterious death during the consecration of the Tabernacle is described in Leviticus, chapter 10, to Phinehas, whose zealous actions are described in Numbers, chapter 25.[30] According to the Zohar, the souls of Nadab and Abihu became impregnated in Phinehas when he faced the lewd exhibitionism of Zimri, the Israelite man, and Cozbi, the Midianite woman.[31] The introduction of *'ibbur* in this context evinces the zoharic tendency to regard reincarnation as an opportunity to rectify sexual transgressions (including sins of omission, such as dying childless).[32] Furthermore, unlike *gilgul*, which was thought to rectify sins, *'ibbur* was regarded by the Spanish kabbalists as a phenomenon that applied primarily to the righteous, in this world and the next. It is with R. Moses Cordovero ("Ramak," 1522–70) that we first encounter the term *evil* 'ibbur—a formulation that signals the consolidation of the kabbalistic conceptual framework underlying early modern *dybbuk* possession.[33]

## Cultivating Connections with the Dead: Spanish Antecedents

Cordovero, Safed's preeminent kabbalist until his death in 1570, distinguished *gilgul* and *'ibbur* clearly and succinctly in his "*Shemu'ah be-'Inyan ha-Gilgul*" (Tradition Regarding Reincarnation), preface 6: "For *gilgul* does not only refer to the [incarnation of the soul at the time of a] person's birth, i.e., at the time of his formation, but also, after his maturity, he may draw a *gilgul* upon himself. The sages refer to this as '*ibbur*."[34] The first kabbalist to discuss the possibility of a deleterious *'ibbur,* Cordovero raised the quotidian possibility of this threat in a fascinating passage in his commentary on the prayer book, *Tefillah le-Moshe* (Prayer of Moses).

According to tradition, the blessings recited upon arising include the following expressions of thanksgiving: "Blessed art Thou, Lord of the Universe, who has not made me a slave," "Blessed art Thou, Lord of the Universe, who has not made me a woman," and "Blessed art Thou, Lord of the Universe, who has not made me a Gentile." This plain sense of this liturgy is to express thankfulness for one's auspicious birth as a free Jewish male. According to Cordovero, however, these daily recitations express one's grateful relief for not having been impregnated by the soul of a slave, a woman, or a Gentile while asleep.

> We may also explain that, even during a person's life, it is possible for one to become impregnated [*le-hit'abber*] in a deleterious manner by the soul of a woman, a slave, or a Gentile. This, God forbid, can harm a person repeatedly. Upon considering these matters, one who is thoughtful will find that at times people change their behavior. At times, they act like women, at times like men. At times they will serve men like slaves, for the inner shows its effects on the outer. At times one will give one's attention to foul matters, like the Gentiles. Thus, when one's soul returns to him and he sees that all is well with him . . . it is upon him to bless his Rock for the good that He has granted him. . . . And this renewal takes place daily for a person, and he must therefore say these blessings daily. One fearful of the word of the Lord, in hearing this, must strengthen himself in his simplicity and not fail, nor heed false words, nor depend upon anything unworthy, God forbid. *And one should intend in these three blessings to nullify any* 'ibbur *of idolators, an* 'ibbur *of a slave, and an* 'ibbur *of a woman from himself.* And he must purify himself through the secret of these three blessings from any grafting [*harkavah*] and evil *'ibbur.*[35]

Cordovero regards the possibility of *'ibbur* as ongoing, even routine. These are not evil souls of the more malicious variety, whom we will meet in later accounts of *dybbuk* possession. Rather, Cordovero seems to have identified the sudden onset of the servile personality traits of the inferior classes of beings—slaves, women, and Gentiles—as symptoms of a deleterious *'ibbur.* In this passage, Cordovero does not identify any particular behavior on the part of the "possessed" that has led to the impregnation; one's actions are not said to attract an *'ibbur* directly, as would be the case in subsequent kabbalistic treatments of the subject.[36] It is also worth noting that in this early discussion, Cordovero entertains the distinct possibility that a male will be impregnated by a woman—a scenario that will be noticeably absent in the later *dybbuk* accounts.[37] Thus, in this kabbalistic rereading of the typical Jewish morning prayer routine, one must, upon arising, thank God for having reentered one's body without unwelcome company. As the soul was thought to depart the body during the night—sleep being one-sixtieth of death[38]—its return to the body could naturally be expected to meet with the occasional complication.

Yet Cordovero's reading of the morning blessings is not merely a novel construal of that for which one's blessings are to give thanks. Rather, the blessings in Cordovero's interpretation serve as a means to nullify *'ibburim,* should one's body have been overcome by unwelcome intruders during the night. Not mere expressions of praise, blessings have become wieldings of power—in this case against any evil soul that has penetrated one's body.[39] In Cordovero's reading, the morning blessings have become liturgical exorcisms. The use of blessings to wield power ought not to surprise, given the well-known and ancient use of the Psalms to magical ends. Drawing on zoharic precedent, blessings would also be hermetically construed as instances of drawing-down (*hamshakhot*) by the Hasidic masters.[40]

Just as certain practices might nullify evil *'ibburim,* other practices were designed by Spanish rabbis to cultivate propitious contact with the dead. These venerable practices were designed to bind the practitioner to the lowest portion of the tripartite soul of a departed saint, the *nefesh.* The *nefesh* was thought to remain in contact with its former body and was thus accessible at the grave. Cordovero's discussion of these practices appears in his commentary on the Zohar, pericope *Aḥarei Mot* [3:70b], in the wake of a discussion of the enduring presence of the *nefesh* near the bodily remains.

The Zohar states:

At the hour when the world requires mercy, the living go and inform the souls [*nefashot*] of the righteous [*ẓaddikim,* pl. of *ẓaddik*], and cry on their graves, and are worthy of rousing them. Why? Because they make it their will to cling to them, soul to soul. The souls of the righteous then awaken and assemble, and go forth to those who sleep in Hebron to inform them of the suffering of the world.[41]

According to the Zohar, in times of crisis, living saints visit the graves of their righteous predecessors. Their cries serve both to bind them (the root *DBK*, as in *dybbuk*, is used here) to the souls of the dead and to rouse them to action on their behalf. The righteous dead then ascend to commune with the souls of the patriarchs and matriarchs of the Jewish people—"those who sleep in Hebron," in the Cave of Makhpelah—hoping to obtain their intervention.[42] In his commentary on this passage, Cordovero is interested in exploring the means by which the living are able to cross the divide that separates them from the dead. How is it that an embodied soul can communicate and commingle with the disembodied souls of the dead? And embodiment is indeed taken to be the heart of the problem; coarse flesh suffices to obscure the refined spiritual form of the dead from the eyes of the living. A metamorphosis of this fleshy garment of the soul is indispensable. So writes Cordovero: "This matter will be apprehended and discovered in the secret of the Garment [*levush*] prior to Adam and the rest of worldly existence, before Adam's sin, the secret 'Garments of Light.' For after the sin and the corporealization [of the Garment] as matter, it was said to him, 'you are dust, and shall return to dust.' "[43] The garment of skin (*'or*) fashioned by God for Adam (Gen. 3: 21) was created first as light (*or*). Sin resulted in its corporealization, and with physicality came opacity and, tragically, perishability.[44] In other words, when Adam was first created, like the dead, he too was formed of a fine, diaphanous body of light, partaking of immortality.

This original Garment of Light was removed from ordinary men as a consequence of Adam's sin, yet remains available to the righteous, whose recovery of this ethereal body enables them to communicate with the souls of the dead. "This Garment and the existence of this subtle world is received by the righteous in the mystery of their soul, and is transmitted only to the refined of mind whose spiritual souls vanquish their corporeality, and who nullify their bodily desires. They then pass beyond the veil and threshold of the physical world and enter the World of Souls."[45] Those who refine their intellects and strengthen their spirits, who manage to overcome their physicality, transmute their Garments of Skin. Attaining the Garments of Light, they become capable of commingling with the souls of the righteous dead. "[There] they apprehend according to the degree of their merit, to hear them [the souls] and sometimes actually to see them, as did R. Shimon and his comrades, as explicated in several places in the Zohar."[46] Once they have exchanged their coarse flesh for ethereal bodies, the righteous find themselves in the world of souls. At this level of spiritual attainment they hear, if not see, the dead. The heroes of the Zohar, explains Cordovero, enjoyed such interaction with departed souls precisely through the process he has described. Yet hearing and even seeing are not enough; in times of crisis, the living righteous must bring about the adhesion of their souls to the souls of their dead predecessors, and arouse them to act on their behalf. This calls for the implementation of a more magical necromantic technique that takes the living *ẓaddik* to the grave of the dead *ẓaddik* whom he seeks to arouse. "This is the secret of the binding of one soul to another, which is given only to one located in this world, who is able to bind his embodied soul with the soul of the righteous. This is done through his pouring out of his soul upon the grave of the righteous, and he clings soul to soul and speaks with the soul of the righteous and informs him. This soul then awakens the other souls, and this is what is said: 'Why? Because they make it their will to cling to them. . . . ' "[47] It is the presumption of the Zohar that the presence of the lower soul (*nefesh*) of the *ẓaddik* remains at the grave; his spirit (*ruaḥ*) is taken to be in *Gan Eden* (paradise), his higher soul (*neshamah*) far beyond. It is the *nefesh* of the living that clings strictly to the *nefesh* of the righteous, which has remained in this world precisely to aid the living when the need arises.[48]

Cordovero's closing remarks on this passage are particularly striking: "This matter was still done in Spain by great men who knew of it. They would dig a trench in the grave over the head of the dead. In it, they would pray for the benefit of the whole community, and they would cling, soul to soul, in solitary meditation."[49] In Spain, the technique is said to have involved laying prone in a trench, head aligned with the head in the grave, the communion enhanced by proximity. A meditative engagement of the practioner's soul with the soul of the dead would then culminate in a state of adhesion, soul to soul. According to Cordovero, then, the technique described by the Zohar was practiced not only by the Tannaitic saints whose exploits were so magnificently depicted in pseudoepigraphic style, but also by the great men of Spain, apparently in the recent past.[50] These men practiced a form of *hishtatḥut*, or gravesite prostration, that was to become extremely popular among the kabbalists of sixteenth-century Safed.[51] Indeed, in his paraphrase of Cordovero's commentary, rather than concluding with the original's recollections of Spanish practitioners, R. Abraham Azulai (1570–1644) substitutes, "And this matter has been verified among us, as this happened in our own times. Speakers of truth have testified to me that they saw this practiced by the AR"I [R. Isaac Luria][52] and his students, the comrades, may the memory of the righteous be a blessing."[53]

Not only did R. Isaac Luria practice these techniques, he broadened their applicability considerably. In his conception, *hishtatḥut* practices were to be undertaken to achieve a positive *'ibbur* in the practitioner, and not only in times of crisis. In his autobiographical dream diary *Sefer ha-Ḥezyonot* (Book of Visions), R. Ḥayyim Vital records that in 1571, Luria sent him to the burial cave of the talmudic sage Abaye so that the latter might penetrate him as a positive *'ibbur.* "In that year, my teacher, may his memory be a blessing, sent me to the cave of Abaye and taught me that *yiḥud* [unification]. I clung to his soul, and he spoke to me of the matters of which I wrote in the aforementioned tract." *Yiḥudim* (pl.) were the staples of Luria's magico-mystical contemplative system. Scholem defined such *yiḥudim* as theurgic acts "based on mental concentration on the combinations of Sacred Names" that "contained . . . an element of magic."[54] Vital's own definition of *yiḥudim* makes it clear that he viewed them primarily as a means for cleaving to souls of the righteous, achieved through a circulation of energies initiated by the intender of the *yiḥud.* Early in the work *Sha'ar ha-Yiḥudim* (Gate of Unifications), Vital promises that he plans to

> explain the matter of *yiḥudim,* what they are and their nature, and how by means of this [practice] one attains revelations of the souls of the righteous. By this we will explain the matter of prostration on the graves of the righteous and cleavage to them, spirit to spirit. . . . [55] For it is impossible for a person to awaken [the dead] without the *yiḥudim,* to ascend in the secret of Female Waters [*mayyim nukvin*]. In this they drawn down illumination below and illuminate the one engaged in the unification [*ha-meyaḥed*].[56]

The *yiḥud* is thus a meditative practice that promises to grant the practitioner clairvoyant contact with the dead and, moreover, to cleave to them in spiritual ecstasy. The *yiḥud* awakens the dead and allows the practitioner to ascend through the energy of his devotion while simultaneously drawing down enlightenment from above. The practitioner-driven devotion is characterized here by the kabbalistic term *Female Waters,* understood as the spiritual arousal and "lubrication" of the practitioner that stimulates the divine partner and calls forth the shower of divine effusion, itself called "Male Waters" in the literature.

In this mystical circle, necromantic techniques such as graveside prostration were not always required to bring about the impregnation of the soul of a departed saint into the body of a living counterpart. Elsewhere in his mystical diary, Vital relates that there were times when he heard voices speaking to him, which he did not know with certainty to be those of visiting transmigrants. He even suspected the voices to be his own. In doubt, he consulted a Damascene sorcerer, who in turn summoned a demonic spirit to appear in a looking glass, in order to respond to Vital's query. "He answered me," writes Vital, "He [the *'ibbur*] is the speaker, and not me. For his soul enclothes itself in my heart, and from there he raises the sound of his words to my mouth and he speaks with my mouth, and then I hear."[57]

Vital devoted much effort to clarifying the subject of transmigration in Luria's thought.[58] In the Lurianic context, a kind of Gnostic structural parallelism between good and evil applies fully to the possibilities of transmigration, a parallelism often associated in kabbalistic works with the phrase from Ecclesiastes, Chapter 7, verse 14: "This opposite that has God made."[59] Both beneficial (often silent) and baneful (often vocal) *'ibburim* exist. The former take up occupancy in a person to do good or to better the host, whereas the latter do so to wreak evil or to catalyze the moral downfall of the host. Thus Vital writes,

> The first [type of deleterious *'ibbur*] are those souls of the wicked who, after their death, do not merit to enter *Gehinnom.* They enter living people's bodies due to our numerous transgressions, speaking and telling all that happens to them there, as is known, may the Merciful save us. The second are those who impregnate themselves in a person in the secret of *'ibbur* . . . and cling to him [*mitDaBKim bo*] in great concealment. Then, if the person sins, this soul impregnated within him will become stronger and bring him to sin [further] and divert him to an evil path in the same way that we have previously explained how the soul of a *ẓaddik* impregnated in a person aids him to become better.[60]

According to Vital, souls of the evil dead impregnate bodies of the living because they are unable to enter Gehinnom. Gehinnom, the Jewish precursor-analogue of the Christian purgatory or the Islamic *barzakh,* was the refinery for a "polluted" soul.[61] There, after death, it could be purged of the dross accumulated over a lifetime of sin before taking its place in the World to Come. The duration of this cleansing was fixed at twelve months according to rabbinic tradition.[62] Without access to Gehinnom, the most the tormented soul could accomplish was a temporary respite from the afflictions associated with its endless limbo state, a respite provided by the shelter of another's body. The idea that a disembodied being might penetrate someone else's body was perfectly natural to medievals, who regarded the body as a highly permeable container.[63] Saint and sinner alike might expect their physical frames to be pierced, if not utterly commandeered by a foreign guest at any time. As Cordovero's recollections so vividly illustrated, however, Luria and his disciples clearly inherited and amplified traditions and sensibilities from remote and more immediate predecessors alike; they did not create them themselves.

Spain was the locus for more than the development of reincarnation theory; there it became a practical matter with both everyday and extraordinary dimensions. An acute sense of the practical implications of transmigration underlies the disturbing concern that in the course of an innocent meal, one might actually devour of one's dear deceased. R. Elazar Azikri (1533–c. 1599) and R. Avraham Galanti, who wrote shortly after Cordovero, tell the following Castilian story: a bull scheduled for a *corrida de toros* appeared to his "son" in a dream. The father, then incarnated in the bull, asked that he be slaughtered in the kosher manner and fed to poor Torah students, in order to return in his next incarnation as a man. "Many events of this kind took place among the people of Israel," testifies Azikri.[64] Such stories indicate that the sources of an "active" understanding of the doctrine of *gilgul* were already present in medieval Spanish Kabbalah, notwithstanding the emergence of *dybbuk* narratives only in the sixteenth century.[65]

The kabbalists of Safed were particularly interested in food and saw eating as fraught with hazardous, yet potentially redemptive, possibilities. Eating with proper *kavvanah* (lit. intention)[66] and sanctity could bring about the elevation of a good soul incarnated in the food.[67] Extreme caution was also advised lest an evil *'ibbur* result from ingesting food in which it resided. Vital, apparently reflecting Luria's influence, stressed the dangers of eating more than any prior kabbalist. According to Vital, for example, eating the hearts of animals or drinking from a well inhabited by disembodied souls might result in an evil *'ibbur* capable of destroying one's life: "Thus, God forbid, if a person drinks such water and a soul which has transmigrated into that water enters him, he cannot rectify the situation, for the evil soul will impregnate him and cause him to sin until it has plunged him down to the nethermost pit."[68] For Vital, the unexpected *'ibbur* that may result from everyday eating and drinking explains why good people may suddenly sin. When the AR"I drank, Vital recalls, he "exorcised" the water first:

Now, my master, may his memory be a blessing, as he traveled and drank water from a spring or a well, he would gaze and intend [*mekhaven*] while drinking so that the power of his intention [*kavvanah*] would expel and repel from [the water] the spirit or soul who had transmigrated in it. Only then would he drink the water. The spirit would afterwards return to its place.[69]

Wells were long considered dwelling places for spirits, and rabbinic literature is not without its tales of these water-based creatures.[70] In his *Ḥesed le-Avraham* (Mercy to Abraham), R. Abraham Azulai discusses the problem in light of Lurianic traditions. According to Azulai, individuals who have not washed their hands in the ritually prescribed manner (for example, upon arising and before eating) and those who have neglected to recite blessings before enjoying food, fragrances, and the like (*birkhot ha-nehenin*) are reincarnated into water as a punishment. As a result,

[k]now that there is no spring, nor well, nor pool of water, nor river which is not infested with countless transmigrants [*megulgalim*]. Therefore it is not fitting that one place one's mouth on the stream to drink, but one should rather take [the water] into one's hand. For it is possible for one of them to transmigrate into him, as is known, and then that evil soul will be impregnated in him. For sometimes through some sin, something evil comes upon a person and then that evil soul impregnates himself in him, and abets him to sin. . . . Thus through his eating and drinking, numerous types of transmigrants reincarnate through a person at all times. One who is learned and who eats with the proper intention is able to elevate and to fix those transmigrants.[71]

These attitudes and precautions exemplify the new centrality of reincarnation in sixteenth-century kabbalistic thought. *Gilgul* stories, like the one from Azikri and Galanti above, were popular, carried pietistic weight, and struck fear in the hearts of their listeners. They may have been even more effective given their undeniable entertainment—and even humoristic—value. Poor sanitation has been considered a primary cause for this suspicious view of food and water, though the personalistic view of reincarnation does not necessarily flow logically from a premodern case of dysentery.[72]

While seeking to avoid evil *'ibburim* by means of these prophylactic exorcism meditations, Luria, like his disciples, also received (and actively sought) holy *'ibburim*.[73] With his disciples, the master discussed methods for inculcating holy *'ibburim* other than the old Spanish techniques of gravesite prostration. Prominent among these was the imitation of the a righteous man (*ẓaddik*) whose soul one wished to draw down as an *'ibbur*.

Occasionally a person will happen to perform a particular commandment [*miẓvah*] in an ideal manner [*ke-tikna*]. Thereupon a certain soul will be called upon him, a righteous man of old who himself ideally performed that commandment. Because of the similarity between them that was established through this commandment, the soul of the righteous man will impregnate him. Moreover, it is also possible for the righteous man to be a contemporary, alive during his lifetime; the soul of this righteous man will become impregnated within his soul for the same reason. For when this man performs any commandment or commandments associated with that righteous man, who, like him, performed them properly, then the soul of that righteous man will impregnate him even while the two are alive simultaneously.[74]

Here is an incubation theory based entirely on the principle of mimesis, colored in kabbalistic hues. The anthropological presumption is that each individual is spiritually rooted in one of the 613 limbs of Primordial Adam (*Adam Kadmon*), the *Macanthropos.* Each limb corresponds to one of the 613 commandments. An individual therefore finds true expression and personal fulfillment through the performance of that special commandment. One's true relatives are those who share one's soul root, rather than one's biological family.[75] Building on these concepts, a practical, natural method for attracting a positive *'ibbur* impregnation suggested itself: imitation of the saint who ranks highly in one's soul family by the fully realized performance of the family commandment. Impregnation would naturally follow, even for one who just "happens" to fulfill the commandment as it should be, for like attracts like. Gary Tomlinson has emphasized "the fundamentally imitative nature of Renaissance magic," and the source of the magician's power in his mimetic abilities.[76] This technique to bring about *'ibburic* possession—the conscious or unconscious imitation of the figure desired as a catalyst to spiritual elevation—is the very essence of mimesis, and reveals the AR"I as close kin of the Renaissance magi.[77]

The tales of the AR"I's elder, R. Judah Ḥallewa, would seem to suggest that the atmosphere in Safed was charged with interest in reincarnation at least a generation before Luria's arrival.[78] Ḥallewa, a rabbi and kabbalist from Fez, Morocco, came to Safed in the early part of the sixteenth century. Upon his arrival, Ḥallewa was dismayed by the lack of disciplinary authority exercised by the rabbis of the Land of Israel. The rabbis of Safed had their hands tied: Turkish authorities granted them little power to punish, while forcing Jews who were turned over for punishment to convert to Islam. Ḥallewa conceived his treatise *Ẓafnat Pa'aneaḥ* (Exposer of Mysteries) as a work to dissuade readers from sin by instilling fear in them.[79] Adducing talmudic and zoharic passages dealing with the punishments awaiting the soul after death, Ḥallewa sought to save his people from the torments of Gehinnom—or worse. Moshe Idel, who brought this work to scholarly attention, wrote of the considerations that would seem to have led to the book's composition:

"In an atmosphere of the weakening of the Jewish tradition and an inability to force it upon sinners through the threat of violence, a unique way of acting arises: persuasion through fear."[80] Ḥallewa's was among the first kabbalistic ethical (*mussar*) books of Safed, which emerged to strengthen religious mores at a time of their weakening.[81] So as to discourage his contemporaries from pursuing their untamed appetites for sexual sins, theft, slander, and apostasy, Ḥallewa focused sharply upon reincarnation and its tribulations.[82] By 1545, Ḥallewa had related a story about a cow escaping to Jews in the hopes of being slaughtered in accordance with Jewish dietary law for transmigratory reasons.[83] In addition to this well-known tale, which Ḥallewa embeds in a discussion of the plausibility of reincarnation into animal bodies, Ḥallewa relates two accounts of spirit possession in which the possessor is a disembodied soul.

One of Ḥallewa's tales of spirit possession features a spirit who declares himself to be the tortured soul of R. Joseph Della Reina. Della Reina, a mid-fifteenth-century Spanish Kabbalist, was the hero of a kabbalistic legend surrounding his failed attempt to hasten the redemption. Although various versions of this Faustian tale are found in sixteenth- and seventeenth-century sources, most scholars believe, with Joseph Dan, that "some factual basis for the story exists."[84] Ḥallewa reports that he was told of this case by two eyewitnesses, but no markers provide further clues as to the provenance of the account, nor confirmation that it took place in a Christian household, which seems to be implied. Although the possessed in Ḥallewa's account is a young Christian servant girl, the exorcist is a Jewish expert.

> Once in the west there was a healthy Gentile maidservant. She suddenly fell to the ground with the falling sickness and said wondrous things. They finally sought out a Jew, from among those who know how to adjure demons, spirits, devils, and destructive beings. He adjured the spirit who entered that Gentile to reveal his name and to depart. The spirit that was in the Gentile's body responded that he should be left in peace in the body of the Gentile, having only now arrived, and that he was weary and exhausted from his journey when he entered the body of that Gentile. [The Jew] adjured him to say who he was, and he responded and said that he was the soul of Joseph Della Reina, who had been punished and driven away by the Supernal Court for having conjoined his soul with demons. For while in this world, he had used Holy Names for his own benefit and for the good of his body, rather than for the sake of the holiness of heaven.[85]

This striking account locates a case of possession by a disembodied soul in preexpulsion Spain. It also suggests, however cryptically, something of a religious syncretism surrounding the possession episode. Christians are said to turn to Jewish experts to treat the possession of one of their own, and the Jewish exorcist is shown revealing the possessing spirit to be none other than a Spanish rabbi of the not-so-distant past. The rabbi has sought refuge in the body of a Gentile girl, having been punished for his abuse of divine names before his death. Although the syncretistic dimension of the account is fascinating, as is its suggestion of a certain ecumenicism in the area of spirit possession in preexpulsion Spain, the account is fragmentary. It neither provides information as to the means of exorcism used nor comments as to the conclusion of the episode. Ḥallewa does not seem to have felt it important to establish that Della Reina was even exorcised successfully from the maidservant's body. For Ḥallewa, the significance of the account was didactic in that it forced his readers to confront the unimaginable suffering that sinners faced after death. Although reincarnation and the possibility of evil impregnation are significant elements in Ḥallewa's thought—and were thus familiar to members of Safed's population in the 1540s—Ḥallewa's discussions and the illustrative and terrifying stories he recounts lack the emphasis upon the rehabilitation or reparation (*tikkun*) of the possessing soul that became central in the literature in the decades to come. In these later accounts, the exorcist often assumed a responsibility for the ultimate welfare of the possessing spirit no less than for the possessed.

Ḥallewa's is not the earliest source that testifies to the association between *gilgul* and some form of spirit possession in the Iberian context. In his midrashic commentary, R. Joseph ben Shalom Ashkenazi recounts a firsthand experience with a woman who died, but whose spirit subsequently returned to her dead body.[86] With the spirit within her, she attained clairvoyant powers associated with the possessed. "Sometimes a spirit will return after its death. I myself saw a woman who had died, and remained so from the beginning of the night until almost the middle of the night, and suddenly she arose and sat aright. She remained mute, however, without speech. Yet she heard, and revealed future events."[87] Ashkenazi's account has much in common with the possession narratives of the subsequent century and constitutes yet another indication that Spanish Jews were not unfamiliar with the idea of a departed soul returning—here to a freshly dead body, emptied of its former soul inhabitant. (It is unclear whether the returning soul was the woman's own.) Although this narrative differs from the standard evil *'ibbur* scenario insofar as the penetrated body is a corpse, the rest of the story is strikingly similar to later accounts. First, the corpse is a woman, and even though women were not the only victims of spirit possession, they were considered to be especially vulnerable to it.[88] Second, the possessing or resurrecting soul is described as manifesting clairvoyant powers—the woman "revealed future events" (*maggedet 'atidot*). Here, Ashkenazi attributes to the woman an ability that was considered by R. Moses Zacuto more than three centuries later to be a distinguishing characteristic of the possessed: "some of them also say something regarding the future."[89] Both Ashkenazi and Zacuto use forms of the Hebrew root *MGD* to describe the manner of speaking associated with clairvoyance in the case of the spirit possessed. *Maggidism,* another kabbalistic phenomenon with strong Iberian roots, was the most significant and recognized form of positively valued spirit possession in early modern Jewish culture.[90]

A *maggid* might be defined as a beneficial *'ibbur,* were it not for the fact that unlike an *'ibbur,* a *maggid* is construed not as a disembodied soul but as an angelic being. Spanish Kabbalists actively sought this form of possession through the deployment of a variety of magico-mystical techniques. An examination of *Sefer ha-Meshiv* (Book of the Responding Angel) reveals the extent to which practices for obtaining revelations through *maggidic* possession were of central importance in fifteenth-century Spanish kabbalistic circles. "This work," wrote Moshe Idel, "represents the first precedent for the rise in the revelatory element in the later Kabbalah of the sixteenth century—as testified to by the work *Maggid Mesharim* [Angel of Righteousness, by R. Joseph Karo]."[91] The aggressive pursuit of revelation through magical means, entailing the supplanting of one's own personality with that of an "other," is not far removed from the cultivation of beneficial *'ibburim* that was a staple of Luria's prescriptions for his disciples. *Dybbuk* possession, which proliferated contemporaneously with *maggidism,* may thus be regarded as "an instance of 'inverse *maggidism.*' "[92] The inversive parallel between *dybbukim* and *maggidim* is most clearly manifest in the eruption of involuntary speech in the host. Like the *dybbuk,* the *maggid* made its presence known through speech. The literature on *'ibbur,* however, indicates that the visiting soul generally remained silent in its temporary abode, discernible only by the clairvoyant (like Luria) and through what presented itself as a visceral influence, the embodiment of the qualities of the departed rather than his (speaking) personality.

Karo would seem to have wedded the two paradigms in an unprecedented manner. The famous recipient of the most famous *maggid* in Jewish history, Karo was also shown by Idel to have been the exorcist in the first known possession narrative in early modern Jewish sources.[93] Karo was not the only recipient of *maggidic* revelations to have been associated with exorcism; Zacuto was also reported to have had a *maggid.*[94] This should not be terribly surprising, given that rabbinic exorcists were as a rule kabbalists—precisely those who would pursue the attainment of a *maggidic* revelation. And a *maggid* could be pursued, unlike Elijah the Prophet, whose revelations were always desired but whose presence was considered impossible to compel. A seventeenth-century purveyor of hagiographic literature, Shlomo ibn Gabbai, discussed the relation between revelations of a *maggid* and those of Elijah in his introduction to his book on the wonders of R. Isaac Luria.

> The level of a *maggid* is not like the level of Elijah, may his memory be a blessing, not even one one-thousandth part. Perhaps he will apprehend something, for a *maggid* is a spark of one's soul that was already in the world, and one can adjure it, and it will appear in one's own form and image, until one becomes bored with the apparition, since it is a shame that it is unable to reveal more, but only that which is within the power of the spark of one's soul and not more. But Elijah, may his memory be a blessing, reveals himself with the *Shekhina*[95] and they do not separate from each other. And the wise will intuitively understand that there is nothing higher than this level.[96]

Karo's own status as a clairvoyant mystic suffered by the comparison. Unlike Luria, Karo's positive possession state, his *maggid*, was not sufficiently rarefied to provide him with the most sublime revelations. His achievement thus paled when measured against that of Luria, as ibn Gabbai was quick to point out: "And you, who are interested, look at the book *Maggid Mesharim* of R. Joseph Karo, of blessed memory, to whom the *maggid* revealed himself regularly and revealed some [mystical] rationales of the Torah [*ta'amei Torah*]. Yet nevertheless, these were as naught before the secrets of the AR"I [Luria], may his memory be for life everlasting."[97] Of course, because Elijah's presence could not be forced, few enjoyed his revelations; *maggidic* revelations were far more common among the mystical rabbinic elite, for whom the *maggid* was a regularized, positive form of spirit possession with clear Iberian roots.

A good deal of the theoretical and practical groundwork for the reconstruction of spirit possession in sixteenth-century Jewish culture can therefore be found in literature written in and recalling preexpulsion Spain. The interest in cultivating positively valued possession states, whether *'ibburic* or *maggidic*, is recalled by sixteenth-century kabbalists as having been part of the Spanish milieu of their fathers. How do such recollections of Spanish antecedents accord with the views of spirit possession prevalent in late medieval Christian Spain? Was the Jewish willingness to accept a disembodied soul as a possessor entirely foreign to Christian contemporaries? Although the Church held that possession by the deceased was impossible—and indeed heretical—sixteenth-century Spanish writers acknowledged that popular notions of possession often presumed precisely that. Souls of the dead appeared frequently in fifteenth-century Spain in the forms of apparitions to the living. These souls, or ghosts, were thought to be in purgatory, in need of assistance from the living to ascend to heaven. Given that requirement, they make their appearance to ask that responses or anniversary masses be said on their behalf. They may also express anger at the dispersal of a patrimony.[98] According to William A. Christian, "medieval theologians accepted that souls could visit the earth in visible form, and these souls seem to have been regarded as good, rather than bad, spirits."[99] Nevertheless, clerical authorities did not consider such ghosts to be capable of possessing the body of a living person—a belief that seems to have been prevalent, despite clerical opposition. Learned demonological works from early sixteenth-century Spain criticize this belief. Two authors of such works, Martin de Castañega and Pedro Ciruelo, sharing common sources and authorities, provided similar descriptions of the possessed.[100] Both Castañega and Ciruelo wrote that souls of the dead professed to occupy demoniacs, compelling them to act as their possessing spirits had acted. If the soul was in purgatory, the possessed would prescribe masses, charity, and fasts. Castañega nevertheless criticizes exorcists for finding the souls of the dead in demoniacs, a phenomenon foreign to the documented experiences of Jesus and the apostles.[101]

Regarding possession phenomena more broadly as forms of prophecy, we may also see Iberian parallels without difficulty. Popular prophecy was a widespread phenomenon in fifteenth-century Spain. Jews who witnessed "plaza prophets" firsthand often suffered as a result of their diatribes.[102] Their experience of prophecy was not merely one of passivity and suffering, however; New Christians were among the active participants in the prophetic revival during this period.[103]

The efflorescence of spirit possession in sixteenth-century Jewish culture resists simple explanation. Although the preoccupation with *gilgul* and *tikkun* in Jewish thought reflected in the idiom of *dybbuk* possession might, like nearly everything else in the period, be seen as a response to the expulsion from Spain, a richer appreciation of the idiom and its emergence requires a more complex historical context. Such a context frames the phenomenon in the broader, shared cultural constructions that characterized the early modern period.[104] Even as they responded to their own crises, Jews nevertheless participated in broad idioms shared by other subcultures. An explanation of the emergence of *dybbuk* possession must therefore take several factors into consideration: shifts in kabbalistic anthropology and demonology, magical practices that closed the gap between the living and the dead, popular conceptions of "ghost" possession, and an appreciation of the indebtedness of sixteenth-century Safedian developments to the cultural climate of fifteenth-century Spain. A mixture of social factors, theory, and practices combined to facilitate the emergence of the classic construct of *dybbuk* possession and render it intelligible in sixteenth-century Safed.

## *Chapter 2*

# *The Dead and the Possessed*

*Several times I was with my teacher, may his memory be a blessing, walking in the field, and he would say to me: "Here is a man by the name of so-and-so, and he is righteous and a scholar, and due to such-and-such a sin that he committed in his life, he has now transmigrated into this stone, or this plant. . . . My teacher, may his memory be a blessing, never knew this person; though when we inquired after the deceased, we found his words to be accurate and true. There is no point in going on at length about these matters, since no book could contain them. Sometimes he would gaze from a distance of 500 handbreadths at a particular grave, one among twenty thousand others, and would see the soul [*nefesh*] of the dead there interred, standing upon the grave. He would then say to us, "in that grave is buried such-and-such a man by the name of so-and-so; they are punishing him with such-and-such a punishment for such-and-such a crime." We would inquire after that man, and found his words to be true. [There are] so many and great examples of this that one cannot imagine.*

*—R. Ḥayyim Vital*[1]

R. Isaac Luria constantly beheld the dead in his midst. So recalled R. Ḥayyim Vital in the preceding passage, among many others. Luria gazed upon the dead, seeing souls suspended over their graves. Vital emphasizes that Luria did not merely feel the presence of the dead, nor did he conjure them up with his "sacred imagination"; he *saw* the souls of the dead "with his eyes."[2] For Luria, the dead mingled with the living. They appeared with transparent immediacy in the rocks and trees of Safed and, of course, in and about its graves, marked and unmarked.

## City of the Dead

Safed, then as now, is a city that lives with its dead, its stone domiciles and synagogues poised on sloping hills that are home to 20,000 dead, whose graves begin only a few steps beyond the homes of the living.[3] Safed embraces its graveyard, which, like the stage of an amphitheater, is always within view, commanding one's attention. Not far in the distance, every denizen of Safed can see hills filled with the graves of rabbinic-era sages, culminating with Mount Meron, graced with remains of the second-century R. Shimon bar Yoḥai, Moses of the mystics, and, in their eyes, author of their bible, the Zohar.[4]

Sixteenth-century Safed was a city shared by the living and the dead, a sacred space that might be compared to sixteenth-century Spanish churches, "where the dead were relentlessly buried under the worshipers' feet."[5] Many who made their way to Safed did so to partake in this sacred space and the special benefits it afforded their souls. R. Moshe Alsheikh, Vital's teacher in rabbinics,[6] described Safed in his *Ḥazut Kasha* (Terrible Vision) of 1591 as a city

> which has forever been a city of interred dead, to which people from throughout the lands of exile came to die. A holy place, a city of our God from the day of its founding, they come to die there and be buried. Within it are many more than 600000 men, not to mention the bones of men continuously brought to the righteous [dead] in its midst, beyond measure, for "there is no end to its corpses." (Nahum 3, 3) Who from all the cities of the exile, near and far, does not have in her a father or brother, son or daughter, mother or sister, or some other kin, them or their bones?[7]

This depiction of Safed by an elder contemporary of Vital could hardly emphasize more vividly the exceptional nature of the place of the dead in the economy of the city, broadly construed. If historians have sensitized us to the regularity of medieval and early modern trafficking with the deceased, few contexts could claim the amplification of this relationship suggested by Alsheikh.[8] According to other authorities of the period, living in Safed was conducive to penetrating the secrets of the Torah. The insights one could expect along scholarly lines were not unrelated to the qualities of the city that promised one a good death as well. R. Abraham Azulai wrote the following about Safed around 1619, some twenty years after his arrival in the Land of Israel:

Safed also adds up [numerically] to 21, and with the word [Safed] itself 22;[9] this corresponds to the 22 letters of the Torah, and alludes to the readiness and receptivity of one in Safed to plumb the depths of the Torah and its secrets. For there is no purer air in the whole of the Land of Israel than the air in Safed. . . . And Safed also adds up to 570 [*TK'A*],[10] to allude that all who dwell in Safed have an advantage over all other cities in the Land of Israel. Since it is a high place with air purer and cleaner than any city in the Land of Israel, the soul of one who dies and is buried there speedily sails and takes wing to the Cave of Makhpelah,[11] in order to pass from there to the lower Garden of Eden.[12]

Mystical hermeneutics and auspicious death, according to Azulai, are Safed's specialties.[13] Its special atmosphere, here associated with the especially refined mountain air, is regarded as conducive to the spiritual study of Torah. This remarkable air also functions as something of a conduit, carrying the dead soul aloft in its breezes along occult passageways, linking Safed to the patriarchal tomb in Hebron, the gateway to Eden. The promise of safe passage, of a good death, may have encouraged the longing for death expressed by so many of its leading lights. This longing could find expression explicitly and literally in R. Joseph Karo's wishes to be burnt at the stake, or esoterically and figuratively in the frequent meditations on death and martyrdom in the prayer meditations (*kavvanot*) of Luria.[14]

With so many interred in her midst, Safed was a natural locus for visionary contact with the dead. Quotidian encounters with apparitions pervade the literature produced in this hothouse of morbid ecstasy. Towering above all stood Luria: his clairvoyance and the visionary powers that enabled him to behold the dead before him (no less than the secrets of the living people and texts that came under his scrutiny) quickly became the stuff of legend. Vital's accounts of his master's abilities repeatedly underscore their exceptionality.[15]

Though few could see the dead quite as Luria seemed to, death was underfoot in Safed and its environs, its proximity never in doubt. The regional relics, the graves of myriad talumudic-era sages, did much to attract the leading lights of the Jewish world in the course of the sixteenth century. By virtue of its unique appeal, as well as its economic health, Safed soon outstripped every other center in the Land of Israel both in the quantity and "quality" of its population.[16] According to the *Mufaṣṣal Defterler*, detailed registers of the cadastral surveys undertaken by the Ottomans in Palestine, Safed's Jewish population tripled between 1525 and 1555, from 232 to 716 households.[17] During that time, the composition of the population changed markedly as well. By mid-century, *Mustarib* (native Arabic-speaking) Jews were no longer the large majority of the Jewish population. Their absolute number declined, as Jews from Portugal, Cordova, Aragon, Seville, Calabria, and other lands added hundreds of new households to the community. Conversos also chose to settle in Safed in substantial numbers.[18] Safed thus took on a cosmopolitan character, with a strong European—and particularly Iberian—component. This Sephardic cultural prominence was not inconsequential in fashioning the particularly intense engagement with the dead we have noted. First there was the orientation to the grave and to death. Among Spanish Jews a positive, sacral orientation is evident, as the zoharic literature of the late thirteenth and early fourteenth centuries exemplifies. Ashkenazic contemporaries, by contrast, regarded the world of the dead as "an abode of dread and danger."[19] It would be the zoharic image of Galilee and its holy relics that attracted many to Safed in the sixteenth century.

Although most did not see the dead hovering over graves or suffering in their transmigrations into the minerals, plants, and animals around them, the residents of Safed did have one way of encountering the dead face to face, "not in a dream, but while wide awake."[20] The dead appeared to the living of Safed through a process of displacement. By commandeering the bodies of the living and making them their own, the dead could become visible to all. The dead appeared to the living Jews of Safed *in* the living Jews of Safed. The episodes of spirit possession recorded by Safedian rabbis of the period—the first such narrative accounts in Jewish literature in more than 1,000 years—are the subject of our analysis in this chapter.

Before we may begin our reading of these narratives, however, we must explore their provenance. The earliest extant manuscripts that include accounts of spirit possession were written in the seventeenth century. These include copies of earlier, no longer extant manuscripts and new works composed in the seventeenth century that include possession accounts. Examples of the former include the 1545 work *Ẓafnat Pa'aneaḥ* (Decipherer of Mysteries) of Judah Ḥallewa and Vital's autobiographical *Sefer ha-Ḥezyonot*, which refers to Safedian cases from the 1570s, as well as to a major 1609 Damascus case.[21] Manuscripts of Jacob Ẓemaḥ's *Ronu le-Ya'akov* (Rejoice for Jacob) and *Meshivat Nafesh* (Restoration of the Soul), and Joseph Sambari's *Divrei Yosef* (Words of Joseph) are among the seventeenth-century works that include versions of possession accounts relating to sixteenth-century Safed.[22] Ẓemaḥ included two Safedian cases in which Vital was the exorcist, and Sambari included four Safedian cases in his chronicle of its "golden age."

Only one work printed in the sixteenth century includes a Safedian case: *Ma'asei ha-Shem* (Acts of the Lord) of R. Eliezer Ashkenazi, published in Venice in 1583. Gedalia ibn Yaḥia's *Shalshelet ha-Kabbalah* (Chain of Tradition), published in Venice in 1586, recounts ibn Yaḥia's own experience with a possessed woman in Ferrara, and mentions a multiple possession case in Ancona, but includes no Safedian cases.[23] At the cusp of the sixteenth and seventeenth century, the *Ma'aseh Buch* (Story Book) appeared in Basel, which featured a possession narrative that, in Sambari's version, was reported as having taken place in Safed.[24] It was only in the seventeenth century that the classic Safedian accounts began to be published widely: from Joseph Delmedigo's 1628 *Ta'alumot Ḥokhmah* (Mysteries of Wisdom), to Naftali Bacharach's 1648 *'Emek ha-Melekh* (Valley of the King), and culminating in Menasseh ben Israel's 1651 *Nishmat Ḥayyim* (Soul of Life). This last work contained a half-dozen accounts of demonic possession among Jews, half of which were said to have taken place in Safed. In the many works published in the latter half of the seventeenth century and beyond containing possession accounts, these early narratives would be reprinted time and again.[25]

To summarize, cases mentioned in contemporary sources include the Karo exorcism in Ḥallewa's work, the famous Falcon case of 1571, copied from Falcon's manuscript by Sambari, and the major accounts of spirit possession involving R. Ḥayyim Vital. Though mentioned in Vital's own manuscripts, these accounts found their way into printed sources only with the efflorescence of hagiographic literature in the mid-seventeenth century; they reflect sixteenth-century Safed as a multicultural, pietistic nexus of the living and the dead.[26]

More than a generation before Luria's arrival in Safed, a case of spirit possession occurred that has been preserved in the unique manuscript of Judah Ḥallewa's *Zafnat Pa'aneah.* "I saw with my own eyes," testified Ḥallewa, that in 1545 a young boy began collapsing and uttering strange prophecies, "grand things." Many rabbis were called to examine the youth, among them the author of the account and the eminent sage R. Joseph Karo. At the threat of excommunication, Karo was able to find out about the nature of the possessing spirit. Answering a series of Karo's questions, the spirit goes through its previous incarnations: just before he entered the boy, he had been a dog; before that, an African; before that, a Christian; and before that, a Jew. A frightening plummet indeed! "Did you put on *tefillin*?" Karo asks him. "Never," answers the spirit. Karo's response: "There is no fixing you, then."[27] The report reveals that Karo accepted the spirit's identity as a disembodied soul and that, in theory, he accepted the notion that the exorcist should assist, not only in the expulsion of the disembodied soul but also in its *tikkun* (rectification). Such a concern for the amelioration of the plight of the spirit is conspicuously absent from ancient narratives of spirit possession. Conceptually this concern flows from the reinscription of spirit possession within the conceptual ground of transmigration. The narrative form highlights this new, pathetic dimension by focusing upon the confession of the spirit, no longer a demonic *shed* but a disembodied soul embroiled in a torturous afterlife.

## Falcon's "A Great Event in Safed"

Elijah Falcon, in the aftermath of a dramatic possession case that began on 16 February 1571, penned what was to become one of the best-known accounts of spirit possession in Jewish history: "The Great Event in Safed."[28] Falcon's account, signed by three other prominent rabbis of Safed who, like himself, were eyewitnesses and participants in the affair, was circulated in the Diaspora as a broadsheet by the late 1570s.[29] R. Eliezer Ashkenazi, writing in Poland after having departed from Italy, wrote that he had heard "in this, our own time" of cases of spirit possession and that only "this year, in 5340 (1579–80)" had he become familiar with the phenomenon upon receiving a broadsheet from Safed that described such a case. In his *Shalshelet ha-Kabbalah*, Gedalia ibn Yaḥia mentions having seen this signed broadsheet as well.[30] Falcon, it would seem, was an early publicist in Safed's bid for acknowledged centrality and preeminence in the Jewish world.[31] Less hagiographic in orientation than we might have expected, Falcon's didactic and dramatic broadsheet asserts Safed's aspirations for leadership on the basis that it was the center of Jewish values and their instruction, as well as a locus of ongoing divine incursion into the historical process. In this case, the divine incursion was seen most vividly in the form of the return of the dead to the society of the living. Constituting a dramatic reification of traditional Jewish values in a period of transition and crisis, spirit possession enhanced the spiritual resources of a community facing conditions of unremitting insecurity as well as swift and disorienting social change.[32]

Falcon opens his account with an exhortative prologue in which he laments human nature for leading people to indulge in the sensory pleasures of the body. Such an indulgence leads to the impoverishment of the soul and to the abandonment of the Torah and its directives. Falcon bemoans that even "believers and the punctiliously observant" generally fail to overcome this vulgar human inclination. Their inability to live up to demands of the holy Torah or to tend to their spiritual edification, writes Falcon, is chiefly due to the profound mismatch in the contest between spirit and flesh. The most sublime elements of the gossamer soul make but faint traces alongside the powerful, coarse desires of the body. Few come to recognize the folly of their material pursuits, the claims of the spirit being uttered in a small voice easily overpowered by the din of the flesh. In Falcon's view, only one conceivable way exists for people to hear the message of the spirit. To overcome the hedonism and epicureanism that naturally vanquish the gentle voice of the spirit in the contest for the shaping of human will, a disembodied spirit must speak from within a living body. Nothing in the Torah, he writes, can possibly make a strong enough impression upon a person to enable him "to remove from himself all traces of evil and wrongdoing: whether in speech, thought, or action." To accept that the soul lives on after the body dies and that reward and—especially—punishment await the sinning soul upon its departure from its short stay in the corrupting body, one must meet a soul that has crossed over into the realm of the dead and returned to tell the tale. "And this is known to him from one who came from that World, and told to him by one who has crossed over. For perhaps the Holy One, Blessed be He, sent him so that they might fear Him, as the Sages of blessed memory said, ' "And God does it, so that men should fear him" (Ecclesiastes 3, 14)—this is a bad dream.' (BT *Berakhot* 55a) And this is not in a dream, but while wide awake, before the eyes of all." Although a nightmare might have sufficed in former good days to inculcate fear of the Lord, such phantasms pale before the persuasiveness of a face-to-face meeting with a denizen of the world of the dead. Here, and throughout his account, Falcon emphasizes the embodied presence of the dead before the living, who, in large numbers, gathered to see the evil dead with their own eyes. He is only one eyewitness among many, and his broadsheet begins and ends with this refrain. "I was there, and my eyes saw and my ears heard all this and more—he who sees shall testify," signed Shlomo Alkabetz. "I too was summoned to see this matter, and my eyes have seen, and my ears have heard," added Abraham Arueti.[33] Lest the reader have any doubts, we are told that some 100 people attended the exorcism, including many sages and dignitaries.[34]

Before this "great assembly," the dead soul appears through the lifeless body of the possessed woman. Responding to the adjurations of the exorcists, a voice erupts from the woman's throat, unformed by any movement of her tongue or lips. This inchoate growl is inhuman, a lion's rumbling. Gradually, the exorcists impose upon it the standards of human language and the voice in the body of the woman becomes "like the voice of men." The exorcist has reinstated within established language that which "manifests itself as speech, but as an uncertain speech inseparable from fits, gestures, and cries."[35] Was the human speech as we have it in the account merely a projection of the anonymous exorcists? A literary invention of Falcon? A faithful record of the words spoken by the possessed woman or by the dissociated personality speaking from within her body? There are no simple answers to these questions. Possession accounts of the early modern period, among Jews and Christians alike, were written up by learned members of the clergy. Nevertheless, many include accounts of possession-speech that give the impression of transcription rather than of literary artifice. In his analysis of the possession of a Silesian girl in 1605, H. C. E. Midelfort notes the theologically learned arguments that the Devil pursued with exorcist Tobias Seiler. These arguments were so complex that "any reader is bound to conclude that Seiler was composing not only his own lines, but the Devil's, too." On the other hand, threats by the spirit to defecate in the pastor's throat "have the ring of spontaneous reporting." Midelfort thus argues that it is possible to "take the shape and color of the lens into account" in order "to say something of what demon possession was like to the demon-possessed, and, more generally, what ordinary people in the German-speaking lands thought of the Devil."[36] Listening for the voice of the possessed in these accounts restores to them a degree of agency denied to them originally on theological grounds, and more recently by historiographical trends that emphasize political and ecclesiastical factors, psychoanalytic subtexts, or, as in Certeau's work, the semantic aggression of the exorcists.[37]

And what does the woman in the Falcon case actually say? What can we find out about her and about her relationship to the soul possessing her? For answers, we must turn to the version of the account preserved in *Sefer Divrei Yosef* by the seventeenth-century historian of Ottoman Jewry, Joseph Sambari. Sambari prefaces his reproduction of this account with the phrase "as I found written in the autograph of the great tamarisk, our teacher the rabbi, R. Elijah Falcon, his memory for life everlasting."[38] Sambari's text alone preserves all names found in Falcon's manuscript, whereas Menasseh ben Israel's *Nishmat Ḥayyim* and subsequent works dependent upon it simply read "so-and-so" wherever the identities of the spirit and the victim's in-laws are mentioned.[39] According to Sambari, the victim is the young daughter-in-law of "the venerable Joseph Ẓarfati."[40] We learn neither the name of the girl nor anything else about her. Might she have been from a converso family? A slender clue points in that direction: the usage of an expression from Esther,

Chapter 4, verse 16 ("What can I do; if I perish, I perish"), which, if not a literary embellishment of Falcon's, may disclose the special identification with Esther known to have existed among conversos.[41] The only thing we learn about her husband, Joseph's son, is that at the time of the episode, he was away from Safed, in Salonika. The spirit, for his part, declares himself to be Samuel Ẓarfati and explains that he died in Tripoli (Lebanon), leaving one son and three daughters.[42] The third daughter was now married to a certain Tuvia Deleiria.[43] Samuel seems to have been well known in the community, as Falcon mentions a number of times that the spirit's words accorded with what people remembered about the deceased. Despite the fact that they were known to many in the crowd in attendance, Falcon asserts that these details were considered validating marks of the authenticity of the possession. "Then we recognized, all of us present, that the spirit was the speaker," he writes after hearing the spirit recount his family tree. In addition to this description of his family, other convincing details were the spirit's identification of his profession—money changer—and his synagogue, the local prayer hall of the Castilian exiles, Beit Ya'akov.[44] Many in attendance also confirmed that the spirit's admission of his most egregious sin was familiar to them: the assertion that "all religions are the same."[45] "Regarding this, many testified before us that he had spoken in such a way during his lifetime," notes Falcon.

The spirit's statement that "all religions are the same" bespeaks a type of popular skepticism that has not been studied sufficiently. Treatments of skepticism in this period have been primarily devoted to the elite, neo-Pyrrhonist skepticism of figures such as Ẓarfati's contemporary, Michel de Montaigne.[46] In his monumental treatment of sixteenth-century skepticism, Lucien Febvre dismissed the historical significance of popular skepticism and viewed it as a response to tragedy, rather than as a reasoned philosophical position. Disbelief had formulated as "a veritable cluster of coherent reasons lending each other support. . . . If this cluster could not be formed . . . the denial was without significance. It was inconsequential. It hardly deserves to be discussed."[47] Febvre's insistence notwithstanding, there has been no little dissent in more recent historiography from his blanket dismissal. In the present case, given our suspicion that key players in the account had converso pasts, it would be shameful to deafen our ears to the spirit's heresy. Indeed, the words attributed to the spirit of Samuel Ẓarfati cannot but bring to mind similar statements of well-known seventeenth-century conversos. Samuel's claim that all religions were equal would be uttered by Dr. Juan de Prado in 1643, according to inquisitorial testimony.[48]

Samuel was familiar for other improprieties as well. Somewhat more prosaically, though no less indicative of his impiety, Samuel was known for taking oaths and breaking them. If the elder Ẓarfati was impious, his son seems to have followed in his footsteps. When asked by the exorcists if the latter should recite the mourner's prayer *kaddish* or learn Torah on behalf of his soul, Samuel replies that such a plan was untenable, given that his son was wholly unsuited to learn Torah. Although the dialogue with the spirit revealed a personality familiar to the onlookers, doubts as to the authenticity of the possession seem to have lingered. The ultimate litmus test was to be administered: the exorcists would assess the spirit's ability to speak the languages Ẓarfati was known to have spoken when alive. In the event, the spirit's successful display of his linguistic prowess in Hebrew, Arabic, and Turkish—coupled with his inability to understand Yiddish—proved to be especially convincing, because "the woman did not know any of these languages."[49]

Did Samuel Ẓarfati have a relationship with Joseph Ẓarfati's daughter-in-law, within whom he had lodged himself? A recent cultural history of ghosts found that in more than three-quarters of the cases studied, percipients of early modern apparitions knew the identity of the spirit before them; possession cases in which the spirit was perceived as a disembodied soul seem to have worked similarly.[50] The fact that the possessed woman was married into the Ẓarfati family would suggest the possibility of familiarity. Many of those present knew Samuel, who would have been an older contemporary of hers (his widow having only recently remarried) or perhaps even her brother-in-law.

Samuel seems to have been quite a cad—he was married three times according to Menasseh's account and was an irreligious skeptic, his spirit relating to the adulterous intimations of his presence with urbane humor. In an exchange deleted from Menasseh ben Israel's version, the exorcists ask the spirit pointedly, "And if she is a married woman, have you no reservations about copulating with her?" The spirit responded, "And what of it? Her husband isn't here, but in Salonika!"[51] Shortly after this remark, the exorcists worked diligently to expel Samuel from her tortured body, and she began to writhe and kick violently. In the process, she exposed herself immodestly, underwear not yet having been invented.[52]

[Samuel] raised her legs and lowered them one after the other, with great speed, time and again. And with those movements, which he made with great strength, the cover that was upon her fell off her feet and thighs, and she revealed and humiliated herself for all to see. They came close to her to cover her thighs, and she was not self-conscious throughout the episode. Those who were acquainted with her knew of her great modesty, but now her modesty was lost.

This image seems to amplify the exorcists' concern and the spirit's admission, that some sort of intercourse was taking place between Samuel and the woman. The possibility that women could have intercourse with spirits was discussed in the rabbinic literature of the period, and rabbis were called upon to determine whether women who had engaged in such forms of deviant sexual behavior were classifiable as adulteresses, prohibited to their husbands—precisely the concern voiced by the exorcists in this case.[53] The final detail suggesting the sexual nature of the relationship between the woman and Samuel—at least in this young woman's mind—was the spirit's chosen point of departure from her body, her vagina. The account is discreet about this point, but the woman seems to have maintained that blood flow from her vagina was due to his departure, and sufficed to demonstrate that he had left.[54] Unfortunately for her, however, he soon returned, and only eight days later, she died. Given the amount of smoke to which she was subjected in the course of the exorcism, it seems likely that irresponsibility on the exorcists' part may have brought about her death—attributed in the account to "choking" at the hands of the spirit.

Whatever the etiology of the affliction that brought so much suffering upon this young woman, the disclosure of a network of associations between the possessed and her possessor certainly suggests that the episode was a meaningful struggle between familiar parties. A psychodynamic reading would highlight the sexual anxiety felt by this woman, left behind by her husband—perhaps away on business—and some lurking feelings of guilt over improper feelings for Samuel. The "other" that has displaced her "self" confesses his lust for her, as well as his utter disregard for her husband. He has also given voice to sentiments at odds with the pietistic standards that climaxed in the years around the possession. Perhaps struggling with a converso legacy, her "other" spoke the voice of Esther, the hidden one, risking transgression in the hope of eliciting the King's compassion.[55] And only a degenerate the likes of Samuel could utter the guilelessly heretical words of a popular *philosophia perennis: all religions are equal.*

Reading the text closely, we have exposed the meaning that this event may have had for the young woman, her family, and others who gathered around her during those difficult days, whether out of concern or curiosity. Yet another distinct meaning may be discerned in Falcon's use of the event in his constructed narrative, printed as a broadsheet for circulation throughout the Jewish world. What was Jewry at large to infer from the suffering and death of this innocent woman?

For those who witnessed this incursion of the dead into the land of the living, several points emerged with palpable clarity:[56]

- *Life persists after death.* No one could scarcely have imagined otherwise then, but the appearance of the dead made the conclusion inescapable. In a later period, when this tenet became contentious, Falcon's account, along with others, was called upon to prove decisively what had once been obvious.
- *The wicked are punished after death.* Judging from Falcon's introduction alone, this tenet was all too imaginable. During the case itself, the exorcists did not miss the opportunity to ask the spirit to describe the punishments he suffered after death.
- *The dead are at close proximity, still embedded in networks of association with the living.* Not only in the graveyard a few paces away, they are in and about the synagogue, blocking Samuel's path as he sought respite within its walls. New associations with the living may also be formed, as with the exorcists who were called in to rectify the spirit's soul even as they ejected it from the victim's body. A certain dependence of the dead upon the living is thus apparent.
- *The dead cast social and ethical ideals into relief by articulating their transgression.* These transgressions emerge in the course of the revelations that the spirit made, including the sins that brought him to his insufferable limbo state and, in other cases, the sins of many in attendance. The spirit's flagrancy encouraged sexual propriety, yet for Falcon at least, there is no more serious violation of communal codes than the subverting of Judaism's exclusive authority. The spirit, in denying this exclusivity and the traditional claim of Judaism's singular truth, and in disregarding the most solemn oaths of the Torah, had placed himself beyond redemption. His inability to enter Gehinnom signifies this unredeemability—rectifiable only through the intercession of the living saints, the kabbalists.

The kabbalists do not, however, always succeed. "One can search in vain," wrote Midelfort, "for Catholic accounts of unsuccessful exorcisms."[57] Not so in the Jewish literature of the period, which begins with failures and is thereafter regularly punctuated with them. The didactic punch of these early accounts might even have been weakened by success, for in becoming a hagiographic genre, the fear of heaven inculcated by the spirit's travails could be supplanted by the hope for miraculous, salvific intercession, regardless of one's sins. For writers like Falcon, religious authority could be strengthened no less by the didactic inculcating of its values (through fear) than by the hagiographic amplification of its leading personalities.

## The Young Man in Safed

Sambari's text appends another possession episode to the Falcon account.[58] This second case does not seem to have been part of the original broadsheet, because the signatories on the latter appear immediately after the recounting of the woman's death. The case, as we have noted, is said to have taken place contemporaneously in Safed by Sambari; other versions omit its location. It certainly pairs well with the Falcon account, in any case, with which it has much in common. This time, the victim is a young man, into whom the spirit of another dead young man entered. The spirit's greatest lament is not his own cruel fate, but that of his young widow. Having died at sea, the young bride is trapped in *'agunah* status. Such a status applies to the wife of a man who has disappeared without granting her a divorce; it is forbidden for her to remarry unless reliable news of his death arrives.[59] Although we are given no details, the account relates that the spirit argued assiduously with the assembled rabbis to permit her to remarry, even invoking rabbinic literature in defense of his position.

Then come the disclosures and revelations: the woman, unable to remarry, is engaged in illicit sexual relationships; the spirit's bitter fate is also a punishment for his having had intercourse with a married woman in Constantinople, a transgression punishable by death in classical Jewish sources beginning in the Bible (Lev. 20:10). His death by drowning thus fulfilled the requirement that one guilty of adultery die by choking, a neat fact that may bespeak the learned construction of the whole account.[60] When a group of young men comes in to examine the possessed, the spirit is quick to reveal clairvoyantly that they too were guilty of adulterous activities, which they immediately confess. Like the Falcon case, then, the case of the possession of the young man in Safed suggests a network of sexual intrigue on the part of the victim, his spirit, and his family—here his wife. If the account is at all factual, it is hard to allay the suspicion that the possessed man was sexually involved with the widow. From a psychodynamic perspective, the appearance of the dead husband made it possible to demand the woman's release from the accursed *'agunah* status, while allowing for the transference of the possessed's feelings of guilt at his involvement with a married woman upon her husband and all the young men who come to see their peer. The ability of the possessed to argue with the rabbis bespeaks a degree of engagement in Jewish sources that would likely have prompted guilt over adultery, if not its avoidance.[61] We ought to note as well the gender of the possessor and the possessed. In this case, we find an example of the somewhat less common scenario, in which male "impregnates" male; the male-in-female scenario is the more common in Jewish accounts, by about a 2:1 ratio.[62]

Although sexual transgression may be most prominent in this account, the Torah is also championed: by the dead who would still abide by its rules and by the implementation of its statutes even when lack of evidence, let alone judicial autonomy, prevented ordained penalties from being carried out. The Torah called for the choking of the adulterer, and choke he did. Thus the dead man continued to live; he was punished; he made claims of, and was dependent upon, the living; and his sins, manner of death, and ongoing participation in learned dialectical modes of argumentation reestablished core values of the religious tradition and its overall cogency.

## The Luria Cases

Although already in Safed, neither Luria nor Vital participated in the exorcism documented by Falcon. They did, however, participate in other exorcisms in 1571, including one or two involving a possessed woman,[63] and another involving a possessed young man.[64] The reports of these cases became standard inclusions in seventeenth-century hagiographic works dedicated to Luria and his circle. R. Naftali Bacharach even went so far as to relate the case of the possessed widow of Safed twice in his 1648 work, *'Emek ha-Melekh*.[65] The other oft-published case involving a woman is so similar to the account involving the widow that it is likely a reworking of the same material. The two cases were not printed alongside one another until 1720, when a collector of these accounts, Shlomo Gabbai of Constantinople, failed to note their essential similarity. In addition to these widely circulated accounts, Vital's "private" diary, *Sefer ha-Ḥezyonot*, provides some external corroboration of this case.[66] Indeed, although the report of the possession of the widow is presented by an anonymous narrator, the other reports purport to be first-person accounts authored by Vital himself.

The possession of the young nephew of R. Yehoshua Bin Nun is preserved in two distinct forms, one reported by an anonymous narrator, the other ostensibly reported by Vital. The two versions have much in common: a young man, suffering for years from a recurring illness, is diagnosed by Luria as possessed. In each, the spirit speaks at Luria's command, and explains that he has possessed the nephew to avenge the wrong committed against him by the young man in a previous incarnation. In that previous life, the spirit had been a pauper in Rome; the young man, a charity warden. The refusal of the latter to provide the pauper with adequate support ended tragically, with the pauper's death. The possession of Bin Nun's nephew, then, is the pauper's revenge. Yet Luria prevails upon the spirit to abandon his quest for vengeance and decrees that he leave the young man voluntarily. The spirit agrees, but on one condition: that the young man have no contact with women for a full week. While recognizing the difficulty of these terms, Luria accepts them. At this point, the spirit departs, and Luria establishes a watch over the boy. According to both accounts, the young man is left alone mistakenly in the course of the watch; during that time, his aunt arrives to celebrate his recovery. Finding the young man, she kisses him with joy. At that moment the spirit returns and chokes the lad to death. Having been associated with the episode, Luria quickly departs from Safed to escape punishment from the Turkish authorities in connection with the young man's demise. According to the accounts, Luria's speedy departure was accomplished through a magical path-jumping technique known as *kefiẓat ha-derekh.*[67]

The Bin Nun account focuses upon the dramatic consequences of sin, exemplifying the indefatigable relentlessness of what we might call transmigrational *lex talionis.* Despite being blessed with magical gifts and extraordinary powers, even Luria is ultimately unable to rescue the poor young man from his deceased avenger. It may be no accident that this account is the only one in which Luria plays the active role of exorcist; in other cases, he provided others with the requisite instruction to expel unwelcome spirits. Despite Luria's magical prowess, his effectiveness in this domain was limited, even he would assert, by his metaphysical nature, by his fundamentally gentle "soul-root." As we will see below, an accomplished exorcist was thought to require the severity borne of more stern metaphysical sources. Moreover, the victim's death could not be strictly attributed to Luria's failure. This account preserves a depiction of the great master that does not detract from his awesome reputation. Luria's account is more hagiographic than the possession accounts of Ḥallewa and Falcon: Luria manages in the course of this account to successfully diagnose the possession by means of his clairvoyant powers, to adjure the spirit to depart voluntarily without resorting to complex magical techniques, and to escape the authorities after the victim's death by performing the famous path-jumping technique that spirits him from Safed to Tiberias "in one second."

Although Luria's role and its depiction in the Bin Nun account are fascinating, so too is the profile of the victim. The young eighteen-year-old is characterized as having suffered from chronic heart pain for a dozen years before Luria's intervention and diagnosis. The victim is asked to cooperate in the exorcism process, an expectation that we have seen neither in the first early modern accounts nor in the classic tales of possession from antiquity. His full participation seems to bespeak the new level of involvement of the victim in the phenomenon, now reconceived as a transmigrational interaction in which possessor and possessed may be conceived as having been historically, even "karmically," linked to one another. As in the account of the "Young Man in Safed" above, here again we have a male-in-male possession scenario. And although less sexually dramatic than the Falcon account, the Bin Nun account does have an obviously suggestive homosexual dimension. In this case, a psychodynamic reading of the story would note not only the male-in-male construction of the possession episode, but no less the terms of the spirit for a successful exorcism: the absolute isolation of the young man from women for a brief, albeit unreasonably difficult, length of time.

With the lengthy account of the possession of the widow of Safed, we return to a case of Falcon-like proportions. Unlike the Falcon report, however, this account opens without any didactic introduction.[68] We are confronted immediately by the penetration of the spirit into a poor widow, which has caused her great suffering. Her suffering notwithstanding, however, we are told that the immediate consequence of this affliction was her transformation into a public attraction in Safed. Visited by many people, the widow answers their questions and reveals their innermost troubles and desires. In two of the three versions of this account, the scene is portrayed in terms that normalize her newfound clairvoyant powers and relationship to her community.[69] These sympathetic versions reveal the spirit to be that of a learned rabbinic student, thus ratifying the integrity of the woman's revelations, and lend support to the arguments in favor of regarding spirit possession as a potentially positive form of womens' religiosity, arguments that will be developed below. In the version preserved in Sambari, however, the problematic nature of the possession episode never abates: the visitors do not cease to implore the spirit to leave the poor widow in peace so that she might support herself and her children. And the spirit's clairvoyance is devoted to exposing the visitor's sins, to their public embarrassment. When a sage finally visits the woman, the spirit indeed declares himself to be this rabbi's former student, yet the spirit admits that he was often rebuked for his foul behavior.[70] In a sense, we can detect equivocation on the narrative level no less than in the reception history of this account. The scenario, by all accounts, is both thrilling and terrorizing, with large crowds gathering to behold a widow with newfound clairvoyant powers. Borne of her "impregnation" by the spirit of a rabbinic student, her impressive powers can also be directed against these voyeurs who have gathered around her in her hour of misery, revealing their sins. And even the character of a rabbinic student-spirit seems to suggest something right that has gone awry.

Finally, according to all accounts, the woman's sufferings become so unbearable that her family seeks out the services of R. Isaac Luria, whom they hope will exorcise the spirit. Unable or unwilling to attend to the matter personally, Luria sends Vital to the woman after empowering him through the laying of hands, and furnishing him with mystical intentions and threats that were capable of evicting the spirit against its will.[71] Thus prepared, Vital makes his way to the widow's house. Vital never forgot this first meeting with the woman, and included a description of the encounter in his diary decades later. This private journal entry reads very closely to the versions presented in the three "popular" accounts.

> The year 5331. When I was in Safed, my teacher of blessed memory instructed me to expel evil spirits by the power of the *yiḥud* that he taught me. When I went to him, the woman was lying on the bed. I sat beside her, and he turned his face away from me to the other side. I told him to turn his face towards me to speak with me, and that he depart, but he was unwilling. I squeezed his face with my hand, and he said to me, "Since I did not face you, you struck me? I did this not out of evil, but because your face is alight with a great burning fire, and my soul is scorched if I gaze at you because of your great holiness."[72]

The clairvoyant powers attributed to the spirit in the woman are unabated, even though she was clearly afflicted and indeed bedridden. Avoidance of face-to-face contact with Vital, the spirit explains, was due to Vital's sublime holiness, a quality of Vital's that seems to have been appreciated primarily by men and women gifted with clairvoyant powers. Although Vital's spiritual stature was recognized by Karo's *Maggid*, Luria, R. Lapidot Ashkenazi, the

Shamanic Kabbalists Avraham Avshalom of Morocco and Shealtiel Alsheikh of Persia, palm readers, Arab seers, and a number of visionary women in Safed and Damascus, he appears to have been underappreciated by those lacking visionary powers.[73] For Vital, this meeting with the possessed widow was recalled precisely because it constituted an encounter with yet another visionary capable of assessing his spiritual stature. Although Vital was quite willing to accept the testimony of visionary women to this effect, this short entry exhibits, through its fluid instability of pronouns, the volatility and ambiguity of customary conceptions of gender when confronting a visionary of this kind—demonic/clairvoyant/female/male: "The *woman* was lying on the bed. I sat beside *her*, and *he* turned *his* face away from me . . . [and] I told *him*. . . ." Clearly, in Vital's view, the woman's body is little more than a physical frame containing the soul of the deceased rabbinic student with whom he is trafficking. Yet it would be wrong to downplay the significance of this bodily frame or to exaggerate Vital's sense of its exceptionality. Far from being a pathological exception, Vital's discussions elsewhere of the problems associated with the "normal" transmigration of male souls into female bodies suggest just how complex his construction of gender was. Vital believed, for example, that his own wife Hannah was in fact a male soul, the reincarnation of Rabbi Akiva's father-in-law.[74]

Vital perceived the refusal to face him as insolence and did not hesitate to use physical intimidation against the disrespectful spirit/woman, forcing him/her to face him. Positioned at the widow's bedside, Vital "squeezed *his* face" to bring about the face-to-face encounter. Indeed, as he himself understood it, Vital's soul genealogy inclined him to violence. Luria required Vital to be especially careful to keep this tendency in check, ordering him to avoid killing even fleas or lice. (Luria himself, Vital reports, killed no creatures intentionally.) Vital was also to remove knives from the table before reciting grace after meals and was never to function as a *mohel* (circumciser) or slaughterer-butcher (or even to observe them at work).[75] In this journal entry, nevertheless, Vital hides neither his immodest approach to the woman's bed nor his assault, albeit limited, upon her body. Moreover, the rare opportunity to compare a revealing first-person description by the exorcist himself with the later popular accounts is particularly telling. Three clear deviations from Vital's account may be discerned, all of which point essentially in the same direction. First, none of the three popular accounts makes mention of the fact that the woman was in bed when Vital arrived. The choreography of the scene is modestly ambiguous. Second, all popular accounts claim that Vital used a "decree" to force the spirit to face him; no physical contact with the woman, which too might have been construed as immodest, was necessary.[76] Finally, it is the spirit's sinfulness that, in popular accounts, explains the spirit's inability to face Vital, rather than its visionary insight of Vital's spiritual grandeur. From these differences, we may see precisely the areas in which accounts that have some factual basis are reported quite accurately, but with omissions and additions that bowdlerize the texts where they might prove embarrassing, or insufficiently didactic. Apparently a portrait of Vital grabbing a visionary woman in her bedchamber was not what the writers and redactors of these accounts had in mind.[77]

And sexual transgression is indeed at the heart of the case, the spirit's sin being the fathering of bastards in an adulterous affair with a married woman. In his conversation with Vital, the spirit recounts his sins and, at greater length, the travails he has undergone since his death by drowning.[78] Refused entry into Gehinnom by 10,000 protesting sinners ostensibly more worthy than he, the spirit attempted to find refuge in the body of a Jewish inhabitant of the city of Ormuz.[79] To his chagrin, not a single Jew in that city could provide him with an inhabitable body. Here again, sexual transgression figures prominently. Owing to their "fornication with menstruating [Jewish] and Gentile women," the bodies of these Jews are contaminated, filled, and surrounded with the forces of defilement. The account of this case, perhaps more than any other, is indeed rife with images of bodies filled—filled with forces of defilement, with souls of the living and the dead, and even with fetuses. When the spirit cannot possess a Jew in Ormuz without harming further his own reprobate soul, he enters a doe in the wilderness of Gaza out of sheer desperation.[80] This doe, however, was itself an unsuitable container—"for the soul of a human being and the soul of a beast are not equal, for one walks upright and the other bent." The spirit, then, is not what would be thought of today as "spiritual"; it has physical form and dimensions, and only the human body is contoured such as to make it an apposite host. It is matter, albeit of a much finer grade than that of which the body is formed. "Also, the soul [*nefesh*] of the beast is full of filth and is repulsive, its smell foul before the soul of a human being. And its food is not human food." In the spirit's description of his travails, he makes clear that the host's pains and pleasures are fully shared by the temporary, unwelcome squatter. And if the mismatch wasn't uncomfortable enough given the differences of form and diet, the spirit explains that in this case, the doe was pregnant and was therefore already quite full. The result was pain for the spirit and the doe alike, for "three souls cannot dwell together" in a single body. The doe, in agony, ran wildly in the hills and through rocky terrain, her belly swollen, until it split open, pouring out the three occupants with her death.[81]

The next bodily container for the spirit was to be a *Kohen* (a Jew of the priestly caste) in the city of Nablus. This gentleman, apparently realizing that he was possessed, called in the local expert exorcists for assistance. In this case, the spirit tells us that Muslim clerics were summoned, not kabbalists. This detail accords well with what we know about Jewish life in mid-sixteenth-century Nablus. Unlike the Jews in Safed who lived in a separate Jewish quarter, the Jews of Nablus lived in mixed Jewish-Muslim neighborhoods.[82] It is also indicative of the acceptance of non-Jewish magical healers in Jewish society that we shall consider at greater length below. The Islamic holy men—using incantations, adjurations, and amulets—do, in fact, succeed in exorcising the spirit from the *Kohen*. Here again, it is the bodily vessel and its contents that determine the matter. Responding to Vital's astonishment that the Muslims' magico-mystical arsenal was capable of effecting the exorcism, the spirit explains that the techniques employed by the Muslims infused the *Kohen*'s body with so many defiling spirits that he had to leave to avoid the kind of contamination he had feared contracting from the impure contents of the bodies of the Jews of Ormuz.[83] This fascinating turnabout takes us from what at first appears to be a model of magico-therapeutic syncretism to a devastating critique of such syncretism. The ambivalence felt in the wake of a successful exorcism performed by the "competition" is articulated in terms that authorize that power while simultaneously undermining its religious credibility; they won the race but failed the drug test. This critique, moreover, is somewhat ironic given the widespread use of demonic adjurations to expel evil spirits found in Jewish magical manuscripts. Such demonic adjurations work along similar lines, essentially forcing out the spirits by their own malevolent presence and potency.[84]

What motivated the spirit's possession of the widow? Early modern Christian attitudes regarding demonic motivations underlying possession reflected theological premises quite remote from Jewish conceptions. In his *Traicté des Energumènes* of 1599, Léon D'Alexis (Pierre de Bérulle) explained the Devil's motives in a manner that reveals how broad the gulf could be between Jewish and Christian views. The Devil, he argued, being "the ape of God," is dedicated to incarnating himself in men, as did Christ himself.[85] This, he suggested, accounts for the proliferation of possession since the birth of Christ.[86] Catholic theologians of the sixteenth century also assumed that demonic possession was most likely to occur as a punishment for the sins of the possessed, whereas popular accounts most commonly portray victims of possession as "pious young Christians." Is there a similar disparity between learned and popular views of this issue in Jewish culture? R. Moses Cordovero stated in his *Drishot be-'Inyanei ha-Malakhim* (Inquiries Concerning Angels) that "the types of *'ibbur* depend on a man's moral and spiritual state, whether his soul is entered by a good soul—because he has done a *mizvah*—or an evil soul—because he has committed some sin. . . ."[87] Even though we have few sources that can directly provide a "popular" Jewish conception of the typical victim of spirit possession, we may be able to infer a disparity of this kind from the degree of inner confusion on this point displayed in Jewish sources. Early modern Jewish possession accounts shift inconsistently between affirmations of the innocence and even piety of the victim, and ascriptions of blame—often of the same person. When the exorcists in the Falcon case asked the spirit of Samuel Ẓarfati what allowed him to possess a "kosher" woman, he replied that the woman had inadvertently cast some mud upon him as he was hovering in her midst.[88] In the case currently under consideration, we know that the most egregious sin of the spirit was sexual, but what of the widow? The sin that allows for the possession to take place seems not much less trivial, though "justifiable" on the basis of the positions staked out in the contemporary Jewish demonological literature. As Vital himself wrote in his treatise on transmigration, "it sometimes happens that notwithstanding the presence in a person of a pure and sublime soul, he may come at some point to anger. Then, [that soul] will depart from him, and in its place will enter another, inferior soul."[89] Before concluding his exorcism of the widow (and the woman in Case 7), Vital asks the spirit how he obtained permission to enter his victim's body: "The spirit responded: 'I spent one night in her house. At dawn, this woman arose from her bed and wanted to light a fire from the stone and iron, but the burnt rag did not catch the sparks. She persisted stubbornly, but did not succeed. She then became intensely angry, and cast the iron and the stone and the burnt rag—everything—from her hand to the ground, and angrily said, 'to Satan with you!' Immediately I was given permission to enter her body.' " What appears to us as a small matter, a casual curse out of frustration, was evidently taken quite seriously. This severe approach to cursing had its basis in the strict enforcement of the third commandment, and traditional Jewish law prescribed penalties for such verbal crimes that paralleled those meted out to witches and idolaters.[90] Sixteenth-century Jews were not alone in regarding the consequences of cursing most gravely; many Christian tales of possession dealt with the consequences of the curse "the devil take you."[91] Maureen Flynn has recently noted that "blasphemy was the most frequently censured religious offence of the Spanish people in the early modern period, far outnumbering convictions on charges of Judaism, Lutheranism, Illuminism, sexual immorality or witchcraft."[92] J. P. Dedieu's work has shown, moreover, that, as in the expression by the woman in the possession case under our consideration, the Spanish Inquisitors were concerned with "petty crimes . . . of the word . . . that never attained the status of formal heresy, much less of unbelief."[93] Concern over these types of verbal offenses, known in Spain as *palabras,* seems to have been particularly prevalent in the mid-sixteenth century. In addition to her angrily spoken words, the woman had thrown down the stone and rag in frustration. Such an act, like cursing, was traditionally considered an invitation to the demonic forces to act, as we read, for example, in zoharic passages.[94] Nevertheless, according to our account, Vital could not accept the idea that a woman could be possessed for letting an ill-chosen word, rock, or rag slip on that cold morning. The spirit, for his part, was forthcoming with a more serious transgression that indeed justified his siege. Here, we return to the issue of skepticism; the curse was merely the outward expression of a deeper heretical posture.

"Know," the spirit tells Vital, "that this woman's inside is not like her outside." Although she participated in the religious observances of Safed's Jewish community, the widow had her doubts. "For she does not believe in the miracles that the Holy One, Blessed be He, did for Israel, and in particular in the Exodus from Egypt. Every Passover night, when all of Israel are rejoicing and good hearted, reciting the great *Hallel*[95] and telling of the Exodus from Egypt, it is vanity in her eyes, a mockery and a farce. And she thinks in her heart that there was never a miracle such as this." At this point, Vital turns his attention away from the spirit and focuses upon the widow.

Immediately the Rav said to the woman, "Do you believe with perfect belief that the Holy One, Blessed be He, is One and Unique, and that He created the heavens and the earth, and that He has the power and capacity to do anything that He desires, and that there is no one who can tell him what to do?" She responded to him and said, "Yes, I believe it all in perfect faith." The Rav, may his memory be a blessing, further said to her, "Do you believe in perfect faith that the Holy One, blessed be He, took us out of Egypt from the house of slavery, and split the sea for us, and accomplished many miracles for us?" She responded, "Yes, master, I believe it all with perfect faith, and if I had at times a different view, I regret it." And she began to cry.

This confrontation concluded, Vital speedily exorcises the spirit with little difficulty.[96] Finally, in an epilogue that again raises the issue of the woman's skepticism and religious identification with the traditional community, we are told that the spirit continued to threaten the woman after its exorcism from her body. Concerned, her relatives returned to Luria, and he again sent Vital as his emissary. This time, Vital was to check the integrity of the mezuzah of her home to ensure that she was adequately protected from evil. Upon inspection, however, Vital discovered that the woman did not even have a mezuzah on her doorpost![97] The mezuzah, a parchment-based phylactery based on Deuteronomy, Chapter 6, verse 9, was regarded as affording protection to those within the houses bearing them, the inscription on the outside of the parchment, *ShD"I* ("the Almighty"), being taken as an acrostic for "Keeper of the Doors of Israel."[98] Tradition also allowed for the possibility that the affixing of a mezuzah might even successfully exorcize one possessed in the house. An eighth-century collection of rabbinic literature, the *Sheiltot*,[99] includes a version of a story from the Jerusalem Talmud, in which Rav's affixing of a mezuzah on the door of the palace of the Artavan, last of the Parthian kings, sufficed to expel the evil spirit that possessed his daughter.[100]

Once again, then, we are confronted with an account that presents a possessed woman who, by virtue of her possession, is able to function as a type of clairvoyant figure in the community, providing "services" not far removed from those provided by figures such as Luria. She attracts many people and is able to discern their hidden sins and desires. Her visionary ability also results in a caustic encounter with Vital, which he recorded in his journal years later. Evident discomfort with aspects of this scenario is suggested by our comparison of the various versions of the account, the bowdlerization of unsavory details, and the heightening of didactic elements signifying later redactions of Vital's original. Moreover, the spirit's presence in the woman fulfills the functions considered above: his appearance before and among the living demonstrates the persistence of life after death, whereas his suffering dramatizes and embodies the doctrine of punishment for the wicked. Although there is little that suggests a relationship between the spirit and the widow, he is not unknown in the community and soon establishes himself as a former student of a leading rabbinic figure in Safed. Finally, the sins of the spirit, and those of the widow no less, by stark transgression, cast in bold relief the values and aspirations of the rabbinic writers who crafted the account, if not broader sectors of the cultural environment. Sexual licentiousness and popular skepticism emerge in this account, as in others we have examined, as fundamental threats to communal leadership struggling to establish a community on the basis of pietistic ideals.

In seeking to understand the apparent proliferation of the phenomenon of spirit possession in sixteenth-century Safed, these efforts to forge a pietistic community cannot be forgotten. In addition to the Iberian cultural influences that we have stressed, Safed was a "pressure cooker," uniquely capable of stimulating apparitional contact with its dead through the idiom of possession. We recall that in northern Germany, Midelfort discovered twice as many cases of possession in this period as in southern Germany, with the greatest frequency "among nunneries and among the most gnesio-Lutheran areas." In his estimation, this concentration was due to the fact that "in both situations the attempt to live an ever more perfect life may have led to stronger temptations [manifested as demonic possession] than those felt in other parts of Germany."[101] How apt is this observation to the religious environment of sixteenth-century Safed, the epicenter of the possession phenomenon in Jewish culture.[102] As Gershom Scholem described it, "Ascetic piety reigned supreme in Safed. At first the religious ideal of a mystical elite only, asceticism now allied itself to an individual and public morality based on the new kabbalism; it struck deep roots in the collective consciousness."[103] The "megalomaniacal" posture that reigned in Safed in this period has been well depicted by Joseph Dan:

> The very pretension of Safed to be a spiritual center and the epicenter of ordination in the Jewish world after the destruction of the center in Spain has within it something of megalomania: a remote village, which even in its apex of development had a population smaller than scores of Jewish communities in Europe—and which lacked the vitality of a large and crowded assembly of Jews, with a high level of culture and organization—dared to aspire to serve as a replacement for the tremendous center that was destroyed in Spain, and to carry the miracle of redemption to the whole community of Israel. [104]

In short, every element was present in the culture of mid-sixteenth-century Safed to make it the epicenter of a resurgence of spirit possession in Jewish society. A substantial number of Iberian refugees, conversos among them, had made Safed their new home. With them, they brought stories and memories, theory and praxis, inner conflicts and turmoil, elation and despair, faith and skepticism. Now in the Ottoman Empire alongside Arabic-speaking coreligionists, they were also in close proximity to Islamic traditions, popular and orthodox alike, sharing similar demonological views and familiar with forms of spirit possession and their magico-therapeutic treatment. For its part, the rabbinic leadership of Safed was leading a campaign to make of this fledgling community a new spiritual center for world Jewry, and producing didactic texts designed to inculcate its values and to discipline its people. Finally, embracing the cemetery at its heart, the people of Safed were living with their dead in exceedingly close proximity. With visionary mystics beholding apparitions at every turn,with farm animals being revealed as deceased relatives, and, no less, with the quotidian brushes with death faced by a society beleaguered by plagues and the tragic mortality of the young, possession by the dead was only natural. Its etiology was certainly familiar to all; if each possession case required careful diagnosis and inquiry to be established as authentic, no doubts were voiced as to its fundamental plausibility. The men and women who were thus possessed were full somatic participants in the ferment that characterized their cultural environment. Their experience and its diffusion through the accounts carefully drafted by leading Safedian rabbis was to resonate for centuries in Jewish communities around the world for whom Safed, itself long since in decline, had come to represent pietistic aspiration and achievement.

# Chapter 3
# *The Task of the Exorcist*

*The material aspects of spells has frequently been described. A list of them will wear down any scholar who takes on the unenviable task of studying them.*

*—Julio Caro Baroja*[1]

Exorcism techniques, as eclectic as they were extensive, were found among the Jews for centuries, a diverse repository deployed by magical experts in their midst. This legacy was inherited by generation after generation of magical practitioners, many of whom were also leading rabbinic figures. In scanning the history of this magico-liturgical material, only one chapter seems to evince signs of internal opposition: the "reform" in technique demanded by R. Isaac Luria. With the reconstruction of the possession idiom, and its reinscription in the field of transmigration, came the need to develop new strategies for exorcising the spirits. Moreover, Luria's new approach reflected his idiosyncratic and ambivalent attitude toward Judaism's magical tradition. Notwithstanding Luria's towering reputation, however, subsequent Jewish exorcists seem to have simply *added* his reformed technique to their arsenals, rather than rely on it to the exclusion of the others.

The Church also initiated exorcism reform in the late Middle Ages. Europeans saw the transformation of exorcism from a spectacle, performed by saints and wonder-workers, into a fixed ritual, performed by priests. This process, an expression of the Church's quest for centralization of authority, and amid a growing suspicion of female spirituality, culminated in the early seventeenth century with the codification of the *Rituale Romanum* (1614), which treated the priestly rite of exorcism in the tenth title.[2] Thus, although there was a concurrent rise in the prominence of spirit possession among early modern Jews and Christians, the Jewish rituals of exorcism did not undergo the kind of revision and standardization that Catholic authorities applied to the exorcisms in their own traditional arsenals. Whereas the Church may have sought to centralize its authority by controlling exorcism, a decentralized rabbinic leadership seems to have favored bolstering its own authority by retaining a broad spectrum of impressive magical techniques to vanquish the spirits.

Despite the warnings of Baroja that open this chapter, in what follows I present the adumbrated results of "the unenviable task" of studying the formulas of Jewish exorcism since antiquity. Such a survey will better enable us to appreciate the context and significance of Luria's reform of exorcism technique in the late sixteenth century, as well as its subsequent absorption in the ever-syncretistic Jewish magical repository.

## Exorcism in the Ancient World: Jewish Dimensions

King David is the first recorded exorcist in Jewish—or at least Judean—history, and King Saul the first demoniac. When King Saul was tormented by an evil spirit, the young David was called upon to heal him with the sweet strains of his lyre.

> The spirit of YHVH departed from Saul and an evil spirit from YHVH tormented him. And Saul's servants said to him, "Behold now, an evil ELOHIM spirit [*ruaḥ elohim ra'ah*] is tormenting thee. Let our lord now command thy servants, who are before thee, to seek out a man, who knows how to play on the lyre, and it shall come to pass when the evil ELOHIM spirit is upon thee, that he will play with his hand and thou shalt be well. [1 *Sam.* 16:14–16]

David is successful: "And it came to pass, when the ELOHIM spirit was upon Saul, that David took the harp, and played with his hand; so Saul found relief [*ve-ravaḥ le-Shaul*], and it was well with him, and the evil spirit departed from him" (ibid., 23). After waves of spiritual elation ("the spirit of YHVH") and affliction ("the evil ELOHIM spirit"), only the strains of David's harp return the king to a state of well-being. Yet diagnosing Saul as a manic-depressive would be anachronistic and insensitive to the biblical valence of the key terms in the account: *ruaḥ ra'ah* and *elohim*. Elohistic spirits are not metaphors, and this passage constitutes an account of an attack of one such evil elohistic spirit upon Saul. Josephus was unequivocal about the nature of the disturbance, and described it as an attack of demons (*daimonia*).

But the Divine Power departed from Saul, and removed to David; who, upon this removal of the Divine Spirit to him, began to prophesy. But as for Saul, some strange and demoniacal disorders came upon him, and brought upon him such suffocations as were ready to choke him; for which the physicians could find no other remedy but this, That if any person could charm those passions by singing, and playing upon the harp, they advised them to inquire for such a one, and to observe when these demons came upon him and disturbed him, and to take care that such a person might stand over him, and play upon the harp, and recite hymns to him.[3]

Josephus's amplified rendering of the biblical passage exemplifies the new spiritual climate in which he wrote. Cosmological shifts transformed a three-tiered hierarchical universe (heaven-earth-underworld) into a universe of concentric spheres, with earth at the center. The newer conception would minimize the direct interventions of the deity, now located at considerable remove, while ramifying the intermediary forces that occupied the nearly endless expanse that separated earth from the remote god.[4] The *elohim* spirit who had overcome King Saul was now understood as a battery of daimones.

Thus spirit possession became more widespread, demonology more complex, and exorcism more magically sophisticated by the Second Temple period. The plethora of accounts of spirit possession and descriptions of exorcism in the literature of the period make this patently clear: from the New Testament and Apocrypha, to the Qumran texts, Josephus, and rabbinic literature.

## Ancient Exorcism

The New Testament features scores of references to spirit possession, with an especially high concentration in the gospels of Luke and Mark. Lest we underestimate the centrality of this phenomenon in early Christianity, note that Jesus' mission on earth was summarized by Peter in Acts as "doing good and healing all that were oppressed by the devil" (Acts 10:38). The Gospel of Mark concludes with a description of the signs that enable one to identify a true Christian, the first of which is the power to exorcise: "These are the signs that will be associated with believers: in my name they will cast out devils; they will have the gift of tongues; they will pick up snakes in their hands and be unharmed should they drink deadly poison; they will lay their hands on the sick, who will recover" (Mark 16:17–18). Exorcistic prowess is the primary mark of the Christian according to this source.[5]

Although less prominent than in the New Testament, exorcism is referred to a number of times in rabbinic literature as well.[6] A well-known example is the case of a Gentile who asked R. Yoḥanan ben Zakkai for an explanation of the customs associated with the Red Heifer, which seemed to him to be magical. The rabbi responded that the process of slaughtering the animal, burning it, collecting its ash, and using the ash to purify was analogous to the Gentile's own customs for exorcising evil spirits.[7]

Meir Bar-Ilan has analyzed a number of rabbinic-era exorcisms recorded in talmudic and midrashic literature. Arguing that in antiquity there was no distinction between religious life and magic, as is commonly assumed by modern scholars, Bar-Ilan claims that exorcism was "an accepted popular practice." It was performed not as a magical act but simply as a healing therapy, "like the war on germs that penetrate the body of modern man."[8] All three of Bar-Ilan's examples of rabbinic exorcism, however, emphasize precisely its *wondrous* dimensions. The first, from a medieval source, deals with R. Ḥanina ben Dosa, who went down to a cave for ritual immersion. When *Kutim* (sectarians) sealed the cave with a large rock, spirits came to remove it, freeing R. Ḥanina. One of these spirits later victimized a girl in his village, and R. Ḥanina's students called his attention to the girl's sufferings. R. Ḥanina went to the girl and addressed the spirit: "Why do you distress a daughter of Abraham?" "Were you not the one who descended to the cave," responded the spirit, "until my kindred spirits and I came and removed it [the stone]? And for the favor that I did you, this is how you treat me?" R. Ḥanina, a wonder-worker and healer in talmudic sources,[9] then began a decree of exorcism upon the spirit, though the formula was not preserved in the account.[10]

Yet another talmudic story recounts R. Shimon ben Yoḥai's successful exorcism of the Emperor's daughter, which led to the rescinding of anti-Jewish legislation.[11] R. Shimon, unlike the wonder-working Ḥanina, was a leading rabbinic figure known for his *halakhic* authority, as well as for his magical prowess. In this case, the demon actually collaborates with R. Shimon; the possession is a "setup" to allow R. Shimon to earn the favor of the Emperor by saving his daughter. This source, and its midrashic parallel,[12] refer to the demon's entering the belly of the girl, the whispering of incantations into her ear by the exorcist R. Shimon, and the breaking of glass in the Emperor's house as a sign of the demon's departure. According to Bar-Ilan, this case exemplifies the centrality of charismatic, shamanistic Jewish leadership in the ancient world.

Josephus provides one of the richest accounts of exorcism in ancient Judaism in his *Antiquitates Judaicae*, describing the exorcism of a demoniac by the Jew Eleazar before Vespasian and his court. As Josephus tells it, "Eleazar applied to the nostrils of the demon-possessed man his own ring, which had under its seal-stone one of the roots whose properties King Solomon had taught, and so drew the demon out through the sufferer's nose. The man immediately fell to the ground, and Eleazar then adjured the demon never to return, calling the name of Solomon and reciting the charms that he had composed."[13] Josephus regarded demons as "spirits of the wicked which enter into men that are alive and kill them," but which can be driven out by a certain root.[14] It has been suggested that Eleazar was an Essene and that the Essenes were in possession of secret works, including one or more works on healing ascribed to King Solomon—perhaps to be identified with the work on healing hidden by Hezekiah.[15]

In the third century, Origen testified to the broad recognition in the ancient world that Jews and Jewish formulas were particularly powerful agents against demons. He was carrying on a trope that shot through Greek and Roman literature for centuries.[16]

> In any event, it is clear that the Jews trace their genealogy back to the three fathers Abraham, Isaac, and Jacob. Their names are so powerful when linked with the name of God that the formula "the God of Abraham, the God of Isaac, and the God of Jacob" is used not only by members of the Jewish nation in their prayers to God and when they exorcise daemons, but also by almost all those who deal in magic and spells. For in magical treatises it is often to be found that God is invoked by this formula, and that in spells against daemons His name is used in close connexion with the names of these men.[17]

Origen is mindful of the fact that the Jews remain the authorities in these matters. "We learn from the Hebrews," he writes, "the history of the events mentioned in these formulae and the interpretation of the names, since in their traditional books and language they pride themselves on these things and explain them."[18] If, as Marcel Simon has suggested, "In the opinion of the ancients, magic was, as it were, congenital in Israel," recent scholars have argued that the very concept of spirit possession is foreign to Greek thought in classical and Hellenistic times.[19] A broad consensus in the ancient world to this effect is indirectly revealed by the many Jewish elements that found their way into both pagan and Christian exorcism rituals, as exemplified so well by the *Greek Magical Papyri* (*PGM*), a body of papyri from Greco-

Roman Egypt dating from the second century B.C.E. to the fifth century C.E. The *PGM* contain a number of exorcism rituals featuring pronounced Jewish elements.[20]

Prominent among these exorcism techniques in the *PGM* are Hebrew magical names, references to the God of Israel and the Patriarchs, and to the saving acts of this mighty God.[21] The following famous passage provides a good sense of the nature of these rituals.

A tested charm of Pibechis[22] for those possessed by daimons: Take oil of unripe olives with the herb mastigia and the fruit pulp of the lotus, and boil them with colorless marjoram while saying, "IOEL . . . come out from NN." The phylactery: On a tin lamella write / "IAEO . . ." and hang it on the patient. It is terrifying to every daimon, a thing he fears. After placing [the patient] opposite [to you], adjure. . . .

[The adjuration:] I adjure you by the God of the Hebrews, Jesus IABA . . . I adjure you by the one who appeared to Osrael in a shining pillar and a cloud by day, / who saved his people from the Pharaoh and brought upon Pharaoh the ten plagues because of his disobedience. I adjure you, every daimonic spirit, to tell whatever sort you may be, because I adjure by the seal / which Solomon placed on the tongue of Jeremiah, and he told. . . . I adjure you by the great god SABAOTH, through whom the Jordan River drew back and the Red Sea, / which Israel crossed, became impassable . . . I adjure you by the one who introduced the one hundred forty languages and distributed them by his own command. . . . I adjure [you] by the one in holy Jerusalem, before whom the / unquenchable fire burns for all time, with his holy name, IAEOBAPHRENEMOUN (formula), the one before whom the fiery Gehenna trembles, flames surround, iron bursts asunder and every mountain is afraid from its foundation. / I adjure you, every daimonic spirit, by the one who oversees the earth and makes its foundations tremble, [the one] who made all things which are not into that which is.[23]

The closing instructions of the exorcism adjure the exorcist himself to abstain from eating pork in order to ensure the effectiveness of the ceremony. He is instructed to keep himself pure, "for this charm is Hebraic and is preserved among pure men."

This procedure combines a number of components: gathering and cooking herbs, along with reciting spells during the process; attaching an amulet to the patient; adjuring the demon to disclose its identity; addressing the deity by various magical names; and recalling His works. As the adjuration in the name of Jesus makes clear, the procedure is not of Jewish provenance, though it obviously has many Jewish elements and is touted as "Hebraic" by the enthusiastic and earnest magician-scribe.[24] Some components, like the use of herbs, may reflect Jewish influence but are nonetheless fairly universal in character.[25] Amulets too were not unfamiliar in Jewish and non-Jewish circles in antiquity, known in such everyday accoutrements of Jewish life as *tefillin* and *mezuzot* (phylacteries for placement on the arm and head during prayer, and upon the doorposts of the home, respectively) as well as in more esoteric forms of Babylonian magical practices.[26]

Our example from the *PGM* also illustrates another characteristic of exorcism rituals that was to remain a constant throughout history: the imperative to force the demon to speak and to name himself. We find this in sources ranging from the Gospel of Mark (5:1–20) to Rumpelstilzkin in Grimm's *Märchen*, as well as in many of the Jewish procedures of the medieval and early modern periods. As Michel de Certeau has written, exorcists respond to the indeterminate "other" that speaks from the possessed

> through a labor of naming or designating that is the characteristic answer to possession in any traditional society. Whether in Africa or South America, therapy in cases of possession essentially consists of naming, of ascribing a term to what manifests itself as speech, but as an uncertain speech inseparable from fits, gestures, and cries. A disturbance arises, and therapy, or social treatment, consists of providing a name—a term already listed in a society's catalogues—for this uncertain speech. . . . Thus exorcism is essentially an enterprise of denomination intended to reclassify a protean uncanniness within an established language. It aims at restoring the postulate of all language, that is, a stable relation between the interlocutor, "I," and a social signifier, the proper name.[27]

Our text's adjuration, "I adjure you by the one who introduced the one hundred forty languages and distributed them by his own command," alludes to this destabilization of "the postulate of all language." In this case, it also asserts an ultimate ordering subject, the "I" of "I am the Lord your God"—guaranteeing order behind the linguistic chaos of Babel.

Finally, we find in the *PGM* passage a recounting of God's mighty works, an example of what has been called "the authoritative discourse of precedent."[28] This particular historiola places significant emphasis upon the crossing of the Red Sea and the Jordan River. In addition to calling upon the power manifested in these great acts, the specific references to bodies of water reflect the widespread notion that demons and witchcraft have no power against water, an idea found in ancient sources from Apuleius to the Talmud, and underlying the twentieth-century icon of the melting wicked witch upon her drenching by Dorothy.[29] It seems to have troubled few that water was also considered a favored domain of the spirits, and drinking a typical way of becoming possessed.

Though magical manuscripts were consigned to destruction repeatedly throughout history, they could never be totally eradicated. Collections were preserved and even enhanced from generation to generation by each recipient of the precious tomes. Ioan Couliano wrote of "an uninterrupted continuity of the methods of practical magic" stretching from late antiquity, via Byzantium, and, through Arab channels, reaching the West in the twelfth century.[30] In Baroja's words, "There is little difference between the spells which Celestina knew and used, and those enumerated in Latin texts."[31] Indeed, magical texts featuring exorcism techniques reveal a consistency over time that is positively unnerving to the historian, who by training and disposition is best equipped to analyze and evaluate change. The preservation of formulas is so significant that scholars have at times been able to reconstruct magical fragments from antiquity by using medieval materials, such as the readings of fifth-century clay tablets assisted by eleventh-century Geniza fragments accomplished by Joseph Naveh and Shaul Shaked.[32]

The use of Hebrew names in non-Jewish rites would continue over the centuries, evincing the enduring and highly syncretistic nature of these traditions. Thus the frequent appearance in Catholic exorcism rites of the Hebrew magical name *AGLA*, the acrostic of the phrase *Atah Gibbor Le-ʿolam Adonai*, "You are mighty forever, my Lord."[33] Jews and Christians used this magical name, connoting as it did divine judgment and severity, in cases of possession, demonic disturbance, or for all-purpose protection. Yet the presence of Hebrew in Christian rites did not find favor in the eyes of all Church authorities. Martín de Castañega, the Franciscan friar whose views on possession by the dead have been noted above, took pains in his *Tratado* to denounce the use of Hebrew words in Christian exorcisms:

> It seems a vain thing, and even a lack of faith, and from the Jewish quarter [*judería*], or superstition, to use ancient Hebrew names in Christian and Catholic prayers, as if the old names were worth more than the new. And such names are especially dangerous for the ignorant who know little, because those Hebrew and Greek names may serve as a cover, so that other unknown, diabolical names are spoken with them.[34]

Castañega's conflation of Judaizing, superstition, magic, and diabolism typifies a critique of the syncretistic tradition going back to the early Christian centuries.[35] It is echoed by Daniel Defoe, who charged in his 1727 work *A System of Magick; or, A History of the Black Art* that magicians depended on books filled with Hebrew and Arabic, alongside altogether nonsensical words and symbols. This, he felt, placed them in league with the demonolatrous necromancers of hoary antiquity. Magicians "make a great deal of Ceremony with their Circles and Figures, with Magical Books, Hebrew or Arabick Characters, muttering of hard Words, and other Barbarisms innumerable; Just, in a word, as the old Necromancers do, when they consult with the Devil."[36] The reputation of Hebrew words for magical efficacy and this syncretic tradition were not limited to the Christian world nor even to the Middle Ages. A more recent witness, from the beginning of the twentieth century, testified that "At present in Cairo, Baghdad and Damascus, Jewish silversmiths carry on a large trade in Moslem amulets. In fact an amulet is supposed to have special power if it has not only Arabic but Hebrew letters on it."[37]

## Medieval Jewish Exorcism

*Shoshan Yesod ha-'Olam* (Lily, Foundation of the World) is perhaps the most comprehensive extant late medieval magical Hebrew manuscript.[38] Most of the manuscript, in its present form, was compiled in the early decades of the sixteenth century by R. Joseph Tirshom, a kabbalist based in Salonika about whom little is known. Tirshom was exposed to magico-mystical traditions from around the Jewish world, and his great manuscript bears witness to this range of experience. In Salonika, Tirshom became acquainted with material that arrived with Spanish exiles as well as with members of the city's Ashkenazi community, including his teacher, R. Meir ha-Levi.[39] Tirshom also traveled widely and discovered magical works in Damascus, Jerusalem, Egypt, and other Jewish communities in the Levant, many of which he copied whole cloth into his comprehensive compilation.[40] Some of these he copied from Judeo-Arabic works, apparently intending to have them translated subsequently into Hebrew; Tirshom does not seem to have understood Arabic himself.[41]

*Shoshan Yesod ha-'Olam* was a pivotal text in the transmission of Jewish magical traditions. First of all, it included significant passages and even entire works from earlier strata in the history of Jewish magic, including material from texts and teachers who played a central role in the development of Safedian Kabbalah. Tirshom copied from *Sefer ha-Meshiv*, perhaps the most important work from late medieval Spain to provide the theoretical underpinnings of *dybbuk* possession as well as traditions in the name of individuals such as R. Ḥayyim Ashkenazi, a mystic acquainted with the father of Vital and whose prophecies regarding Ḥayyim Vital are noted in the latter's journal.[42] Second, *Shoshan Yesod ha-'Olam* was clearly an important manuscript for the mystical inheritors of Luria's legacy. Autographs and annotations in the margins indicate that it passed through the hands of important redactors of Lurianic literature, including R. Ya'aqov Ẓemaḥ, and even caught the attention of no less a striking figure than Sabbetai Sevi, whose signature appears on page 522![43] Additions to the manuscript—including a commentary on Luria's sabbath meal hymns—are in a mixture of Spanish and Ashkenazic handwriting, indicating that it found a home among the Ashkenazi sages who studied with Sephardic authorities in Jerusalem in the early seventeenth century; other additions exhibit a liberal use of Ladino.[44] In short, just as Tirshom copied copiously from earlier works as well as from his contemporaries, his great manuscript became an important source for subsequent generations of practical kabbalists and copyists.

*Shoshan Yesod ha-'Olam* is full of exorcism rituals. Although many techniques are suggested in the manuscript, the ingredients that go into most of them would be found in every good magician's cabinets. The procedures almost universally call for the adjuration of spirits, some angelic and some demonic, in the classic form "I adjure you angel so-and-so to come and to do such-and-such." The exorcist must adjure the appropriate angel for the job, because each day has its own angel who must be enlisted for the operation to be a success. The procedures have much in common with those found on the magical bowls of antiquity as well as with those of the *PGM.* Bowls are still very much in use—they are written upon, erased, and filled with living waters made murky by the erasure. The potion is then given to the possessed to drink. Other passages suggest that deer skin be used in lieu of a bowl or that the magical names be written directly upon the forehead and arms of the possessed. Psalms, foremost among them the famous antidemonic Psalm 91, also have their uses here, suggesting parallels going back to Qumran and forward to the *Rituale Romanum.*[45] Elsewhere, the exorcist is advised to supplement the recitation of two chapters of Psalms with the use of leaves from a date palm that has not yet produced fruit.[46] Finally, it is important to note that most techniques suggested for treating spirit possession have other uses as well—they are truly broad-spectrum remedies. *Shoshan Yesod ha-'Olam* includes a technique that promises to offer protection from injuries, doubts and fears, bad dreams, business negotiation problems, crying children, women having difficulty in labor, dangers of travel, and demonic afflictions.[47] Another technique is said to have the power to confuse and confound one's enemy, while also being capable of exorcising a demon and exiling someone from his or her place of residence.[48] The ability to treat disparate problems with one solution stems from a belief that the problems had a common etiology, often astrologically or sympathetically understood.

Quite nearly at random, then, we may choose from the many techniques of adjuration exorcism in *Shoshan Yesod ha-ʿOlam* to exemplify the "pre-Lurianic" approach. Little had changed in the composition of such techniques since antiquity, as a cursory comparison with our *PGM* text well demonstrates. In one exorcism technique recorded by Tirshom (§511), the exorcist-magician is given the following instructions in order "[t]o remove a demon [*shed*] from the body of a man or woman, or anything into which a male or female demon has entered":

Take an empty flask and a white waxen candle, and recite this adjuration in purity:

I adjure you, the holy and pure angels Michael, Raphael, Shuviel, Ahadriel, Zumtiel, Yeḥutiel, Zumẓiel. . . . By 72 names I adjure you, you all the retinues of spirits in the world—Be-ʿail Laḥush and all your retinue; Kapkafuni the Queen of the Demons and all your retinue; and Agrat bat Malkat and all your retinue, and Zmamit and all your retinue, and those that were made on the eve of the Sabbath[49]—that you bring forth that demon immediately and do not detain the *mazzik* of so-and-so, and tell me his name in this circle that I have drawn in your honor. . . .

Immediately they will tell you his name and the name of his father and the name of his mother aloud; do not fear them.

Immediately recite this adjuration in such a way:

I adjure you the demon so-and-so, by the utterance of the watchers and the holy ones [cf. Dan. 4:14] by YHVH God of the Heavens, with these names I adjure you the demon so-and-so, son of so-and-so and so-and-so, that you now enter this flask immediately and immediately the flask will turn red. Immediately say to him these five names YHV YHV. . . . That demon will immediately cry a great and bitter cry from the great pressure; do not believe him until he swears by YUD HA VAV HA explicitly.[50] Then leave him alone and pay him no further heed.[51]

This procedure again contains familiar elements, many of them ubiquitous in exorcism techniques. Hardware requirements are minimal—the standard glass flask, common in Arabic magic for these types of applications, and a white candle. Holy angels and demonic spirits are adjured by the exorcist, enlisted to assist him by forcing the penetrating demon to disclose his name and the names of his parents. Once the demon has been named, it becomes vulnerable to adjurations that force its departure and subsequent capture in the flask. At this point, with the demon quite literally in the exorcist's hands, the exorcist makes his final adjurations and is "left alone." Although this formula does not include instructions for disposing of the flask, options ranged from disposal in a barren place to a thorough rinsing in water.

In all, exorcism techniques preserved in late medieval Hebrew manuscripts indicate that little had changed since antiquity. Comprising both adjurations and operations based upon the occult properties of objects, these exorcism techniques blend natural and demonic magic to full effect.[52] Moreover, the ceremonies retain the theatrical power that had made them the miracles par excellence of antiquity. This theatricality and the powerful impression made by public exorcisms almost certainly led to the interest in their control by elites, no less than it did to their success as a healing modality.[53]

When the kabbalists of sixteenth-century Safed were faced with cases of spirit possession in their midst, techniques such as those in *Shoshan Yesod ha-'Olam* constituted their paradigms for conducting exorcisms. At this point, we return to the cases considered in the preceding chapter, but rather than focusing upon the possessed, we shall examine in detail the techniques of exorcism deployed in these accounts and compare them with the more extensive formulas preserved primarily in magical manuscripts.

The first early modern account, as we have noted, features R. Joseph Karo as exorcist. How did the rabbi exorcise the unknown spirit possessing the small boy who came before him? First, Karo forces the spirit to speak by threatening it with *niddui*, a form of excommunication. Discovering the spirit to be a hopeless soul, he works to expel it by reciting *Aleinu Leshabeaḥ* ("It is incumbent upon us to praise the Master of All"[54]), an ancient prayer that concludes all Jewish liturgical services, composed by the talmudic sage Rav of third-century Babylonia. Karo's intonation is not petitional, however, but magical: the passage is recited seven times, and it is recited both forward and backward.[55] Forward and backward recitation was not unique to Jewish magic; it could be found in widespread use, even among Christian commoners. Jean Bodin, in his demonological treatise of 1580, *De la Démonomanie des sorciers*, discussed the magical effect of saying verses from the Psalms forward and backward and claimed that the technique was known to every village peasant.[56] Its apotropaic function is founded upon the assumption that encrypted into sacred texts are strata even more powerful than the "outermost" semantically intelligible layer. Like the mysteries revealed when spinning a vinyl Beatles album in reverse, reciting a sacred text backward was bound to unleash its fullest energies.[57]

This rather modest technique is effective enough; according to the account, the boy recovers. Nevertheless, although Karo evinces an interest in ameliorating the plight of the spirit—a sinning soul in limbo—his technique does not rise to the challenge of expelling *and* rectifying the soul. Although we hear nothing of his use of venerable and elaborate magical procedures, there is no indication that a new approach had been worked out to deal with the new twofold challenge.

The exorcists in the cases of the 1570s that did not involve Luria seem to have used techniques akin to those used in antiquity. In the 1571 broadsheet written by R. Elijah Falcon, the exorcists are referred to as "two men, knowledgeable in adjurations." They made extensive use of sulfurous fumigations, burning the acrid element into the nostrils of the possessed. The Spanish *halakhic* authority R. Isaac ben Sheshet Perfet (1326–1407) believed that fumigations were an integral part of demonic-magical exorcism techniques, rather than natural curatives. "There is no doubt," he wrote, "that these spices do not work magic due to their natural properties, but they fumigate with them, and with them recite adjurations and incantations."[58] Such fumigations were also a mainstay of Catholic exorcism.[59] Although widely used, opinions differed as to the purpose and effectiveness of "smoking out the demons." Thinkers such as Martín Del Río (1551–1608) insisted that the victim only deteriorated through heavy exposure to the foul smoke, whereas Piero Antonio Stampa believed that fumigations were absolutely necessary, though with the provision that they be administered "rarely and cautiously, lest we bring graver disease on those we seek to help."[60] Some believed that the smoke provided relief to the possessed, whereas others held that the demon was offended by the smoke's foul smell and its similarity to the hell fire that he sought to avoid. Other authorities reassured, however, that remedies such as fumigations were endowed by God "with power against demons, and this the more so, if they are piously offered and duly blessed and exorcised."[61] William Winston also made extensive use of fumigations in his propagandist exorcism tours of England in this period.[62]

Although fumigations were a component of exorcisms going back to antiquity, the exorcists in the Falcon case would seem to be the first on record to have supplemented age-old techniques to take the spirit's identity as a disembodied soul into account. To ameliorate his condition, the exorcists trouble themselves to perform a penitential service for the spirit's rectification, complete with shofar blows and the traditional *sliḥot* liturgy.[63] A full penitential service has thus been incorporated into the rite of exorcism, a striking departure from ancient precedent. Strikingly, though perhaps not surprisingly, this innovation came at the request of the spirit himself, the service having been conducted "in accordance with the spirit's will."

A good deal of negotiation went into planning the penitential ceremony. If the request for such a ceremony was new—predicated as it was upon the spirit's human background and afterlife needs—the idea of negotiation between spirit and exorcists was most certainly not. Negotiation played a central role in both Jewish and Catholic exorcism, and there was much to be negotiated: the departure location, together with the agreement over the sign of the spirit's departure, were often only the last of the items on the table. Jewish and Catholic thinkers regarded such negotiation as a licit component of any exorcism. In the event, possessing spirits often "choreographed" their own exorcisms, specifying which exorcist was most suited to their expulsion.[64] In the Jewish cases, the spirits, now disembodied souls seeking salvation, concerned themselves with which rabbis might best petition God for their rehabilitation.

Upon concluding the penitential service on behalf of the spirit, the exorcists return to their labors directed to expel the spirit and refocus their attention upon the young woman. She is bombarded with adjurations and worse apparently, by a great deal of noxious smoke. The exorcists do everything they can to remove the foreign soul from her body. Physical manipulation was considered a licit component of this therapy, and in this case, the exorcists massage the victim's legs to move the spirit down to her toes for departure.[65] The spirit, however, is "noncompliant" and refuses to leave by way of the victim's toes. Instead, the cruel intruder departs by way of her vagina, causing an embarrassing hemorrhage at the spot. The final stage in the exorcism process involved the preparation of amulets to prevent repossession. According to the account, the exorcists in this case did not make up amulets with this girl's particular spirit in mind but instead relied upon generic formulas. The spirit returns, leading to further fumigations; the young woman's death followed a few days thereafter.[66] "They say that the spirit choked her," wrote Falcon, "and went out with her soul." These exorcists, like Karo, accepted the twofold goal of exorcism as rectification and expulsion. Their technique, however, remained classical, though with the addition of a penitential service for the rectification of the unwelcome soul.

## Lurianic Exorcism

That same year another woman became possessed in Safed.[67] This time, the relatives of this woman approached R. Isaac Luria and requested that he examine her and prescribe appropriate treatment. A check of her pulse led Luria to confirm that she was indeed possessed and that an exorcism was in order. Luria himself, however, did not perform the exorcism but instead sent his disciple R. Ḥayyim Vital to do so.[68] Luria armed Vital with only one weapon with which to accomplish the exorcism: *kavvanot* (pl., intentions), the component parts of a *yiḥud*, to exorcise the possessing soul. Although versions of these meditative techniques were used to promote positive *'ibburic* impregnation, here they were used to repel the negative analogue. Whereas Vital recorded at least eight Lurianic *yiḥudim* to exorcise a *ruaḥ ra 'ah* that Luria taught him, we shall focus on the first and most extensively developed *yiḥud*. All share a basic structural similarity, but according to Vital, this first *yiḥud* was "the most essential [*'ikkar*] of them all."[69]

### [Introduction]

A *yiḥud* that my teacher, of blessed memory, taught me to remove an evil spirit, may the Merciful save us. For sometimes the soul [*nefesh*] of an evil person is unable to get into Gehinnom because of his many transgressions. He wanders continuously, and sometimes enters the body of a man or a woman and overcomes[70] him, which is called the falling sickness. By means of this *yiḥud*, his soul is somewhat fixed, and he leaves the person's body.

### [Overview]

Now this is how it works, as I myself have done it and tried it. I would take the arm of that [possessed] person and place my hand on the pulse of his left or right forearm, for there is the garment [*levush*] of the soul, and there it is clothed.[71] I then intend [*mekhaven*] that the soul enclothed in that pulse should depart from there through the power of the *yiḥud*.

While still holding his arm on his pulse, I then say this verse ["Appoint over him a wicked man, and may Satan stand at his right" (Ps. 109:6)] forward and backward. I intend those names that emerge from it: the numerical values of each word, the first letters of the words and the last letters of the words, as you know. By means of this I intend that he depart.

He then speaks from within the body, everything that you ask of him. Command him to depart.

It is sometimes necessary to blast the *shofar* [ram's horn] next to his ear and to intend the name *KR'A STN*, vocalized throughout with *Sh'va*, as well as its permutation through *A"T B"Sh*, vocalized throughout with *Sh'va*, the name being *DGZ BNT.*

[Significance of Ps. 109:6 explained]

Know that this spirit does not come alone, but a *satan* holds him and drags him here and there, to complete the punishment for his transgressions. [The spirit] is unable to do anything without [the *satan*'s] permission, for God has made him a watchman over him, as it is written in the *Zohar* [2:41b]: "The evil one—the evil inclination is his judge" [BT *Berakhot* 61a]. King David, of blessed memory, in the verse "Appoint over him a wicked man, and may [a] *satan* stand at his right" [Ps. 109:6], was cursing the wicked that the Blessed Holy One should appoint a wicked soul [*nefesh*] over him, to penetrate and to harm him, and that a *satan* should come along to stand at the right of this evil soul, to assist him to stand there. Sometimes the soul departs and the *satan* remains alone guarding its place. Thus the transmigrated soul [*ha-nefesh ha-mitgalgelet*] is not there at all times, and when he departs and travels at known hours for them to punish him, he must depart from there to receive his punishments. Either way, that *satan* who is assigned to him dwells there, to keep his place; and one does not recuperate from that sickness until both of them depart. And you know that the Blessed Holy One sweetens bitter with bitter [Midrash *Tanḥuma, Beshallaḥ* §24]. Thus, counter-intuitively, this verse, which seems to be a command to appoint over him this wicked soul, on the contrary, here alludes to its rectification, by means of the *kavvanot* that we will write. And I cannot elaborate further on this matter given how much there is to say about it.[72]

[Technique]

I shall copy before you the version of the *kavvanah*, and you will understand on your own how it derives from the verse. And it is possible that from SGZGIEL[73] on, they [the *kavvanot*] do not derive from the verse "Appoint. . . ." And this is the verse: "Appoint [*HFKD*] over him [*'ALAV*] a wicked man [*RSh'A*], and may Satan [*V'STN*] stand [*Y'AMD*] at [*'AL*] his right [*YMINV*]."

[Reverse word order:]

*YMINV 'AL Y'AMD V'STN RSh'A 'ALAV HFKD*

[Reverse letter order within reverse word order plus sefirotic vocalization:]

*VNIMY* [*kamaẓ*] *L'A* [*pataḥ*] *DM'AY* [*ẓiri*] *NTSV* [*segol*] *'AShR* [*shva*] *VAL'A* [*ḥolam*] *DKFH* [*ḥirik*]

And these are the vowels of *Keter* [Crown], *Ḥokhmah* [Wisdom], *Binah* [Understanding], *Ḥesed* [Love], *Gevurah* [Severity], *Tiferet* [Beauty], *Neẓaḥ* [Eternity].

SGZGIEL

*MTTRON* [Metatron] *NORTTM INNGFT* (This name is Metatron permutated with *A"T B"Sh*)

[Permutations of the tetragrammaton and the forty-two-lettered name:]

*YYH YHV YHVH*
*YOD*
*YOD HA*
*YOD HA VAV*
*YOD HA VAV HA*
YVAḤẒẒBIRON
KR'A STN
ILI (via *A"T B"Sh*) *MKhM.*

Know that I have forgotten what [this last portion] is about, for I found it written as I heard it, with great brevity, when I copied the matter at the time. And it appears to me that this is the manner of proceeding: first you say the verse, "Appoint over him a wicked man . . ." forward, then backward, i.e., reverse the words and begin with "right his at stand . . ." and then backward, so that the order of the letters is reversed from the end of each word to its beginning, as in "thgir sih ta dnats. . . ." But each letter of the word "right" should be vocalized with a *kamaẓ*, and all the letters of "on" with a *pataḥ*, and all the letters of "stand" with a *ẓiri*, and all the letters of "*satan*" with a *segol*, and all the letters of "evil" with a *shva* and all the letters of "upon him" with a *ḥolem*, and all the letters of "appoint" with a *ḥirik*, and so throughout. And all this will be understood when they are reversed, as mentioned, in this manner, *VNIMY* through *DKFH*. And the order of these seven vowels is the order of the seven Sefirot from *Keter* to *Neẓaḥ*, as mentioned in the *Tikkunim* [*Tikkun* 70], "*Kamaẓ* in *Keter*, *Pataḥ* in *Ḥokhmah*, etc. And know that these seven words, when reversed along the lines noted, are holy names, which emerge from this verse. I am in doubt as to whether one is to intend these names while one is reading the verse in reverse word order, or whether after one says the verse forward and backward, he should intend these names. The latter seems more correct to me. Afterward, intend the rest of the names with their vocalizations in the manner copied out above; these do not emerge from the verse, "Appoint over him. . . ." Intend first the name *SGZGIEL* vocalized throughout with *ḥolam*. Then *MTTRON* forward, vocalized throughout with *shva kamaẓ*. Then *MTTRON* in reverse (*NORTTM*) vocalized throughout with *shva kamaẓ*. Then *MTTRON* permutated with *A"T B"Sh* (*INNGFT*), vocalized throughout with *shva*. Then the simple posterior quadratic expansion [*ribu'a*] of YHVH, vocalized throughout with *shva kamaẓ*. Then that expansion filled with ALEFs, vocalized throughout with *shva kamaz*. Then the name *YVAḤẒẒBIRON* in the vocalization there. Then *KR'A STN*, vocalized throughout with *shva*. Then *ILI*, vocalized throughout with *shva*. Then the name *MKhM*, vocalized throughout with *shva*.

[Additional Instructions]

Intend that the spirit depart by the power of these names. If it does not depart, return to the aforementioned verse, and intend all the names again. At the conclusion of each round, say with strength, "Depart, depart, quickly!" You should know that everything depends on your firming and strengthening your heart like a mighty one, with no fear, and let your heart not soften, for he will become stronger and not heed your words.

You must also decree upon him that he leave from no place other than the space between the nail of the big toe and the flesh, in such a manner that he not damage the body in which he stands. Also decree upon him with the power of the aforementioned names that you intended, and by the power of *ḥerem* and *niddui* that he not harm, nor enter any Jew's body ever again.

Know that he will strongly resist speaking, so as not to be embarrassed before the listeners.

Know that when he speaks, the body of the person remains like a lifeless rock, and the voice of the spirit goes out of his mouth, without movement of the lips, in a fine voice, like the voice of a small child. Also when it rises from the body to the mouth to speak, it will rise in the shape of a round vertebra arising by way of the neck through the skin of the neck. So too when it descends to the nail of the toe of the foot to depart.

Know, too, that when you ask him who he is and what is his name, he will lie to you and say someone else's name, or insult you, all in order to avoid the decree that you will decree upon him to depart. Thus you must decree upon him *ḥerem* and *niddui* and with the power of the names mentioned that you intended, so that he not lie, and so that he tells you who he is and his name with utter truthfulness. Moreover, this matter must be done with purity, immersion, holiness, and the utmost intentionality.

Thus the "most essential" Lurianic exorcism, from etiologic introduction to didactic epilogue. Vital opens with a brief explanation of the causes of spirit possession. His explanation reflects the understanding of the phenomenon that we have seen in the Safedian narratives and stresses the pathetic plight of the sinning soul. Trapped in a hopeless limbo state, unable to secure admission to Gehinnom, his purification and redemption cannot progress sufficiently to enable him to transmigrate normally, as a newborn baby.[74] This would appear to be the first example of the new etiology of spirit possession conjoined to a technical presentation of exorcism procedure. This etiology presents the classic symptomatic manifestation of the syndrome—"falling," or epileptic seizures. As with hysteria and melancholy, the other diseases mentioned repeatedly in possession literature, epilepsy was commonly viewed as an ailment reflecting or accompanying possession.[75] Illness left the subject more susceptible to demonic victimization than would be a healthy person. Indeed, Vital writes that "when a person is sick the spirit penetrates him, and also in the case of falling sickness. Also, sometimes when a good spirit enters a person, a spark of an evil spirit enters him as well. And in order to expel the evil one, one must sit behind the person and grasp his two arms. . . ." At this point, Vital records the technique that we have reproduced above and will now analyze in depth.[76]

## Pulse and Kabbalistic Diagnostics

In the first section, Vital places the exorcist behind the possessed, holding the arms of the victim by the wrists while engaged in pulse-based diagnosis.[77] The pulse, according to Vital (and Galenic medical opinion), is felt in the arteries from the heart that do not contain blood, as opposed to those from the liver that do (but which do not pulsate).[78] The arteries from the heart "contain only vitality and spirituality [*ruḥniyut*] drawn from the spirit [*ruaḥ*] that is within the heart, branching out throughout all the organs in their inward dimension, as is known, for under the blood vessels are the pulsating arteries."[79] Vital, early in *Sha'ar Ruaḥ ha-Kodesh*, explains his master's use of the pulse as an indicator of ailments of the soul. Vital provides a theosophical explanation of the basis of this technique, though I will not undertake an analysis of its details here.

> Know, that also in the pulse of a person—just as through it physicians of the body know and recognize ailments of the body—my teacher, may his memory live in the World to Come, recognized ailments of the soul when he touched a person's pulse. . . . [Here follows a lengthy theosophical explanation of the relationship between the Divine Wisdom and its process of concatenation into human veins.] For according to the transgression and the sin that a person commits, he will lack the corresponding light and vitality in his pulse.[80]

Vital continues with an explanation of the ten varieties of pulse identified in the *Tikkunei ha-Zohar* (Tikkun 69). Each variety is named after the Hebrew vowel with which it has a rhythmic affinity. This rhythmic affinity is expressed graphically in the spatial/temporal relationships between the lines and the points that make up the vowel signs. The pulse can thus be read/felt as a kind of musical notation or rhythmic braille. The vowels in turn have sefirotic associations, as we shall see below.[81]

## Permutating Psalms

While still gripping the possessed from behind, the exorcist recites Psalm 109, verse 6, into his or her ear. "Appoint over him a wicked man, and may Satan stand at his right." This verse is said forward and then backward—a common magical technique that figured in Karo's exorcism as well. The verse is also permuted numerically, and its posterior and anterior acrostics contemplated. These Psalms in reverse were only the first of the "nonsensical" linguistic elements in Lurianic—and pre-Lurianic—exorcism techniques. Discussing Sinhalese mantra in his important essay on the linguistics of magic, "The Magical Power of Words," anthropologist Stanley Tambiah has examined the apparent unintelligibility of words and formulas addressed to demons by exorcists. His illuminating analysis is worth considering in light of the many semantically unintelligible elements in the Lurianic rite.

> When demons are directly addressed and commanded, the words are a polyglot mixture and therefore unintelligible. . . . This exotic and powerful mixture is the "demon language." . . . The "demon language" is consciously constructed to connote power, and though largely unintelligible is nevertheless based on the theory of language that the demons can understand. Thus, far from being nonsensical and indiscriminately concocted, the spells show a sophisticated logic. The logic of construction must of course be separated from the problem of whether the exorcist actually understands all the words contained in the spell. From his, as well as the audience's, points of view, the spells have power by virtue of their secrecy and their capacity to communicate with demons and thereby influence their actions. However, *mantra* do not fall outside the requirements of language as a system of communication, and their literal intelligibility to humans is not the critical factor in understanding their logic.[82]

The similarities and differences between the nature of the linguistic sensibility (or lack thereof) between the Sinhalese mantra and the Lurianic *yiḥudim* are worth considering. The polyglot mixture of the mantra—composed of Sinhalese, Tamil, Pali, Sanskrit, Malayalam, Telegu, Bengali, and even Persian—has more in common with the magical exorcisms we have seen in the *PGM* and medieval manuscripts such as *Shoshan Yesod ha-'Olam*, with their frequent and garbled use of Latin and Arabic words within larger Greek, Hebrew, or Aramaic contexts.[83] Luria's *yiḥud* marks a departure from that tradition, though without abandoning the use of unintelligible linguistic elements. Although semantically nonsensical, most of these elements nevertheless carried symbolic meaning to the practitioner steeped in kabbalistic learning, if not to the victim in whose ear the strangely vocalized syllables would be intoned. In the Lurianic case, the spells show a sophisticated logic that would be largely intelligible to the exorcist. Largely, but not entirely, for as Vital makes perfectly clear, he did not understand all portions of the exorcism *yiḥud.* He had taken notes on the procedure, but by the time he redacted them, he could no longer remember precisely how the portion beginning with the angelic name *SGZGIEL* had been derived. Indeed, even after noting this in his preamble, he further underscores his doubts as to the meaning and performance practice of the technique twice in the course of its exposition. Nevertheless, it would seem that it was more the performance practice about which he had his doubts. The meaning of various expansions of the tetragrammaton, the forty-two-lettered name, or angelic names such as Metatron—however inverted and permutated—retained their basic intelligibility to this highly versed kabbalistic scholar. Like the *mantra*, the *yiḥud* neither falls outside the requirements of language as a system of communication, nor is its literal intelligibility to humans the critical factor in understanding its logic. The *yiḥud* is more or less understood by the kabbalistic exorcist and, given its effectiveness, by the spirit it addresses. It is not, however, an ordinary human language and could not be fathomed by most victims or onlookers. And most of this kabbalistic "demon language" would have been whispered into the ear of the victim rather than intoned aloud. At most, the onlookers would have heard whispers—aptly the ancient Hebrew word for *spells.*[84]

According to Vital, the verse "Appoint over him a wicked man, and may [a] *satan* stand at his right" (Ps. 109:6) represents King David's curse against "the wicked that the Blessed Holy One should appoint a wicked soul over him, to penetrate and to harm him. . . ."[85] The key verse of the exorcism technique, from which so many of those potent names are derived, thus appears to be a curse on the victim! King David himself cursed the wicked to be penetrated and harmed by the evil dead. And the foul ghost is not to come alone but accompanied by a satanic watchman charged with keeping him in place. The shift from previous etiologies of spirit possession is subtle but sure. Although a demonic being, the *satan*, is found alongside the penetrating ghost, it is the latter who is doing the possessing. The *satan* has been relegated to the role of enforcer and gatekeeper.

The verse in question would seem to represent a classic case of "blaming the victim." As a punishment for wickedness, the victim is invaded by foreign spirits and is subjected to the attendant suffering entailed by their presence. Although penetration of a *satan* would seem to add insult to injury, Vital argues that its appointment over the soul dialectically led to the liberation of the latter from endless, tormented wanderings. By extension, it also ultimately contributed to the liberation of the possessed from his or her tormentor. This service removed the demonic sting from the *satan*'s presence in the body of the possessed. "And you know that the Blessed Holy One sweetens bitter with bitter. Thus, counter-intuitively, this verse, which seems to be a command to appoint this wicked soul over him, here alludes to its rectification by means of the *kavvanot* that we will write." The use of Psalm 109, verse 6, in this context is explained elsewhere by Vital as an example of how "with what God crushes, he heals."[86] These passages exemplify the proximity of Neoplatonic sympathetic magical beliefs to kabbalistic theosophy.[87] It is thus possible to see in our passage a similar *mentalité*, one that assumes, as in the famous cure of the weapon-salve,[88] that only by harnessing the powers that inflicted the wound can the wound itself be mollified. Hebrew magical handbooks suggest much the same when, for example, the suggested cure for a scorpion bite is to panfry a number of them in olive oil and then anoint the wound with the infusion. "The cure for its bite," we are told, "is from it and of it [*minay u-vay*]."[89] *Dinim* (judgments) must be countered and rectified through *Dinim*. Another example of this sensibility is to be found in the Lurianic *kavvanot* against plague, which has a great deal in common with the exorcism *yiḥud* we have translated above.[90] As if to vaccinate oneself against the plague, Vital records the instruction he received from Luria to meditate constantly during a plague on the "holy name" *NGF*, vocalized as in the modern Hebrew *nagif*, or virus![91] Theoretically minded kabbalists articulated this principle explicitly, as did R. Joseph ben Shalom Ashkenazi, who explained that "the similar aspect will be awakened when acted upon by that similar to it. And this is the opening to all sorceries and adjurations, and their secret."[92] This emphasis on resemblance is characteristic of the epistemology of premodern Western culture, guiding exegesis, organizing symbols, and granting knowledge of things visible and invisible.[93]

This view is also reflected in Luria's decision to deputize Vital to perform exorcisms because of the latter's spiritual genealogy. While Luria understood himself to be a reincarnation of Abel, and thus a manifestation of the divine attribute of compassion, Vital was considered to be a reincarnation of Cain, and therefore a manifestation of the divine attribute of judgment and severity.[94] The presumption was that the success of the exorcist was dependent in no small part upon the nature of his soul. As he was called upon to confront the "left side," the dimension of evil in the theosophical terms of the kabbalah, the exorcist could most effectively do so if he were himself a manifestation of this dimension.[95] Thus, as in Islamic traditions in which exorcists were thought to require "plenty of *jinn* themselves" to expel the *jinn*, or genies, in others, Vital was marked as the ideal exorcist by his master, Luria.[96] As Vital explained it, "For so was my teacher's, of blessed memory, custom to send me for these types of actions, and he would explain to me that it was because I derive from Cain, the left side of *Adam ha-Rishon* [the First Adam[97]], which is *Gevurah* [Severity[98]], and the judgments are only sweetened at their source, and therefore I have this power."[99] Subsequent editions of this Lurianic exorcism technique would take this particular spiritual-genealogical virtue of Vital's and generalize it, as we read in the eighteenth-century *Mishnat Ḥasidim* (Teaching of the Pious) by R. Emanuel Ḥiriki. At the conclusion of his review of the technique, Ḥiriki writes, "And if one has done this and the spirit has not left, do not be surprised, for perhaps he is not capable [*mesugal*] of expelling *klippot*. For those who are capable are ones who have this power, like those whose souls are from the root of Cain, of whom the *klippot* [evil 'shards'] are greatly afraid."[100]

There is a striking parallel to this notion in Christian sources as well, though without the transmigratory dimension. After the institution of the order of exorcist in the third-century Catholic Church, laypeople as well as clerics continued to engage in the exorcism of demoniacs. Ecclesiastical law, however, restricted the use of the power of exorcism to "priests of piety and prudence" and made the "personal victory over the temptations of the evil spirits" a prerequisite "in those who receive the power to expel them from others." In the technical language of the Church, therefore, administering an exorcism to a demoniac (as opposed to the exorcisms that often precede baptism) was considered to be *ex opere operantis* (lit., from the work of the doer) rather than *ex opere operato* (lit., by the work done).[101] Moreover, according to *L'Histoire des diables de Loudun* (1716), "exorcists almost all participate, more or less, in the effects of the demons, by vexations which they suffer from them, and few persons have undertaken to drive them forth who have not been troubled by them."[102] Indeed, in a startling letter to his spiritual advisor, Father Jean-Joseph Surin, the exorcist at Loudun, wrote that

> during the exercise of my ministry, the Devil passes from the body of the possessed person, and coming into mine, assaults me and overturns me, shakes me, and visibly travels through me, possessing me for several hours like an energumen. I would not know how to explain to you what occurs inside of me during this time, and how this

> Spirit unites with mine, without depriving me either of the knowledge or the liberty of my soul, while nevertheless making himself like another me, and *how it is as if I had two souls, one of which is deprived of its body, or the use of its organs, and stands apart, watching the actions of the one which has entered.* . . . I feel the state of damnation and am frightened by it, and I feel as if I were pierced by sharp points of despair in *this foreign soul which seems to be mine*, and the other soul, which is full of confidence, makes light of such feelings, and in full liberty curses the one which causes them; verily I feel that the same cries which leave my mouth come equally from these two souls, and I am hard-pressed to discern if it is the mirth which produces them, or the extreme fury which fills me. The tremblings which overcome me when the Holy Sacrament is bestowed upon me come equally, it seems to me, from horror at its presence, which is unbearable to me, and from a sweet and gentle reverence, without my being able to attribute them more to one than to the other, and without its being in my power to restrain them. When one of these two souls moves me to want to make the sign of the cross on my mouth, the other turns my hand away with great speed, and seizes my finger with my teeth, in order to gnaw on it in a rage.[103] [Emphasis added]

This revelatory first-person account of Surin's experience illustrates the extent to which a Christian exorcist might participate in the very phenomenon that he was charged to eradicate, albeit this marks an exceptional extreme.[104] What was an extreme in Christian circles appears to have been more the norm among kabbalistic exorcists. Their considerable personal experience with possession states made sixteenth-century Safedian exorcists ideally suited to the task. Vital even alerted his disciples to the likelihood that as they began to practice *yiḥudim* to cling to righteous souls—en route to even higher prophetic states—they would experience a number of possession-like symptoms. "It also happens that one who begins to attain a little attainment and the spirit will rest upon him, though without the perfection necessary to settle a voice of prophecy and the holy spirit on his lips and tongue, does not talk and only feels for himself at the time of the *yiḥud* that his hair is on end, his body and limbs quaking, and his lips moving though his mouth lacks the power of speech."[105] In the following chapter, Vital provides remedial *yiḥudim* that aim to restore the power of speech and "to cut down the power of the outside forces [*ḥiẓonim*]," the latter being demonic spirits who seize the opportunity of any opening—even toward holiness—to invade and afflict.

The demonic dangers facing exorcists were articulated most directly in Jewish magical literature outside the Lurianic corpus. Techniques in such magical texts regularly combine adjurations to expel the demons with personal supplications for protection against these same forces, particularly in the wake of their expulsion. Thus the exorcist in a late compilation is instructed to plead with God, to "spread over us the *ḥashmal* [electrum] of *Binah* [the mother sphere of Understanding] to protect us so that the foreign spirit that is in the body of so-and-so not harm us now, nor after his departure, and that he not order any *mazzik* from among his comrades to harm us, not now nor at any time after he leaves quickly from so-and-so."[106]

The *kavvanot* based upon Psalm 109 are said to have the power to force the spirit to speak "from within the body, everything that you ask of him." Although the need to obtain specific information, and especially a name, from the possessing spirit is treated in more detail later in Vital's instructions, this phrase indicates an interest in communication with the spirit for its own sake. Even though this curiosity is understated here, it plays a large role in other possession accounts dating from this period. In a case in Ferrara, a Jewish woman was possessed by the soul of a certain Batista of Modena, a Gentile who had been hanged for theft.[107] Gedalia ibn Yaḥia, upon hearing that a possessed woman was accessible to him, let his curiosity get the better of him and immediately realized the great opportunity before him to find out secrets of life after death. "This is the day I have hoped for—to know new discoveries regarding the soul's parting from the body!" he wrote of his reaction at the time. He proceeded to interrogate the spirit at length, though with disappointing results. Elijah de Vidas, a student of Cordovero and a contemporary of Vital, evinced similar curiosity. De Vidas wrote that the soul of a person three months deceased appeared to him in a dream. He did not miss the opportunity to ask him questions about the next world, the torments of the grave, and other punishments inflicted upon the soul.[108]

Indeed, nearly every Hebrew possession account includes extensive interviews with the possessing spirit, in which questions are asked that are of no immediate relevance to the exorcism itself. Such curiosity seems to have been condoned by the rabbis, in stark contrast to the warnings against such interviews for curiosity's sake to be found in learned Christian literature. Although this learned literature was coming out against a practice that was probably the norm, the fact remains that Christians were much more wary of what was going to be said by their possessing spirits than Jews seemed to be of theirs. The possessing spirits in the Jewish cases, generally souls gone astray—and sometimes, in cases of "good" possession, even righteous souls—were hardly the demons of their Christian counterparts.[109] By contrast, in the *Rituale Romanum* and earlier exorcism manuals, curious questioning is discouraged.[110] Such curiosity was also discouraged by Del Río, who writes, "Exorcizers should be warned not to interrogate the demon from motives of curiosity; there should be no familiarity with him nor should aid or counsel be sought of him."[111]

Of course, the primary reason to converse with the spirit remains here, as it had been since antiquity, to obtain the spirit's true name. By this period, however, Jewish exorcisms begin to use the name, once obtained, somewhat distinctively. For Catholic exorcists, the discovery is an essential component of a punitive process. Catholics use the name magically in the exorcism by writing it down and then showing and burning it before the victim.[112] Jewish exorcists, by contrast, use the name in order to decree upon it bans of expulsion—as well as to pray for its rehabilitation.

According to Vital, in stubborn cases, it is necessary to combine the meditations with a blast from a *shofar* (ram's horn) in the possessed's ear. The notion that the blast of the *shofar* is capable of putting demons to flight is evident in the earliest strata of rabbinic literature. *Mishna Rosh ha-Shanah,* Chapter 3, mishna 7 notes the use of a *shofar* to vanquish demons dwelling in a well before drawing water on the Jewish New Year.[113] The trumpet of a ram's horn can easily be understood as having played a cathartic role in the healing of the possessed, a purging that, in the Aristotelian sense, had religious as well as medical connotations. Lévi-Strauss explained the power of dramatic performances to heal as stemming from "the efficacity of symbols."[114]

The deployment of a ritual object charged with religious meaning at the center of a miraculous healing rite also bore symbolic significance. Catholic exorcisms in the post-Reformation period made extensive use of the sacraments, and the Eucharist in particular. In a letter to Pope Gregory XIII from the Bishop of Soissons, the Bishop "emphasizes the happy effect of these exorcisms in confirming the Catholic faith and the power of the Eucharist in these calamitous times, when so many are leaving the true Church."[115] Nicole Obry, a sixteen-year-old girl in the diocese of Laon in Picardy, encountered a spirit in November 1565; she was subsequently diagnosed as possessed. The priests who exorcised the demons made extensive use of the Eucharist. Prior exorcisms had used Holy Water, Crosses, and saints' relics.[116] Although not a symbol under contention, as was the Eucharist in this period, the *shofar* was a clear marker of Judaism. Its effectiveness to help vanquish the spirits would be certain to shore up the flagging communal self-image and confirm its power as a ritual object even in its normative application.

The *shofar* blast was to be accompanied by a series of *kavvanot* based on the words *KR'A STN,* the second of the seven sestets that form the forty-two-lettered name.[117] This sestet was considered effective against the powers of evil, as it may be read as "Rend Satan." Moreover, as the second of seven, it corresponds in kabbalistic theosophy to the divine attribute of *Gevurah* (Severity), the attribute Vital (qua Cain) manifested in Luria's eyes. The *kavvanah* calls for the exorcist to contemplate this sestet vocalized with the *shva,* the vowel associated in kabbalistic sources with severity.[118] Such a vocalization would serve to amplify the power of the already-severe formula *KR'A SaTaN.* A further permutation-amplification of this formula is accomplished by the letter-exchange technique known as *A"T B"Sh.*[119]

The meditation then continues by requiring the exorcist to contemplate a number of alternative permutations of Psalm 109, verse 6, in a meditation that involves associating each of the seven words of the verse with one of the seven lower Sefirot. The final assault on the spirit comes with the meditation on the names Sagzagiel, Metatron, and YVAḤẒẒBIRON, as well as on a quadratic expansion of the tetragrammaton. The *satan*-rending second sestet from the forty-two-lettered name concludes the meditations, again transformed by letter-exchange techniques and vocalized with the piercing *shva.*

How should we characterize this kind of exorcism technique? We might start by mentioning what the procedure does not include: sulfurous fumigations, deer skin, bowls written upon, erased, and filled with living water. It contains no adjurations to angels, holy or demonic, to assist in the expulsion of the possessing spirit. It is also not a multipurpose, "broad-spectrum" procedure. On the contrary—Luria seems to have provided custom-made *kavvanot* appropriate to individual circumstances. According to *Eleh Toledot Yiẓḥak* (The History of Isaac [Luria]), an early hagiographic work attributed to R. Ḥayyim Vital, "[Luria] knew the secret of *'ibbur* and would speak with the reincarnated spirits [*ha-ruḥot ha-megulgalim*], whether a good spirit or an evil spirit, and he would remove an evil spirit from the body, each and every one with a *kavvanah* unique to that spirit."[120]

These novel exorcism techniques distill to the level of ritual the radical conflation of cosmology and anthropology characteristic of Lurianic Kabbalah. This system calls for the application of the same hermeneutical principles to the reading of books, the world, the human soul, and, of course, the divine. Sharing the same basic signatures,[121] they lend themselves to a common hermeneutical strategy. Luria's diagnostic and healing techniques, then, might best be thought of as "somatic exegesis."[122]

For each of the 600000 interpretations of the Torah, one soul of Israel was created, and in the future, every Jew will know the entire Torah according to the interpretation attuned to his own soul root, from which he was created and came into being. . . .

> And my teacher, may his memory be a blessing, would gaze every evening at his students who stood before him, and see upon them which verse was shining inordinately upon each one's forehead from his soul's illumination there. He would then explain to him something of the interpretation of that verse according to the interpretation belonging to his soul, as we have mentioned.[123]

Luria reads people as composites of divine names and configurations; when one person's soul invades another's body, one had therefore to engage in a theosophical-exegetical assault. One might think of Lurianic exorcism, then, as an act of radical deconstruction (or higher criticism) that was good for the Jews.

Luria's transformation of exorcism was less a critique of the old ways than it was an outgrowth of his understanding of possession, now inextricably bound up with the doctrine of transmigration. Luria brought Safed's decades-long obsession with transmigration (and its attendant concept of personal perfection) to its most sublime conceptual development. His achievement was to articulate the deep structure shared by God and the created universe; the human soul was its mirror and gateway. When individual souls went astray, then, their rectification required the exorcist to engage with this deep structure. To perform the requisite magical act of exorcism, a mystical act was needed. This logic explains the transposition of classical magical goals into theosophical meditations throughout such works as *Sha'ar Ruaḥ ha-Kodesh* and *Sha'ar ha-Yiḥudim.*

Is Luria's technique less magical than those that preceded it? Luria was opposed to the use of *kabbalah ma'asit* ["practical" kabbalah] and forbade students from adjuring demons and writing most amulets. Luria explained his reticence in different terms to different disciples, and it may be that as in other aspects of his teaching, this "antimagical" approach to exorcism was developed with a specific disciple or disciples in mind.[124] To Vital, Luria insisted that without the ashes of the Red Heifer, the defilement of death clung to all, rendering even the most pious unfit to use divine names. To Elijah de Vidas, Luria insisted that a person had to be entirely free from sin to use holy names to avoid divine punishment; another time, Luria told de Vidas that the names could not be used because all of the magical manuscripts were full of errors. Whatever his reasons, the fact that no such adjurations occur in his exorcism techniques is sufficient to confirm his disavowal of these methods. Yet Luria's *yiḥudim* were clearly magical in their own right. The mechanistic aspects of the *yiḥudim* indicate a coercive rather than supplicatory relationship to the divine powers, and Luria's understanding of language attests to his belief in its intrinsic occult power. Such an understanding might be classified as a type of natural magic.[125] In Luria's mind, however, and from an internal kabbalistic perspective, it is also clear that Luria effectively transferred the techniques for exorcism from the realm of Kabbalah *ma'asit* to the realm of Kabbalah *'iyyunit*, or contemplative kabbalah. This transformation would have struck a Renaissance contemporary as a shift from demonic to natural magic. Like a Renaissance magus, Luria "looked with suspicion on much of the magic of his immediate predecessors but at the same time merged many of its elements with more distant traditions that might purify and transform them."[126] This transposition resulted in the attenuation of the dramatic features of classical exorcism in which magical rites and formulas were displaced by contemplative exercises. This development seems to have pleased neither exorcists nor their communities. The old methods retained their broad appeal despite Luria's authority and towering reputation.

## The Afterlife of Lurianic Exorcism

Upon examining the exorcism techniques that the kabbalists used after Luria's death, we find that they conspicuously made peripheral the distinctively Lurianic elements. Despite having remained a figure of imposing authority, whose teachings governed the lion's share of their spiritual lives, the AR"I's reconstruction of exorcism technique was either assimilated or ignored by later Jewish exorcists. This process is vividly captured in two striking documents from kabbalist-exorcists a mere generation or two removed from the period of Luria and Vital's activity. The first is the account of an exorcism in Cairo during the summer of 1666 by R. Samuel Vital (1598–c. 1678), the youngest son of R. Ḥayyim. The liturgical and ritual setting in which R. Samuel carries out the Lurianic technique would seem to indicate his appraisal of its usefulness as a "stand-alone" rite. The second document, a 1672 letter of R. Moshe Zacuto (c. 1620–97), provides a rare opportunity to examine the conscious inscription of the AR"I's technique in a broader, magical context, one that further betrays signs of its Italian baroque provenance.

R. Samuel Vital's oft-published account—typically appearing at the end of the tractate on reincarnation, *Sha'ar ha-Gilgulim*—documents the possession of a young woman by the name of Esther Weiser.[127] In fact, it tells us little about her possession but a great deal about the development of exorcism technique since his father's exorcisms in Safed nearly a century earlier. After a Gentile expert (*palil*)[128]—who was recommended to the family by

R. Samuel—failed to remove the spirit, R. Samuel arrives on the scene to interview the spirit "in the body of this maiden." With his recitation of "*Shm'a Yisrael*," the spirit demonstrates that he is a Jew to the exorcist's content. Unlike the Gentile soul who possessed a young Jewish girl in Ferrara in the case documented by Gedalya ibn Yaḥia, this ghost was able to answer the curious questions that his interrogator posed to the latter's satisfaction.[129] The spirit begs R. Samuel to carry out a *tikkun* for him while removing him from the girl's body, and the rabbi agrees. At this point, R. Samuel summons ten scholars and begins to carry out the Lurianic exorcism. Combining the key Psalms verses, the forty-two-lettered divine name, and threats of excommunication, the junior Vital (at this time already an elder himself) follows his father's notes closely. Nevertheless, in this gathering of scholars, Vital adds a lengthy prayer, the likes of which we have not seen in anything recorded by his father. The central passage of this prayer is a plea for the admission of the possessing soul to Gehinnom, woven into a penitential setting.

In the name of the unique God, You are great, and great is Your Name in strength. Please Lord, the honored and awesome, the majestic and beautiful and sanctified, the exalted and blessed, the examiner and inquirer, the straightened and the lofty, the hidden and concealed, the mighty in 72 names, the one unique, clear and pure, the hearer of cries, the receiver of prayers, who answers in times of suffering, incline Your ear to my prayer, to my supplication, and to my plea that I pray before You and ask of You. And You will hear from heaven, the place of Your dwelling, and receive with mercy and good will this spirit who remains before us, transmigrated in this maiden, who is called so-and-so daughter of so-and-so, who is called so-and-so, and receive our prayers that we pray for him to fix his soul and his spirit. Remove him from this transmigration, and bring about his admission to the judgment of Gehinnom, and allow his soul and his spirit to escape from the catapult of the *mazzikim* and from the suffering in which he wallows. May this transmigration and this humiliation be considered an atonement for all of his transgressions, his sins and his crimes. May these words of ours be words of advocacy before You for this soul and this spirit, and may Your mercy prevail over Your attributes [of judgment] upon him, in our recalling before You the "Thirteen Attributes of Mercy": God King sitting on the Throne of Mercy etc.; And he passed over etc. . . . And while saying the thirteen attributes, Lord, Lord, God merciful and forgiving (Ex. 34, 6–7), blow the *shofar* as is the custom of all the penitential prayers (*sliḥot*) and afterwards say the thirteen attributes of Micha the prophet: Who is God like You, etc. . . . (Micha 7, 18).

A few more apt verses and the command to depart from the young woman's body was all it took to bring the possession episode to a happy end. The spirit left through her smallest toe, while crying out "*Shalom aleikhem*!"

("Peace unto you!"), as he had agreed with R. Samuel to do upon departure. The young woman awoke, seemingly unaware of anything that had transpired, asking why so many had gathered around her.

When we consider the experience of R. Samuel as an exorcist, it appears that he was largely content to follow his father's instructions. We would expect little else from a devoted Lurianic kabbalist, heir to his master, and redactor of so many of his father's writings. Yet there *are* additions to the strictly Lurianic *yiḥud*. First, in Luria's instructions, we hear nothing of the need to gather a large group to be present for the exorcism. Second, Luria's approach deals with the rectification of the possessing soul, though without incorporating a penitential service. Such a service, we recall, had been used by the exorcists in the Falcon case but does not seem to have been deemed necessary by Luria. Finally, the entire dramatic liturgical setting bespeaks a theatricality utterly absent from Luria's method. I would speculate that all three of these additions represent, at least on an intuitive level, the sensibility of a kabbalistic healer who fully appreciates the contribution that cathartic drama makes to a successful exorcism. Moreover, although R. Samuel adds dimensions to the Lurianic technique that would otherwise be lacking, none of his additions would seem to violate the spirit of Luria's *yiḥud* nor any of his explicit prohibitions.

We find a somewhat bolder approach to this material in the Zacuto letter, written to a colleague on 27 June 1672. Zacuto was a Venetian rabbi, born in Amsterdam to a family of former Portuguese conversos. He enjoyed a broad education in religious and secular subjects and made his way to Italy through Poland, where he studied in various rabbinic academies.[130] Zacuto's letter was a response to a query from R. Samson Bacchi of Casale, asking Zacuto to provide him with an "Order" (*seder*) for a woman in Turin possessed by an evil spirit.[131] The order, of course, was an exorcism ceremony.

To the eminent sage, his honor our rabbi, Rabbi Samson Bacchi of Casale, may the Compassionate One keep and preserve him. . . .

Regarding that evil spirit in the woman in Turin, of whose case you have informed me: You have already performed the Order [exorcism] of the Rav *zlh"h* [R. Isaac Luria, may his memory live on in the World to Come] for her, which neither helped nor produced lasting results.

This surprised me, for this *kavvanah* has great power to subjugate the spirit to the strong Judgments, particularly given his being from *Sitra Aḥra* [*lit.*, "the Other Side"; *viz.*, the demonic realm], as you have inferred from his name. You did not, however, inform me of the signs that indicate that it is to be diagnosed as a spirit rather than as madness. The outstanding sign that a spirit is present [and not madness] is when its voice is heard through a part of the body other than the mouth, and when its location is seen in the swelling of some place like the throat, the breasts of a woman and the like. Some of them also say something regarding the future.

In any case, you may afflict it through the burning of sulfurous wicks. If, when the smoke reaches the nostrils, it becomes angry and enraged, continue [to apply the smoke] and say the verse, "He will rain down upon the wicked blazing coals [and sulfur; a scorching wind shall be the portion of their cup]" (Ps. 11, 6). If he has not been subdued into declaring himself, have ten scholars and God-fearers assemble. The greatest of them should first ritually bathe, and all should don phylacteries. When they come to them [*sic*] they should begin [saying] "May the pleasantness" (Ps. 90, 17) quietly, and when they say "only with your eyes will you behold" (Ps. 91, 8) they should intend the name *KhH"Th*[132] according to the words of the Rav *zlh"h*. Afterwards, they should all say "It is incumbent upon us to praise . . ." with the known *kavvanot*, and also "And therefore we hope to you. . . ." When they reach "But we bow down . . . ," one of them should blast a great blast [from a *shofar*]. After this, they should all say the verse "Appoint over him a wicked man, [and may a *satan* stand at his right]" (Ps. 109, 6) and intend the *kavvanot* of the judgments alluded within it. They should all look in his face when saying this verse forward and backwards. If he is not subdued, the greatest should powerfully fortify himself, with great concentrated *kavvanah*, and say in his ear the verse "Appoint" with its vocalizations, forward and backwards, with the *kavvanah* of all the names.

Everything must be prepared before him in writing, lest there be anything whatsoever missing of the names or the *kavvanot*, in the first letters, or the last letters, or the middle letters. If any change or sign of submission is seen in him, repeat the verse and its *kavvanah* two or three times, along with similar material like the amulet I gave to the friend of God R. Benjamin Kohen of Reggio,[133] according to the Rav, of blessed memory. You should write it in purity upon clean parchment and hang it upon her to help her.

If none of this helps, let me know if there are any of the signs I have mentioned, and whether she tears her clothing, or whether her form changes, her eyes are bloodshot, and so forth—all the details you can specify. Then I will know what to do for her.

Zacuto begins and ends his letter with discussion of the diagnostic problems involved in exorcism. Perhaps, he supposes, the Lurianic ritual did not succeed because the individual was not possessed but mad (that is, naturally rather than spiritually afflicted). "You did not, however, inform me of the signs that indicate that it is to be diagnosed as a spirit rather than as madness," he wrote Bacchi. The Church too required that exorcists recognize the symptoms that distinguish someone who is possessed from those suffering from melancholia or other illnesses, maintaining, like Sir Thomas Brown, in his 1642 *Religio medici* (1642), that "the devil doth really possess some men; the spirit of melancholy others; the spirit of delusion others."[134] Zacuto suggests that the exorcist examine the woman for the classic signs of true possession: the voice speaking from a part of the anatomy other than the mouth; swelling, indicating the spirit's location; and clairvoyance. Zacuto's attempt to distinguish possession from a form of natural mental illness is very much consonant with main trends of the Christian demonology of his time. Most manuals of exorcism include extended discussions of this problematic issue and provide lengthy lists of symptoms that indicate the nature of the victim's affliction. As we recall from our discussion of Vital's diagnostic techniques, it was assumed that natural and supernatural "diseases" could afflict a victim simultaneously, since the mentally ill, the hysteric or depressed, were considered suitable and easy targets for the Devil.[135]

. . .

Although Jewish sources distinguish spirit possession from mental illness, many of them propose treatments ostensibly effective for either. Thus a procedure in the early medieval Babylonian magical compendium *Ḥarba de-Moshe* (Sword of Moses) is claimed to be effective for people bewitched, suffering from an evil spirit, or from madness.[136] *Shorshei ha-Shemot* (Roots of Names), a magical anthology compiled originally by Zacuto, includes an amulet designed for use by one who is possessed or mad.[137] Some techniques pair clearly psychological problems with demonic afflictions, suggesting a certain linkage between the two. Thus *Shoshan Yesod ha-'Olam* provides a technique that one can use on oneself when suffering from bad thoughts or from an evil spirit.[138] The fact that possession was distinguished from "natural" forms of mental illness by early moderns and their predecessors should give us pause as we translate the possession idiom into modern psychological terms, substituting current clinical diagnoses for the "wrong" understandings of the phenomena held by the "primitives" of the past.[139]

In addition to the symptoms noted by Zacuto, Jewish and Christian possession victims shared numerous other symptoms, including egg-sized lumps moving about the body from which the voice was sometimes heard, catatonia, violent fits, speaking in strange voices, clairvoyance, and speaking in languages unknown to the victim (xenoglossia), as well as the sudden onset of symptoms.[140] Zacuto's list of symptoms reads very much like those in the many exorcism handbooks that circulated widely in seventeenth-century Italy. These works were already popular in Italy in the sixteenth century, as we learn from the distribution of Girolamo Menghi's works. At least forty-two editions of two of his handbooks for exorcists came out between the end of the sixteenth century and the beginning of the eighteenth.[141] Valerio Polidoro, nearly a century before Zacuto, noted the following symptoms in his treatment of possession:

> In addition to the ordinary signs the body and limbs are swelled and the victim can scarcely move; sometimes the face is cedar-colored and there are pains of different kinds in the limbs; the heart seems to be compressed or pricked, or as if gnawed by a dog; the orifice of the stomach seems constricted; digestion ceases and food is vomited; a ball seems to rise from the stomach and descend; there is severe colic in the lower belly and wind seems to pass, sometimes very cold and sometimes burning. There is also a loss of reasoning power and idiocy, at intervals, sometimes longer or shorter.[142]

Because all physical symptoms might be viewed as arising due to natural illnesses, many regarded xenoglossia as the surest sign that possession was involved rather than, or in addition to, natural illness. Christian as well as Jewish sources regarded it as a symptom that was irrefutable evidence of possession, as we saw in the Falcon case above.[143] The striking affinities between Menghi's manuals and Zacuto's letter point to the common cultural background against which the possession idiom became intelligible to them both.

## Exorcism and the Freedom to Heal

The core of the procedure that Zacuto recommended in his letter remained the meditations and *kavvanot* presented by Vital in Luria's name discussed above. In a departure from the Lurianic procedure, however, Zacuto prescribes the extensive use of sulfurous fumigations, a mainstay of Catholic exorcism and earlier Jewish magic. Amulets were used by Jews and Christians (including many Protestants, though with certain stipulations) to protect the victim from relapses (that is, "repossession") after the completion of the exorcism, as Zacuto's letter also explains. Relapses might be blamed on the failure to hang such amulets around the necks of victims or on deficiencies in the amulets themselves. In the Falcon case, the young woman was repossessed because the amulets she was given were generic, rather than written especially for her.[144] Nevertheless, Luria did not prescribe the use of amulets in exorcisms.[145] Indeed, Luria prescribed *tikkunim* (penitential reparations) for those who made use of amulets, requiring penitents to roll in the snow nine times while naked, from head to toe.[146]

Although Zacuto does not call for adjurations, his description of the expected effects of the Lurianic *kavvanah* that was used suggests that he had come to regard it as a kind of adjuration. "I was surprised by the matter, for the strength of this *kavvanah* is very mighty to subjugate that spirit to the strong judgments." Thus, Zacuto assumed that the *kavvanah* would function precisely the way adjurations do in most magical exorcisms—to summon demonic (and holy) angelic beings to be the exorcist's "hit men" in his assault on the possessing spirit. The exorcist adjures them to enlist their assistance in his difficult task. Luria notably omits this element from his technique, whereas Zacuto reintroduces it, reconstruing the very essence of Luria's *yiḥud.*

In Zacuto's instructions we thus find elements familiar both from the Jewish magical tradition and from the exorcism manuals of his Catholic contemporaries. At first glance, Zacuto's openness seems expected; his enthusiastic integration of Italian baroque culture has been noted by several scholars.[147] In this case, however, Zacuto has adopted precisely the elements notably absent from Luria's technique. This would not be surprising, were it not for the fact that, his baroque literary tastes notwithstanding, Zacuto was an "orthodox" Lurianist—"orthodox" insofar as he was consistently unwilling to innovate in the lacunae of the Lurianic system and was conservative in his exegetical deployment of Lurianic principles.[148] How, then, did he come to adopt non-Lurianic and, effectively, *anti*-Lurianic practices? What accounts for Zacuto's willingness to integrate "foreign" practices into his own prescriptions? Why would Zacuto, dedicated to strict and conservative Lurianic exegesis and practice, be willing to ignore Luria's vocal opposition to the techniques of practical kabbalah?[149]

This willingness is made apparent not only in this letter, but also in the large collections of magical formulas assembled by Zacuto—*Shorshei ha-Shemot* and *Sefer ha-Sodot she-Kibbalti mi-Rabbotai* (The Book of Secrets I Received from My Masters). Collecting most of the magical material that makes up the latter work during his stay in Poland, Zacuto gathered amulets, adjurations to angels and demons, and natural magical procedures. *Segulot ha-teva* (virtues of nature), as he referred to the last, are based primarily on the use of herbs and stones in accordance with sympathetic and astral magical principles. They are of use, according to Zacuto, whether a person suffers "from illness or from sorcery."[150] In a number of places Zacuto notes, "tested by me"; from this we may gather that Zacuto assembled this magical material for practical and not merely theoretical purposes.

How could a strict Lurianic Kabbalist ignore the AR"I's warnings against magical pursuits? Perhaps Zacuto understood Luria's opposition to magic as directed especially toward R. Ḥayyim Vital and less so toward his other disciples.[151] Luria's *yiḥudim* could after all also be regarded as magical in their own right, making it difficult to accept the image of Luria as antimagical in the extreme. And Luria's actions may have spoken louder than his words; the hagiographic literature that coalesced around his figure emphasized precisely his tremendous supernatural powers. In the eyes of the readers of this literature, Luria was a powerful magician.

Yet Zacuto did not know Luria through hagiographic literature. On the contrary, his fluency in Lurianic theosophy is obvious in his highly technical commentary on the Zohar.[152] It is therefore difficult to explain his indifference to the AR"I's opposition to magic on the basis of the image of Luria as reflected in hagiography. To answer this question, we must take a step back and examine the issues in a broader context.

Exorcism is a therapeutic act that takes place in a religiously sensitive area. The question of how to act in this area necessarily arises. Which interest will triumph—the desire to heal the possessed or the requirement to refrain from performing suspect procedures?[153] Among Christians in the early modern period, the latter interest generally prevailed. This was a result of the traditions of Augustine, Thomas Aquinas, Bonaventura, and others who claimed that "it was forbidden to do evil even to good ends, and it is preferable that a person die rather than be liberated from the domination of spirits by means of vain and foolish actions."[154] This approach was adopted by Heinrich Kramer and James Sprenger in their *Malleus Maleficarum*, the infamous demonological work of the period. The authors of this work knew well to what extent people availed themselves of suspect means of healing: "Again it is pointed out that the common method in practice of taking off a bewitchment, although it is quite unlawful, is for the bewitched persons to resort to wise women, by whom they are very frequently cured, and not by priests or exorcists."[155] In spite of this, there were Christian thinkers who sought to permit magical procedures to the extent that they successfully countered *maleficia*. This pragmatic approach is associated in the demonological tradition with Henry of Segusio, John Duns Scotus, and the Canonists, and it reflects the more benign evaluation of "white magic" found in Roman law.[156] Jews were clearly inclined toward pragmatism in magico-medical matters. Because treatments were evaluated according to their success, it was possible to choose from a wide range of healing strategies. This eclectic approach to healing in the early modern period has been called "medical pluralism" by Peter Burke.[157] Not only were modalities of therapy varied, but the healers themselves might come from outside the faith community of the patient. Gentile sorcerers might be consulted, a phenomenon well attested to in our sources. Thus Ḥayyim Vital and his son Samuel had no reservations about collaborating with or receiving treatment from Islamic magicians.[158] Menasseh ben Israel reports, without aspersion, on the failure of a Jewish "adjurer" to exorcise a young man successfully in a mid-seventeenth century North African case. This young man suffered for more than two weeks, until "an old Arab, an eminent sorcerer, came and cured him within a half an hour."[159] Like Jewish law, Islamic law was generally pragmatic in its approach to these issues. An Ash'ari jurist of the thirteenth century, Al-Djuwayni, is typical. "God has merely prohibited what is harmful and not that which is useful; if it is possible for you to be useful to your brother, then do it."[160] This common pragmatism no doubt facilitated the collegiality between Jewish and Arab sorcerers.

Yet Jews in Christian lands might also avail themselves of local magical healers, as we read in the "Tale of an Exorcism in Koretz" dating from the 1660s. In this account, the parents of the afflicted girl are said to have taken her "to witches and doctors," though to no avail.[161] Moshe Rosman has noted of the eighteenth-century Carpathians that "when it came to fending off supernatural predators, religious lines could be crossed. . . . At least sometimes, members of each group viewed the holy individuals of the other as possessing theurgic power."[162] This posture was shared by Ashkenazic authorities centuries earlier, as testified to by a fascinating responsum of R. Solomon Luria, known as Maharshal (c. 1510–74). This rabbi, known for his rejection of the "pilpul" style of learning then popular in Poland, discussed whether it was permissible for a sick person to have recourse to the services of non-Jewish sorcerers.[163] In his consideration of the question, Maharshal notes the history of laxity with regard to this possibility, notwithstanding the biblical injunctions against magic[164]—rabbinically interpreted as referring to graver practices than the ones under consideration.[165] Where a sick person is concerned, questions of theological propriety are suspended. Maharshal's decision is actually stricter than many earlier rulings. Only in the case of life-threatening illness may magicians be consulted, he concludes. In cases where sickness has been brought on by magic or an evil spirit, however, Maharshal makes an exception:

> Nevertheless, it seems appropriate to permit [consultation] occasionally, even where there is no threat to life, but only danger to a limb. For example when it is known that the illness came upon the person through magic, chance, or evil spirits, then it is

permissible to consult them according to Maimonides. For about those matters and their like, most of the sorcerers are knowledgeable and find help and remedy. And it may be that even according to Maimonides we may find a way to permit, if we say that the Torah did not prohibit sorcery in this manner, which comes only to expel and to nullify sorcery and evil spirits. For the Torah only prohibited inquiring after them, pursuing them, and believing in them as being in themselves substantial. A small proof to this effect is that the Sanhedrin used to learn sorcery in order to nullify the sorcery of those sentenced to death. I also found such an approach in a responsum of R. Menachem Metz, [in which he wrote] that it was permissible to learn sorcery from sorcerers in order to save oneself or others.

This bold pragmatism stemmed from a number of factors. The rich Jewish magical tradition furnished sufficient proof that magical activity was considered licit by a sizable portion of leading rabbinic figures. Moreover, if Christian thinkers tended to be sensitive to theological contradictions and heresies, Jewish thinkers were more pragmatic. The very structure of Judaism as a performative religion also lent it to magical reinterpretation.[166] In short, there was no problem with undertaking magical activity so long as such activity did not vitiate divine service. According to Maharshal's abovementioned responsum, "The Torah did not forbid sorcery" if its purpose was "to expel and to nullify sorcery and evil spirits . . . for the Torah only forbade inquiring after them, pursuing them, and believing in them." The Torah forbade engaging in magical practices associated with inquiry, pursuit, and belief—all of which would be in tension with divine service. Magic for treating victims of witchcraft or to exorcise spirits was, however, permissible. Similar discussions are found in the works of R. Joseph Karo, R. David ibn Zimra, and others.[167] Even the *Kitzur Shulḥan Arukh* (Abridged Ordered Table), the highly conservative 1864 work of R. Solomon Ganzfried (1804–86), rules that "It is forbidden to consult sorcerers except in life-threatening situations, or if a sickness was the result of witchcraft, chance, or an evil spirit. In such a case, it is permissible to be treated by a non-Jewish sorcerer."[168] The ultimate rabbinic roots of this acceptance of magical healing techniques are, in fact, already implicit in the Babylonian Talmud. There we find the teaching of the fourth-century rabbis Abaye and Rava, according to which all concerns that a particular practice is illicit because of its magico-idolatrous character are suspended when healing is at stake: "Anything of a medical nature is not [in conflict with the biblical prohibition of the] ways of the Amorites.[169] Zacuto's willingness to ignore Luria's opposition to practical kabbalah where healing was at stake thus made rabbinic sense. When magical praxis constituted an effective treatment, any reservations regarding its propriety were to be suspended. Healing magic was judged according to its terrestrial success, even in the opinion of the famously antimagical Maimonides.[170] In all that pertained to theosophical questions, Zacuto was careful not to stray from the instructions of Luria. Zacuto's additions to Luria's technique were therefore undertaken not out of disregard but from a conviction that in these matters pragmatism reigned. Whether his approach to exorcism was influenced by his Catholic environment or by the Jewish magical tradition—and it is reasonable to assume a confluence of influences—his options were open. Zacuto, like kabbalist-exorcists before and after him, did not hesitate to deal with exorcism with flexibility and openness. The main thing was, as they say, to be well.

## The Reformation That Wasn't: Jewish Exorcism and Magical Recidivism

A mutual indebtedness to magical traditions, Arabic and ancient, as well as an awareness of the practices of contemporary colleagues, accounts for the many similarities between the Jewish and Christian approaches to exorcism in the early modern period that we have observed. Yet there were also key differences, owing to the very different historical and doctrinal contexts in which Christianity and Judaism found themselves in the period. As the Church sought to transfer the prerogative to exorcise from wonder-workers to priests, techniques of exorcism went through a process of standardization, as many popular practices and practitioners were condemned as "superstitious" by the post-Tridentine authorities. With the Reformation, Protestants and Catholics developed competing models of exorcism, thrusting the dispossession of the demoniac to center stage in this essential conflict. The theatricality of the Catholic approach to exorcism is generally considered to have triumphed the more introspective Protestant alternative both as propaganda and as treatment. [171]

Although Judaism did not undergo a parallel reformation in the period, it is not difficult to point to the need to reassert rabbinic authority and to demonstrate the power of Jewish symbols in this unstable period.[172] In the Jewish case, Luria played the role of reformer, going quite nearly so far as to condemn the plethora of magical Jewish exorcism practices as "superstitions" to be avoided.[173] This introspective refashioning of exorcism was not to displace the broad range of techniques in the Jewish magical arsenal going back to antiquity. Perhaps due to their pragmatic approach to all things related to healing, perhaps out of an intuitive sense of the importance of the theatrical to the effectiveness of exorcism, Luria's reform was not respected as much as reinscribed. Demonstrating their perennial capacity to assimilate the widest variety of practices in syncretistic hybrids, Jewish magical practitioners swallowed up the AR"I's techniques and made them their own.

## *Chapter 4*

# Dybbuk *Possession and Women's Religiosity*

Our study has, thus far, introduced us to a number of women whose clairvoyant abilities in the course of their possession attracted considerable interest and attention. At the very least, their possession experience entailed a certain ambiguity along the fault lines of gender (male/female) and spirit (divine/demonic). Here we must pose the question more directly: what was the relation of spirit possession to broader notions of women's religiosity, as perceived and experienced by women as well as by the male religious elite?

## Comparative Perspectives

The past decades have seen a renaissance in the study of women's religiosity in medieval and early modern Europe. Since Caroline Bynum lamented that women's spirituality was "a surprisingly neglected field,"[1] countless studies have redressed that neglect and provided us with thoughtful discussions of its distinctive features from the thirteenth to the seventeenth centuries. These studies have taught us that despite systemic discrimination, repression, and suppression, women succeeded in forging individual and collective forms of religious expression. These enabled them to pursue their own spiritual development with passion and integrity, while commanding the respect, attention, interest—and not infrequently the suspicion—of male religious and secular authorities.

Distilling "a typology of female sanctity," Gabriella Zarri identified its distinctive contours.[2] As complemented by the studies of Bynum, Jodi Bilinkoff, Alison Weber, and others, the following might be taken as the characteristic features of Christian women's religiosity in this period:

- affective piety, involving a personal, emotional engagement with Jesus;[3]
- somatic spirituality: ritual eating, fasts, and feasts, along with ecstatic raptures, trances, seizures, and stigmata;[4]
- clairvoyant abilities and prophetic powers;[5]
- divine inspiration yet lack of formal education;[6]
- being active in the secular domain, not having taken the vows of any order;[7]
- intense involvement with their spiritual director-confessors, whose devoted writing about them is often our only window into their lives.[8]

Given the ecstatic, experiential nature of women's spirituality in late medieval and early modern Europe, it is not surprising that the problem of identifying the source of their inspiration—the discerning of spirits, as it was known—was a critical one for religious authorities.[9] The problem was so complex and acute that a woman could begin her spiritual career as a living saint and end it imprisoned, exiled, or at the stake. Conversely, a woman could emerge to prominence as a demoniac and, mastering the spirits, go on to a career of spiritual leadership. Magdalena de la Cruz is but one example of the former trajectory, Jeanne des Anges, abbess of the Loudun convent, of the latter.[10] Given the fact that the source of visions was always open to question, saints' lives might be constructed to emphasize the orthodoxy of their subjects. Thus in his book on the life of Catherine of Sienna, Tommaso Caffarini downplays her inspiration, while casting Catherine as a "doctor saint."[11] Although contemporaries struggled with the problem of discerning the saint from the witch, ecstasies from possessions, recent historians stress the inherent structural ambiguity of these categories, regarding them as inextricably bound inversionary parallels.[12]

Bearing these features of late medieval and early modern Christian women's spirituality in mind, it would seem instructive to compare them with what we know about the characteristics of Jewish women's spirituality in the same period. Unfortunately, however, the two schools of Jewish historiography where we would most expect to find treatments of this topic—the historiographies of Iberian Jewry and of Jewish mysticism—are of little assistance.

## Women's Religiosity and Jewish Historiography

The prophetess Inés and her followers among the conversos of Herrera, Segovia, and the surrounding areas at the cusp of the fifteenth and sixteenth centuries have been the subject of numerous studies by the eminent historians Yiẓḥak Baer and Ḥaim Beinart. At the outset of his work on Inés, Baer states that he intends to treat "only the messianic essence" of the movement surrounding the young prophetess.[13] Shortly thereafter, he cites at length from the inquisitorial testimony of a man from Segovia who was introduced to Inés by her father, shortly after her visions and prophecies began. The man testified that Inés told him of her ascent to heaven, and

> how her deceased mother appeared and held her hand, telling her, "Don't be afraid, for it is the will of God that you ascend to heaven and see the secrets, and see wondrous things." Her other hand was also held by a youth who had died a few days before, and by the angel who guided them. And so she said that they raised her to heaven, and that she saw Purgatory and the souls who suffered there, and also, how in another department others sat with honor upon golden thrones. . . . Among the things that the girl said to me, was that she asked the angel for a sign so that her statements would be believed, and that the angel said that he would bring her an approbation from God.[14]

In subsequent studies, Beinart adduced additional evidence of gatherings around Inés and among her followers that included ecstatic dancing, song, mystical marriage, and calls for fasting and repentance.[15] Despite these descriptions, the women's religiosity that finds expression in nearly every document remains to be analyzed as such, while attempting to contextualize Inés in the environment of Magdalena de la Cruz, María de Santo Domingo, and the other prophetic *beatas* (holy women) of late medieval Spain.[16] Jewish historians have until now chosen to focus on the messianic dimension of the phenomenon and the eschatological orientation of the conversos. Concluding a study that includes extensive documentation of the ecstatic experiences of Inés and many of her female followers, Beinart thus summarizes, "The story of the activities of the prophetess Inés in her hometown of Herrera teaches us the great extent of the excitement that gripped the conversos in their expectation of redemption."[17] The lack of any analysis of the mystical religiosity of the women who participated in this movement stems from multiple causes. The emphasis on the nationalist-messianic dimension of the phenomenon that we find in Baer and Beinart is typical of the Israeli historiography of their generations.[18] Both men also conducted their research before women's religiosity was recognized as an important topic in European historiography.

When we inspect the historiography of Jewish mysticism, we find not so much an overlooking of women's mystical religiosity as a fundamental denial of its existence. Gershom Scholem, the modern founder of the field of kabbalah studies, concluded the opening chapter of his magisterial *Major Trends in Jewish Mysticism* with the following remark:

> One final observation should be made on the general character of Kabbalism as distinct from other, non-Jewish, forms of mysticism. Both historically and metaphysically it is a masculine doctrine, made for men and by men. The long history of Jewish mysticism shows no trace of feminine influence. There have been no women Kabbalists; Rabia of early Islamic mysticism, Mechthild of Magdeburg, Juliana of Norwich, Theresa de Jesus, and the many other feminine representatives of Christian mysticism have no counterparts in the history of Kabbalism. The latter, therefore, lacks the element of feminine emotion which has played so large a part in the development of non-Jewish mysticism, but it also remained comparatively free from the dangers entailed by the tendency towards hysterical extravagance which followed in the wake of this influence.[19]

It is impossible to exaggerate the impact of such a definitive statement by Scholem, whose work effectively defined the parameters, methodology, and goals of the field for more than fifty years. Having defined Jewish mysticism as an exclusively textual-ideational phenomenon, Scholem could recognize only the primary producers and consumers of mystical texts and their ideas as Jewish mystics.[20] It was not ideology that impeded Scholem here so much as his philosophical-doctrinal approach to the study of Jewish mysticism, an approach that slighted its magical and experiential dimensions as well.[21] The study of gender in kabbalah studies has thus remained almost exclusively a matter of assessing the gender valence of theosophical symbols.[22] And although American and French feminist scholarship long assumed a correlation between the prominence of female symbolism in religion and improved cultic and social opportunities, recent studies suggest otherwise.[23] In short, so long as the mystical religiosity of men constitutes the standard of reference, women's mystical religiosity cannot be an object of research—it cannot even be said to exist.[24]

## Mystical Women in R. Ḥayyim Vital's *Sefer ha-Ḥezyonot*

If few women participated in the textual culture of Jewish mysticism in the late medieval and early modern periods, many, it would seem, were nevertheless spiritual adepts with a religious profile distinctly their own.[25] This chapter represents an attempt to begin to identify that religious profile, to assess its social dimensions, and to reflect upon its effective disappearance from Jewish historical memory. Although rich material from the fifteenth and seventeenth centuries must certainly be marshaled for any comprehensive history of Jewish women's mystical piety—the inquisitorial records pertaining to Inés and her prophetic movement on the one hand, and Sabbatian sources on the other—the present inquiry will draw primarily from an exceedingly rich source, which has yet to be appreciated for its potential contribution to such a history.[26] This source, *Sefer ha-Ḥezyonot*, is the mystical diary of R. Ḥayyim Vital, a ubiquitous character in the preceding chapters.[27] The diary of the foremost student of R. Isaac Luria, who became the preeminent Kabbalist of the late sixteenth and early seventeenth century, is of immeasurable historical value and is one of the few significant mystical diaries authored by a kabbalist.[28] Vital's diary was clearly unintended for broad consumption, and its inclusion of painful and embarrassing self-disclosures bespeaks an essential honesty of presentation.[29] Thus, although the work would be of historical significance if only for its exposure of Vital's mentality, there is no prima facie reason to discount the historicity of the events and personalities it describes.

Of interest to us are the women of *Sefer ha-Ḥezyonot*, women with whom Vital had contact throughout the course of his life in Safed, Jerusalem, and Damascus. In addition to revealing his unabashed acceptance of their religious integrity and mystical prowess, a close examination of Vital's descriptions of these women discloses a great deal about the nature of their spirituality and reveals the network of relations that bound and supported them.

Vital describes women whom he consulted for their divination skills, for their ability to mediate contact with the dead, and for their clairvoyant ability to assess his own condition. He also records the dreams that many women shared with him, in which he played a meaningful role. Who were these women?

We may begin with the "dreamer," Soñadora. "In the year 5330 [1570]," writes Vital, "there was a wise woman, who predicted the future, and who was also expert in the art of oil-gazing. They called her Soñadora. I asked her over the oil by means of an incantation, as is customary, about my attainment in the art of the Kabbalah. She did not know how to respond to me, until she was imbued [*lit.* enclothed] by a zealous spirit, and strengthened herself in her incantations. She then stood on her feet, and kissed my feet. . . ."[30] Soñadora goes on to tell Vital of the greatness of his soul, as she has seen it written with Ashurite letters formed by the oil.[31] She also interprets a dream of Vital's at his request. Vital also consults other experts in divination, including the wise women Mira and Mazal Tov. Mazal Tov, sought out for advice by Vital, "hears voices,"[32] whereas Mira's dreams impose missions upon her, their grim prophecies coming to pass in harsh plagues that strike the city of Damascus.[33] From what Vital tells us about them, it would seem that Soñadora, Mira, and Mazal Tov had more in common with Iberian witches than *beatas.* The former were distinguished by their mastery of techniques in the realms of love magic, divination, and communication with the dead.[34] That said, in a community in which religious authorities were themselves deeply engaged in magical theory and practice, the distinction between useful witch and female saint would be difficult to make.

Francesa Sarah of Safed seems to have been a religious adept very different from Soñadora and the other sorceresses consulted by Vital. Tellingly, Vital describes Francesa as having been present in the study hall when he taught his students in Safed in 1594. Seated beside her, conversing with her at the time, was the daughter of R. Shlomo Alkabetz. Vital records, "Francesa Sarah was there. She is a pious woman, who sees visions while awake, and hears a voice speaking to her. Most of her pronouncements are true."[35] Vital notes Francesa's piety, her waking visions, her attentiveness to a divine voice, and the accuracy of her prophecies. These are exceptional attainments by any standard, and they certainly demonstrate that as far as Vital was concerned, women could be mystical virtuosi of accomplishment.[36] Joseph Sambari (c. 1640–1703), writing his history of the Jews under Muslim rule some sixty years later in Cairo, referred to Francesa as well. According to his account, "In those days there was a woman, wise and great in her deeds in the Upper Galilee, Safed, may it be rebuilt speedily in our days. Her name was Francesa. She had a *maggid* to speak to her and to inform her of what was to be in the world. The sages of Safed tested her several times to know if there was substance to her words, and everything that she said came to pass."[37] The ambiguous voice mentioned by Vital is identified by Sambari as a *maggid,* an angelic revelatory agent considered nearly as exalted as Elijah the Prophet, and associated with the male rabbinic elite of this period.[38] Sambari included two lengthy stories about Francesa in his treatment of the sages of sixteenth-century Safed. The historicity of these stories is almost incidental to the very fact that Sambari saw fit to include them alongside the classic hagiographic accounts of Luria and other mystical luminaries.[39] Sambari's stories give us a fuller picture of Francesa than does Vital's complementary, telegraphic description. These accounts underscore Francesa's spiritual prowess and her high standing in the community. The first recounts her summoning of the sages of Safed to order them to decree a fast. The Jews of Safed must fight for their lives, she explains, as she has been informed from behind the heavenly curtain that a plague has been decreed against them. The rabbis, we are told, immediately decreed a public fast for young and old, man and woman alike. At the penitential service, Francesa mournfully foretells the death of the preacher, R. Moses de Curiel, eight days later. And indeed Curiel passes away on the eighth day, dying for the sins of his community, which was saved from the plague—"just as the woman had said."[40] The second account relates the conversion of a doubting rabbi, R. Abraham Shalom, into a believer. Shalom planned to leave Safed to resettle in Ankara, where he had a business partner. Curious to hear what Francesa would say, he went to ask her opinion of the idea. Francesa tells him bluntly, "The man you seek is already dead . . . and your trip will not succeed." Furious, Shalom returns home, bewildered, and begins to reconsider his trip. That night, asking God to be his witness, he decides that he should travel to Ankara to collect his investment and then come home to Safed, his birthplace, to live out the remainder of his life. In the morning, he returns to Francesa. "I am going," he says:

> "Indeed, know, and see what word you will bring back for me." And she placed her hand upon her eyes, and waited a bit, and said: "Hear now the word of the Lord! The man whom you seek is certainly dead, but should you desire to go, the Lord will make your journey successful." "Yesterday you told me not to go, since I would not succeed, and now you tell me to go, for the Lord will make my journey successful?" "That is true. Yesterday you thought to leave Israel and dwell abroad, while last night you repented and made the Lord your witness that if He grants you success, you will return to Safed. Since the will of the Lord is that you not uproot your home from the Land of Israel, he will grant you success." Upon hearing the words of the woman, he fell flat on the ground, and bowed in worship to the Lord for having given his wisdom to this woman of valor.[41]

The next day, documents arrived from the executors of the dead man's estate in Ankara telling him to come get his money. "From then on, faith in her was fixed in his heart like a trusty stake, and he believed her, and she said many different things."[42] Far more than "an indication of Sambari's opposition to the abandonment of the Land of Israel, this story presents the conversion of a great Safedian rabbi from an unbeliever to a believer in a female mystic; it portrays a mystic-prophetess enjoying revelatory experiences, summoning rabbis, decreeing fasts, foreseeing death, forestalling plagues, and being privy to man's midnight secrets with God."[43]

*The Oracle of Damascus: The Daughter of Raphael Anav*

Only now may we consider perhaps the two most accomplished female spiritual adepts described in Vital's diary—Rachel Aberlin and the young daughter of Rabbi Raphael Anav.[44] We begin with the young girl, whose first name we never learn; she will be referred to throughout simply as "Anav." Vital devoted no less than seven pages of his tightly written, eighty-page manuscript to an account of this girl's possession and subsequent mediumship in Damascus during the fall of 1609. Like Elizabeth de Ranfaing and Jeanne des Anges, Anav mastered her spirits and, like many former demoniacs, became a holy woman admired and sought after.[45] Although the spirit that possessed Anav was benign, the initial episode is portrayed as having come about involuntarily; only later would the girl learn to communicate with this and other spirits at will. Anav's experience thus appears to conform to patterns observed by the anthropologist Esther Pressel in her field work in Brazil.[46] Pressel found that "initial possessions tended to be involuntary and subsequent ones voluntary as the host gained control of his or her spirit." Although we would do well to recall Vincent Crapanzano's observation that the phenomenon of spirit possession rarely obeys the neat classificatory models developed by anthropologists and scholars of religion,[47] this trajectory from victim of possession to shamanistic master has indeed been discovered by anthropologists in a wide variety of cultures. Generally the development from victim to master takes place in cultures that have an established, positively valued, and at least semi-institutionalized possession cult.[48] Given the lack of such a setting in Jewish culture, this trajectory seems to have been rather unusual, with few additional examples coming readily to mind.[49] At the same time, the reception of Anav by Vital and other Damascene sages would seem to indicate an acceptance of the legitimacy of this sort of phenomenon and of the possibility of a young woman's becoming an accomplished master of the spirit world. Although a certain theatrical novelty may be inferred from the large crowds that gathered to witness the prophecies and contumelies, leading rabbis nevertheless gathered without protest to collaborate with, and be subjected to, this young woman.

In the account, the so-called evil spirit of a sage[50] possesses Anav. This possession by a good soul is most unusual, as this awkward, oxymoronic phrase suggests. Few contemporary parallels of such a possession have been found by early modern historians, a notable exception being the seventeenth-century Sardinian cases discovered by Peter Burke—the only cases he discovered of possession by saints or good spirits in a European context.[51] In the Anav case, the good spirit—that of "Ḥakham [Rabbinical Sage] Piso"—descends from his station in heaven to the Anav residence over the Sabbath of 1 August 1609, aptly known as Shabbat "*Masei*" (Journeys), after the Biblical reading of the week (Num. 33–36), which adumbrates the journeys of Israel through the wilderness. The journey of Ḥakham Piso, through the waters of the Euphrates, into a fish, and ultimately, via ingestion,[52] into the body of Anav, was instigated in order for him to proclaim through the young girl that the Jews of Damascus must repent. As a reward for his couriership and for having suffered the travails of the descent, Ḥakham Piso was to be purged of the final gossamer sins that partitioned him below his rightful heavenly station. A point of further ambiguity: the kabbalists deemed it necessary to use exorcistic adjurations to "assist" Ḥakham Piso's departure from the girl's body, even though he was a good spirit, suggesting the difficulty of severing soul from flesh—this, even when the soul has not lodged itself within the living for its own shelter or the other's harm.

Again, the Jews are faced with a decree of pestilential destruction, which must be averted; Vital further stresses the need to remove the obstacles blocking the redemptive arrival of the Messiah. While in the girl's body, Ḥakham Piso provides ritual direction on the Sabbath and gathers the souls of a half-dozen deceased sages to be present as he dispatches his mission. The spirit summons Vital, promises to reveal secrets beyond anything he ever learned from Luria, and harshly chastises the rabbinic establishment of Damascus. Finally, the spirit loses patience with Vital, who fails "to see the great fire burning the world" and neglects an opportunity to receive the mystical secrets he was to have disclosed. With the spirit's departure, the first chapter of the account—indeed its overture—comes to a close. It was a form of this overture that became a popular addendum to Lurianic hagiographic literature, first appearing in R. Jacob Ẓemaḥ's *Ronu le-Ya'akov*

The popular version of the account concludes with the departure of

Ḥakham Piso on the Sunday following that rather "enthusiastic" Sabbath. The closing of the account at the end of merely the overture to the extraordinary saga of Anav's mediumship in itself suggests a strong editorial hand. What is omitted is Anav's emergence as herself. No longer involuntarily possessed, Anav, with experience, gradually becomes a medium capable of interacting with the dead and the divine—Elijah and the angels—while awake. One possibility that suggests itself, then, is that the degree of female agency evident in this case was discomfiting and played a role in the editorial decision. Was the cultural context of the redaction of this account different from the one that prevailed as the case unfolded in the Damascus of 1609? Or were there perhaps different standards in a given environment for narratives intended for private and public consumption? Were accounts of certain phenomena simply deemed inappropriate for the printing press? Of course, it is entirely plausible that the popular account was concluded where it was for other reasons: aesthetic-dramatic considerations might also support the choice to popularize the overture, just as opera overtures are commonly programmed in orchestral "pops" concerts today. Moreover, to the extent that the account was crafted to maximize its didactic force, the continuation of the saga might have had a subversionary effect, including as it does harsh critiques of rabbinic figures made by a young woman who, no longer possessed, was now accountable for her words and actions.[53]

With the departure of the spirit, the agency of the young woman comes to the fore as she moves from passive to active engagement with the spirits and her community.[54] Now, Vital tells us in the continuation of the account preserved only in his diary,

> other things happened, not by means of that spirit while he was still lodged [*lit.* enclothed] in her—for he had already departed, and the young woman remained entirely healthy—but she says that she sometimes sees visions while awake, and in dreams, by means of souls [of the departed] and angels, and also by means of that spirit on occasion.[55]

Although he did not see the girl in person after the spirit departed, Vital kept in touch with her father and other men who furnished him with accounts of her activities and who mediated exchanges between them. Among the first reports were her statements that she constantly beholds an angel who leads her, in her dreams, through Paradise and Hell and shows her the stations of the righteous. Angels and disembodied souls she encounters along the way frequently implore her to warn Vital that he must bring the Jews of Damascus to repent. They also explain the cessation of Vital's own revelations and the cause of his daughter's death in the plague. Over the following days, in a dramatic escalation of her prophetic gifts, Elijah the Prophet reveals himself to her with a message for the sages of Damascus, warning them of the consequences of their not having taken to heart the admonitions of the spirit who had possessed her. At this point, Vital writes that he relayed a question to her through her father about the absence of his own revelatory spirit, the soul of a sage with whom he had had a long association.

The 10th day of Av. I asked her via her father why the righteous one who is known to me has desisted from speaking with me, and what was his name, and whether there was any hope of bringing about his return. She responded to me that on the eve of the 11th of Av she saw my teacher, may his memory be a blessing, and he said to her, "Tell him in my name that he should not continue to ask these questions so many times, and that I cannot respond to him with any response other than this—are they not these three words: *Ashrei* (happy) *maytim* (the dead/those who die) *be-veitekha* (in your house). He will understand the meaning of the things himself."[56]

Luria's enigmatic response to Vital's persistent questioning, "Blessed are the dead in your house," a macabre variation on Psalm 84, verse 5 ("Blessed are those who dwell in your house"), may have been meant to strengthen Vital's resolve to restore contact with the dead who had, in former days, been regular *'ibburic* occupants of his "house"—that is, his body.[57] Vital, however, records that he himself was unable to fathom the import of his master's cipher. For her part, Anav offered nothing beyond the message. She is told merely what to convey to Vital, and not its interpretation; Vital would do the construing. These three words, moreover, amount to the recorded "positive" teaching accomplished by Anav while in a possessed or obsessed state (most everything else being personal criticisms, revelations of sins, and prophetic prognostication). How could Vital have understood speaking to his master through this young woman without understanding three simple words, practically biblical, from him? They were not three words Vital had seen together before, and seem absent from the talmudically vast Lurianic corpus.[58] Luria via Anav was not speaking Lurianically.

When Anav sees Luria again the next time, Luria asks her how Vital responded to his message.

The night of the 12th of Av. In a dream, she saw my teacher, may his memory be a blessing, in a cave. He said to her: "How did Rabbi Ḥayyim respond to you?" She told him, "He said to me that he did not understand those three words." He said to her, "Something so simple as this? Has his intellect been sealed, that he did not understand? Where is the wisdom that I taught him? And he should well remember that same evil spirit that I removed from him. It has now been four years during which time he has not seen me in a dream. Now, I had considered returning to him, but because he did not understand the words of my response I do not want to return to him."[59]

Vital here records this second visitation of his master to Anav, as the latter slept. Anav sent word that, according to Luria, the three words were simple and had something to do with an exorcism Luria had once performed for Vital. "Happy are the dead in your house!"—evil spirits and souls of the righteous. Anav brings more than disappointment, however, and conveys Luria's declaration that he has no intention of revealing himself to Vital again. Vital continued recording the visionary encounters between his master and the young girl for months. As much as a half-year later, R. Raphael told Vital that Luria was now appearing to his daughter while awake, discussing with her the community of Damascus and its fate, as well as Vital's own spiritual fortunes.

The public climax of this episode seems to have come nearly three weeks after Ḥakham Piso's initial departure. On Monday, the seventeenth of Av, the spirit revealed himself to the Anav girl and demanded that she charge her father in his name to summon before her R. Jacob Abulafia (c. 1550–c. 1622) for chastisement.[60] Rabbi of the Spanish congregation of Damascus, Abulafia was something of an Urbain Grandier of Damascus, blamed for calling down God's wrath upon the community by Vital and, it would seem, by a number of the city's ecstatic women as well.[61] Abulafia arrives at a house full of men and women; even the roof is overflowing with people trying to hear. "Tuesday morning, after the prayer, he [Ḥakham Piso] called him, and he [Abulafia] sat for fully half the day being admonished. Raphael and his daughter, and all their household, and other women, and R. Y. Bom and Beẓalel and Frajalla his brother were present; other people stood on the roof in order to hear."

With the assistance of Kabbalist Joshua Albom, the girl summons Ẓadkiel and the souls of four deceased sages to appear in a magical mirror to chide Abulafia. There is no indication in Vital's diary that any of those present felt uncomfortable engaging in necromancy or disapproving of the girl's collaboration with Albom.[62] Anav gazes into the mirror, sees the angel and souls, and converses with them. Ẓadkiel, however, soon declares his unwillingness to reprove Abulafia in this manner, as the latter was unlikely to believe chastisements that only Anav could hear from the figures/reflections in the mirror. Instead, Ẓadkiel suggests that the original spirit reenter Anav so that he might speak through her once again and address Abulafia directly.

Taking direction from the spirits, Anav orders Abulafia and his associates to leave the room. Upon their departure, "the spirit enclothed itself in the young girl, and she collapsed in the manner of the epileptics." Anav had been repossessed. This time, Anav's soul remained alongside that of Ḥakham Piso, the two consciously sharing her body. This type of dissociation is comparable to that reported by R. Joseph Karo, who could take dictation from his *maggid*.[63] It is distinct from most negatively valued cases of spirit possession, in which the personality that normally occupies the body is ousted, suppressed, or eliminated during the period of the spirit's activity. Ḥakham Piso begins by instructing the girl, telling her what to say before launching into his own prolonged jeremiad. Vital's entry continues, "After the spirit had enclothed itself [in Anav's body], he began to speak, addressing himself to the girl, saying, 'Tell Abulafia to come close to the window from outside.' [Abulafia] drew near and said [to the spirit], 'Why did you not enclothe yourself until I left?' " A literal translation of Ḥakham Piso's reply seems most apt here: "Because you are not worthy to see me when I am dressing, as you are a sinner." One hardly knows whether Vital's transcript is to be read tongue-in-cheek, given the natural double entendre of traditional kabbalistic jargon. (There is little else in Vital's oeuvre that would indicate a sense of humor on his part, though it is hard to read this passage straight.) Whatever the case, Ḥakham Piso continued to dress down Abulafia for his ignorance and liability for the community's dire plight. From Abulafia, the spirit made the rounds of many other leading rabbinic figures, exposing the saints and especially the sinners, of Syria, Egypt, and even Venice. This diatribe against the scholars and common-folk exposed a variety of sins, ranging from reheating food on the Sabbath, to encouraging false oaths (by requiring a sworn declaration of financial worth for tax purposes), to sodomy. The overwhelming majority of accusations are sexual in nature and include allegations of immodest dress on the part of many women, adultery committed by women (with servants), and frequent sexual relations between Jewish men and Gentile women. Out of a tirade many pages in length, the following represents but a small sample:

"The people of Egypt have servants serving them, and when the men leave their homes, the servants sleep with their wives. They also warm the food on the Sabbath day, and more of the same. . . . Now, you [Abulafia] and the inhabitants of Damascus have no share in the World to Come, God Forbid, for a few reasons: For causing the people to sin by making them take oaths over taxes and their worth. . . . What is more, your wives go about brazenly with brazen garments and shameful jewelry, like with those *firengis* [silk brocades[64]] upon their heads, their breasts revealed and bosoms filling clothes to show off their large breasts, with trailing shawls and fine veils to show off their bodies. Moreover, they put on wild orange and other varieties of perfumes and scents to arouse the evil inclination in men. In all of this they parade through the markets and streets to show the nations their beauty. . . . Now, 48 people transgress with Gentile and married women, and sodomize [men], aside from other transgressions." And he counted all of them, but they told me about these alone, and they are: "Elijah Hafetz and the Gandor boys and a son of Koreidi and Avraham Mozeiri—these sleep with Gentile women; and the daughter of Komeiri the apostate fornicates with Joshua Koresh and many other men; and R. Jacob Monedas sodomizes Nathan Kulif, and now he has given him his daughter and she still fornicates with him. . . . And Rafael Kulif and his son Michael transgress with Israelite and Gentile women. Now, on the last Sabbath eve a scholar referred to as a Sage among the community of Sefardim slept with a Gentile woman in Gubar. . . . And the wife of Meir Peretz and her daughter are utter prostitutes, bringing many to sin. And R. David Gavizon sins much, for he left his modest wife here and married a whore in Egypt; because of his sins, his modest wife and daughter-in-law died. . . . Now, there is much sodomy in these parts, and there is also much perversion of justice here." R. J. Abulafia responded to him: "And how do you know all of this?" He said to him, "Your son Moses, he and Menachem Romano brought a Gentile woman to a certain house on the last festival of Shavu'ot, before going to Ẓovah, and slept with her." He said to him, "Is it possible that my son sinned this way?" He said to him, " 'The sons have inherited the acts of their fathers.' Did you not do foul deeds in your youth?"[65]

Vital punctuates his accent with the periodic interjection that upon subsequent investigation, the allegations made by Ḥakham Piso through Anav were indeed corroborated.

Although Ḥakham Piso identified many individuals by name, perhaps none was of the stature—nor enjoyed the posthumous fame—of R. Israel Najara (c. 1555–1625). Najara was "the best known and, in Schechter's phrase, most 'vividly erotic' of . . . [Safedian] mystic bards."[66] Najara was subjected to especially harsh criticism, and even though the popularized account of Anav's possession omits many proper names included in Vital's journal, the criticism of Najara remained personal and fairly scathing.[67] In *Ronu le-Ya'akov*, the criticism is voiced by the spirit in the midst of the original possession episode, as Vital queries the spirit regarding a suitable group of men to form a "watch" over the possessed girl. Among the possible candidates for this group, Vital mentions Najara. To this suggestion, the spirit responds venomously, "Do not call this man, for he is disgusting. For although the songs that he composed gladden God and man, and are received before the Lord, nevertheless he incurs dishonor for eating at the altar of the Lord [viz., the table] with his head uncovered, wearing only a red *'arkia* upon it, and his arms are uncovered.[68] And he sits with the naked [souls?[69]], and he and they eat and drink, and he is not careful about the company of the naked."[70] Although the full denunciation of Najara in Vital's journal occurs in the context of the Abulafia episode, Vital notes that during the weekend of the initial possession, the spirit told him explicitly that the watch must be made up of only Sefardic scholars "except for Israel Najara—he must not see my face."[71] When the critique of Najara finally arrives, it is considerably more vicious than the somewhat restrained invectives of *Ronu le-Ya'akov*:

> And now R. I. Najara. It is true that the songs that he composed are good in themselves, but it is forbidden for anyone to talk with him or for anyone to allow one of the songs he composed to come out of his mouth. For Najara's mouth is constantly speaking filthily, and he is perpetually drunk. Now, on such-and-such a day, which was during the period of mourning "between the straits,"[72] he made a feast at such-and-such a time at the home of Jacob Monedas, and placed his hat on the ground and sang songs in a loud voice and ate meat and drank wine, and even got drunk—and how does he decree watches in Guvar and preach repentance to them?" And I, Ḥayyim, told him about this matter and he acknowledged that such indeed had happened. "Now too, when he was fleeing from the plague, he engaged in sodomy from the extent of his drunkenness. And on the Sabbath day he sinned twice: first, when he fought with his wife and expelled her from his house, and second, afterwards, when a Gentile woman came into his house and roasted fresh figs on the fire on the Sabbath; afterwards he slept with her. Therefore it is forbidden to act in any way that is beneficial to him, and it is forbidden to give him marriage or divorce contracts to write; it is almost appropriate to invalidate those written by him. His young son also copulated with a Gentile and is a total sinner, may his bones be pulverized. But his eldest son does not sin.[73]

R. Israel Najara—the greatest Hebrew liturgical poet of his era; rabbi, scribe, preacher. R. Israel Najara—a filthy-mouthed drunkard, who feasts rather than fasts, sings loudly, eats meat and drinks wine during the period of mourning; a sodomist, wife-abusing, Sabbath-violating fornicator with Gentile women. "And I, Ḥayyim, told him about this matter and he acknowledged that such indeed had happened," Vital wrote in his diary. Here again we confront a scene not bereft of ironies, as the most erotic Hebrew poet of the age is condemned via a young girl, for sins of a largely sexual nature. Have we here a confrontation between competing images of religiosity: Ḥakham Piso/Anav, austere and Ḥasidic,[74] Najara a rabbi of *'amkha*, the people, whose flaws are those of so many of "the people of Egypt . . . and the inhabitants of Damascus?" Are the critiques voiced *against* the establishment, or are they *of* the establishment? The spirit in Anav, for all the inversionary radicalism entailed in the use of a woman's body as a vehicle for revelatory public preaching, speaks with a voice that is reaffirming of traditional mores and piety. Even as he or she attacks individual rabbis, the attacks assert the ultimate authority of the rabbinic system in its most puritanical guise. This critique is not directed against men but against men and women, and is voiced by an essentially androgynous creature who champions the pietistic ideal of the religious establishment. Like the seventeenth-century Quaker female prophets studied by Phyllis Mack, the presence of Anav in the public arena "constrained her as firmly, in some ways more firmly, than the walls of the nunnery did the behavior of the Catholic visionary of the Middle Ages."[75]

Clearly, the possession and repossession of Anav was originally understood, as well as publicized, for its didactic value. Through Anav, Ḥakham Piso was to bring the Jews to repent. This penitential emphasis has much in common with what we know of many contemporary possession episodes in sixteenth- and seventeenth-century Europe. Perhaps ironically, in both Jewish and Christian settings, "evil" spirits provided a powerful spur to repentance.[76] The spirit would identify the transgressions of unrepentant sinners in his audience, leading to large-scale confessions, as many attempted to avoid the public revelation of their sins. Priests were stationed at every pillar in the cathedral at Laon, and "thousands confessed for fear that their sins would be revealed during the exorcisms."[77] Often, the spirit would directly call upon people to repent. H. C. E. Midelfort tells the story of a pious girl in 1559 who was possessed by the Devil, who claimed that God had sent him "in order to warn people to give up their godless pride, gluttony, and drunkenness." A similar case in 1560 led Luther's student Hieronymous Weller to accept the Devil's words as "a serious sermon of repentance, which should move us as directly as if it were a good angel's voice."[78] Although Vital reports that Abulafia and others broke down on the spot in contrition after being subjected to Anav, the case ended with mutual recriminations between the spirit and Abulafia. Abulafia went on the offensive to salvage his own maligned reputation and the reputations of his colleagues, excommunicating the spirit. For her part, Anav sent word from Tripoli that in the "Supernal Study Hall" the spirit pronounced a ban on Abulafia and his associates on a daily basis.

Even though the system as a whole may have been strengthened, Anav denounced individual authorities and exposed the ugly secrets of leading personalities and common folk alike. It would be wrong, moreover, to construe Anav as merely a pathological agent of rabbinic authority. In her vituperative clairvoyance, Anav expressed more anger than hope. Yet the sense of mission to community, of the possession of secrets to be vouchsafed to the worthy, of mediation between the living and the dead all indicate just how complex was the religious profile of the young daughter of R. Raphael.

In Anav, then, we find a fiercely independent young woman, unafraid and viciously critical of the rabbinic leadership of her generation. While possessed, she assumes a variety of male behaviors from the prosaic (sanctifying the Sabbath over a cup of wine) to the elite (pledging to vouchsafe secrets the likes of which he has never known to Vital).[79] Once exorcised, Anav's oracular career begins in earnest, and through Vital's diary, we find her undertaking tours of heaven and hell, meeting hosts of angels and souls of the righteous, and mediating between the living and the dead, who charge her with the mission to bring the Jews of Damascus to repent, thus saving them from destruction. Among the living, she sees the sins of others with penetrating clairvoyance; she encounters Luria and Elijah the Prophet while awake (experiences, incidentally, that Vital despairs of attaining again himself according to entries throughout his diary); and, like the prophetess Inés, she finds in her father her most loyal advocate. Finally, we must note, Anav is not alone—she has a mentor among the women of Damascus: Rachel Aberlin.

### *Rachel Aberlin and R. Ḥayyim Vital*

On the twenty-fourth of Av, nearly a month after the weekend of the possession, R. Raphael and his daughter went to the coastal city of Tripoli, perhaps to rest and recuperate by the sea. Rachel, Vital tells us, went to visit them and spoke to Anav about her experiences. Who was Rachel Aberlin? After about 1582, Rachel was the widow of Judah Aberlin, a wealthy man who had emigrated to Safed from Salonika in 1564 and become the head of its Ashkenazic community. A principled and strong-willed man, he led the campaign to require Safed's rabbis to pay full taxes when the tax burden on the city's Jews forced a financial crisis, enduring their vehement protests and bans of excommunication.[80] Judah was also on close terms with the kabbalists of Safed, who apparently thought highly of him despite his efforts to make them into taxpayers. Luria himself considered Judah to be a reincarnation of Yair, son of Menasseh—a figure regarded in the rabbinic tradition as a heavyweight whose opinion was as decisive as a majority in the Sanhedrin, Israel's ancient supreme court and legislature.[81] Judah married the sister of an eminent kabbalist: Rachel's brother was R. Judah Mishan, an ecstatic mystic and one of Luria's most devoted disciples, and was among those who pledged their loyalty to Vital after Luria's death.[82] This devotion to mystical pursuits—and to Vital in particular—seems to have been shared by Rachel. By 1590, Rachel had established a *ḥaẓer*, or court, in Safed, where Vital and his teacher in exoteric studies, R. Moses Alsheikh, lived and studied.[83] She had become Vital's patron and would remain in close contact with him for decades to come.

Vital's earliest mention of Rachel was his recollection of her presence at a Sabbath morning service in Jerusalem in 1578. As he preached, Rachel saw a pillar of fire hovering over his head and Elijah the Prophet supporting him throughout his sermon. A revelation of Elijah was accorded a much higher status than maggidic revelation, owing to the fact that no preparatory steps were considered sufficient to ensure his appearance. Other forms of revelation, by contrast, could be forced by diligent application of magico-mystical techniques.[84] Twenty-three years later, at the Yom Kippur services at the Sicilian synagogue in Damascus, Vital notes that Rachel again saw the fiery pillar upon his head. Concluding his entry, Vital notes, "And this woman is accustomed to seeing visions, demons, souls, and angels, and most everything she says is correct, from her childhood and through her adulthood."[85]

Vital was not alone in his high regard for Rachel. We recall that she served as a kind of spiritual elder to the Anav girl during the period of the latter's ecstatic and visionary activity. Other women dream of Rachel. The wife of Uziel, the caretaker of the Sicilian synagogue, dreamt of a number of deceased sages whose appearance in heaven seemed odd to her. Still in her dream, she approaches Rachel and asks her to explain this odd phenomenon. Rachel replies that "in the next world, all are healed from their defects. The heavy in this world are thin in the next, by means of the Torah, which weakens the flesh of man."[86]

Rachel and Vital were close, relating to one another in a manner reminiscent of the bonds between the tertiaries and their confessors with whom we began.[87] When Rachel was in Safed, so was Vital; when Vital was in Jerusalem, Rachel was there; at the end of his life, Vital was in Damascus, and Rachel was there as well. Their shared wanderings bespeak deep devotion, and, given the dynamics of patronage, there is no way to know who followed whom. Vital was married—three times over the years—and when he lived on Rachel's premises, he did so with his entire family. Their closeness, however, was likely of another order. Might Vital and Rachel have been the great male and female Jewish mystics of their age? Each recognized the greatness of the other and was nourished by the recognition of the other. In 1607, while in Damascus, Rachel dreamt that she was on her porch in Safed "where I lived," writes Vital, "and she saw me flying and descending from the sky, and I descended there. And I told her how great my rank was there and the great visions I had witnessed there."[88]

Their mystical virtuosity took different forms, and the male was not always on top. In the spring of 1609, Rachel had a dream. In the dream, she entered a room and saw Vital learning at a table piled high with books, snacking on radishes and lettuce. Rachel thought this a strange meal, though Vital insisted that it was his chosen dietary regimen. This multivalent detail resonates in ways both complementary and critical. Although in keeping with ascetic guidelines modeled upon Proverbs chapter 15, verse 17 ("Better is a dinner of herbs where love is, than a fatted ox and hatred with it") as well as more contemporary recommendations for the pious to avoid eating meat,[89] these foods might also represent something of a symbolic critique of the meager nourishment Vital was drawing from the many books with which he occupied himself. Radishes and lettuce were also the foods said to have always graced the tables of the Roman Caesar Antoninus and Rabbi Judah the Prince, patriarch of Judea and redactor of the Mishnah (BT *Avodah Zarah* 11a), each of whom could afford the luxury of foods that had no nutritional (i.e., caloric) benefit. Whatever the case may be, behind him, Rachel saw a large heap of straw burning, unconsumed; its light illuminated the house. Rachel asked Vital to explain the dream, and he replied with a verse: "And the house of Jacob shall be a fire [and the house of Joseph a flame] and the house of Esau for straw [and they shall burn them, and consume them . . . ]" (Obad. 1:18).[90] "And she said to me," Vital recalls, " '*You tell me the words of the verse as it is written, but I see the matter itself in practice, completely manifest.*' "[91] Vital sits at the table with the books piled high and knows the verse referring to the fire and to the light. Rachel sees the very fire and light to which the books refer. Vital may have been the master of the mystic sign, the sacred text, but Rachel saw that which they signified.

## Female Jewish Mystics?

How might we account for the religious activity of these sixteenth-century Jewish women? Empowered religious behavior among women has been understood in functionalist terms by many European historians who have stressed the social, educational, and sexual deprivation that women in this period suffered.[92] There is, in fact, no denying that the possession idiom afforded women the opportunity to enjoy, at least temporarily, the advantages of being a man.[93] The anthropologist I. M. Lewis has argued that the predominance of women in cases of spirit possession reflects "changing aspirations and attitudes towards their traditional status on the part of women. . . . [I]n many cases there is direct evidence of spirit-possessed women seeking to assume male roles which they specifically covet, and their exclusion from which they explicitly resent."[94] While acknowledging the pietistic use of possession by its victims, D. P. Walker follows Lewis in placing his emphasis squarely upon its deployment by women who would otherwise have had no opportunity to preach. He adduces a number of fantastic examples of the paradoxical preaching of the devil. In 1611, for example, at Aix-en-Provence, Verrine, a devil possessing the nun Louise Capeau, waxed eloquently on the Virgin Mary and concluded with the exclamation: "A miracle, an un-heard of miracle, and which will never happen againe that the Divell should convert Soules." The same devil, preaching on the imminence of the Day of Judgment, explained that human wickedness had reached its peak. It was therefore necessary to resort to heretofore unknown measures: "Behold the last remedy is, that God would convert soules unto him by the Divell. Be ye therefore penitent." Walker proceeds to argue, "It is, I think, clear that Louise Capeau's sermons are an only slightly disguised attempt at a good possession. If a woman wanted to preach, this was perhaps the only way open to her, and to Louise must go the credit of having first fully exploited it."[95] Yet not all agree that women "used" the possession phenomenon to overcome social or sexual deprivation. Contra Lewis and those historians who have followed in his analytical footsteps, the anthropologist P. J. Wilson has argued that women are completely socialized in their roles in traditional societies and that possessed women must not be viewed as frustrated protofeminists chafing at the bit.[96] Moreover, recent scholars have questioned whether the idiom of possession can even be said to be "usable." Moshe Sluhovsky has argued that women could not manipulate the idiom of spirit possession given the fine boundaries that distinguished licit possession, mental illness, and illicit witchcraft. Sluhovsky argues that sexual anxiety precipitated most of these cases, rather than a cleverly disguised bid for power by the "weaker sex."[97] Against those who would regard possession as the mental illness of primitive cultures, the anthropologist Janice Boddy, in her study of the *zār* possession cult, has noted that "successful negotiation of the possession context requires the patient to have or develop considerable cultural awareness. It is thus inapplicable to those who suffer severe psychological disturbance."[98]

It would seem prudent to resist adopting as our "default" assumption the view that women's religious behavior derives from social and psychological motivations, rather than religious ones. It is far more common for anthropologists and historians to adopt such an assumption when the actors involved are women. I therefore concur with the assessment of anthropologist Susan Sered that "religiously active women should be understood as having chosen to be religiously active (unless in a specific instance there is clear evidence to the contrary)."[99] Were one to examine the case of Anav in isolation, a functionalist explanation of her career would be difficult to resist. By associating her with a larger circle of nonpossessed, yet religiously active women, we gain the perspective necessary for contextualizing her as an active participant in a major religious idiom of her day. Like Vital, Anav is the beneficiary of "positive [*'ibburic*] possession," and though she did not participate in the literate mystical culture of her male counterparts, her religious prowess was no less daunting. Given the attention, collaboration, and cooperation she received, Anav's spiritual leadership in her community seems unquestionable, if only during the fall months of 1609. (We unfortunately know nothing of her subsequent whereabouts.)

Clearly, the women we have encountered in *Sefer ha-Ḥezyonot* were religious adepts of different types, of varied accomplishment. Some excelled only in the fields of magic and technical divination, whereas many others combined magical prowess with clairvoyance, ecstatic trance states, visionary activity in dreams and while awake, and prophetic gifts. Revelatory experiences charged leading women with communal responsibility, bringing them to initiate penitential revivals with public fasts, contrition, and chastisements. Like their elite male contemporaries, these women were overwhelmingly of European, primarily Sefardic origin, rather than members of the indigenous Mustarib Jewish community.[100] Although the strong Iberian and Ashkenazic subcultures that Jewish immigrants retained in places like Safed, Jerusalem, and Damascus justify European comparisons and contextualization, our understanding of these Jewish women will certainly be enriched by studies of Muslim women's religious lives in early modern Ottoman centers. As in Jewish historiography, this type of work remains largely a desideratum in Ottoman historiography.[101]

Although their socioeconomic status was variegated, prominent Jewish female pietists were generally related by birth or by marriage to the financial or scholarly elite. Whereas Rachel Aberlin emigrated to the Holy Land with her husband in 1564, many pious women, mostly widows, were attracted to the Land of Israel in the sixteenth century.[102] This influx of pietistic women, alongside the better-known male pietists who flocked eastward after the Ottoman conquest of Palestine in 1516, certainly contributed to the fashioning of a dynamic and intense religious culture, exceptionally self-selecting and self-demanding. Safed might thus be best understood as having been something of a Jewish "open monastery." In this hothouse of pietistic aspiration, ecstatic religious sensibilities were expressed in divine no less than demonic modes, not infrequently with some measure of the ambiguity characteristic of this divide.[103] Like their male counterparts, pietistic women interacted regularly with one another. Francesa and Rachel may have been informal leaders of these female magico-mystical pietists in successive generations; their spiritual aptitudes were recognized and revered by other women and by the rabbinic elite alike.

Having brought these women into focus, we are in a better position to assess the role of women in Sabbatianism on the one hand and the apparent suppression of Jewish women's mystical pietism on the other. Might not the unleashing of the full energies of female ecstatic spirituality in the Sabbatian movement have led to a backlash devoted to the eradication of the very memory of such a tradition?

Yet even before the Sabbatian movement took wing only to crash, skeptical winds had begun to blow. For a moment, it seemed that narratives of spirit possession might be wielded to advantage against these incipient doubters in life eternal. The most ambitious effort along these lines would be made by R. Menasseh ben Israel, whose mid-seventeenth-century treatise on the afterlife deployed the largest collection of *dybbuk* stories ever assembled in a single work. At this point, then, we move from the history of spirit possession to a history of its representation. In effect, what we are examining is the very beginning of the afterlife of spirit possession in Jewish culture.

*Chapter 5*

# *Skeptics and Storytellers*

*But souls that of his [God's] own good life partake*
*He loves as his own self; dear as his eye*
*they are to him: He'll never them forsake;*
*When they shall dye, then God himself shall die. . . .*
*—Henry More (1614–87),* Psychozoia or the Life of the Soul *(1642)*[1]

The classic tropes of European demonological literature were significantly altered in the seventeenth century—and the cause was the rise of skepticism. This shift might be described as a retreat from the offensive posture of most late fifteenth- and sixteenth-century treatises, to a new defensive stance.[2] *Maleficia*, witches, and demons were no longer the main foils of religion in this literature. Instead, by the mid-seventeenth century, disbelief had become the enemy; *maleficia*, witches, and demons were now being summoned to rescue religion from skeptical clutches. The contours and context of this new breed of demonological literature—what might be called "polemical demonology"—are what I hope to illuminate through an analysis of Menasseh ben Israel's *Nishmat Ḥayyim*,[3] which exemplifies this genre, while bearing witness to the unique cultural profile of the Jewish community of seventeenth-century Amsterdam.

A characteristic feature of this new genre is its reliance on stories, dubbed "exempla of the weird" by one historian of the Cambridge Platonists.[4] Indeed, until Gedalyah Nigal's anthology of *dybbuk* tales appeared a decade ago,[5] Menasseh's work could claim the distinction of having assembled the largest collection of possession narratives in the history of Jewish literature. In *Nishmat Ḥayyim* are the classic tales of spirit possession in Safed, as well as accounts that Menasseh heard from acquaintances who had traveled the globe in true seventeenth-century Portuguese fashion. Galilean stories thus appear alongside anecdotes from Africa, South America, and Asia.

## Menasseh ben Israel in Seventeenth-Century Amsterdam

Before undertaking an analysis of *Nishmat Ḥayyim*, however, we must take a brief detour to meet its author, one of the most studied figures of seventeenth-century Jewish culture.[6] Born Manoel Dias Soeiro to conversos around 1604, Menasseh was spirited out of Portugal as a newborn by his parents, who sought religious freedom away from the dangers of the Portuguese Inquisition.[7] The family, including Menasseh's siblings Efraim and Esther, soon found its way to Amsterdam, which at the time hosted a modest, but growing community of former conversos. Menasseh was educated by fine scholars and, in a manner that was typical rather than exceptional in his cultural environment, attained proficiency in "secular" as well as rabbinical studies. Indeed, in addition to classical literature, the libraries of many children of Iberian exiles provide ample evidence of an ongoing immersion in the works of the prominent Spanish and Portuguese authors of the seventeenth century.[8] Menasseh's broad education prepared him to serve the unique community of former conversos that grew swiftly in the first decades of the seventeenth century. Such a community was unprecedented in Jewish history: conversos, with little or no exposure to actual Jewish life and lore, reconstituted themselves en masse as a traditional Jewish *kehillah* (community).[9] Much of Menasseh's life was devoted to abetting this exceptional endeavor. In addition to writing works with conversos specifically in mind, Menasseh's printing house was principally dedicated to publishing works designed to provide them with sophisticated, if remedial, Jewish education.[10]

The challenge of serving the spiritual needs of this odd community were great, however, and though the overall project was surely a remarkable success, it was not without complications. Clearly, for some conversos the experience of living as inauthentic Catholics, of engaging in ongoing religious dissimulation, particularly in an era of violent wars of religion and inquisitorial persecutions, was conducive to the development of a skeptical view of religion and religious authority.[11] Upon arrival in the new Jewish community of Amsterdam, yet another difficulty faced the converso: assimilating traditional (i.e., rabbinic) Judaism after having long nursed idyllic (mis-) conceptions of its character. Naturally, conversos, whose knowledge of Judaism was limited to what they could glean from available Catholic sources, were apt to conceive of Judaism as a Christless Christianity, the religion of the "Old Testament."[12] Those who imagined Judaism to be a more "natural" or "reasonable" religion than Christianity on the basis of their sense of the this-worldly character of the Hebrew Bible were dismayed by the rabbinic religion they encountered upon gaining religious freedom. We need only situate Menasseh ben Israel as a young rabbi during the Uriel da Costa affair,[13] and as Spinoza's tutor, to get a sense of how acute this challenge was for him and his communal peers.

Indeed, nearly thirty years before Menasseh wrote *Nishmat Ḥayyim*, controversies in the community over the nature of the soul and its afterlife—over the eternality of punishment, that is, whether eternal damnation was a Jewish doctrine, and over the heretical assertions of da Costa (including his thesis that the soul perished with the body)—had led to the penning of a series of polemical tracts by the sages of Amsterdam. The treatise by R. Isaac Aboab da Fonseca, also entitled *Nishmat Ḥayyim*, was analyzed and published for the first time in a classic study by Alexander Altmann that explored the complex theological and pragmatic issues raised by the controversy over eternal damnation in the community of former conversos. Altmann revealed the extent to which the invocation of the kabbalistic notion of *gilgul* allowed former conversos to escape the tormenting doctrine of eternal damnation—a doctrine that had contributed to da Costa's discarding of Christianity, according to his autobiography.[14] Moreover, Altmann suggested that this kabbalistic escape hatch from this doctrinal "dead end" had something in common with the Socinian writings that were then being published in Holland, writings that presented religious doctrines "as consolatory rather than terrifying truths."[15] Although Jewish historians since the nineteenth century had viewed the kabbalah as a retrograde body of knowledge that promoted a primitive, ethnocentric isolationism among its adherents, Altmann was among the first scholars to recognize its equivocal nature. In this case, Aboab's kabbalism "happened to resound . . . with echoes of kindred spirits in the contemporary world at large."[16] This finding anticipated recent work by Robert Bonfil and Allison Coudert, who have argued that the kabbalah functioned as a modernizing force in early modern Jewish culture.[17]

Menasseh's *Nishmat Ḥayyim* is certainly replete with lengthy quotations from the Zohar, as well as from works by other kabbalists: Recanati, Ẓioni, Ḥayyat, Luria, and others.[18] The frequent invocation of these kabbalistic sources is undoubtedly the reason why attention to this work has been confined to scholars of Jewish mysticism. Although these discussions have shed light on the work and its author, they have left many questions unanswered.

## Nishmat Ḥayyim: What Kind of Work, and for Whom?

Joseph Dan and Moshe Idel have recently examined the question of whether Menasseh ought to be considered a kabbalist, primarily on the basis of their respective appraisals of *Nishmat Ḥayyim.* As Dan sees it, "Ben Israel presents in this work a curious attitude of non-kabbalistic Kabbalism—accepting the Kabbalah as a revelation of ancient divine truth, while completely disregarding the contents of this truth, save for the few elements of demonology and psychology needed directly for this thesis."[19] Menasseh's failure to adduce the dualistic Sefirotic ontological schemes of the Zohar ("the contents of this truth") thus disqualifies him as a kabbalist and *Nishmat Ḥayyim* as a kabbalistic work. Although Dan notes that *Nishmat Ḥayyim* was "one of the most significant post-Renaissance Hebrew works reflecting the cultural attitudes of the Renaissance period in which, both in general and in Jewish culture, are found a strong opposition to Aristotelianism and a new embracing of Platonic and neo-Platonic philosophy," he nevertheless concludes by slighting the significance of Menasseh's extensive use of non-Jewish sources. Because Menasseh believed that whatever is true in them ultimately derived from Jewish roots, he was "no closer to the spiritual world of the enlightenment than any other medieval Jewish thinker." Among thinkers of the enlightenment, the reigning view was that "non-Jewish methods, scholarship and sources . . . [were] different from the Jewish ones and [were to be regarded] as realms of culture to which the Jews must adapt while changing their own culture."[20] Although Menasseh may not have been "ahead of his time" (a notion that is highly problematic theoretically, in any case), Dan's analysis fails to show adequately just how much his concerns and presentation were precisely of his time.

Idel responded to Dan's characterization of Menasseh as a nonkabbalist by situating Menasseh in the history of Jewish intellectuals who adopted neo-Platonic perceptions of the kabbalah, and emphasized the "legitimacy" of these thinkers as a kabbalistic school. According to Idel, Menasseh adduced only the kabbalistic lore that was pertinent to his neo-Platonic psychological discussions of the nature of the soul, metempsychosis and exorcism.[21] Among these Platonizing Kabbalists, there was a pronounced tendency to advance syncretistic intellectual genealogies that advocated a common font of spiritual wisdom: *prisca theologia.*[22] Menasseh, Idel demonstrates, was of this breed of kabbalist; *Nishmat Ḥayyim* is certainly replete with statements identifying the views of Plato with those of the prophets and the kabbalists.

Although he frequently referrs to kabbalistic works and concepts, Menasseh clearly addresses his readers as nonkabbalists. Thus, rather than explaining the meaning of the forty-two-lettered divine name that he mentions, he refers to it simply as the name "whose power is known to the enlightened."[23] In his discussion of the edenic reward of the righteous after death, he writes, "it is fitting that you should know that the masters of the wisdom of the Kabbalah have agreed that there is a higher garden of Eden, and a lower garden of Eden, and the truth is with them."[24] It is evident in these and many other passages that Menasseh did not conceive of his work as intended for elite kabbalists. But who were his intended readers? To paraphrase Judah Leib Gordon (and Eccles. 4:8), for whom did Menasseh labor? We recall that Menasseh was a prolific writer, though, unlike Gordon, most of his works were written in languages other than Hebrew—whether in Spanish, Portuguese, or Latin. Of these works, many were intended for a non-Jewish scholarly readership—for example, the Latin works *De Creatione* (1635), *De Termino Vitae* (1634), *De Resurrectione Mortuorum* (1636), *De Fragilitate Humana* (1642), and the Spanish *Esperanza de Israel* (1650).[25] This last work, as well as *De Termino Vitae*, was written in response to a specific request by a non-Jewish scholar. Yet other works of Menasseh's were written for the converso community, whether exclusively or alongside a Gentile readership. *De Fragilitate Humana* was thus published simultaneously in Spanish as *De la Fragilidad Humana y Inclinacion del Hombre al Peccado*, with the conversos very much in mind, as N. Yosha has recently shown.[26] Menasseh, therefore, devoted himself almost exclusively to a non-Hebrew literate readership, Gentiles, as well as present and former conversos. So, then, what of *Nishmat Ḥayyim*? We might begin to assess the audience Menasseh had in mind when writing the work by evaluating a number of passages in which Menasseh himself addresses the issue, whether explicitly or implicitly.

In his introduction, Menasseh describes his distress over what might be called the "naturalization" of man, of the reduction of man to the level of a beast, and the denial of man's partaking in divinity by virtue of his Godly soul. It is his first challenge, writes Menasseh, to find "triumphant answers to show to all the nations the precious, beautiful greatness of man owing to his soul."[27] This remark indicates not only a declaration of Menasseh's intended audience but also a certain universalization of his subject. It is the greatness of man he is to champion, rather than the greatness of the Jew and his distinctive soul (a leitmotif in much of the kabbalistic literature he cites in the work). As for his intended audience, Menasseh's declaration is clear enough here: he has written this work for all nations (*le-khol ha-ʿamim*). This objective is reiterated later in the introduction. After reviewing a number of the works he has previously authored and noting of one that it was written "as a light to the nations," of another that it was composed for the benefit of the conversos, and of a third that it was authored at the request of "the minister and great man of the nations of the world," Menasseh writes somewhat ambiguously of *Nishmat Ḥayyim*, "I have written this book to assist all of my contemporaries."[28] In addition to his defense of the "divinity" of man, Menasseh declares his determination to respond to a specific charge that Gentiles leveled against Judaism: namely, that the Torah itself presents a naturalized view of man, of man devoid of a divine soul destined to receive spiritual reward (or punishment) upon the perishing of the body. The first of the four discourses that make up *Nishmat Ḥayyim* is largely devoted to arguing the contrary, as Menasseh writes, "to remove the grievance of the nations who have set themselves in array at the gate [cf. Isa. 22:7] in their claim that the Torah of Moses contains no spiritual reward after death."[29] In addition to his comprehensive demonstration of the spiritual dimension of the Hebrew Bible against these charges, Menasseh's treatise makes frequent (critical) reference to Christian doctrines that were being hotly debated in his time, rejecting the doctrines of predestination, of original sin, and perhaps even of preadamitism.[30]

All of these direct statements by Menasseh would suggest that he wrote *Nishmat Ḥayyim* for a Gentile readership, and were it not for the fact that we are dealing with a Hebrew book, we might consider the case closed. Given the very limited number of potential Gentile readers of this work, however, we would best entertain alternatives—while recalling that he need not have written exclusively for one kind of reader. There are certainly a number of reasons to believe that *Nishmat Ḥayyim* was penned for Jewish readers. Clearly our presumption with regard to any Hebrew book, until proven otherwise, is that it was written for Jewish readers. Is it to be regarded as another of Menasseh's converso-oriented works? Did enough have sufficient Hebrew literacy to have managed the learned Hebrew and Aramaic text? Menasseh begins his formal address to the reader of the introduction, "In the name of our God set up our banners (Psalms 20, 6), for the eyes of the children of my nation (Genesis 23, 11)."[31] Furthermore, Menasseh's defense of his frequent citations from non-Jewish sources, "the testimony of authors who are not of the sons of our nation" (*asher lo mi-bene ʿamenu*) suggests a Jewish readership sensitive to this issue, defending his approach against their potential objections. It is precisely in this context that Menasseh often invokes the notion of *prisca theologia*, for if Plato were understood as Jeremiah's faithful student, who could object to the invocation of Platonic material?[32]

Given these mixed messages, we may assume that Menasseh had multiple readers in mind: his Christian Hebraist friends, conversos who had acquired a facility in Hebrew literature, and his rabbinic peers. As for the converso readership, the fact that these readers were informed by "the grievance of the nations" (having received a Catholic education and having generated their expectations and formative impressions of Judaism through this lens), while remaining "the sons of our nation" suggests a good fit, were it not for the fact that *Nishmat Ḥayyim* was written in a language inaccessible to so many of these potential readers. (Da Costa, for example, whose early "Sadducean" heretical position advocated a naturalistic reading of the Torah devoid of a next-worldly reward, never learned Hebrew.[33])

In composing *Nishmat Ḥayyim*, Menasseh may have been attempting to produce a magisterial Hebrew work that would earn him greater respect in the eyes of a rabbinic establishment that repeatedly failed to honor and remunerate him adequately (even putting him under the ban [*Ḥerem*] for a short period). *Nishmat Ḥayyim* represents something of a summation and expansion of Menasseh's earlier treatments of topics related to the soul. In his *De Creatione* of 1635, he had argued for the preexistence of the soul on the basis of biblical and rabbinic statements, as well as logical demonstration, whereas in *De Resurrectione Mortuorum* (1636) he had defended the doctrine of resurrection against "Sadducees" (likely referring to da Costa). Certainly, Menasseh's Hebrew work would assist his fellow rabbis, girding them for their encounter with heretical elements in their own communities. *Nishmat Ḥayyim* fortified rabbis with critical information and provided them with means of defense—"Know what to say in response."[34]

*Nishmat Ḥayyim* was not, however, a typical kabbalistic or philosophical treatise taking up the fight against heterodoxies. Menasseh's Hebrew magnum opus was a "native" Hebrew version of a variety of treatise that was becoming increasingly significant in the mid-seventeenth century—an attack on "atheism" grounded in a demonstration of the existence of the demonic. The denial of the immortality of the soul was not a new heresy in the mid-seventeenth century. Disbelief in personal immortality among the Latin Averroists had been so widespread over a century before that the Lateran Council of 1512 "found it necessary for the first time to establish the immortality of the soul as a dogma of the Church."[35] Conversos seemed to have had a special propensity to deny this doctrine, as evinced by the significant attention to it in the Portuguese tract *Spiritual Merchandise* (*Ropica pnefma*) of 1532 by João de Barros, written for the religious edification of recent converts.[36] The new Jewish community of Amsterdam, composed chiefly of former conversos, was thus especially vulnerable to this heresy, though Christianity no less than Judaism was threatened by it. In the face of a threat that had a special urgency in his Jewish community, Menasseh crafted a treatise that was at once universal and particular, wedding a broad range of sources, fashionable rhetorical strategies, and Jewish testimonies from Biblical times to his own.

## Demonological Hermeneutics

Debates in the secondary literature that focus upon how to classify *Nishmat Ḥayyim* within the history of the kabbalah miss the essential point that it is first and foremost a work of "polemical demonology." As such, the heresy against which it is polemicizing is evident throughout. Beyond the particular heresy of denying the immortality of the soul lies, however, an abiding preoccupation with heresy per se. Menasseh begins *Nishmat Ḥayyim* with a prologue in which an angel goads him to write against those heretics who claim "that in the Torah of Moses there is no indication of an afterlife," whether to justify their own disbelief or to criticize Mosaic materialism.[37] Book One then begins with a discussion of the potential for heretically misconstruing the plural grammatical constructions relating to God in Genesis. Later in the work, weighing in on the issues that had occupied the polemicists years before in the da Costa controversy, Menasseh reaffirms the rabbinic dictum that opens *Perek Ḥelek* (Mishna Sanhedrin Chapter 10): "All Israel have a share in the World to Come." "For each of them has certainly fulfilled one of the commandments of the Torah, through which he will merit life in the World to Come."[38] Eternal life for modest achievements is a compassionate position by any standards. Menasseh, in a Pauline sounding flourish, is quick to point out the catch, however: not every Jew is worthy of the name "Israel." "Not all of the progeny of our father Abraham and the Children of Jacob His chosen are worthy of being called by the honorable name of Israel, for some transgressions are so severe that they obliterate the commandment; those who commit them no longer profit from their labors."[39] The name "Israel" does not apply to the sinners—"thought-criminals" would be more precise—noted in *Perek Ḥelek*, namely, one who denies the biblical basis of resurrection, the divine origin of the Torah, and a heretic (*apikorus*).[40] Menasseh regards these sins as fundamental, because the doctrines in question are foundational to Judaism: "the religion and its very existence are contingent upon them."[41] In his treatment of *Gan Eden* and Gehinnom, Menasseh again emphasizes the overarching significance of doctrinal fidelity. In a discussion structured by the metaphor of the ritual purification necessary when acquiring used vessels from a Gentile—an interesting choice given his situation within a converso environment—Menasseh equates those who commit thought crimes with earthenware vessels, which when polluted are not purified, but destroyed (cf. Lev. 11:33; Num. 31:22–23). "Such are the souls that have become dirtied by foul views and left the community of Israel, such as heretics (*apikorsim*), sectarians (*minim*), apostates (*meshumadim*), and informers (*mosrim*). These are punished eternally."[42]

Reading further in *Perek Ḥelek* we arrive at the particular views of Rabbi Akiva, recorded just after the enumeration of heresies over which there is ostensible consensus. According to Rabbi Akiva, one who reads "uncanonical books" (*sefarim ḥiẓoniim*)—identified in the talmudic discussion (BT *Sanhedrin* 100b) as works written by *minim*, or schismatics[43]—as well as "one who whispers [a spell] over a wound" is also liable to forfeit his share in the World to Come. The juxtaposition of heresy and magic in this rabbinic text is not atypical, though by no means did the rabbis equate all magical activity with heresy.[44] Although an association between magic and heresy is implicit in passages such as the famous rabbinic definition of *sorcerers* as those who oppose or weaken the heavenly powers,[45] rabbinic views of magic were generally permissive, if not encouraging.[46] Classical rabbinic treatments of magic were nuanced, recognizing the possibility of natural as well as demonic magic. (This distinction is suggested in a teaching of R. Ḥiyya bar Abba, who suggested that certain forms of magic were inherently efficacious, whereas others worked by means of demonic intervention.[47]) Given this tradition behind him, the extreme degree to which Menasseh conflated heresy and magic in *Nishmat Ḥayyim* is remarkable. Menasseh's position represents a retreat not only from these classical rabbinic positions, but from the more proximate Renaissance cultural environment that construed magic as the highest actualization of human potential.[48] Although, as Joseph Dan and Moshe Idel have shown, *Nishmat Ḥayyim* exemplified typically cultural attitudes of the Renaissance, the Menasseh did not adopt the positive view of magic typical among the critics of Aristotelianism and the embracers of Platonic and neo-Platonic philosophy.[49] Quite the contrary: Menasseh thoroughly demonized magical activity, aligning himself with the most severe early modern demonological theorists and their scholastic predecessors. Like Martín Del Río, whose *Disquisitionum magicarum* he cites repeatedly,[50] Menasseh believed that magic implied heresy, trafficking with the demonic rather than with the divine.[51] "Know," he writes, "that there are many varieties of magic, and *all* operate by means of demonic power."[52]

A number of phenomena that were commonly understood in the literature of his day as operating on the basis of natural magical principles were thus demonized, or spiritualized, by Menasseh. Thus, in his treatment of sympathetic bleeding—the bleeding of the corpse of a murder victim in the presence of his killer—the typical neo-Platonic categories of sympathy and antipathy are rejected in favor of a spiritualistic explanation.[53] Whereas figures such as Reginald Scot and Francis Bacon upheld the veracity of this phenomenon on the merits of its natural, albeit occult explanation (occult influences were considered part of the natural world[54]), Menasseh, though fully conversant with their views, argues that the ghost of the victim alone is responsible for this fresh bleeding, concerned as he would be to point out his murderer.[55] As in the case of corpse bleeding, the crime of ligature, magically induced impotence (*asirat ḥatanim*), was also discussed without invoking the common category of sympathy.[56] Ligature was generally accomplished by the tying of knots, a procedure based on the assumption of a sympathetic link between the knotted rope and the fettered sexual function of the victim.[57] All sudden illness, as well as illness caused by the evil eye, are ascribed by Menasseh to demonic affliction. To these phenomena we could easily add reviews of Menasseh's treatment of physiognomy, metamorphosis (magical shape shifting), and magical illusion (*aḥizat 'ainayim*)[58]—all of them accepted uncritically and explained in demonic-spiritualist terms rather than in the natural, occult terms common in the literature of his day.

Here we ought to stress that Menasseh's thorough-going demonization of magic included the repeated endorsement of a key component of the intellectual foundation of the European witch-hunts that plagued Europe between 1450 and 1750: the demonic pact.[59] In calling upon the demons, one effectively cast off the divine and served a new master. Thus, Menasseh explains, the Jerusalem Talmud justifiably asserts that one who engages in ligature forfeits his share in the World to Come. "For one who gives himself over to demons, the yoke of the Kingdom of Heaven is removed from him, and he accepts instead the yoke of the Kingdom of Evil Wickedness."[60] If the transfer of yokes implies the notion of a pact, elsewhere Menasseh is more explicit. After discussing the magical murder of children by witches through the demon Lilith, he concludes, "And it is known that all sorcerers and witches make a pact [*t'nai*] with the demon, and give over their souls to them. [The demons'] first words deceive them away from the fear of the Lord, and they deny His providence."[61] This passage presents a radical alignment of Jewish and Christian demonological traditions. I would go so far as to say that if the characters are Jewish (Lilith), the script is clearly Christian. The emphasis on heresy and the demonic pact are the hallmarks of Christian discussions of magic from Augustine to Gratian (twelfth century), Aquinas (thirteenth century), and a myriad of writers in the subsequent centuries.[62] Menasseh not only subscribes to the notion of the demonic pact, he endorses the entire complex of learned witch beliefs and goes so far as to justify the executions of his age.[63]

Now, all of the land of Ashkenaz (Germany) and Alsace, France, and other nations know the deeds of the witches, who are called in their language *sagi* or *hexerei*,[64] and they are women who have made a pact [*brit*, covenant] with devils [*shedim*] and they have a special time and meet in a certain place, in covens [*ḥavurot ḥavurot*]. There they dance and caper throughout the nights and have intercourse with satyrs, these being spirits who appear in the guise of he-goats. Every day they are arrested and interrogated. If they deny the matter, they are tried by water, for those innocent of the charge sink and are saved and redeemed, while the guilty float, and fly like birds. Thus their sentence [lit. law] is uniformly to be burnt, even if they are lovely maidens. Every day these trials are conducted and many books have been published on their ways and deeds.[65]

Here we find all of the components of what Brian Levack has called "the cumulative concept of witchcraft": the pact, the witches' sabbath, flight, and intercourse with demons. Quite matter-of-factly Menasseh mentions the daily ordeals to which even "lovely maidens" are subjected, as well as their subsequent execution by fire.

Menasseh is not, however, unaware of the critique of the witch-hunt voiced by men such as Johann Weyer and Reginald Scot. Scot's *Discovery of Witchcraft* had already come out in two Dutch editions by the mid-seventeenth century,[66] whereas Weyer's works on witchcraft were well known to Menasseh in the original Latin.

And legal experts ask and question whether they deserve death or not, for it appears in the eyes of their great sages that they do not sin in action nor gather in a place to conjoin with spirits, but on the contrary, they do not budge from their beds and merely act in their imaginations. For they have forced and compelled their minds to believe that Satan will couple with them and satisfy their desire in fornication, as he has more strength than any man in size, hardness of instruments, and prolongation of the exercise, and other types of pleasure. And it seems to them in their dream that they travel and dance with the spirits, and in the course of the imaginary intercourse, they become hot and come to ejaculation and have great pleasure, as some of them have admitted under investigation. And it is not true, but the act of spirits, worthless imagination. . . . And according to this opinion, they are killed and burnt unjustly, for in no book of laws is there a punishment proscribed for the hidden thoughts of the heart.[67]

This argument most closely approximates the objections of Weyer, who accepted the reality of the devil's existence while arguing that witchcraft merely amounted to the hallucinations of pitiful women. Against this critique of the witch-hunt, Menasseh emphasized the insurmountable significance of the pact, a feature of witchcraft more significant than maleficia to nearly all learned demonological writers.[68] "To this [call for mercy, others] answer that it is just nevertheless, for they are judged for having made a pact with Satan in their wanton hearts, and it is as if they have given themselves up body and soul to him, and cast off the yoke of the Lord from their necks. And the Torah says, 'Thou shall not suffer a witch to live. (Exodus 22, 17)' "[69] Concluding his discussion of the witch-hunt by invoking the position of Weyer and Scot's critics and the Biblical call for execution, Menasseh effectively posits the identity of Christian and Jewish demonological traditions in their most intemperate modes.[70]

No discussion of Menasseh's demonological hermeneutics would be complete without consideration of his biblical hermeneutics, and no biblical text would seem better suited to reveal a commentator's demonological beliefs than 1 Samuel Chapter 28, the famous account of the "Witch of Endor." In this text, King Saul consults a witch known for her necromantic prowess—a *ba'alat ov* (lit., mistress of necromancy[71])—who summons the recently departed soul of Samuel to prophesy to Saul regarding his imminent fate. Given the biblical view of the underground netherworld of the dead, or Sheol, in which the dead "continue to live a shadowy, ghostlike existence . . . [in] a region of darkness and silence deep within the recesses of the earth,"[72] there is nothing inherently unintelligible about Samuel's return to the land of the living. Nevertheless, biblical exegetes, Christians and Jews alike, had long found much that was troublesome about this account. Menasseh captured at least one essential aspect of this discomfort when he introduced his own treatment by remarking that Samuel's appearance was "a difficult matter, and among the strangest things found in the Bible. For the intellect cannot bear [the notion] that refined and pure souls should fall under the rule of ov."[73] A history of the exegesis of this chapter would certainly reveal the extent to which commentators of the broadest philosophical diversity attempted to mitigate the plain sense of the text and to substitute a construal of the events that was palatable to them, compatible with their "reality map."[74] To this end, essentially all the imaginable possibilities were suggested by the exegetes.

Menasseh critically reviews a number of these interpretations in his own treatment of the chapter. Among them appear the dominant alternatives to the plain sense of the text: the illusion theory (the woman acted deceptively and created the illusion of Samuel's presence), the imagination theory (the entire event was a figment of Saul's imagination), the God theory (God, rather than the witch, summoned Samuel to appear before Saul), and the *shed* theory (a demonic spirit, rather than Samuel himself, appeared in the guise of Samuel).[75] Menasseh cites the illusion theory in the name of R. Samuel b. Ḥofni Gaon, and rejects it for its lack of scriptural basis and as an insult to Saul's intelligence. The imagination theory is drawn from Gersonides (1288–1344), and Menasseh seems to concur with the critique of it by Don Isaac Abrabanel (1437–1508) on the basis of the capacity of any healthy person to distinguish the actual from the imaginary; moreover, such a theory rendered Saul's visit to a witch entirely superfluous. As for God, rather than the witch, being the agent of Samuel's return, Menasseh cites David Kimḥi (c. 1160–c. 1235) against this position, attributed by Kimḥi to Sa'adia and Ḥai Gaon (late ninth–early tenth century). Had God desired to communicate prophetically to Saul, he could have figured in a dream or by means of the Urim and Tumim (see, e.g., Num. 27:21; 1 Sam. 28:6). The *shed* theory was also rejected by Abrabanel, who attributed it to Augustine. Nevertheless, Abrabanel himself concludes his commentary on the chapter by suggesting that a demon entered Samuel's physical remains and animated them temporarily. Menasseh regarded this position as essentially identical to the Augustinian position Abrabanel himself rejected. In the wake of all these attempts to evade the plain sense of the narrative, Menasseh champions the approach of the talmudic sages: "We will not budge from the view of our rabbis whose little finger was thicker than our loins [cf. 1 Kings 12:10]." Menasseh cites approvingly the talmudic treatment of this subject in BT *Shabbat.* This discussion suggests that souls do not find their way to the Throne of Glory until twelve months have elapsed since their death. Until that time, they are vulnerable to necromantic manipulation.[76] "Therefore," Menasseh concludes, "you see how souls are still alive after their separation from the body, and they may be summoned. *Ov* divination is not vanity and chaos as many have thought. . . . And it is enough for us to have shown how this episode is a great instruction in the immortality of the soul."[77] Menasseh's championing of the plain sense of this narrative was in keeping with a tendency among seventeenth-century commentators to reject the venerable tradition of mitigating the theologically and philosophically disturbing aspects of this story, from the forbidden consultation with the necromancer, to her successful raising of a prophet of God from the grave and Samuel's subsequent revelations to Saul in this context. Writers keen on demonstrating the reality of witches and witchcraft, as well as those who sought to prove that a personal soul survived the death of the body, could scarcely do better than to invoke 1 Samuel chapter 28 in its plain sense.

Menasseh's commitment to preserving the plain sense of scripture, however, "absurd" in philosophical terms, extended as well to his treatment of *Gan Eden* and Gehinnom. Rejecting writers who offered metaphorical interpretations of Gehinnom, philosophical or psychological, for example, as a state of sadness and concern over one's separation from the Godhead,[78] Menasseh argued for a literal understanding. "However . . . the Sages . . . taught and concluded that there is a Gehinnom below, and that there the souls of the wicked are sentenced to real fire."[79] Might one detect here the beginnings of a "fundamentalist," or perhaps "Protestant" Jewish response to modernity, its heterodoxies and heresies?

So far, we have exposed Menasseh's demonological hermeneutics, highlighting his thorough adoption of the heretical reading of witchcraft that was so prominent a part of learned Christian demonology. Although such a conception of witchcraft may be found in classical Jewish sources as well, Menasseh's comprehensive demonization of all forms of magical practice is highly unusual in Jewish intellectual history. It is even more surprising given Menasseh's extensive investment in Platonic thought, which was closely linked with natural magic in the early modern period. The heretical reading of witchcraft espoused by Menasseh reveals not only an underlying preoccupation with heresy in the wake of skeptical crises within Amsterdam Jewry but also a sustained attempt on Menasseh's part to emphasize the role of demons and spirits in the operation of the world. Witchcraft and magic were stripped of their natural, occult dimensions and associated almost exclusively with the demonic. Thus understood, witchcraft provided tangible evidence of the world of the spirits. Here the two issues come together: if the existence of this spirit (albeit demonic) realm could be effectively demonstrated, Menasseh believed, the heresies rife in his community could be answered and overcome. We now begin to see Menasseh's strategy for coping with his primary epistemological problem—how can we know that divine souls exist? As Henry More and other contemporaries of Menasseh would repeatedly write, revealing the existence of the demonic was the surest way to reestablish faith in the existence of the divine.

## Ghost Stories and the Epistemology of Experience

Menasseh believed that there were three ways of knowing something: on the basis of authoritative tradition, by means of logical demonstration,[80] and by direct experience, or sense perception. Invoking authoritative tradition in a battle against heresy was clearly problematic. The story of a poor Ḥasidic water carrier who planned to undermine the Viennese *maskilim* (Jewish enlightenment thinkers) conference comes to mind. "What are you going to tell them?" his rabbi asks him as he boards the train for Vienna. "I'm going to tell them that God created the heavens and the earth!" he answers. "But . . . they don't believe in God." "Nu, so that's why I'm bringing a *ḥumash* [Pentatuch] so that I can show them inside!" "But . . . they don't believe in *ḥumash*." "They don't believe in *ḥumash*?! . . . so I'll show them Rashi." "They don't believe in Rashi either. . . ." "What . . . they don't believe in Rashi?!?"[81] More sophisticated than the water carrier, Menasseh nevertheless invested a great deal of effort in demonstrating that biblical and rabbinic texts supported the Platonic metaphysics he sought to affirm, often quite convincingly. As for logical demonstration, Menasseh made modest use of it to assert his claims, knowing full well that others, (for example, Aristotelians like the Latin Averroists) could use it even more effectively to promote their heterodox positions. As a result, it was clear to Menasseh that his best, and perhaps only means of proving the existence of a divine, immortal soul was through recourse to experience and sense perception—no simple matter when the object to be experienced and sensed was invisible and immaterial.

In fact, throughout *Nishmat Ḥayyim*, Menasseh invokes experience as the decisive factor of his arguments. For, as he says, it is inconceivable to deny "that which has been apprehended by sense perception, for it is impossible to say about it that it is not."[82] Thus, justifying the traditional Aramaic translation of Leviticus, chapter 18, verse 5—"And live by them [the commandments]" as "And live by them eternally"—Menasseh writes that experience proves that Jewish dietary laws do not promote long life; on the contrary, Gentiles are clearly healthier and live longer:[83] "The reason certain foods are prohibited is not related to the body, *for experience proves* that the nations of the world eat pork, vermin, and rodents while living healthily, with none tired among them, and none failing. If so, their prohibition must be for the perfection of the intellective soul."[84] Menasseh reiterates this position in subsequent considerations of theodicy. The fact that experience shows that the wicked prosper while the righteous suffer proves that the rewards promised the latter in the Bible must be enjoyed by the soul after death.[85] For Menasseh, the very notion of authoritative tradition is to be understood in reference to its founding experience. In an argument reminiscent of Judah ha-Levi's *Kuzari*, Menasseh writes, "that which has been apprehended by the senses at a particular time by many people . . . passed down as a received tradition from father to son, must be believed, for it is the absolute truth and an incontrovertible matter."[86] Ultimately, the reader was to recall, what lay at the root of tradition was the real experience of people, an experience transmitted through the medium of tradition.

Here we might note that in his spiritualist-demonic interpretations of natural magical phenomena that we considered above, Menasseh frequently deployed a rhetoric of experience to make his point. Thus, although astrological principles might indicate that twins would lead identical lives, "experience shows the contrary."[87] In his discussion of the bleeding corpse, he counters the usual sympathetic explanation that the victim's blood on the murderer attracted the blood of the corpse by noting that experience shows that corpses bleed even when no such stains are present; thus the vindictive soul of the victim had to be the true cause.[88] In the days before inhaled Viagra, ligature too was to be regarded as an experience proving the power of demons summoned by efficacious, if immaterial, words and acts.[89] And, of course, there were always magnets to provide a handy experience of immaterial power. Menasseh's colleague Joseph Delmedigo invoked the magnet in his own discussion of the power of experience to override reason in his *Maẓref la-Ḥokhmah* of 1629: "With our eyes we see things daily that reason refuses to accept; yet they actually appear to be true, and perhaps our judgment is determined by our imagination rather than by our reason; moreover, it is further substantiated by wondrous activities [of nature], like the magnet that possesses many great and wonderful properties, as I wrote in a long composition on it."[90] The magnet provided empirical evidence of immaterial attraction and repulsion, sympathy and antipathy. Though part of the natural world, it also pointed beyond it.

Menasseh's strategy of deploying a wide range of non-Jewish literary sources also played a role in his empirical approach. Although fluency in classical and contemporary literatures was not unusual in his environment, Menasseh's broad sweep of Gentile authors may also have been intended to have a specific rhetorical effect. The assertion of near-universal consensus with regard to the core issues of *Nishmat Ḥayyim* added empirical weight to his position. As each of these sources is adduced, the position advocated could be taken as more natural and less constructed. Although skepticism asserted the constructed nature of particular doctrines or phenomena, Menasseh defended them by asserting their axiomatic status, as evinced by overwhelming consensus. Thus a discussion of *terafim* (speaking statues) begins with a rabbinic discussion of their preparation (killing someone, chopping off his head, pickling it in salt and spices, writing a demonic name on a golden plate, and placing it under its head or tongue, mounting it on a wall, lighting candles and prostrating before it), and then continues with a discussion of the creations of Albertus Magnus and the views of many classical and contemporary authors on such phenomena. As for why there seem to be no *terafim* today, Menasseh cites the opinions of Plutarch and Cardano, as well as a Jewish concept that linked the end of divine prophecy with the end of demonic prophecy. Menasseh then anticipates the objection that demonic prophecy still exists, because "in the West Indies when people want to ask about something from the Satan, one of them drinks the herb called 'peyote' and becomes intoxicated, falls down, is possessed, and answers questions."[91] He also relates that Portuguese conversos were told by the natives of India upon arrival that their coming had been predicted by their oracles. Menasseh accepts these testimonies as evidence of the ongoing power of Abraham's famous gifts to his concubines.[92] The correlations between Jewish and Classical literature, contemporary ethnographic reports, and the testimonies of his brethren constitute a kind of empirical mass that Menasseh hoped would naturalize the questioned phenomena.

If *terafim* were his daggers in the struggle against the heretics, the possessed were his canons. In the phenomenon of spirit possession experience, demons, souls, universalism, and particularism all conjoined. Menasseh writes repeatedly in *Nishmat Ḥayyim* that the fact that "spirits of men who have died enter the bodies of the living is a complete proof, over which there can be no doubt, for the immortality of the soul."[93] *Dybbuk* possession, the penetration of a living body by a ghost, is tangible evidence of the soul's survival of bodily death. Because, to paraphrase Eric Clapton, we cannot see the soul in heaven (would it be the same?),[94] meeting it as a *dybbuk* is the best we can hope for. As in his discussion of *terafim*, the breadth of Menasseh's treatment is vast. In this case, the suggestion of axiomatic status for the phenomenon is explicit; Menasseh declares it to be "*min ha-mekubalot*," an axiom "for which no proof is necessary. For do not all the books of adjurations extant in the Christian language called '*Exorcismi*' testify and preach on this matter, as you may see in Martín Del Río, Bodin, Weyer, and many others, old and new?"[95] His discussion of spirit possession ranges from these exorcism manuals to the classic accounts from Safed and Ferrara, to talmudic passages, to a recent case on the Barbary Coast, and Josephus, and then to recent cases, including one that took place in Seville, reported to Menasseh by over twenty conversos who were there and witnessed the possession firsthand. In this case, a black girl from Angola was possessed by a demon and subsequently displayed clairvoyant powers. She was arrested by the Inquisition, later released, and according to the latest reports, had been beaten severely. Menasseh then notes the possession of a sixteen-year-old boy in Tituán of which he had just been informed, along with the information that the boy was exorcised by an old Arab sorcerer. Historical writers provide him with information on Chinese divination practices that involve induced possession, whereas Del Río, Augustine, and Aquinas figure in his discussion of demonic illness. Menasseh asserts here what could be called a "towering edifice of authority" supporting the existence of spirit possession, which in turn demonstrated the existence of an imperishable soul.[96] Possession stories—ghost stories, really—were the strongest weapons in his arsenal against the "Sadducees" of his day, as they were often called. These stories were histories, as undeniable as the evening news.

Here we ought to meet a few of the works that were published in the mid-seventeenth century that had more than a little in common with *Nishmat Ḥayyim.* Taken together, they allow us to form an impression of the larger genre to which it belongs. Their titles alone tell us a great deal about them: there is Henry More's *An Antidote against Atheism*, published one year after *Nishmat Ḥayyim*, the title page of which boasts of its relating "strange . . . and undeniable Stories of Apparitions." Meric Casaubon's *A Treatise Proving Spirits, Witches and Supernatural Operations by Pregnant Instances and Evidences* was published a few years thereafter.[97] Richard Baxter began writing this type of literature in 1650; his most famous work is entitled *The Certainty of the World of Spirits. Fully evinced by unquestionable Histories of Apparitions and Witchcrafts, Operations, Voices &c. Proving the Immortality of Souls, the Malice and Miseries of the Devils and the Damned, and the Blessedness of the Justified. Written for the Conviction of Sadducees and Infidels* (1691). Perhaps no work bears a greater resemblance to *Nishmat Ḥayyim* than Joseph Glanvill's *Saducismus Triumphatus: Or, Full and Plain Evidence Concerning Witches and Apparitions*, which first appeared in the late 1660s.[98] Examples of works of this kind could surely be multiplied. As C.O Parsons pointed out in his analysis of Glanvill's work, the underlying theory of this genre was that a propagandist might "gain entry to the hard Sadducean consciousness through the senses." The primary means of doing so was by relating "true histories," "exempla of the weird." Of course the possibility that these stories might simply be read as entertainment was an inherent problem faced by authors working in this genre. "As a sensationalist and an empiricist," observed Parsons, "Glanvill argued from sense data, but the danger was that his public might feed on the bait and not submit to the doctrinal hook."[99] Thus we find repeated declarations by authors like Glanvill and More to clarify their intentions: "I have no humour nor delight in telling Stories," wrote Glanvill in the preface to his *Blow at Modern Sadducism* of 1668, "and do not publish these for the gratification of those that have; but I record them as Arguments for the confirmation of a truth." In the third edition of this popular work, Henry More's additions to Glanvill's original text made this point with special clarity:

> Wherefore let the Small Philosophick Sir Foplings of this present Age deride them as much as they will, those that lay out their pains in committing to writing certain well-attested Stories of Witches and Apparitions, do real service to true Religion and sound Philosophy, and the most effectual and accommodate to the confounding of Infidelity and Atheism, even in the Judgment of the Atheists themselves, who are as much afraid of the truth of these Stories as an Ape is of a Whip; and therefore force themselves with might and main to disbelieve them by reason of the dreadful consequence of them as to themselves.[100]

This was not to be a winning strategy for long, however. Although Menasseh's ghost stories were certainly intended to provide confirmation of a truth, by the 1660s, possession stories were being published in Prague as *Maaseh Buchl* for their entertainment value.[101]

Menasseh's strategy, at bottom, was that of this genre as a whole: to lead the reader from demons to souls, and from souls to God.[102] In his prefatory letter to Glanvill's *Saducismus Triumphatus,* More put it this way: "the confession of Witches against their own lives [is a] palpable Evidence, [along with] the miraculous feats they perform, that there are bad Spirits, which will necessarily open a door to the belief that there are good ones, and lastly that there is a God."[103] Sir Thomas Browne, in his *Religio Medici* (1636–43) argued simply that "if there are no witches, we have no assurance that God exists."[104] Menasseh is quite explicit about this orientation throughout *Nishmat Ḥayyim.* Introducing his discussion of the different forms of biblically prohibited magic (fully conflated with idolatry), Menasseh writes, "Having proven the existence of demons in what has preceded on the basis of sense, received tradition, and logical demonstration, I will now speak about additional demonic activities so as to further strengthen your faith in the immortality of the soul."[105] Elsewhere he argues that when he succeeds in proving the existence of demons "though they are unseen," people will justly acknowledge the existence of souls—which are also unseen.[106]

Although the parallel strategies adopted by Menasseh and his contemporaries, the Cambridge Platonists, and their extended supporters (such as Glanvill) bespeak deep affinities between them, Menasseh was not a Jewish affiliate of the group. If Glanvill seemed to maintain something of Menasseh's brand of empiricism, Henry More and Ralph Cudworth are recalled for having anticipated Leibniz and Kant in arguing that senses do not judge, whereas knowledge requires judgment. According to Cudworth's rationalist paradigm of knowledge, true knowledge derives from deduction—a position obviously at odds with Menasseh's own skeptical posture with regard to reason.[107] Moreover, we ought not to discount the importance of earlier demonological literature in the shaping of Menasseh's defense of tradition. Walter Stephen's treatment of the history of witch-hunting and religious doubt is particularly illuminating in this regard, arguing for a considerable "prehistory" of the attempt to infer the existence of God from a demonstration of the reality of the Devil.[108] According to Stephens, witch-hunters were less interested in eliminating demonic and Satanic activity than in proving that it existed.

Menasseh's strategy has, at any rate, become clear: to lead his readers to accept the tangible evidence for the existence of a demonic realm, which will in turn provide them with the certainty they lack with regard to the existence of the divine realm, the realm of the immortal human soul. Combating a heresy that struck his community with particular force, Menasseh's defense of tradition was not chiefly accomplished through the reiteration of Jewish doctrine but through the invocation of at least a rhetorical empiricism, as well as the assertion of a demonology that reflected Menasseh's profound assimilation of Christian traditions. In this sense, *Nishmat Ḥayyim* provides another example of the converso propensity to internalize cultural paradigms that were previously used against them. Demonology may thus be added to such notions as purity of blood, for example, which Dutch Sephardim adopted to the detriment of their Ashkenazi coreligionists.[109] In crafting *Nishmat Ḥayyim*, Menasseh fashioned a defense of traditional Jewish doctrine that might best be shelved alongside the most fashionable, if retrograde, Christian demonologies of his day.

# *Arrival*

The preceding chapters are stations of a broader, sweeping and singular history, as well as miniature histories in their own right. The grand narrative of the early modern reemergence of spirit possession in Jewish culture begins in preexpulsion Spain. With the exiles, the phenomenon travels clear across the Mediterranean, where it climaxes in the charged, pietistic atmosphere of late sixteenth-century Safed. In the seventeenth century, the trajectory again moves westward, as the narratives of spirit possession are assembled and disseminated by Menasseh ben Israel in his campaign to arrest the skeptical trends plaguing the new Iberian Jewish community of Amsterdam.

At this point, two Spanish diasporas converge: the pietistic diaspora of fifteenth-century exiles and the converso diaspora of the seventeenth century. As far as Menasseh was concerned, this latter diaspora desperately needed to bolster its fragile faith through an engagement with those same sources. Menasseh was not, of course, merely a literary conduit faithfully carrying these accounts to a new audience. It is true that his transcriptions of the sources are faithful. Indeed, Menasseh's "fundamentalism" expressed itself in a forceful devotion to the plain sense of the most awkwardly "irrational" narratives. Nevertheless, in Menasseh's work, these literary artifacts of the pietistic Sefardic Diaspora, known for its particularistic (and especially anti-Christian) orientation, are brought into unmitigated engagement with classical and current Christian demonological thinkers, from Augustine to Del Río and Weyer. The narratives of spirit possession among the Jews of Safed are thus marshaled to ensure the fidelity of the Jews of Amsterdam through an act that is at once transmission and translation. There is no lack of irony in this "Protestant" wielding of sources to salvage Jewish faith.

The implications of this study for a phenomenology of early modern Jewish religiosity are significant. We have seen the extent to which notions of spirit possession suffused Jewish society across a broad socioeconomic and educational spectrum. Although little doubt exists that learned male élites were the predominant beneficiaries of divine possession and unlearned females the most common victims of spirit possession, we have also exposed a heretofore unappreciated domain of positive spirit possession among some very powerful early modern Jewish women. The exposure of these women in itself raises for the first time the issue of the "discernment of spirits" in a Jewish cultural setting. We may now see more clearly the extent to which behaviors recognized as possession were subject to diagnosis and classification by the males who crafted the accounts at our disposal. Among the possible implications of this discovery is the existence of a realm of positively valued possession-centered religiosity among early modern Jewish women. This mode of religiosity, whatever its actual proportions may have been, has been all but forgotten, its memory likely eradicated in the wake of the Sabbatian debacle.

Spirit possession, in conjunction with the host of related prophetic-necromantic-revelatory phenomena that were prominent in so many genres of Jewish literature, may thus be seen as having occupied a central place in the construction of Jewish religiosity in the late medieval and early modern periods. Marvin Becker advised me many years ago to "take a small mirror and use it to reflect something much larger." The study of spirit possession has been a prism no less than a mirror, refracting and reflecting the intersections of ancient magic and modern skepticism, of the ever-present and interlaced worlds of sex and death, of religious piety reaching perhaps a pathological extreme. Diverse as our sources may be, however, they have a common, albeit threatened conviction: that life will ultimately defeat death. If there is much in their world impossible to embrace in my own, to this conviction I offer my prayerful assent.

# *Appendix: Spirit Possession Narratives from Early Modern Jewish Sources*

## 1. Joseph Della Reina, Possessing Spirit

I will now adduce an obvious proof, for we have seen with our own eyes and also heard from reliable witnesses—according to two witnesses—that once in the west there was a healthy Gentile maidservant.[1] Suddenly, she fell to the ground with the falling sickness and would say wondrous things.

Finally they sought out a Jew from those who know how to adjure demons, spirits, devils, and destructive beings. He adjured the spirit who entered that Gentile to say who he was and to depart. The spirit that was in the body of the Gentile responded that he should be left in peace in the body of the Gentile, since he had only just arrived, weary and exhausted from his journey, and entered the body of that Gentile.

And he adjured him to say who he was, and he responded and said that he was the soul of Joseph Della Reina, who had been punished and driven away by the Supernal Court for having conjoined his soul with demons. For while in this world, he had used Holy Names for his benefit and for the good of his body and not for the sake of the holiness of heaven. Furthermore, he had desecrated the Name when, with the king of the Christians, he adjured Amon Ma'aya [*sic*] and the form of a snake descended, took the pen in its mouth, and wrote, "I am your servant Joseph Della Reina." "For this, [he said,] I was punished by the judgment of Gehinnom and expelled to wander, conjoining with the demons." These are their [the witnesses'] words.

## 2. Joseph Karo, Exorcist

I further testify that in that year, the year 5305 from the creation (1545 C.E.), here in the upper Galilee, a spirit entered a small boy, who, while fallen, would say grand things.[2]

Finally, they sent for and assembled many great sages, along with men of deeds—myself among them.

The sage R. Joseph Karo, may peace be upon him, came and spoke with that very spirit. [The spirit] did not respond to him until he decreed the punishment of *niddui* upon him unless he spoke. He then spoke and responded.

The sage said to him, "What is your name?" He said, "I do not know my name." "Who are you?" "I am a dog." "And before that what were you?" "A Black Gentile." "And before that what were you?" "An Edomite [Christian] Gentile." "And before that what were you?" "From those people who know the Holy Tongue."

He said to him, "What were your first deeds?" He said, "I do not remember." "Did you know Torah or Talmud?" "I used to read the Torah but I knew no Talmud." "Did you pray?" "I did not pray except on the Sabbath and festivals." "Did you don phylacteries?" "Never did I don phylacteries." He said to him, "There is no fixing you." He said, "They already decreed on me . . ."—that he cannot be fixed.

He said that it had been two years since he departed from the body of the dog, and that since the father of the boy killed the dog, he said to the boy's father, "Just as you distressed me when you killed the dog that I was within, so I will kill your one and only son."

At that moment the sage R. Joseph Karo recited over him, "It is incumbent upon us to praise . . ." seven times, forward and backward, and he decreed upon him a *niddui* to depart from anywhere in the Galilee. And so it was that the young man was healed. This is what I saw with my own eyes at that Holy Convocation.

## 3. A Great Event in Safed

A Great Event in the Holy Community of Safed, *may it be rebuilt and reestablished speedily and in our days* [hereafter *tvb"b*].[3] For man is more attracted to the pleasure of his body for his sensory pleasure than he is inclined to follow the advice of his soul and the direction of the Torah—even believers and those most punctilious in all things. For the matters of the World to Come are not felt; thus who can establish them in his heart so that they might make an impression upon him to abandon any aspect of evil or wrongdoing—whether in speech, thought, or action? Not every person merits this. Therefore, in order to bestow merit upon others, I concluded to commit to writing that which transpired before me today, 11 Adar I 5331 [16 February 1571]: the case of a woman, the daughter-in-law of the venerable Joseph Ẓarfati, into whom entered a spirit of a man of Israel, as I will describe below. In truth, whoever was there at the time and heard from the spirit what he said and what he revealed, and whoever heard it from him, ought to subdue their hearts to heaven and have fear and dread of the Day of Judgment on account of their actions. For all comes to account, and there is no House of Refuge in Sheol (cf. *Avot* 4:29). And this is known to us from one who came from that World, and told to us by one who has crossed over there. Perhaps the Holy One, blessed be He, sent him so that they might fear Him, as the Sages of blessed memory said, " 'And God does it, so that men should fear him' (Eccles. 3:14)—this is a bad dream." And this is not a dream but while awake, before the eyes of all.

I was amid a great gathering, for there were more than 100 people there, Torah scholars and heads of communities. Two men, knowledgeable in adjurations and many matters, approached the woman so that the spirit within the woman would speak, by means of the smoke of fire and sulfur that they would make enter her nostrils. She was like naught, for she would not push herself away—not even her head—from the fire, nor from the smoke. By means of the adjurers the voice would begin to be heard, "like the voice of the Almighty," drawn out like "the roar of a lion and the howl of a fierce lion" (Job 4:10) without any movement of the tongue or opening of the lips. When this voice began to be heard, the two aforementioned men would strengthen and intensify themselves quickly and diligently so as to act rapidly. They would quarrel with him with a loud voice and say to him: "Evil one, speak and say who you are in a clear tongue!" Then the voice would reveal itself and show itself to all that it was like the voice of men.

Again they spoke to him in a great voice and by means of all the aforementioned: "What is your name, evil one?" He responded, "Samuel Ẓarfati." They asked him, "How can we be sure that your name is Samuel Ẓarfati?" He responded that he had died in Tripoli and that he had left one son, whose name is So-and-so; that he had had three daughters, the name of the first being So-and-so, the name of the second So-and-so, and the name of the third So-and-so; and that from the third he died, and she is now married to Tuvia Deleiria. And on all of the signs that he said, [his] word [was] correct and veracious, a word of truth. Then we recognized, all those present, that the spirit was the speaker.

They asked him, "For what deed do you reincarnate in the world in reincarnations such as these?" He responded, "For many sins that I have committed during my life." In turn, they demanded, "Be explicit about them." He said that he did not want to, for what purpose would be served? They then compelled him to state at least the greatest transgression of them all, and he answered and said that he had been a type of *apikorus* [heretic] and that he had said that all religions are the same. Regarding this, many testified before us that he had spoken in such a way during his lifetime. And they asked him, "And now of what mind are you regarding this?" And he responded like one groaning with a voice crying and raging and said, "I recognize that I sinned, transgressed and wronged." And he asked for forgiveness from the Holy One, blessed be He, and of His perfect Torah for his many transgressions.

Then the aforementioned two men began to entreat him and to ban him to depart from within her and to go to a place of barren wilderness, by means of the techniques mentioned above. They also [promised that they] would petition for mercy upon him and pray for him and blow the shofar. He said, "What I wouldn't give for that!" They asked him: "Who should blow the shofar?" He said: "The sage, his honor the rabbi Shlomo Alkabetz." The aforementioned sage responded that he was unable. They again said to him, "Request another." The spirit said, "Let it be the sage, his honor the rabbi Avraham Laḥmi." They asked him, "Who should request [mercy] for you?" The spirit responded, "Let it be the rabbi Elijah Falcon."

And then we said "*El melekh*" and "*Va-ya'avor* [Exod. 34:6]" thrice with the blast of the shofar. And all was done according to the revelation of his will. Then they said to him once again that he must depart, as they had acted in accordance to his will. The spirit responded,"Let a little time pass; then I will depart." They asked him, "Do you want your son to say *kaddish* for you or learn Torah?" He said that it would not help it at all and that his son was unsuited to learn Torah.

They asked him about the matter of "the beating of the grave." And one of those seated there responded, "This one never entered the grave!" Then the spirit said—and refuted his words: "I entered on the day of my burial, and on that same night they removed me, and I did not enter again. And from that very time, which was nearly three years ago, I have gone from mountain to mountain and from hill to hill. I did not find rest in any place, except that for a period of time I was in Shekhem, where I entered into one woman, and they removed me through the aforementioned and placed amulets upon her so that I was unable to return upon her further." And all this is true from what we knew from the mouths of others that such had transpired. "After that I was roving through the city to enter synagogues [thinking that] perhaps I would find rest and comfort there for my soul, but they did not allow me to enter any synagogue." And they asked him, "Who prevented you?" The spirit said, "The sages." They asked him again, "Were they alive, or were they dead?" He said, "Dead. And they trampled me and said to me, 'Depart from here, wicked one!' " The questioner asked further, "To which synagogue did you go first?" He said, "To my own congregation." They said to him, "Which is it?" He responded, "Beit Ya'akov" They asked him further, "Your seat: who sits upon it?" He responded, "If they did not allow me to enter, how am I supposed to know who sits in my place?" They asked him further, "Who sat by your side when you were alive?" He responded, "So-and-so." And all that he said was true.

Then they said to him, "And how did you enter this woman? Is she not forbidden for you?" He said, "What can I do, for I found no rest anywhere other than inside her, for she is a kosher woman." "And if she is a married woman, have you no reservations about copulating with her?" The spirit responded, "And what of it? Her husband isn't here, but in Salonika!"

The two men asked further, "How did you enter this house, which has a mezuzah?" He answered, "I came in via a lower entrance which did not have a mezuzah." And they asked him, "And how was it that you entered her, being that she was kosher?" He said, "There was a difficult time and she threw a little mud on her [*sic*] head, and for that, I was able to enter inside her." And all this was on Thursday of last week in the evening. All this the spirit himself said, and thus it was that from that moment she had felt it herself. While still compelling him to depart, they said to him, "And why have you not feared the *ḥerem* that you received yesterday, to depart and not to return again inside her? How could you transgress it?" He responded, "I did depart but did not find rest in any other place, until I saw that they did not put amulets upon her; then I was able to enter her another time." Then they strengthened themselves and said to him, "Depart, evil one! If not, we will decree upon you the '*ḥerem Kol-Bo*' that you depart in any case." And they cast the "*ḥerem Kol-Bo*" since he had been adjured by the Ten Commandments to depart after one hour. Many testified that such was his custom while alive, to take this oath. And they delayed among themselves for a short time and reproached him and spoke harshly against him: "Is it that you do not fear from any man, nor even from your vow, and not from the '*ḥerem Kol-Bo*?' " And the spirit would say, "What can I do; if I perish, I perish (cf. Esther 4:16)."

After this, they wanted to test whether this speech was spoken by the spirit. They spoke with him in the Holy Tongue, and in the Arabic tongue, and in the tongue of Ishmael, called *Moorish*. To each and every language, he responded in a clear tongue, as he did while alive, as his acquaintances said of him. The woman did not know any of these languages. Thus, when they spoke with him in the Ashkenazic language, he would not respond to them in it, because he did not know or understand that language.

They asked him, "Who am I?" To each he responded with their names. They also asked him, "What was your trade when you were alive?" "Money changing," he answered. And so it was. They also asked him about Ibn Musa, whether he had seen him, and the course of his transmigration. He responded that he had not seen him at all.

They pressed him with the aforementioned adjurations, with the aforementioned smoke, and with the Names, that the spirit should depart through the big toenail of one of her feet. He then tried to deceive them into believing that he had departed the way in which we told him; he raised her legs and lowered them one after the other, with great speed, time and again. And with those movements, which he made with great strength, the cover that was upon her fell off her feet and thighs, and she revealed and humiliated herself for all to see. They came close to her to cover her thighs, but she had no self-awareness in any of this. And those who were acquainted with her knew of her great modesty; now her modesty was lost to her. All this because she was like dead and naught, as we said above.

They said to him, "The sign and demonstration by which we shall know that you indeed went out completely is that when you go out you must extinguish the candle hanging on the wall at a distance of roughly three cubits from him [*sic*]." And by those movements that we mentioned he wanted to extinguish the candle. But although he strengthened himself and hurried and warmed himself to show us that he was going out through the aforementioned nail to extinguish the candle that hung on the wall, nevertheless he did not go out. For he did not want to go out but wanted to mock us. Many times he said, "Bring the candle nearer, to the place where it was yesterday," so as to extinguish it there. And they said to him, "If you extinguish the candle where it is, we shall know with certainty that you departed, but if you do not, then you are mocking us." He again strengthened himself to make movements and shakings with the legs until he blew the air with those movements. Because [he did not] want to depart and abandon his dwelling there, he was unable to extinguish the candle from there. Had the candle been nearer, he could have extinguished it, for the spirit was on top of her feet as he said. The two adjurers and we saw the spirit going out, close to her feet. They again adjured him and gave him smoke, fire, and sulfur into her nostrils so that he should go out completely through the aforementioned nail and should uproot himself with a total uprooting and extinguish the aforementioned candle, which was at a distance of three cubits, on his way out from there while going to the desolate desert place. He said many times, "Let this poor Jewish woman be, and do not hurt her!" And they said to him, "It is you who hurts her; depart if you have pity on her." And he answered, "Do not continue to force me, for if you force me to go out, I shall take out her soul with me." Nevertheless the aforementioned adjurers decreed upon him that he should go out unfailingly. But he did not go out. They said to him, "Sit up on the bed and then go out, and if you do not want to, then we will force you with all the things mentioned. He sat up on the bed without any help. Then, when he was seated, they said to him with a great voice, "Go out, you evil one, quickly, without her soul."

Then he himself touched her feet with his fingers, as if to push the spirit that was in the flesh through the nail by means of that pressure. And then suddenly she began to speak. She was sitting and saying, "He has already left." And they did not believe her, for they suspected that perhaps the spirit himself was speaking. For they saw that he did not extinguish the candle. And she said that he forgot to extinguish the candle because of the great confusion and the great hurry to go out. Nevertheless they still did not believe her, and they wanted to do again as they had done before, and she cried to her father-in-law and her grandmother, "Why do you let them burn me, for he has already left, and they do not leave me alone!" And she said, "I know that it is true that he indeed has left." And they said to her, "What is the truth?" And she answered, "I cannot tell you." "And then they understood that it was a matter that cannot be told in public, and they said to a woman, "Go to her and she will reveal the matter to you." And so it was done, and it became known that the spirit went out through that place and drew blood as he went out. And all this cogent evidence made all of them accept that there was truth in her words. And they placed the amulets upon her that were ready in the house, and she was assumed to have recovered.

An hour later the sages came to her, when the cry went out in the city: "Behold, the spirit of a man from Israel speaks in a woman." And when they saw her they said, "He certainly did not leave–and if he ever left, he has returned." [They said so] because of the signs they saw, such as glazed eyes and labored breathing. And from these signs they knew that he was still in her. And then the voice [in the city] told about the ruination, a voice which did not cease, that the spirit was still in her. But the two adjurers said that he surely had gone out but that he subsequently returned, because, for one thing, the amulets that they put on her were not written with her name and, for another, because of the confusion, because the whole city, Jews and Turks, were coming one after the other to her, to see the terrible thing that was astonishing to the eyes of every man. They hushed up the matter because of the danger on the part of the nations who would have wanted to burn her, until all was forgotten after a few days; then the matter could be corrected. Eight days later, the poor woman died because of the spirit that did not leave her, and they say that he choked her and went out with her soul.

Everything I wrote above, every detail is written precisely as it was. One must not doubt anything in it, because it is written accurately, and there is no addition in it nor any deletion, for I wrote exactly what I saw and heard. I further request the sages who were there that they, too, should put their signatures on this, for by their mouths we live, that they verify my words through their signatures. And the eye that sees this writing of mine and the ear that hears it should believe with complete faith as if he had heard it from the mouth of the spirit, and should fear and be afraid and believe everything written in the Torah and in the words of our rabbis of blessed memory, and then he will rest on his couch in peace and three groups of ministering angels will go out before him, one will say, "Peace etc. . . ." and no plague will go near his tent, and his soul will cleave to God and will return to the place whence it was hewn. Thus says the writer, the young and the poor among the thousands, the devoted servant of the fearers of the Lord, and those who think of His name, Elijah Falcon.

I was there, and my eyes saw and my ears heard to instruct all this and more—he who sees shall testify, your servant SHLOMO LEVI BEN ALKABETZ (author of the book *Shoresh Yishai* on Ruth)

- These words are words of truth that have no measure so that every man should know about this event and leave his evil ways, and every man [should give up] the wrong of his thoughts before he goes and is not, and he who knows will return, and repent, and come back, and will be healed. The youth ABRAHAM HA-LAḤMI
- SHMUEL BUENO
- I too was called to see this matter, and my eyes have seen and my ears have heard, and it is a miraculous thing, to teach us that we should turn back in repentance. Says ABRAHAM ARUETY.

## 4. The Possession and Death of the Young Man in Safed

Again a similar event happened a second time in Safed.[4] Once a spirit entered a young man, and they adjured him by all the conditions mentioned above, and he too recalled his name and the name of his city and the name of his wife.

(Every time he recalled his wife, he would weep and say that his wife remained an *'agunah* after him, because he drowned at sea. The sages are unable to permit her to marry, and she whores. He would beg of the sages who were standing there to permit her [to remarry], and he gave many signs [attesting to the truth] of what he said. They said to him that, all of that notwithstanding, she was still forbidden. He debated with them over this, invoking rabbinic teachings.) They asked him what his sin had been. He said that he had relations with a married woman in Constantinople. (And that the statement of the Sages' to the effect that the four manners of execution had not been nullified, had been the case for him. They said to him, "What was the name of that woman?" He did not want to expose her, for she too had already died, and there was no purpose in exposing her.)

In the midst of all of this, he stood up on his feet. They said to him, "Why did you arise?" He said to them, "Because the Sage so-and-so has now come." (And so it was, for immediately after this he came, as he had said.) After that a group of young men entered his midst. He said, "Why are these coming here to see me? The cup shall also pass over to them as well! (See Lam. 4:21–22.) For we all share the same transgression. I am shocked by these, for matters of common knowledge need no proof! But I am astounded by this man, who makes himself appear as though he were a pietist, dressed in white, and he is blanched by evil: he commits the acts of Zimri and requests the reward of Pinḥas! Did he not have relations with a married woman in Constantinople? And all those present expressed their shock to one another. The one dressed in white clothes began to weep with great weeping, and all admitted and confessed their actions. Then one of the sages there asked him, "How do you know?" He said to him, "And does the verse not say 'he places a seal upon the hand of every man' (Job 37:7)?" And I know even what is in the innermost chambers." (One of the sages standing there said to him, "Tell me my actions." He said to him, "Regarding our master we have no permission to say anything." And they asked that same young man inside whom was the spirit, "Why does this spirit speak with your mouth and lips as if you were the speaker? Let him speak for himself." He again began to laugh and said, "And did not the Sages say in [Babylonian Talmud tractate] *Baba Kamma* 'the agent of the person is like him. . . .' ")

They then asked him to tell them in what way he entered into this young man. He answered that he drowned at sea at a particular place, and fish ate his flesh. His spirit wandered in the land (hiding and concealing itself from the eye of every creature, for all would torment him with all types of suffering). He finally entered a cow. The cow then went mad. When the owner of the cow saw its actions, he sold her to a Jew, and that Jew slaughtered her. When he slaughtered her, the young man was there; he left the cow and entered into him. Many testified that such was the case (and that immediately after the slaughtering of the cow, the young man felt the spirit that was tormenting him).

Within eight days this young man passed away. Thus, one fearing the word of the Lord should return and regret the sins he has committed and plead with his maker; perhaps the Lord will hear and return and heal him.

## 5. The Spirit in the Widow of Safed

There occurred an event at the time that the holy and pure Rav, the divine kabbalist Isaac Luria Ashkenazi, his memory for a blessing [hereafter *z"l*], was in Safed, *tvb"b*.[5] A spirit entered one woman, a widow, and made her suffer very great and enormous suffering. Many people assembled about her, and spoke with her and the spirit replied to each and every one, making known the wounds of his heart and all of his needs for that which he lacked. And among those who came one sage entered his midst, and his name was our teacher, the rabbi R. [hereafter *mvhr"r*] J. I., may the memory of the righteous be a blessing [hereafter *zt"l*]. Immediately the spirit said to him, "Blessed is he who comes, my master, my teacher and my rabbi! I recall my master, for I was his student in Egypt for a long time, and my name is so and so, and my father's name is so and so.

Now, when the relatives of the woman saw her suffering and her pain, that it was very great, they went to the Holy Rav, *mvhr"r* Isaac Luria *zt"l*, to beg him to go with them to the woman and to remove this spirit from the woman. Being that the Rav *zt"l* was not free to go himself, he sent his student, *mhr"r* Ḥayyim Calabrese *zt"l*, and laid his hands upon him and transmitted to him *kavvanot* with Names. He also commanded him to decree upon him bans and excommunications and to remove him against his will.

As soon our teacher the *mhr"r* Ḥayyim Vital *z"l* entered her midst, the woman immediately turned her face away to the wall. The Rav *z"l* said to her, "Evildoer, why did you turn your face away from me?" The spirit replied to him and said, "I am unable to gaze upon your face, for the wicked are unable to gaze upon the face of the *Shekhina*!" Immediately our teacher the *mhr"r* Ḥayyim *z"l* decreed upon him that he turn his face, and he then immediately turned his face. He said to him, "What is your sin and your transgression for which they have punished you with this severe punishment?" The spirit replied to him and said, "I sinned with a married woman and fathered bastards. It has now been twenty-five years since I began wandering in the land, and they have given me no respite, neither for an hour nor for a minute. For three angels of destruction go with me to all the places to which I go, and punish me and beat me with exceedingly hard blows, and declare before me, 'Such will be done to one who multiplied bastards among Israel.' And these three angels of destruction are alluded to in the verse: 'Appoint over him a wicked man, and may Satan stand at his right' (Psalms 109:7–8)." And the spirit also said to the Rav *z"l*, "Do you not see one angel of the angels who stands on my right, and one on my left, and they decree, and the third strikes me death blows?" The Rav asked him and said to him, "Did our sages *z"l* not say, 'The sentence of the wicked in Gehinnom is twelve months'? (*Eduyot* 2:10)." The spirit responded to him and said to him,

My master was not precise in this statement, for when our sages *z"l* said that "the sentence of the wicked in Gehinnom is twelve months," it was after they have suffered the punishments outside of Gehinnom, in reincarnations and through other hard judgments. Then they are admitted to Gehinnom, and there they spend twelve months. They whiten and wash them in order to remove from them the stains of their souls, in order for them to be summoned and prepared to enter *Gan Eden*. This is like an expert doctor who first administers stinging substances upon the wound, which consume the living flesh, and afterward he administers good salves and bandages in order to cool and restore the flesh to its former state. So is the matter of Gehinnom, for the suffering of Gehinnom is not one fiftieth part that the soul endures before it enters Gehinnom.

The Rav *z"l* then asked him, "How did you die?" He responded and said to him, "My death was by choking, for although the four manners of death of the *Bet Din* (Supreme Rabbinical Court) have been abrogated, the four types of death have not been abrogated. When I left from Alexandria in a boat to go to Egypt, my boat was sunk in the Nile delta region, where the Nile enters the sea. We drowned, other Jews who were with me on the boat and I." *Mhr"r* Ḥayyim *z"l* then asked him, "Why did you not say the confession at the hour of the departure of your soul from your body; perhaps it would have helped you." The spirit responded to him, "I did not manage to confess, for immediately the water choked me in my throat. Also immediately in the drowning in the sea my mind became confused, and I was not in my right mind to confess."

The Rav then asked him, "Tell me what happened to you after you drowned in the sea and after the departure of your soul from your body." The spirit responded and said,

Know that when the matter of the sunken boat became known in Egypt, immediately the Jews of Egypt went into the sea and took all of us out of the sea and buried us. Immediately thereafter, when the Jews left the cemetery, a cruel angel came, with a staff of fire in his hand, and he struck my grave roughly with that staff. Immediately the grave split in two from the strike, which was so very great and strong. That angel said to me, "Evil one, evil one, arise in judgment!" Immediately he took me and put me in the hollow of the sling and slung me in one shot from Egypt to before the opening of Gehinnom in the wilderness. And as I fell there before the opening of Gehinnom, immediately 1,000,000 souls of evildoers who are being judged there came out of Gehinnom, all of them shouting against me and saying to me, "Depart, depart, man of blood, depart from here evildoer, tormentor of Israel!" And they cursed me with vehement curses and said to me, "You are still unworthy of entering here, and you still have no permission to enter Gehinnom." Then they cast me from mountain to mountain and from hill to hill, those three angels of destruction ever with me, decreeing before me and striking me always. And at each and every moment other angels of destruction, evil spirits, demons, and she-devils injure me. And upon hearing the decree that they decree before me, they beat me with great and difficult blows as well. These pull me here, and that one pulls me there, until all the knots of my soul are unwound.

In this way, I went wandering to and fro in the land, until reaching the city of Ormuz, a large city close to the land of India. My intention was to enter into the body of some Jew, perhaps to be saved from those blows, sufferings, and torments. Now, since those Jews are evil and sinning to the Lord exceedingly, fornicating with Gentile women and committing other transgressions, I was unable to enter even one of them due to the many spirits of impurity that dwell in them and around them. Had I entered the body of one of them, I would have added defilement to my defilement and injury to my own injury. For that reason I returned, and went from mountain to hill and from hill to mountain, until I came to the wilderness of Gaza. There I found a pregnant doe; due to my great suffering and pain I entered her body. This was after seven years during which I went through many terrible troubles. When I entered the body of this doe, it was tremendously painful for me, for the soul of a human being and the soul of a beast are not equal, for one walks upright and the other bent. Also, the soul of the beast is full of filth and is repulsive, its smell foul before the soul of a human being. And its food is not human food. I also had great pain from the fetus in her belly. The doe also had great pain because of me; her belly swelled, and she ran in the mountains and in the rocks until her abdomen split and she died. From there I left and I came to the city of Shekhem, where I entered the body of a Jew, a *Kohen*. And that *Kohen* immediately sent after the holy men and clerics of the Ishmaelites, and from the number of their incantations and adjurations of impure names, and also the amulets of unholy names that they hung from his neck, I was unable to bear it and to remain in his body. I immediately left there and fled.

Immediately the Rav said to him, "Is it really the case that there is something to the forces of impurity to injure and to ameliorate by themselves?" He said to him, "No, but because the clerics, through their adjurations, infused so many spirits of impurity into the body of that *Kohen*-Jew, I saw that if I continued to stay there all those spirits would cling to me. Thus I was unable to stay with them.

"I then came to Safed *tvb"b*, and I entered the body of this woman. For me, as of today it has been twenty-five years that my suffering persists." The Rav said to him, "For how long will you have this suffering, for have you no recovery forever?" The spirit responded to him, "Not until all the bastards whom I fathered have died. For as long as they live and exist, I have no reparation." Then all those who were there, a very great multitude, all of them cried many cries, for fear of judgment fell upon them. A great awakening took place throughout the region from that very occurrence. The Rav then asked him, "Who gave you permission to enter the body of this woman?" The spirit responded, "I spent one night in her house; at dawn this woman arose from her bed and wanted to light a fire from the stone and iron, but the burnt rag did not catch the sparks. She persisted stubbornly, but did not succeed. She then became intensely angry and cast the iron and the stone and the burnt rag—everything—from her hand to the ground and angrily said, 'To Satan with you!' Immediately I was given permission to enter her body." The Rav *z"l* asked him and said, "And for a minor transgression such as this they gave you permission to enter her body?" The spirit responded and said, "Know, my master the sage, that this woman's inside is not like her outside, for she does not believe in the miracles that the Holy One, blessed be He, did for Israel, and in particular in the Exodus from Egypt. Every Passover night, when all of Israel is rejoicing and good hearted, saying the great Hallel and telling of the Exodus from Egypt, it is vanity in her eyes, a mockery and a farce. And she thinks in her heart that there was never a miracle such as this."

Immediately the Rav said to the woman so-and-so, "Do you believe with perfect belief that the Holy One, blessed be He, is One and Unique, and that He created the heavens and the earth, and that He has the power and capacity to do anything that He desires, and that there is no one who can tell him what to do?" She responded to him and said, "Yes, I believe in it all in perfect faith." The Rav *z"l* further said to her, "Do you believe in perfect faith that the Holy One, blessed be He, took us out of Egypt from the house of slavery, and split the sea for us, and accomplished many miracles for us?" She responded, "Yes, master, I believe in it all with perfect faith, and if I had at times a different view, I regret it." And she began to cry.

Immediately the Rav decreed a ban on the spirit to depart, and he decreed upon him that he not depart by way of any limb other than via the little toe of the left foot, because the reason is that from the limb that it departs, that limb is ruined and destroyed utterly. And the Rav intended the Names that his teacher *z"l* had transmitted to him, and immediately the little toe swelled and became like a turnip, and [the spirit] left by that way. After that, on a number of nights the spirit came to the windows of the house and to the entryway and terrorized the woman [threatening] to return and to enter her body. The relatives of the woman returned to the Kabbalist the AR"I *zt"l*. The Rav sent his student *mhr"r* Ḥayyim *z"l* to check the mezuzah, and he found the entryway without any mezuzah. Immediately the Rav commanded that a kosher mezuzah be affixed to the entryway, and so they did. And from them on, the spirit did not return.

## 6. The Spirit in the Nephew of Rabbi Yehoshua Bin Nun

An event in Safed, *tvb"b*, in the time of my teacher, may his memory be for life in the World to Come [hereafter *zlh"h*]. 'There was a young man eighteen years of age in the yeshivah, the son of the sister of Rav Yehoshua bin Nun *z"l*. My teacher *zlh"h* saw him and said to his father, "Your son—a spirit is in him; do not waste your money on doctors." The father of the young man answered and said to him, "Do not say that, master, for he only has occasional heart pain. He has had this pain for twelve years, and he is healed by the doctors, but then the heart pain then returns." My teacher *zlh"h* answered him, "Now you will see that it is a spirit." And he decreed upon him, and the spirit spoke and said to him that he had been impregnated within this young man for twelve years. The Rav *zlh"h* said to him, "And why have you been here for twelve years?" The spirit responded, "I was a pauper in Rome and supported myself on charity in that incarnation. This young man was also there, and he was a charity warden in that incarnation. I cried out to him, 'Help me!' but he refused. I died of hunger. Now the Supernal Court has decreed that just as he killed me in that incarnation, I may now kill him."

Then the Rav *zlh"h* decreed upon him that he not do him any harm. The spirit said, "If you want me to leave here, agree with me to one condition—that after I depart from here, this young man not see the face of a woman for three days; if he transgresses this condition, I will kill him." The father asked the son if he had heart pain, and he said no. The Rav *zlh"h* ordered that there be a watch over the young man, and not to allow him to depart from the House of Study, nor [to allow] women to come to him. The spirit, he said, was a scoundrel, for he demanded of him a condition difficult to fulfill.

And the first day was *Rosh Ḥodesh* [New Moon] and I, Ḥayyim, went to make a feast. I left the Rav Rabbi Yehoshua Bin Nun in my place for the watch. He too left afterward and left the young man in the House of Study. His mother and aunt then came to see the young man, saw his face, and kissed him. At that same moment the spirit returned, entered him, and strangled him.

And out of fear of the nations of the world—that they would say that we killed him—the Rav *zlh"h* made a magical jump over two reeds and traveled to Tiberias in one second, at dusk. In Tiberias, the Rav *zlh"h* prayed that the matter not spread among the nations and that there be no informing against the Jews. And thus it was. After eight days we returned to Safed, *tvb"b.*

## 7. The Possessed Woman of Safed

One day when we were in the study hall of my teacher [the AR"I], they brought one woman before him to know whether she was ill, or whether some spirit had enclothed himself in her.[7] They said to my teacher *zlh"h* that she had been free from sickness and pain and that suddenly she was transformed to this state. Her whole body shook. My teacher *zlh"h* checked her pulse and said that it was a spirit who enclothed himself in her. He sent her home and told me to go there in the evening to remove the spirit from her. He also told me to be particularly wary of that spirit because he is a great deceiver, and when asked his name, lies up to three times; he also gave me *kavvanot* to remove him. For it was my teacher's custom to send me to carry out this kind of mission, the reason he would give me being that I am from the soul-root of Cain, the left side of the Primordial Adam, which is severity, and judgments are only sweetened at their source. For this reason I have this power.

Now, I only left at dusk on Thursday night. Before I went in to the house of that woman, the spirit said to those standing there, "See that the Sage Rabbi Ḥayyim Vital has come here to remove me from here. We will see what his power is and what he is able to do. I am not afraid of him; what power has he to remove me from here?" When I entered and the spirit saw my face and I greeted them, the spirit paid me great respect. And half his body arose, and he began to quake. I asked him who he was, and he responded, "I am so-and-so." I said to him, "Lies you speak; that is not your name." And thus he lied three times, and on the fourth time he said his true name, as my teacher *zlh"h* had said he would. Then I drew close to his ear, and I said a few *kavvanot*, and the spirit panicked and spoke abusively and wanted to depart until I thoroughly rebuked him, and he gave me a sign that he wanted to depart by way of the little toe of the foot. This was a lie, for I saw that he was standing entirely in the throat and that he wanted to depart and extinguish the candles and to harm those standing there. Seeing this, I decreed upon him a *niddui* that he not depart from there. I left things in this state and went to pray the evening prayer in the home of my teacher *zlh"h*.

After we prayed and the comrades left, I told my teacher *zlh"h* the entire episode. He said, "I am surprised at you; for I told you to go in the evening and you went at night, which is the time when all the spirits and *klippot* [demonic 'husks'] have dominion. It is no time to act upon them, for then is their time." In the meantime, it had become very late, and rain was falling. My teacher *zlh"h* told me, "Go in peace," and he walked with me a little, which he never did any other time. And he said to me, "You need to protect yourself from that spirit very well, for he is extremely angry with you for wanting to remove him from his place. And I want to reveal one thing to you, and do not allow it to make your soul grow haughty: See the power that is yours, and how many *klippot* flee and fear you; for even if all the *klippot* in the world came, they would be unable to harm you. If you shake the corners of your garment, all will flee from you and be unable to stand before you."

After this, I went to my house by way of the Jewish market, for that is my path. It was then already one o'clock at night. When I wanted to go up to the market, a dog came before me at close range, black and huge as a mule. I was shocked before him and could not recall any *kavvanah*, for upon seeing him I forgot everything. I walked with great fear. I was close to him in a narrow place, fenced in on both sides; it was night, dark and raining, and I could not turn back from fear of the Turkish sergeants and also because the *klippot* are *aḥorayim* ("rear-beings") and adhere to and harm the back more than they do the front. I passed across from the dog and, behold, he cried out in a great voice. I was startled, and I fell upon the ground, and my hand touched the hand of the dog. When I arose, the corners of my garment were full of mud and I shook them—without the intention of one performing a *kavvanah*—and behold, the dog fled immediately and did not stand before me any longer. I walked to my home. The hand that touched the hand of the dog was withered. In the morning, I walked to the house of my teacher *zlh"h* and he said to me, "Did I not tell you to shake the corners of your garment? I also accompanied you and did not enter my house until I saw that you had already entered your house, and my heart was with you." Then my teacher *zlh"h* held my hand, and it returned to its original state.

After this, my teacher gave me different *kavvanot*, and I went and spoke into the ear of the woman within whom was the spirit. The spirit did not want to leave. I went to my teacher *zlh"h* and told him this, and he said to me, "The spirit did just as you decreed upon him—he did not depart." He also gave me different *kavvanot*, and they are written in their place. I went to the woman, and the spirit started to quake, and I recited those *kavvanot* into the ear of the woman. I then asked the spirit through which place he entered the house. He responded that there was a small hole in the wall, and from there he entered, because he was unable to enter from the entrance, upon which there was a kosher mezuzah, nor by way of the windows, for they are not for the comings and goings of men and do not require a mezuzah. I also asked him in what way he entered this woman. He said that he had been in that same house for three days before he entered that woman, and was seeking some opportunity to enter her. Finally, on Thursday night, that woman wanted to arise early and to busy herself with her labor. When she was striking the steel and stone to release the fire, the spirit was sitting upon the stone, and the woman would strike, but no sparks would emerge. After she troubled herself greatly and there was no fire, she threw the steel from her hand in anger, and then he entered her—for he found an opening to enter her. Afterward I asked him what he did during those three days that he was in the house and in what place he dwelled. He responded that he was hiding in a beam from which candles are hung; he entered the beam because the guards appointed over him came and he entered there and they did not find him. I said to him, "Give me a sign that this is true." He responded to me that the sign was that on such-and-such a day you all ate such-and-such, and that on such-and-such a day the woman said such-and-such to her husband, and he responded to her such-and-such. And they acknowledged that such had been the case. Afterward I released him from the *niddui* that I had decreed upon him. Then, I caused him to go out and he went away by means of the *kavvanot* that my teacher *zlh"h* had given me.

## 8. The Spirit in Ferrara

Now, after God has made known to you all of this by means of the toil of my hands, having gathered and bound them together, may the strength of my hand grow to write to you and to present before you the answer to your question regarding the foreign spirits that enter the bodies of humans, which by the power of adjurations reveal their names and say that they are people who have died in strange deaths.[8] With the power of our intellects, it is difficult to understand how it is possible that the spirit of one who died can act in another body that lives, and use all of its limbs and senses. The truth is that it would appear to be one of the wonders of our time and exceedingly strange.

And I myself experienced the phenomenon in the month of Tevet 5335 [December 1574–January 1575], while I was in Ferrara. I went to visit a young woman 25 years of age, a young wife, in the company of many distinguished people.

I found her stretched out on her bed, lying on her back, like a body without soul. Her eyes were closed, her mouth was open, and her tongue was very thick from the lip inward. The men and women supporting her said that the spirit was then situated in her tongue. Then I said to myself, "This is the day I have hoped for, to know new revelations regarding the departure of the soul from the body!"

After I begged the spirit and strongly implored him to respond to my questions, he responded in Italian with clearly enunciated letters, well heard, that his name was Battista de Modena, who had been hung as a punishment for theft. He began to make a crying voice and groans, and I comforted him with good words, and he was comforted. I began to ask him questions regarding the soul, in order to know its essence and the manner of its departure from the body at the time of death, its paths thereafter, and what was Gehinnom. I did not ask about *Gan Eden*, for I knew that it was inaccessible to him, nor other questions like that. To them all, he answered common words, and the seal of his words was "I don't know," saying that he was a man of the field and a shepherd of beasts. And in the course of his words, I came to regard him as a beast.

He had the power to rule and force the young woman according to his will, like not eating meat on Friday, and saying their prayers upon the early evening ringing of the bell on Saturday, and things according to the customs of the Christians. I asked him what it mattered to him if that [girl's] body ate meat on Friday. He responded that it was a sin for him, because he also derived pleasure from her eating.

I asked him what was the essence of his body, and he responded, "I don't know." I asked him his size—whether it was like the egg of a goose, a chicken, or a dove—and he responded, "Of a chicken." I asked him where he was situated in the body of the woman, and he responded, "Between her ribs and loins on the right side." I asked him who put him there, and he responded, "I do not know." I asked him to depart from there and he responded, "I cannot."

I asked him why he entered the body of a Jewish woman. He responded that it pained him, that she was not aware of his entrance there, and that had he been able [to avoid it], he would not have entered there. I asked him from what place he entered. He responded, "Through her nakedness." He also informed me how it was, as we heard later from the young woman.

I asked him with great pleading that he leave the girl quiet until I could speak to her, and he was pacified. In his movement to his place, we saw the throat of the woman swell greatly. The woman felt great pain in all of her limbs and shook and quaked with difficulty and wondrous strangeness, prompting great compassion among all observers. When the spirit entered his place, the girl's entire body, and that side in particular, would shake and quake continuously, like the consumption before the fever. Immediately she opened her eyes and saw us.

I asked her what had happened, and she responded that after returning from immersing herself in the ritual bath, she descended out of her house to the courtyard at two o'clock in the morning with a lit candle in her hand, to draw water from the well in order to prepare food for her husband. She placed the lit candle in a hole near the well. Her husband, who had been with her, went away, and she took the pail to draw the water. Suddenly the candle extinguished, and she was taken by the spirit and lowered to the midst of the well. She was then lifted up from there into the air; she did not know what he was, nor why, nor how. She screamed and fainted. The members of her household carried her to her bed and sought a remedy for her wound. Suddenly the spirit reascended before our eyes, causing great pain and suffering to that girl. He did not allow her to speak further.

This was what happened, and other events of this kind—and even more shocking—were told to me, and I have also seen them signed, one of them from the sages of Safed *tvb"b*, that happened there. Another was from the sages of Italy, regarding a case in Ancona involving the spirits of men executed by hanging that entered the people's bodies; by means of adjurations and fumigations of sulfur and such in their nostrils, the spirits would make known and reveal their names and tell of their matters, of all their experiences, of the place of their dwelling, and of the sins for which they have [been punished to] enter the bodies and wander. Others have testified that all their words are true and that by means of adjurations they expelled them from the bodies and that the place from which the spirit exits swells.

## 9. The Spirit in the Daughter of R. Raphael Anav: The Popular Account

An event in Damascus involving the daughter of the precious and elevated Rabbi Raphael Anav, while she was still a virgin in her father's house.[9] Sabbath eve at dusk she ate the head of a fish and suddenly fainted and fell upon the sick bed. They covered her face.

They lit two candles, as was their custom every Sabbath. Now, her father and mother and the servants standing there, seeing this, they grieved and were shocked. Rabbi Jacob Aliman Ashkenazi was also there.

Now, before the day was sanctified, they heard a voice speaking from within her mouth, from that same daughter. It called for Rabbi Raphael and told him to come close to her. Then, when he had drawn closer, it said to him, "Why did you set up only those two candles?" Rabbi Raphael responded and said to him that he had done so because such was his custom every Sabbath. The spirit said to him that this Sabbath was not like other Sabbaths and that it was necessary to be exceedingly joyous. R. Raphael said to him that another candle would be set up. Thus was it done. They then lit the candles. Afterward, he requested a chair for Elijah the Prophet, remembered for good; he requested another chair for the sage Rabbi Joseph Karo *z"l*, and another chair for the sage Rabbi Isaac Karo *z"l*. Thus until seven chairs [were set], for seven sages.

Afterward, he sent them to the synagogue to pray *'aravit* [the evening prayer], and commanded Rabbi Jacob not to reveal a thing of what he had heard and seen. When he went to his house to dress in his Sabbath clothes, his wife asked him why he had been delayed in coming. He responded to her that he had been with his honor Rabbi Raphael Anav, engaging in business.

His wife said to him that this could not be true, for on the Sabbath it is forbidden to speak about business. She pressured him greatly until he said to her that he had been delayed because the evil spirit of a sage had entered the daughter of R. Raphael. His wife said to him, "If he is a sage, why did you call him an evil spirit?"

In the meantime, they left the synagogue. Rabbi Jacob came and called to the doorway for R. Raphael. The spirit said, "This one who calls, R. Jacob, is a fool, for I commanded him not to say a word—and he told everything to his wife. She is more astute than he, for she objected to his words and told him, why did he say 'evil spirit' if he is a sage?" And the spirit was angry at him and cursed him. Everyone pleaded with the spirit and kissed his hands and his feet until he forgave him. Afterward, Rabbi Jacob came in and hid himself between the barrels of wine that were in the storeroom. The spirit said that they should call him. He also said, "Behold this man, who in his limited knowledge thinks that I do not see him among the barrels."

Afterward, the spirit requested a cup full of wine, over which to say kiddush. He sat upon the bed and said kiddush in a loud voice, and they all ate. They then said *birkat ha-mazon* [grace after meals]. All night, no one was able to sleep, [so anxious were they] to see what would be the end of this affair.

Now, immediately after the middle of the night, the spirit called out to them and said, "Go after our teacher, the Rav Rabbi Ḥayyim Vital, and tell him that I want to speak to him." And they responded to the spirit that they were afraid of encountering the Sovasi [Turkish police]. He told them not be afraid, for he would go with them. All this notwithstanding, they did not go. Some two hours before daybreak, he called them a second time and said to them that they should go and see our teacher the Rav Rabbi Ḥayyim Vital, for the Sovasi have already departed from the Jewish market. They responded that they knew that the Rav would not come with them. Then the spirit said to them that they should go and that they would find him awake from his sleep, on his bed, with his head resting upon his hand; they should tell him that he should come, for he has now dreamt and is startled over not remembering the dream. He should come to me, and I will remind him of it and explain the dream to him.

Now, this time they listened, and they went to our teacher, the Rav Rabbi Ḥayyim Vital *zlh"h*, and found him just as the spirit had said. They conveyed to him the message of the spirit who sent them. He donned his clothes and came to the spirit, who paid him great respect. They greeted one another.

The spirit said to him, "The dream that you dreamt was that a man sent you seven sages along with one sick person so that you might heal him. You forgot the dream, and this is it. Its solution: the person who sent you the seven sages is the AR"I, your teacher; the seven teachers are Elijah *z"l* and the sage Rabbi Joseph Karo *z"l* and the sage Rabbi Isaac Karo, etc. . . . And the sick person is me."

And your teacher sends you his greetings and tells you to take care to do such-and-such a thing and not to forget to do them. Now, I expect you to heal me and, in order to discharge the obligation of my mission, I will reveal to you now what is my concern.

Know that I am so-and-so who lived in Safed *tvb"b amen*. It is now forty years since my soul departed from my body. During those years, they raised me from one partition to the next. At each and every ascent they punished me for what remained, until, at the end, when they wanted to elevate me to a special partition for my type, they were punctilious over the lightest of matters. And they did not allow me to ascend, because they still found in me such-and-such a sin, which is a matter of the least significance.

Now, being outside my partition and close to it, I heard, from behind the curtain, the Supernal Court saying, "Who shall we send and who will go for us and inform the Children of Israel in Damascus that because of their sins and transgressions a plague has been decreed upon them? And someone must go and inform them so that they might repent, to fix their transgressions in order to nullify this decree from upon them." When I heard this, I said, "Here I am; send me!" They said to me, "Go and say to them all that you heard, and through this mission your damage will be fixed. And when you return from this mission, you will enter your partition."

And I left from there and sought a path to come to this world. I came by way of the Euphrates River to Botzra, near Damascus. There, I entered a fish, and a fisherman came after him and caught me. I prayed to the Lord that I not fall into the hands of Gentiles, but rather into the hands of an Israelite. The fisherman brought me with the other fish to your market. There also I pleaded and prayed to the Lord that I not fall into the hands of Gentiles, but into the hands of an Israelite, a meritorious man. It was close to sunset when Solomon Tagweil came to buy me. I prayed to Hashem that he not put me into the hands of an evil one like him. And Hashem heard the voice of my plea and gave my soul for my request. Then this honorable man came, the kosher man, Rabbi Raphael. He took me, brought me to his home, and commanded his wife to hurry to prepare it to honor the Sabbath. Seeing this, I was glad. When they removed the scales from the fish, I felt great pain and entered the head of the fish. When they had cooked the fish, this young virgin came and ate from its head. Since I was there, I became impregnated in her—for she is pure, a spark of Queen Esther.

After all of this, the spirit said to the sage Rabbi Ḥayyim, "Go to pray, and then immediately come back to me and I will reveal to you things that your rabbi has not yet revealed to you. And warn the people to repent, to give charity, and to fast." And the rav responded, "Who are fitting to perform a watch?" The spirit said, "The sage rabbi Jacob Abulafia would be good, but he is in Safed. And the sage Rabbi Hoshiayahu Pinto, and call the sage R. Joseph of Taron, who is a perfect man."

The sage said to him, "I will also call the sage R. Israel Najara." The spirit said to him, "Do not call this man, for he is disgusting. For although the songs that he composed gladden God and man and are received before the Lord, nevertheless he incurs dishonor for eating at the altar of the Lord with his head uncovered, wearing only a red *'arkia* alone upon it, and his arms are uncovered. And he sits with the naked [souls], and he and they eat and drink, and he is not careful about the company of the naked."

Afterward the rav R. Ḥayyim went to pray and left the synagogue and ate his feast—and did not return to the spirit.

When the time for the afternoon prayer came, he did not come. They wanted to send for him, but the spirit commanded that they not call him. "See," he said, "that the sage R. Ḥayyim acts with arrogance toward me, waiting until I call. I already told him to come immediately following the prayers. Now, I have already explained to him the whole matter of my mission and have thus fulfilled my obligation. Therefore he alone loses that which I said I would reveal to him. Now I ascend to my partition."

At the time of the afternoon prayer, a Torah scholar was preaching at the synagogue of the Sephardic Jews. The spirit said, "See this man preaching, how he chastises people for their transgressions—and he is full of various transgressions, like this and that, that he has done in his time."

When the time for *havdalah* [prayer ending the Sabbath] arrived, he said to them, "Recite *havdalah*, for the time has come for my departure from here to my portion."

"Now, in the morning, the sage R. Ḥayyim will come to speak with me. Tell him that the day that was the Sabbath I had permission to reveal secrets to him that he has never heard—and I already told him that, yet he did not come."

They said *havdalah*, and the spirit was silent. Now, in the morning, the sage R. Ḥayyim came, and they told him everything the spirit commanded, and he did not speak to him at all.

The sage R. Ḥayyim called to Joshua Albo, and he came before him and gave him a *kavvanah* so that the spirit would come and leave by way of the small toe of that girl.

Afterward, the girl began saying contradictory things. The sage R. Jacob Abulafia came from Safed, and when he heard what had happened, he went to speak with the spirit and found that its words were senseless. He told this to the rav R. Ḥayyim. He replied that the first spirit had been that of a great sage and was holy, that all of his words were true, and that he had already left and gone on his way. What the girl was saying now was due to the fact that in every place where holiness has resided, there it leaves its residue, to which impurity is attracted and to which it wishes to cling. Thus with the other holy spirit's departure from her, a spark from the *sitra aḥra* entered there, and for that reason there is now no substance to her words. Now, with the departure of that latter spirit from the maiden, she remained well and healthy as before.

## 10. *Ḥakham* Piso in the Daughter of R. Raphael Anav: Vital's Account in *Sefer ha-Ḥezyonot*

The year [53]69.[10] Something great happened in Damascus, and I will write only that which involved me. Now, on the eve of the Sabbath, the twenty-ninth of Tammuz, traumas and faintings came upon the daughter of Raphael Anav. They took her to the sorcerers, but it did not help at all. That night, which was Sabbath night and *Rosh Ḥodesh* [New Moon] of Av, after lighting the Sabbath lamp, she was stretched out like a corpse, without any feeling.

And Raphael heard a voice emerging from her mouth and saying, "Raphael, come here." And he asked, "Who are you?" And he said, "I am *Ḥakham* [Sage] Piso. Why did you light only two lamps, as is the custom—you ought to have lit many lamps in honor of the angels and the souls of the righteous who came with me to accompany me and to protect me. Therefore, prepare chairs for them, for they are six souls." And they prepared [the chairs] for them.

And he said,

Now, I am not like the rest of the spirits, for I am a sage and a righteous man. I have come only because of a minor sin that remains for me to rectify and also to be a messenger to you, to bring you to repentance given the preponderance of sins among you.

Now, it has been twenty-one days since I departed from *Gan Eden* by way of the rivers of *Gan Eden*, and I traveled underground to the rivers of Damascus. There I entered a fish, and I was caught by a fisherman. He took me to be sold on the Jewish street, on the eve of Sabbath after the afternoon prayer. And a great evildoer came there, Al Tawil, the son-in-law of Sheikh al-Yahud, and he wanted to purchase me. And Hashem, may He be blessed, sent Raphael Anav there, and he purchased me. They cut [me] into a number of pieces and gave one piece to R. Jacob Ashkenazi. On the Sabbath night they ate me, and I was in the head of the fish, and his daughter ate me and I entered her. But I did not harm her at all, for I am unlike the rest of the spirits.

They did not give me permission to reveal myself and speak until now, for it is the Sabbath and *Rosh Ḥodesh*, and I am very upset that I did not merit to ascend on this holy day to my place in *Gan Eden*. And Joshua Elbom will be in *ḥerem* for not having assisted me by means of the techniques in the book in his possession so as to bring about my ascent on the eve of the Sabbath; perhaps I would have merited to ascend. Now, I will be delayed only this one day, for on it alone they have given me permission to speak, and immediately on Sunday morning I will return to *Gan Eden* to my place. Now, all the angels and aforementioned souls wait for R. Ḥayyim the kabbalist to do his bidding by means of him. So call him, and he will come.

And Raphael did not want to come then, for it was at night.

He said to him, "Do not worry about what has happened in your house, for I am a holy spirit; eat and say *kiddush* [sanctification of the day over a glass of wine]." He said *kiddush*. He said to him, "Why were you not careful to place water in the *kiddush* cup?"

And R. Jacob went to his house, and he said to him, "Beware of [my placing you under] *ḥerem*, and do not say a word."

When he returned after eating, he said, "Do not allow this excommunicate in here, for he transgressed my [threat of] *ḥerem*." Raphael also said to him, "Do not come in; perhaps you ate saffron, which is bad for these things." He said, "I did not eat saffron." The spirit said to him, "You are also a liar—for indeed you ate fish! Also, your wife is better than you are, for when she asked you why you were delayed, you said, 'Because of the evil spirit that went into so-and-so.' And your wife was more correct than you were, and said to you, 'If you say that he is a sage, how do you refer to him as an evil spirit?' " Afterward he said to him, "I knew you were a simpleton and a fool, so come in." He came in.

He began telling all of the members of the household a few of their sins. He also told the sins of those who died in that plague. Throughout the first half of the night, it seemed to them that there were flames of fire in the house. R. Jacob dozed and felt as if he were being strangled. He awoke. In the middle of the night he said, "I have already fasted for three days over the pain I went through in this *gilgul* and it is inappropriate to fast on Shabbat as well. Give me water to drink and an apple to eat." They gave him. He said to them, "Now sleep a little."

They slept until daybreak. He awakened them and said, "The morning is approaching; call for R. Ḥayyim." They did not want to, until he decreed *ḥerem* upon them and said to them, "If he does not believe you, give him a sign, for this night at the morning watch he dreamt a great dream and he does not know its meaning and is upset. Now, you will find him dressed with his head upon the ground, thinking about that dream. Let me come to me and I will tell him."

Now what I myself dreamt was that I saw six righteous men coming from the World to Come to my house, and they brought me a scholar to heal. And I forgot who they were.

Then Raphael and R. Jacob came and they told me all that was mentioned, and I went with them. When I entered the doorway, he said to me three time, "Blessed is he who comes!"

I came near to the girl; there was a veil upon her face, and she was like a dead corpse. I said to him, "From where do you know me?" He said, "Are you not R. Ḥayyim the kabbalist?" I said to him, "And who are you?" He said, "I am *Ḥakham* Piso." I compelled him to tell me his name, until he told in a whisper: "I am Jacob Piso, and, in Jerusalem, I was married to the daughter of the sage R. Isaac Ashkenazi. My wife's sister is Esther. I passed away 35 years ago and ascended to my place in *Gan Eden*, and there I remained until now. There remains for me to fix one small matter, and I have come now to fix it. Therefore, woe to him who is not careful in this world about even the lightest sin, so that he not come to this ordeal that I am now undergoing." And it appears to me, Ḥayyim, that his sin was that he made the masses sin by blocking them from paths of repentance, and that he has now come to fix the matter of repentance.

"Now this is the dream that you dreamt: I am the scholar sent to you from the heavens for you to heal and for whom you must pray by means of the six souls who are sitting by you, and they are Elijah *z"l*, and the sage R. Joseph Karo, R. Samuel Amron, R. Aaron ibn Tipah, the sage Atiah, and the sage Arḥa. And even though I learn with *mhr"r* Isaac Luria, your teacher *z"l*, he did not come with the aforementioned souls, but he is there above praying for me. Now, you know that there is no ability in the supernal realms to improve except by means of the prayers of the righteous in this world. Therefore all are waiting upon you and are in need of you. Thus pray for me and heal me. For does his honor [lit., the honor of his Torah] not see the great fire burning the world?"

I said, "Would you like me to gather all the inhabitants of the city before you?" He said to me, "Would that they would come and fast for three fasts of Monday, Thursday and Monday, just like Yom Kippur, men and women—perhaps the Lord will return from his wrath upon you over the numerous sins among you." Said the writer, Ḥayyim, "This teaches what I wrote above, that his sin was impeding repentance and that he came to fix that. It had to be through me, however, because I am still in this world. Enough said for one who understands." I said to him, "But the people of Damascus do not value my sermons." He said to me, "All of this is already revealed before the Blessed Holy One." I said, "If so, I will gather the scholars alone." He said to me, "That is good." I said, "I do not know whom to gather."

He said to me, "Do not bring before me any sage from the *Mustaravim* but only Sephardic scholars, except for Israel Najara—he must not see my face."

I said, "I will go and pray." He said to me, "This matter is greater than prayer." I said, "I do not cancel prayer under any circumstances; thereafter may the Lord have mercy." He said to me, "And does not his honor want to have mercy on my suffering and fix that which I have said? What shall I do?" And I went to pray. I went and ate the morning meal, and I expected Raphael to come back to call me—but he did not come. I could not decide whether to go there or not. So I sent for R. Jacob, and he came and said to me, "I did not go there."

We sat until *Minḥa* [the afternoon prayer]. Then the spirit said to Raphael, "See, the sage thinks about coming here and sent for so-and-so." After *Minḥa*, R. J[acob] went there and the spirit said to them, "Now, the sage did not want to come and scrupulously avoided coming to me—and pride is unfit for anyone besides the Holy Blessed One. A person should not say, 'I do not want to drink from those waters,' for perhaps he will have to drink from them. Now, the whole matter of my mission was only for his sake, for they sent me from the heavens to reveal to him mysteries of the supernal heavens, matters that he did not know from his teacher *z"l*, and also to bring the world to repentance, for the fixing of the whole world depends upon him, and I came to reveal to him matters pertaining to the Messiah, for his coming hangs only upon a hair.

Now, he always preaches that people ought to repent so that the Messiah might come, and R. J. Abulafia, out of envy, says to the people, "Lies he speaks, since the Messiah is not coming in this generation." Woe to him, for his punishment is great, for because of his words and the great sins of this city, heavy and thick chains of iron have been fastened upon the Messiah, and he will be delayed for another twelve years. And during this time many sufferings will befall Damascus and it will be overturned like Sodom and also Jerusalem will be burnt—but Safed will survive. Thereafter Gog and Magog will come, and then the Messiah will come with "eight princes of men" (Mic. 5:4). And the sage preached three sermons last year before the plague and they repented a bit. Since he prevented himself from preaching further, his beloved daughter died in the plague—and she was a great soul. However, his small son will be a great rabbi in Israel.

Here, however, he has lost a chance to hear supernal mysteries—for on that account they sent me from the heavens—and when he seeks me he will not find me, for I was given permission to speak on this day alone and tomorrow I will return to my place.

Saturday night after the Sabbath he did not speak any more. In the morning, they came and told me all that he said and I went there. And he did not want to speak further. He said to me, "I now return to my place." And he gave signs like the spirits when they depart, and he departed and did not return again.

However, when he said himself that he was leaving, Joshua Bom was standing there and carried out his adjurations, and afterward he left.

Upon his departure, I said to him, "Write such-and-such an amulet that is in your book such-and-such and hang it upon the girl, so that harmful spirits do not harm her after his departure." And so he did.

I will now write that which I did by means of R. J. Bom. Thereafter I will write other matters relating to the girl above. And this is the matter:

**§23.** On the Friday of the aforementioned Av, Rabbi J. Bom brought down an angel from the servants of Ẓadkiel, the minister of that day, and he was revealed in a glass mirror, as is the custom. I asked him whether the wisdom of my teacher *z"l* the Ashkenazi—and also that about which he spoke with me regarding my soul and my apprehension—was true. He said, "All of his words are true." I said, "With regard to the soul of a *ẓaddik* speaking to me by means of *yiḥudim*—is that true, or imaginary?" He said that the speech was true, but that sometimes the soul of a *ẓaddik* enters my heart and raises his speech to my mouth and I hear; at other times he remains outside and comes close to me and speaks to me. I said, "Why has he [the AR"I] distanced himself from me for such a long time?" He said to me,

It is your own fault. Since in the beginning you distanced all matters of this world from your heart and adhered supremely to your maker. You would unify *yiḥudim* and engage all day in Torah study and admonish the people. Now you have abandoned everything, and he too has abandoned you. For you know what your teachers and others said to you also—that all of the world depends upon you, and that you did not come into the world but to bring the people to repentance, and that redemption depends upon you. And you have already tried this for ten years, during which time you lectured and admonished the people. Some repented, and your words were heeded; yet when you abandoned them, they strayed from the path and many of them died in their sins. The transgression is hanging from your neck. And now you have distanced yourself entirely and you have isolated yourself in an unobtrusive corner.

A number of people dream wondrous dreams and tell them to you. All of this is from the Lord, may He be blessed, in order to strengthen your heart. Nevertheless your heart still dithers and you do not believe strongly in those dreams. Know that your place in the Garden of Eden is beside your Rabbi the Ashkenazi and two other *ẓaddikim* from the great ancient *Tannaim*. And you are a perfect *ẓaddik* before the Blessed Holy One, except for that which I have said, and this is the cause of the silence of that *ẓaddik* [who has entered you as an *'ibbur*] by means of the *yiḥudim*. Your rabbi is also a bit angry with you and you therefore do not have dream contact with him as you did at first. But if you return to your devotions, you will attain all that you desire without a doubt. But there is still one other small sin in you, and we have no permission to reveal it before those standing here, without your permission. Now, your beloved daughter was a great soul and died in the plague for that sin. Also, we have no permission to reveal the name of the *ẓaddik* who speaks with you before these people, because of his honor. Nevertheless, his name has four letters. Now, the *yiḥud* most appropriate for you now is the seventh *yiḥud* of *MT"T* that is written in your book, and also the *yiḥud* of your rabbi *z"l*. So too the *ẓaddik* most appropriate for you now is Samuel the prophet, notwithstanding that he is very great in your eyes.

Know that if you do not heed our words—and bring the nation to repentance, having them fast Monday and Thursday and Monday, just as on Yom Kippur, with fasting and crying . . . —great sorrow will come upon you. Those who dwell in Damascus will also be visited by tremendous sorrows.

Now, the Holy One, blessed be He, only sent the spirit into the daughter of Rafael Anav in order to bring the people of Damascus to penitence, for he was the spirit of a great pietist in his place in *Gan Eden*. For a minor sin that he still had to fix they sent him down a river to receive his punishment. There he became enclothed in a fish, and Raphael purchased him. When his daughter ate his head, he entered her and dwelled in her for twelve days. On Sunday, *Rosh Ḥodesh* Av, the time for his ascent arrived and he arose on his own, rather than by means of any person. On the Sabbath day before, he sent after you in the morning and you went there. After that, you did not return there until Sunday, when the time for his ascent had already arrived. He had wanted to reveal to you supernal mysteries. His intention was entirely that you bring the world to repentance. A number of souls and angels descended with him on Sabbath eve, and they all were waiting for you, to speak with you about this, and you did not believe their words, and you lost all of those mysteries. Now, the Blessed Holy One sent them only so that the people might hear the act of God, for He is awesome, and thereby repent—perhaps the Lord will turn back from His wrath upon them, for in the future a great evil will come upon them from the number of transgressions that are among them. The Holy One, blessed be He, also knows that the men of Damascus will not listen to your voice, for there are great transgressions in their hands that impede their repentance. Do that which it is upon you to do, and gather ten men, the worthiest that you can find—even if they are not fully worthy—and bring them to repent. Also do that which it is in your power to do to bring the people to repentance. And the hearer will hear and the fearer will fear, and you—you will have saved your soul.

Now, in §22 I wrote regarding the spirit itself in the daughter of Raphael Anav, that which I saw with my eyes, and that which R. Raphael and R. J. Ashkenazi told me. All of this was on the Sabbath, *Rosh Ḥodesh* Av. On Sunday morning he departed without a doubt and ascended to his place.

Afterward, other things happened, and not by the aforementioned spirit while he was still enclothed in her, for he already departed and the maiden remained completely healthy. But she says that sometimes she sees visions, while awake and in the dream state, by means of souls and angels and also, infrequently, by means of the aforementioned spirit.

For that reason, I have doubts about whether these words of hers are truthful or if they are a mixture of good and evil for the above reason, and also for another reason: since I did not see this with my own eyes, as I saw at first. What astounded me, however, was that all of her words are only for repentance and fear of God and words of admonition. For that reason I will not desist from writing them from the mouths of men of truth who were there.

And these are those [words]: She said that after the spirit left her, she would always see a particular angel in her dream leading her to *Gan Eden* and to Gehinnom and who would show her the places of the righteous. In most of these visions, they tell her that she should warn me to bring the men of Damascus to repentance—perhaps the Lord will turn back from his wrath upon them.

On the Sabbath day, the twenty-eighth of Av. The spirit said that it was true that he was unable to ascend to his place in the Garden of Eden until Sunday morning. However, if R. J. Bom had assisted him to depart by means of adjurations on Friday, he would have then entered a glass vial and dwelled there all day on the Sabbath. After that they would wash it inside before using it, so that they would not be harmed, for he had entered it.

The night of the seventh of Av. They told her to tell me that at first the soul of one Tanna would always be revealed to me by means of a unification with which I would bind myself to him. It has now been a long time—two and one-half years—that, for two reasons, he is not revealed to me. First, that I abandoned the aforementioned unifications, and second, that I abandoned my sermons of admonishment to the people, and [my attempt] to turn them in repentance as in former days. And for these very two reasons, my daughter died in this plague.

The night of the eighth of Av. Elijah, may he rest in peace, said to her while awake at the time of the Holy Sabbath, "Tell Rabbi Ḥayyim and the rest of the sages of the city how they are failing in all that they heard, and that now a great evil will come on account of this to those who dwell in Damascus, and in particular to R. Ḥayyim. Also tell him: Why did you sin on that Friday in [the month of] Av to bring down an angel in a flask to question him—does he not believe in all of the words that we spoke to him by means of the aforementioned spirit? And verily his teacher too, *z"l*, in his lifetime told him that he did not come into the world for any reason other than to bring the people to repentance, and also the angel that he drew down told him all of this, and still he wavers and does not believe entirely? I fear for him that there will come upon him, God forbid, many sorrows, for his stubbornness."

The tenth day of Av. I asked her via her father why the righteous one who is known to me has desisted from speaking with me, and what was his name, and whether there was any hope of bringing about his return. She responded to me that on the eve of the eleventh of Av she saw my teacher, may his memory be a blessing, and he said to her, "Tell him in my name that he should not continue to ask these questions so many times, and that I cannot respond to him with any response other than this—are they not these three words: *Ashrei* (happy), *maytim* (the dead/those who die), *be-veitekha* (in your house), and he will understand the meaning of the things himself."

The night of the twelfth of Av. In a dream, she saw my teacher *z"l* in a cave. And he said to her, "What did Rabbi Ḥayyim respond to you?" She told him, "He said to me that he did not understand those three words." He said to her, "Something so simple as this? Has his intellect been sealed and he did not understand? Where is the wisdom that I taught him? And he should well remember that same evil spirit that I removed from him. It has now been four years during which time he has not seen me in a dream. Now, I had considered returning to him, but because he did not understand the words of my response I do not want to return to him."

And it seems, to the extent of my poor knowledge, that the meaning of the matter of the evil spirit mentioned is the matter of the resurrection of the dead. For he revived me when we went to Kfar Akhbara, since that spirit in the grave of the Gentile injured me. Otherwise, it refers to how my mouth was bent during the first unification I practiced.

The twenty-forth day of Av. Raphael went to Sinim [Tripoli El-Sham], and Rachel Aberlin went to visit them. And his daughter told her that on the Sabbath of *Rosh Ḥodesh* Av all of the sought-after intention of that spirit was toward me, and to me he was sent. Afterward, when I did not want to do his will, as said above, and I did not return there, he denounced me over three things. First, when I went there I thought he was an evil spirit, like the other spirits of evil people. Therefore I did not pay respect to him and spoke to him degradingly. Second, I did not believe his words when he told me that there were angels and souls there who were all waiting for my prayer, and I did not remain there, and I departed. Third, I did not return there afterward to speak with him. Now, he came on the mission of the Holy One, blessed be He, to tell me wondrous things and supernal mysteries. Therefore I have lost them, and I shall ultimately regret this; and when I seek, I shall not find.

*Rosh Ḥodesh* Kislev 5370 [Friday, 27 November 1619]. Raphael came from Sinim and told me that my teacher *z"l* appeared to his daughter while awake and said to her, "Say to Rabbi Ḥayyim that he is sad that he did not succeed with his sermons before the people of Damascus in the month of Elul. At first I was angry with him, because he did not want to listen to the words of that spirit, and he waited until Abulafia would come from Safed, and thereby ruined the matter. For when the spirit spoke with him it was a time of grace, and afterward his time passed; for that reason he did not succeed in his sermons. However, all of that notwithstanding, his sermons already have been found acceptable before the Holy One, blessed be He, even though they did not succeed."

I will now write that which happened to Rabbi Jacob Abulafia with that spirit, after he already departed from her body, as said above. Now, I was prevented from bringing the people [to repent] because he was not then in the region, and I thought that by the two of us the matter would be fixed. The reverse was the case. For with his coming, everything was destroyed.

Now, he came on Sabbath eve, the fifteenth of Av, and so that I not accrue honor by the words of that spirit, he made a vanity of it all in the eyes of the people.

Then, on Monday the seventeenth of Av, that spirit was revealed to the daughter of Raphael, and told her that she should decree a *niddui* upon her father in his name, that he not taste a smidgen Tuesday morning until bringing Abulafia there after the [morning] prayer to admonish him on what has been mentioned. Tuesday morning, after the prayer, he called him, and he sat for fully half the day being admonished. Raphael, his daughter, all their household, other women, R. Y. Bom, and Bez̤alel and Farjalla his brother were present; other people were on the roof in order to hear. Then the maiden said to R. J. Bom, "Bring the glass mirror before me and I will draw down the angel Z̤adkiel who rules this day." That angel then became visible, and four souls of sages are witnesses to the matter, and they are R. Joseph Z̤iag and Rabbi Yiz̤ḥak Karo and Rabbi Samuel Amron and Rabbi Aaron ibn Tipah. The maiden looked into the mirror and saw them and spoke with them. The angel said to her, "I do not want to admonish him myself, since R. J. Abulafia will not believe wondrous things through allusion in a mirror but only clear words from the mouth of the spirit who has enclothed himself in the mouth of the girl. Also, since from the beginning he himself came on this mission from above, I shall therefore ascend to summon him." Then he went, and was delayed there a little, and returned and descended into the mirror with the four witnesses. He said to her, "Tell R. Jacob Abulafia, Bez̤alel, and Farjalla that they should go out to the courtyard until the spirit enters the maiden." The three of them went out to the courtyard, and the spirit enclothed itself in the maiden, and she fainted in the manner of the falling. Afterward, the spirit enclothed himself, started to speak, and said, "Tell R. J. Abulafia to come close to this window from outside." He drew close and said to him, "Why did you not enclothe yourself until you sent me out?" He said to him, "Because you are not worthy to see me when I am dressing, for you are a sinner. And now the Messiah is angry with you, for you always jest about the matter of the coming of the Messiah, and say, 'The Messiah will not come in this generation.' And when Rabbi Ḥayyim the kabbalist preaches repentance to the people together with matters of the Messiah, you ridicule him and make his words vane because of your envy of him. If you are a sage in your own eyes, give me a reason for the commandments of Passover and Shavuot and Rosh ha-Shanah and Sukkot. . . ." And he told him those same simple reasons that everybody knows. He said to him,

Those things are known to simpletons; if you want to know the truth, what you ought to do is to listen to the mysteries of Torah from Rabbi Ḥayyim. Now, he had wanted to preach before and to admonish the people on the Sabbath day, and you prevented him, and withheld repentance from Israel. Woe to you, the sages of this era, who do not turn the people in repentance!

Now, I have also seen abominations among the sages of Egypt, for there is no wisdom among them at all, and they destroy the city with perversions of judgment. And the people of Egypt have servants serving them, and when the men leave their homes, the servants sleep with their wives. They also warm the food on the Sabbath day, and more of the same. Now, anyone who goes to Egypt at present, even to engage in trade, they ban him from above, and ultimately he will lose all of his money because of the evils there. Moreover, the sword will also fall in Venice in the future for seven consecutive days, and great righteous sages, the likes of which are not in this city, will be killed there. The end of the matter: woe to you, sages of the generation, that you have pride and contempt, and you do not watch over the honor of the Holy One, blessed be He, to bring the people to repentance; you cause great evil in the world.

R. Jacob Abulafia was then somewhat humbled, and tears dropped from his eyes. He said to him, "Since you have been humbled and humiliated by my having expelled you outside, it is enough." He gave him permission to enter. After he entered, he said to him,

Now, you and the inhabitants of Damascus have no share in the World to Come, God forbid, for a few reasons: for causing the people to sin by making them take oaths over taxes and their worth, that is, how much money each one has, [causing them] to make false oaths—and you already know that they take false oaths. What is more, your wives go about brazenly with garments and jewelry of shame—like those with caps upon their heads and revealed breasts—and whose bosoms are filled with clothes to show their large breasts; with trailing shawls and fine veils to show off their bodies. They put on wild orange and other varieties of perfumes and scents to arouse the evil desire in men. All of this they parade through the markets and streets to show the nations their beauty. They also admonished your sons and prevented them from transgressions. And now forty-eight people perform transgressions with Gentile women, and married women, and sodomize, aside from other transgressions.

And he counted all of them, but they told me about these alone, and they are:

Elijah Ḥafetz and the Gandor boys and a son of Koreidi and Avraham Moẓeiri—these sleep with Gentile women; and the daughter of Komeiri the apostate fornicates with Joshua Koresh and many other men; and R. Jacob Monedas sodomizes Nathan Kulief, and now he has given him his daughter and she still fornicates with him—and woe to Jacob, for his cheeks are black in the World to Come as tar from the number of his crimes and he has no portion in the World to Come; and Jacob Uzida, your brother-in-law, transgressed with the girl so-and-so; and Nissim Menasseh has no share whatsoever in the World to Come and he has no advocate in heaven, and anyone who does a favor for him, even to heal him from this sickness which has befallen him from heaven by means of the evil spirit, is worthy of being split by a saw. And Rafael Kulif and his son Michael transgress with Israelite and Gentile women. Now, on the last Sabbath eve a scholar referred to as a "sage" among the community of Sephardim slept with a Gentile woman in Gubar.

Afterward we investigated who was there on the stove that was there, and it became known that it was Avraham the son of R. M. Galante, for he and his wife slept there along with a Gentile woman, the owner of the house. "And the wife of Meir Peretz and her daughter are utter prostitutes, bringing many to sin. And R. David Gavizon sins much, for he left his modest wife here and married a whore in Egypt; because of his sins, his modest wife and daughter-in-law died." And another person said to me that he also said about him that in Egypt he sinned with prostitutes and lost his World [to Come]; perhaps that is the matter of the wife he took in Egypt.

And now R. I. Najara. It is true that the songs that he composed are good in themselves, but it is forbidden for anyone to talk with him or for anyone to allow one of the songs he composed to come out of his mouth. For Najara's mouth is constantly speaking filthily, and he is perpetually drunk. Now, on such-and-such a day, which was during the period of mourning "between the straits," he made a feast at such-and-such a time at the home of Jacob Monedias and placed his hat on the ground and sang songs in a loud voice and ate meat and drank wine, and even got drunk—and how does he decree watches in Gubar and preach repentance to them? And I, Ḥayyim, told him about this matter and he acknowledged that such indeed had happened. "Now too, when he was fleeing from the plague, he engaged in sodomy from the extent of his drunkenness. And on the Sabbath day he sinned twice: first, when he fought with his wife and expelled her from his house, and second, afterward, when a Gentile woman came into his house and roasted fresh figs on the fire on the Sabbath; afterward he slept with her. Therefore it is forbidden to give him any benefit and forbidden to give him any marriage or divorce contracts to write, and it is almost appropriate to repudiate them. His young son also copulated with a Gentile and is a total sinner, may his bones be pulverized. But his eldest son does not sin.

"Now, there is much sodomy in this region, and there is also much perversion of justice in the region." R. J. Abulafia responded to him, "And how do you know all of this?" He said to him, "Your son Moses, he and Menachem Romano brought a Gentile woman to a certain house on the last festival of

Shavuot, before going to Ẓova, and slept with her." He said to him, " 'Is it possible that my son sinned this way?" He said to him, " 'The sons have inherited the acts of their fathers.' Did you not do in your youth things that were not good?" He said to him, "If so, then I will go to Safed." He said to him, "You have destroyed Damascus, and you want to go now to destroy Safed as well? First fix the destruction of Safed, and afterward go wherever you want." He said to him, "I will wait until the month of Elul, which is the time for repentance." He said to him, "You have spoken well, but your mouth and your heart are not the same, for you do not believe in those very words. Now, when I spoke with R. Ḥayyim the kabbalist he was shilly-shallying at first, until he drew down the angel, and then he believed and accepted [his responsibility] to bring the people to repentance. But you do not believe at all. Therefore, in any case, gather together all the sages of the city and bring the people to repentance. Leave R. Ḥayyim the kabbalist and do not summon him since he did not believe at first, and fast seven days." He said to him, "But the seventh day is Shabbat!"[11] He said to him,

> And is it as if you keep all of the commandments? Now, for the needs of the present, as the wrath of the Lord is upon you, you must all fast on the Sabbath as well. But do not preach sermons. Rather, prolong penitential prayers all day, supplications, and cries. And if you do not do this, know that harsh decrees will come upon the dwellers of Damascus, in particular a fierce starvation, during which people will eat the flesh of their own arms. And this matter I decree upon you with *ḥerem* and *niddui*. Now, if there was among you a perfect righteous and holy person, a holy angel would reveal himself to him to speak with him mouth to mouth of all these things.

Also among his words [he mentioned] that Joshua Bom knows and is expert in the matter of adjuring spirits and demons from that which he received from R. David the Mughrabi his teacher, who was a God-fearer and an expert sage. And this student of his, if he so desires, could heal Simon the epileptic, the brother of Beẓalel.

After the spirit ascended, R. Jacob Abulafia decreed a *ḥerem Kol-Bo* on those standing there that they not reveal a word because of his honor and the honor of others mentioned by spirit. And they did not respect his *ḥerem* and revealed the matters; it was then necessary for him to acknowledge [what happened]. However, he cast aspersion upon the holy, since his honor was damaged, and he let out about him a rumor that he said "as if all the Torah is true?" And on this he built traps and bans, and he banned the aforementioned spirit before the community for having slandered the righteous. Afterward the daughter of Raphael sent him a message from Sinim, in the name of the spirit, that the aforementioned spirit stood every day in the Supernal Yeshiva, banning him and all who agree with him in what he did.

## 11. The Spirit in Egypt

Said the youth Samuel Vital: today I will give expression to enigmas, as I relate that which happened to me in Egypt [Cairo], may God protect it.[12] This happened to Esther, blessed among women, daughter of R. Yehuda Weiser, may the Lord protect him and grant him life; she was stricken and remained in her stricken state with heart pain for more than two months following her marriage.

One day thereafter, they compelled me to go and visit her. I went to visit her and found her in the manner of the stricken, and I was in doubt as to whether it was a *mazzik*, or a demon, or an evil spirit of an Israelite.

I advised them to bring a cleric from the Gentiles to visit her, and thus they did. In the middle of the matter, the *mazzik* which was within her spoke in a loud voice and said that he was a Gentile and that he had entered her out of his lust for her. Among other things, he said that he had, with a small blow, struck me in my thigh—for that reason I have had pain in my thigh—so that I would be unable to go to heal her.

Afterward, the Gentile cleric toiled over her and said that he had already conquered the *mazzik* with a small flask and buried it in the earth, which is how he deals with them.

Then, all of the sudden, a voice cried from the mouth of the maiden and spoke and said, "I have been left by myself, alone in the body of this maiden, and I am the spirit of a Jew! Therefore hurry, and call to me the Sage R. Samuel Vital, may the Lord protect him and grant him life, in order that he heal me and remove me from this."

Immediately they called me, and I was obliged to go to her out of the honor of those who came. At the time I approached her, I was still uncertain as to whether it was a Jewish spirit, or a demon, or a *mazzik*, and I sat by his side. She was lying like a silent stone, covered in a white sheet. Out of uncertainty I said, "*Shalom* upon Israel." Immediately, the lips of the maiden moved and she responded to me, "Blessed is he who comes, *shalom* upon you, blessing and goodness." I said to him, "You are a Jew?" He responded, "Yes." I said to him, "If you are a Jew, say *Shema Yisrael* (Deut. 6)." He then said *Shema Yisrael*. . . .

I then began to speak with him, and he responded to me appropriately, all that I asked of him, until I had asked him who he was, and who his father was, and what land he came from, and when he died, and how he was buried, and how many years he lived, and what his punishment was, and what his sin was, and who the transmigrant here was, whether the soul [*nefesh*] or the spirit [*ruaḥ*], and who was appointed over him, and whether he sits alone here, or if he has a watchman over him. To everything he responded properly and rightly, with nothing perverted or twisted about his words, and without my having had to decree upon him a decree like the rest of the spirits, their ways being known to all those cognizant of science.

Afterward I asked him, "Now what do you want?" He responded that I fix him and remove him from this body with my great wisdom, for he recognized me from that which they decreed upon me in heaven. I said, "If so, how did you praise yourself, and say, 'I struck the sage Samuel in his hip, so that he would not come to me again'?" He responded that it was not him, God forbid, but "that Gentile *mazzik* who was with me." It was he who said that he struck me, and he lied and deceived; in order to glorify himself he said this. But he does not have the ability, God forbid, to touch me. I said to him, "If so, why did you come to me in a dream of the night on Monday night, the seventeenth of Tammuz, and afflict me?" He responded, "True, I was the one who came, but the one who afflicted you was that Gentile *mazzik*; I did not sin against you at all."

I said, "And you, why did you come with him?" He responded, "To request of you that you fix me, finally." I said, "Now, what do you want?" He responded, "It is my will that you fix my soul and my spirit and that you remove me from this body." I said, "Thus will I do tomorrow." He answered back and said, "Why delay, with two suffering spirits like this, my spirit, and the spirit of this maiden? It is within your power to do so." He petitioned me greatly. Finally, I adjured him with a severe adjuration not to deceive and depart, only to return and (re)enter her; and also that in his departure he not injure the maiden herself, nor her family, nor those standing there at the time of his departure from the body, nor anyone of Israel; and also that he not remain any longer here in Egypt but rather that he go immediately on his way to Gehinnom to be healed there. Aside from this, I decreed upon him all of the above with *ḥerem* and *niddui*. . . . Afterward, I said to him that he give us a true sign in his departure and that he say "*shalom aleikhem*" during his departure. And thus he did, and thus he spoke, three times.

Afterward, I summoned ten scholars to be present, and I started to feel his right pulse, and I intended the verse "Appoint over him a wicked man, and may Satan stand at his right" (Ps. 109:6) as it is written by me at length, and also other intentions known to me to fix his soul and his spirit. His lips then fluttered, and he said aloud with us first the Psalm "The Lord answer thee in the day of trouble" (Ps. 20) in its entirety. And the Psalm "let the graciousness of the Lord our God be upon us" (Ps. 90), "O thou that dwellest in the covert of the Most High" (Ps. 91), [and] *Ana Be-koaḥ* [the prayer of R. Neḥuniah ben HaKana, the acrostic of which forms the forty-two-letter divine Name], in its entirety. And I intended the name *KR"'A ST"N.* And afterward "Answer me when I call, O God of my righteousness, [Thou who didst set me free when I was in distress]. . . ." (Ps. 4)

And afterward this prayer: In the name of the unique God, You are great, and great is Your Name in strength. Please Lord, the honored and awesome, the majestic and beautiful and sanctified, the exalted and blessed, the examiner and inquirer, the straightened and the lofty, the hidden and concealed, the mighty in seventy-two names, the one unique, clear and pure, the hearer of cries, the receiver of prayers, who answers in times of suffering, incline Your ear to my prayer, to my supplication, and to my plea that I pray before You and ask of You. And You will hear from heaven, the place of Your dwelling, and receive with mercy and goodwill this spirit who remains before us, transmigrated in this maiden, who is called so-and-so daughter of so-and-so, who is called so-and-so, and receive our prayers that we pray for him to fix his soul and his spirit. Remove him from this transmigration, and bring about his admission to the judgment of Gehinnom, and allow his soul and his spirit to escape from the catapult of the *mazzikim* and from the suffering in which he wallows. May this transmigration and this humiliation be considered an atonement for all of his transgressions, his sins, and his crimes. May these words of ours be words of advocacy before You for this soul and this spirit, and may Your mercy prevail over Your attributes [of judgment] upon him, in our recalling before You the "Thirteen Attributes of Mercy": God King sitting on the Throne of Mercy etc. . . . And he passed over. . . . And while saying the thirteen attributes, Lord, Lord, God merciful and forgiving (Exod. 34, 6–7), blow the *shofar* [ram's horn] as is the custom of all the penitential prayers (*sliḥot*), and afterward say the thirteen attributes of Micha the prophet: Who is God like You. . . . (Micha 7:18).

Afterward say, "The tale of iniquities is too heavy for me; as for our transgressions, Thou wilt pardon them" (Ps. 65:4) and the verse "Happy is the man whom Thou choosest, and bringest near, that he may dwell in Thy courts; may we be satisfied with the goodness of Thy house, the holy place of Thy temple!" (Ps. 65:5) and the verse "And all these thy servants shall come down unto me, and bow down unto me, saying, 'Get thee out, and all the people that follow thee; and after that I will go out.' And he went out from Pharaoh in hot anger" (Exod. 11:8), and say this verse three times. Afterward say "Depart! Depart! Depart!" and intend the intentions that are in this verse, as written by me.

And immediately as I was finishing the word "Depart!" three times, he lifted the left foot of the maiden up before all the people and left from the little toe of her foot and shouted in a loud voice and said, "Unto you, peace!" three times, and I responded to him, "Go in peace! Go in peace!" three times. Immediately the maiden sat and opened her eyes and looked at me, and she was embarrassed. And she said, "What are these people doing?" For she did not know a trace of what we had done. She then kissed my hand and ate and drank.

This I accomplished on Thursday, 26 Tammuz 5426 from creation, here in Egypt. I have written all of this as a memorial to those who come after us, so that they might know that there is a God in Israel. The youth Samuel Vital.

# *Notes*

## *Introduction*

1. Michel de Certeau, "Discourse Disturbed," in *The Writing of History* (New York, 1988), 254–55.

2. For the sake of simplicity, I shall make anachronistic use of the term *dybbuk* throughout this work to refer to the Jewish possession idiom. *Dybbuk*, from the root meaning "adhere," is the abridged manner of referring to a penetrating disembodied soul, or ghost, lodged in a human body. This short form came into common usage only in late seventeenth-century Ashkenazic circles. On the history of the term, see Gershom Scholem, " '*Golem*' and '*Dibbuk*' in the Hebrew Lexicon" (in Hebrew), *Leshonenu*, 6 (1934): 40–41.

3. See Erika Bourguignon, "World Distribution and Patterns of Possession States," in *Trance and Possession States*, ed. Raymond Prince (Montreal, 1968).

4. Janice Boddy, "Spirit Possession Revisited: Beyond Instrumentality," *Annual Review of Anthropology* 23 (1994): 407–34.

5. The phrase first appears in E. W. Monter, *Witchcraft in France and Switzerland* (Ithaca, 1976), 60.

6. See Moshe Idel, "Jewish Magic from the Renaissance Period to Early Hasidism," in *Religion, Science, and Magic, in Concert and in Conflict*, ed. Jacob Neusner, Ernest S. Frerichs, and Paul Virgil McCracken Flesher (New York, 1989), 107.

7. Ibid., 108. This issue was treated in more depth in Idel's subsequent article, "On Mobility, Individuals and Groups: Prolegomenon for a Sociological Approach to Sixteenth-Century Kabbalah," *Kabbalah: Journal for the Study of Jewish Mystical Texts* 3 (1998): 145–73.

8. See H. C. Erik Midelfort, "The Devil and the German People: Reflections on the Popularity of Demon Possession in Sixteenth-Century Germany," *Religion and Culture in the Renaissance and Reformation*, vol. 11 of *Sixteenth Century Essays and Studies*, ed. Steven Ozment (Kirksville, 1989).

9. Gedalia Ibn Yaḥia, *Shalshelet ha-Kabbalah* (Venice, 1586), 86b. Ibn Yaḥia (1515–87) was an Italian Jewish loan-banker, historian, and talmudist.

10. Eliezer Ashkenazi, *Ma'asei ha-Shem* (Venice, 1583), 5a. On the circumstances surrounding Ashkenazi's receipt of the broadsheet, see Meir Benayahu, *Toledot ha-Ari, Studies and Texts* (Jerusalem, 1967), 105 n. 3. On Ashkenazi, see *Encyclopedia*

*Judaica*, s.v. "Ashkenazi, Eliezer"; Meir Benayahu and Yosef Laras, "On the Appointment of Ministers of Health in Crimona in the Year 1575" (in Hebrew), *Michael* 1 (1972): 78–133.

11. I would thus question the assertion that "all the first cases were written in a matter-of-fact style, with no evidence of wonder at the bizarre, unprecedented occurrence." See Yoram Bilu, "The Taming of the Deviants and Beyond: An Analysis of *Dibbuk* Possession and Exorcism in Judaism," in *The Psychoanalytic Study of Society*, ed. L. Bryce Boyer and Simon A. Grolnick (Hillsdale, 1985), 20 n. 9.

12. The eleventh-century work *Megillat Aḥima'aẓ* contains a story of the possession of the daughter of Emperor Basil I and her exorcism by R. Shephatiah (d. c. 886), a story that closely parallels a talmudic story (BT *Me'ilah* 17b) involving R. Shimon bar Yoḥai and the possession of another emperor's daughter. Benjamin Klar, ed., *Megillat Aḥima'az*, 2nd rev. ed. (Jerusalem, 1974), 18–19, 144–45. In this story, the emperor's daughter is being tormented by a *shed*. R. Shephatiah exorcizes the *shed* with adjurations and, upon its departure, traps it in a leaden jar, which he throws into the sea.

13. See André Goddu, "The Failure of Exorcism in the Middle Ages," in *Soziale Ordnungen im Selbstverständnis des Mittelalters*, ed. A. Zimmermann (Berlin, 1980). For a critique of this thesis, see Nancy Caciola, "Discerning Spirits: Sanctity and Possession in the Later Middle Ages" (Ph.D. diss., University of Michigan, 1994).

14. On the history of the doctrine of reincarnation in Judaism, see Gershom Scholem, "Gilgul: The Transmigration of Souls," in *On the Mystical Shape of the Godhead*, ed. Jonathan Chipman (New York, 1991).

15. My early research along these lines was published as J. H. Chajes, "Judgments Sweetened: Possession and Exorcism in Early Modern Jewish Culture," *Journal of Early Modern History* 1, no. 2 (1997): 124–69.

16. The historiography treating the European witch-hunts is vast. Among the most interesting recent works are Robin Briggs, *Witches and Neighbours: The Social and Cultural Context of European Witchcraft* (London, 1996); Stuart Clark, *Thinking with Demons: The Idea of Witchcraft in Early Modern Europe* (Oxford, 1997); Carlo Ginzburg, *Ecstasies: Deciphering the Witches' Sabbath*, trans. Raymond Rosenthal (New York, 1991).

17. The importance of this distinction has been stressed in recent historiography. See David Harley, "Explaining Salem: Calvinist Psychology and the Diagnosis of Possession," *American Historical Review* 101, no. 2 (1996): 307–30.

18. See, e.g., G. L'Estrange Ewen, *Witchcraft and Demonianism* (London, 1933), 169–73, 76–81; Brian P. Levack, *The Witch-Hunt in Early Modern Europe* (New York, 1987), 155, 58; D. P. Walker, *Unclean Spirits: Possession and Exorcism in France and England in the Late Sixteenth and Early Seventeenth Centuries* (Philadelphia, 1981), 1, 8ff.

19. The possibility that spirit possession might be brought on by maleficence indeed arises in a reponsum of the fourteenth-century Spanish scholar R. Isaac ben Sheshet Perfet. See R. Isaac ben Sheshet Perfet, *She'elot u'Teshuvot ha-RIVaSh* (Constantinople: 1547), §92.

20. Classical Jewish sources on witchcraft include, e.g., Exod. 22:17; Lev. 20:27; BT (Babylonian Talmud) *Sanhedrin* 7:4; BT *Sanhedrin* 7:11 and 67b. For a talmudic-

era "witch-hunt," see Mishna Sanhedrin 6:4, which notes the execution of eighty pagan witches in Ashkelon on a single day at the order of Simeon ben Shetaḥ.

21. See Joseph Dan, "Demonological Stories from the Writings of R. Judah the Pious" (in Hebrew), *Tarbiz* 30 (1961): 273–89. Reprinted in I. G. Marcus, *Dat ve-Hevrah be-Mishnatam shel Ḥasidei Ashkenaz* (Jerusalem, 1986), 171 n. 9.

22. See, e.g., Reuben Margalioth, ed., *Sefer Ḥasidim* (Jerusalem, 1957), §411, §680.

23. See the manuscript material adduced in Dan, "Demonological Stories from the Writings of R. Judah the Pious," 279–80 §2, §5, and n. 18.

24. On the legal developments that served as a "necessary precondition" of the great witch-hunt of early modern Europe, see Levack, *The Witch-Hunt in Early Modern Europe*, 63–92.

25. See Caciola, "Discerning Spirits: Sanctity and Possession in the Later Middle Ages."

26. See Lyndal Roper, *Oedipus and the Devil: Witchcraft, Sexuality and Religion in Early Modern Europe* (London, 1994).

27. This popular mode of analysis may be found in Midelfort, "The Devil and the German People: Reflections on the Popularity of Demon Possession in Sixteenth-Century Germany"; Walker, *Unclean Spirits: Possession and Exorcism in France and England in the Late Sixteenth and Early Seventeenth Centuries.*

28. See, e.g., Bilu, "The Taming of the Deviants and Beyond: An Analysis of *Dibbuk* Possession and Exorcism in Judaism."

29. This last phrase is Lyndal Roper's. See Roper, *Oedipus and the Devil: Witchcraft, Sexuality and Religion in Early Modern Europe.*

30. This broad issue is raised in Moshe Sluhovsky, "A Divine Apparition or Demonic Possession? Female Agency and Church Authority in Demonic Possession in Sixteenth-Century France," *Sixteenth Century Journal* 27, no. 4 (1995): 1036–52.

31. On the problem of documentation and the small number of cases on which a history of spirit possession must invariably be based, see Walker, *Unclean Spirits: Possession and Exorcism in France and England in the Late Sixteenth and Early Seventeenth Centuries*, "Introduction".

32. Midelfort, "The Devil and the German People: Reflections on the Popularity of Demon Possession in Sixteenth-Century Germany," 101, 107.

33. Walker, *Unclean Spirits: Possession and Exorcism in France and England in the Late Sixteenth and Early Seventeenth Centuries*, 3–5, 68.

34. A number of historians have adopted and refined Walker's position. See, e.g., Gregory Hanlon and Geoffrey Snow, "Exorcisms et cosmologie tridentine: trois cas agenais en 1619," *Revue de la Bibliothèque Nationale* 28 (1988): 12–27; Jonathan L. Pearl, " 'A School for Rebel Soul': Politics and Demonic Possession in France," *Historical Reflections* 16, no. 2/3 (1989): 286–306; Phillip M. Soergel, *Wondrous in His Saints: Counter-Reformation Propaganda in Bavaria* (Berkeley and Los Angeles, 1993); Marc Venard, "Le Démon controversiste," in *La controverse religieuse (XVIe–XIX siècles): Actes du ler Colloque Jean Boisset* (Montpellier, [1980]); Henri Weber, "L'Exorcisme à la fin du seizième siècle, instrument de la Contre Réforme et spectacle baroque," *Nouvelle Revue du seizième siècle* 1 (1983): 79–101.

35. Clark, *Thinking with Demons: The Idea of Witchcraft in Early Modern Europe*, 389.

36. A recent, English-language treatment of the history of the Jewish community of Safed in the early modern period may be found in Abraham David, *To Come to the Land: Immigration and Settlement in Sixteenth-Century Eretz-Israel*, trans. Dena Ordan (Tuscaloosa, 1999).

37. The literature is vast and will be cited as appropriate below. For now, in the European historiography, see, e.g., Alastair Hamilton, *Heresy and Mysticism in Sixteenth-Century Spain: The Alumbrados* (Cambridge, 1992); Richard L. Kagan, "Politics, Prophecy, and the Inquisition in Late Sixteenth-Century Spain," in *Cultural Encounters: The Impact of the Inquisition in Spain and the New World*, ed. Mary Elizabeth Perry and Anne J. Cruz (Berkeley and Los Angeles, 1991); Geraldine McKendrick and Angus MacKay, "Visionaries and Affective Spirituality during the First Half of the Sixteenth Century," in *Cultural Encounters: The Impact of the Inquisition in Spain and the New World*, ed. Mary Elizabeth Perry and Anne J. Cruz (Berkeley and Los Angeles, 1991). According to McKendrick and MacKay, visionaries must be placed "within the context of the nature and influence of Franciscan spirituality. Above all, the anti-intellectual and affective thought espoused by the Franciscans made them favorably disposed to certain aspects of female spirituality. . . . The Franciscans' attachment to an intuitive and emotional religiousity also led them to value the gift of prophecy." It would indeed be ironic if modes of Jewish spirituality in this period were influenced by Franciscan spirituality given the order's notorious hostility to Jews.

38. On Cordovero, see Bracha Sack, *Be-Sha'arei ha-Kabbalah shel Rabbi Moshe Cordovero* (Beersheva, 1995).

39. On Azikri, see Mordechai Pachter, *Milei de-Shemaya by R. Elazar Azikri* (Tel Aviv, 1991).

40. See Moshe Idel, "Investigations in the Methodology of the Author of *Sefer ha-Meshiv*" (in Hebrew), *Sefunot* 2, no. 17 (1983): 185–266; Moshe Idel, "R. Yehudah Ḥallewa and His *Ẓafnat Pa'aneaḥ*" (in Hebrew), *Shalem: Studies in the History of the Jews in Ereẓ-Israel*, edited by Joseph Hacker, 4 (1984).

41. Yosef Kaplan, "Political Concepts in the World of the Portuguese Jews of Amsterdam during the Seventeenth Century: The Problem of Exclusion and the Boundaries of Self-Identity," in *Menasseh ben Israel and His World*, ed. Yosef Kaplan, Henry Méchoulan, and R. H. Popkin (Leiden, 1989), 47–48.

42. See Dale Eikelman, "The Islamic Attitude towards Possession States," in *Trance and Possession States*, ed. Raymond Prince (Montreal, 1968). On the tension between high Islamic teaching and popular beliefs with regard to the evil dead and their ability to harm the living, as well as a treatment of the Islamic view of the permissability of adjurations, see Rudolf Kriss and Hubert Kriss-Heinrich, *Amulette, Zauberformeln und Beschwörungen, Volksglaube im Bereich des Islam* (Wiesbaden, 1962), 16; Ernst Zbinden, *Die Djinn des Islam und der altorientalische geisterglaube* (Bern, 1953), 94ff. On the similarity between Christian and Islamic notions of spirit possession, see R. Campbell Thompson, *Semitic Magic: Its Origins and Development*, Luzac's Oriental Religions Series (London, 1908), 101. On the complex relations be-

tween *jinn* possession, madness, and prophecy, see Michael Walters Dols and Diana E. Immisch, eds., *Majnun: The Madman in Medieval Islamic Society* (Oxford, 1992).

43. For examples of Pines's view of Jewish intellectual history and its contexts, see the essays collected in Shlomo Pines, Warren Harvey, and Moshe Idel, *Studies in the History of Jewish Thought* (Jerusalem, 1997). Recent historical work to take more nuanced views of acculturation include Robert Bonfil, *Jewish Life in Renaissance Italy*, trans. Anthony Oldcorn (Berkeley and Los Angeles, 1994); Ivan G. Marcus, *Rituals of Childhood: Jewish Culture and Acculturation in the Middle Ages* (New Haven, 1996); Kenneth R. Stow, *Theater of Acculturation: the Roman Ghetto in the Sixteenth Century* (Seattle, 2001). See also the essays in Yosef Kaplan and Menahem Stern, eds., *Hitbolelut u Tmi'ah* (Acculturation and Assimilation) (Jerusalem, 1989).

44 .Particularly helpful and illuminating treatments of this issue may be found in B. J. Good, *Medicine, Rationality and Experience: An Anthropological Perspective* (Cambridge, 1994); Stanley Tambiah, *Magic, Science, Religion, and the Scope of Rationality* (Cambridge, 1990).

45. Diane Purkiss, *The Witch in History: Early Modern and Twentieth-Century Representations* (London, 1996), 77, 79.

46. Ibid., 78.

47. Michel de Certeau, *The Mystic Fable: The Sixteenth and Seventeenth Centuries*, trans. Michael B. Smith (Chicago, 1992), 1.

48. Purkiss's attempt to use feminist psychoanalytic theory does not seem to overcome the basic problem she articulates in her critique of the historiography. See Purkiss, *The Witch in History: Early Modern and Twentieth-Century Representations*, 79–83. Purkiss relies heavily upon Hélène Cixous and Catherine Clément, *The Newly Born Woman*, trans. Betsy Wing (Manchester, 1986).

49. See the thoughtful discussion of this problem in witchcraft studies in Clark, *Thinking with Demons: The Idea of Witchcraft in Early Modern Europe*, 4–10.

50. Ibid., 389–400.

51. For a short biography, see Gershom Scholem, *Kabbalah* (New York, 1974), 420–28.

52. See Bilu, "The Taming of the Deviants and Beyond: An Analysis of *Dibbuk* Possession and Exorcism in Judaism"; Gedalyah Nigal, *Sippurei Dybbuk be-Sifrut Yisrael* (Dybbuk Stories in Jewish Literature), 2nd ed. (Jerusalem, 1994).

## *Chapter 1*

1. For Plato's views, see "Cratylus" in *The Collected Dialogues of Plato*, trans. Benjamin Jowett, ed. Huntington Cairns and Edith Hamilton (New York, 1961), 435, §397–§398. For Josephus, see *The Jewish War*, trans. H. St. J. Thackery, 3 vols., vol. 3 (Cambridge, 1997), 559 (7:185). These views and others on the rise of demonology are summarized in Naomi Janowitz, *Magic in the Roman World: Pagans, Jews and Christians* (London, 2001), 27–35.

2. See David Luria, ed., *Pirkei de Rabbi Eliezer 'im Beur ha-Radal* (Warsaw,

1852; reprint, Jerusalem, 1969), 79a §34. For an English edition, see Gerald Friedlander, ed., *Pirke de Rabbi Eliezer* (New York, Imc., 1971), 253.

3. Zohar III 70a (adduced in the context of a description of a classic witches' sabbath). Cf. Zohar 1 29a, 100a, and 3: 16b and the discussion in Yehudah Liebes, "Perakim be-Milon ha-Zohar" (Chapters of a Zohar Dictionary) (Ph.D. diss., Hebrew University, 1977), 54–55, 190; Yehudah Liebes, "How the Zohar Was Written" (in Hebrew), *Meḥkerei Yerushalayim be-Maḥshevet Yisrael: Sefer ha-Zohar ve-Doro*, 8 (1989): 12–14. This idea is also expressed in Reuben Margalioth, ed., *Sefer Ḥasidim* (Jerusalem, 1959), §1170. For an introduction to this thirteenth-century work, see Isaiah Tishby and Yeruham Fishel Lachower, *The Wisdom of the Zohar: An Anthology of Texts*, trans. David Goldstein (Oxford, 1989). A recent and compelling theory of the authorship of the Zohar may be found in Liebes, "How the Zohar Was Written."

4. See Moshe Hallamish, ed., *A Kabbalistic Commentary of Yoseph ben Shalom Ashkenazi* (Jerusalem, The Hebrew University, 1985), 79. Cf. Menasseh ben Israel, *Nishmat Ḥayyim* (Jerusalem, 1995), I 14, IV 19. On Menasseh ben Israel (1604–57), see Chapter 5 below.

5. On Ashkenazi's view that all forms in the cosmos, from the highest to the lowest, were in constant flux, movement, and change, see Melila Hellner, "Transmigration of Souls in the Kabbalistic Writings of R. David ibn Zimra," (in Hebrew), *Pe'amim*, 43 (1990): 26; Moshe Idel, "The Meaning of *'Ta'amei ha-Ofot ha-Temaim'* of Rabbi David ben Yehuda he-Ḥasid," in *'Alei Shefer: Studies in the Literature of Jewish Thought Presented to Rabbi Dr. Alexandre Safran*, ed. Moshe Ḥallamish (Ramat Gan, 1990).

6. Eliezer Ashkenazi, *Ma'asei ha-Shem* (Venice, 1583) 5b–c. This work was printed a number of times, including editions from Cracow (1584), The Hague (1777), Zolkiew (1802), Lemberg (1852 and 1858), and Warsaw (1871). In the Warsaw edition, the reference to the possessing spirit being the soul of a non-Jew was edited out, along with the information that the non-Jew's identity was recognized by the group in attendence at the exorcism. Unfortunately, the edition of *Ma'asei ha-Shem* currently available is a photo-offset of this censored edition.

7. Lit., "a pearl in the mouths"; this is a rabbinic idiom for a favorite or common saying. See, e.g., BT *Berakhot* 17a and the comments of Rashi.

8. A particularly enlightening discussion of the natural setting within demonic activity was believed to occur in early modern European thought and may be found in Stuart Clark, *Thinking with Demons: The Idea of Witchcraft in Early Modern Europe*, (Oxford, 1997)161–78, "The Devil in Nature."

9. Charles Ber Chavel, ed., *Perushei ha-Torah le-Rabbenu Moshe ben Naḥman (Ramban)*, 2 vols. (Jerusalem, 1959), 89 (commenting on Lev. 16:8). For an English translation, see Charles Ber Chavel, ed., *Naḥmanides' Commentary on the Torah*, 5 vols., vol. 3 (New York, 1971).

10. Rashi, active in Troyes, France, is the preeminent figure in medieval rabbinic hermeneutics, the author of the definitive rabbinic commentaries on the Bible as well as the Talmud. See his commentary on BT *Sanhedrin* 109a. On this terminology, see L. Blau, *Das altjüdische Zauberwesen* (Budapest, 1898), 14–15; Joshua Trachtenberg, *Jewish Magic and Superstition: A Study in Folk Religion* (New York, 1939), 27–28,

274 n. 6. Islamic demonology had a similar tradition of terminological confusion, with attempts made at by commentators such as Al-Djahiz to provide precise definitions of terms, including *jinn, shayṭan, marid,* and *'ifrit.* Like the figures of Jewish demonology, these Islamic demons have many human characteristics, and scholars have noted that, in the Egyptian context, *marid* may connote the spirit of a deceased person and an *'ifrit* the soul of one who has died a violent death. See *Encyclopedia of Islam, New Edition,* s.v. " 'Ifrit"; *Encyclopedia of Islam, New Edition,* s.v. "Shaytan"; *Encyclopedia of Islam, New Edition,* s.v. "Djinn"

11. See Nancy Caciola, "Discerning Spirits: Sanctity and Possession in the Later Middle Ages" (Ph.D., University of Michigan, 1994), part 2; William A. Christian, Jr., *Apparitions in Late Medieval and Renaissance Spain* (Princeton, N.J., 1981); Jean-Claude Schmitt, *Ghosts in the Middle Ages: The Living and the Dead in Medieval Society,* trans. Teresa Lavender Fagan (Chicago, 1998); Pierre-Andre Sigal, "La Possession Démoniaque dans la Région de Florence au XVe Siècle d'après les Miracles de Saint Jean Gualbert," in *Histoire et Société: Mélanges Offerts à Georges Duby* (Aix-en-Provence, 1992). See also Introduction above.

12. See Augustinus Hipponensis, *De Cura pro Mortuis Gerenda Liber Unus,* ed. J. P. Migne, 217 vols., vol. 40, *Patrologiae Cursus Completus, sive Bibliotheca Universalis . . . Omnium S.S. Patrum, Doctorum, Scriptorumque Ecclesiasticorum Qui ab Aevo Apostolico ad Innocenti III Tempora Floruerent . . .* Series Prima (Patrologiae Tomus XI, S. Patrologiae Tomus IX, S. Aurelii Augustini, Tomus Sextus) (Paris, 1844), cols. 591–610. See also the discussion in Schmitt, *Ghosts in the Middle Ages: The Living and the Dead in Medieval Society.*

13. Abu Ameenah Bilal Philips, *The Exorcist Tradition in Islam* (Sharjah, 1997), 22.

14. See David B. Ruderman, *Kabbalah, Magic, and Science: The Cultural Universe of a Sixteenth-Century Jewish Physician* (Cambridge, Mass., 1988), 54–55. A more recent Jewish thinker argued that it was the contemplation of the corpse of one's loved one that brought man to invent demons: "[i]t was his sense of guilt at the satisfaction mingled with his sorrow that turned these new-born spirits into evil, dreaded demons." See Sigmund Freud, "Thoughts for the Times on War and Death," in *Collected Papers,* ed. Joan Riviere and James Strachey (New York, 1959), 304–5.

15. For biographical information on Vital, see Gershom Scholem, *Kabbalah* (New York, 1974), 443–48. Bibliographical information may be found in J. Avivi, "The Works of R. Ḥayyim Vital in Lurianic Kabbalah" (in Hebrew), *Moriah* 10 (1981).

16. Musayoff Ms. 219, 5:121a. On the importance of using the technique appropriate to the type of possessor, see Musayoff Ms. 219, 3:54a. These sources are cited in Meir Benayahu, *Toledot ha-Ari* (Jerusalem, 1967), 297, 99.

17. Ḥayyim Vital, *Sefer ha-Goralot* (Book of Lots) (Jerusalem, 1997), 30–31 §35. Scholem questioned the attribution of this work to Vital. See Scholem, *Kabbalah,* 447.

18. See Abu Ameenah Bilal Philips, "Exorcism in Islam" (Ph.D. diss., University of Wales, 1993), 62–75.

19. See Benayahu, *Toledot ha-Ari,* 297–301.

20. The popular Islamic etymologies for the terms *jinn* and *thakalyan* assume a derivation from the root means of "to hide, cover, or conceal" and include the cognate word for *fetus.* See Philips, *The Exorcist Tradition in Islam,* 41; Samuel M.

Zwemer, *The Influence of Animism on Islam: An Account of Popular Superstitions* (London, 1920), 126.

21. On late medieval necromancy see Richard Kieckhefer, *Forbidden Rites: A Necromancer's Manual of the Fifteenth Century* (University Park, Pa., 1998).

22. C. D. Chavel, ed., *Kitvei Rabbeinu Moshe ben Naḥman*, 2 vols., vol. 1 (Jerusalem, 1963), 186. G. Scholem's view that these two terms have only been distinguished since 1300 must be corrected in light of Moshe Idel, "We Have No Kabbalistic Tradition on This," in *Rabbi Moses Naḥmanides (Ramban): Explorations in His Religious and Literary Virtuosity*, ed. Isadore Twersky (Cambridge, Mass., 1983), 53 n. 8. On the doctrine of *gilgul* in the thirteenth century, see Michal Oron, "The Doctrine of the Soul and Reincarnation in Thirteenth-Century Kabbalah" (in Hebrew), in *Meḥkarim be-Hagut Yehudit* (Studies in Jewish Thought), ed. S. O. Heller-Wilensky and Moshe Idel (Jerusalem, 1989); Gershom Scholem, "Towards the Study of Transmigration in Thirteenth-Century Kabbalah" (in Hebrew), *Tarbiẓ* 16 (1944): 135–50.

23. Gershom Scholem, "Gilgul: The Transmigration of Souls," in *On the Mystical Shape of the Godhead*, ed. Jonathan Chipman (New York, 1991), 207.

24. On the Jewish-Christian polemic in the Middle Ages, see David Berger, *The Jewish-Christian Debate in the High Middle Ages: A Critical Edition of the Niẓẓaḥon Vetus* (Philadelphia, 1979; reprint, Northvale, 1996). The disputation between Ramban and Pablo Christiani may be found in Chavel, ed., *Kitvei Rabbeinu Moshe ben Naḥman*, 299–320.

25. On the controversies surrounding the doctrine of transmigration within Jewish culture, see Ḥaggai Ben-Shammai, "Transmigration of Souls in Tenth Century Jewish Thought in the Orient" (in Hebrew), *Sefunot*, n.s., 5 (1991); Efraim Gottlieb, "The Gilgul Controversy in Candia in the Fifteenth Century" (in Hebrew), in *Meḥarim be-Sifrut ha-Kabbalah*, ed. Joseph Hacker (Tel Aviv, 1976); Dov Schwartz, "The Critique of the Doctrine of Transmigration in the Middle Ages" (in Hebrew), *Maḥanayim*, n.s., 6 (1994): 104–13 Cf. Yehudah Arieh Modena, "Ben David," in *Ta'am Zekainim*, ed. Eliezer Ashkenazi (Frankfurt am Main, 1854), 61–64.

26. Michal Kushnir-Oron, ed., *Sha'ar ha-Razim le-R. Todros ben Yosef ha-Levi Abulafia* (Jerusalem, 1989), 24. See also Oron, "The Doctrine of the Soul and Reincarnation in Thirteenth-Century Kabbalah," 289.

27. Trachtenberg, *Jewish Magic and Superstition: A Study in Folk Religion*, 61.

28. These three strata derive from various biblical verses and were imbued with particular meaning and a hierarchical order by medieval Jewish thinkers, neoplatonists, and kabbalists. See Scholem, *Kabbalah*, 152–65.

29. See Scholem, "Gilgul: The Transmigration of Souls," 217.

30. For introductory bibliography, see n. 3 above.

31. See Zohar 2: 26b.

32. See Scholem, "Gilgul: The Transmigration of Souls," 209. On the notion of *'ibbur* in the Zohar, see also Liebes, "Perakim be-Milon ha-Zohar," 278. In the Zohar, see pericope *Mishpatim* for the astounding chapter known as *Saba de-Mishpatim*.

33. See Scholem, "Gilgul: The Transmigration of Souls," 223.

34. Moses Cordovero, "*Shemu'ah be-'Inyan ha-Gilgul*," in *Or Yakar* (Jerusalem,

1991), 79–80. On this work, see Bracha Sack, "Some Remarks on Rabbi Moses Cordovero's 'Shemu'ah be-'Inyan ha-Gilgul,'" in *Perspectives on Jewish Thought and Mysticism—Proceedings of the International Conference Held by the Institute of Jewish Studies, University College, London, 1994* (Amsterdam, 1998).

35. Moses Cordovero, *Tefillah le-Moshe*, 2 vols., vol. 1 (Przemysl, 1892), 11a.

36. On the mimetic dimension of *'ibbur*, see below.

37. On the decidedly heterosexual character of most Jewish possession accounts, albeit without exception featuring male *dybbukim* penetrating female victims, see Yoram Bilu, "The Taming of the Deviants and Beyond: An Analysis of *Dibbuk* Possession and Exorcism in Judaism," in *The Psychoanalytic Study of Society*, ed. L. Bryce Boyner and Simon A. Grolnick (Hillsdale, 1985), 6–14.

38. See, e.g., BT Berakhot 57b.

39. Jonathan Garb has recently treated the subject of power in rabbinic thought and kabbalah. See Jonathan Garb, "Power and Kavvanah in Kabbalah" (Ph.D. diss., Hebrew University, 2000), 34–68 (rabbinic power), 232–59 (power in the thought of Cordovero).

40. On the magical use of Psalms, see below, Chapter 3 n. 45. For the notion of blessing as a "drawing-down" in the Zohar, see, e.g., 3: 190b; in Ḥasidism, see Moshe Idel, *Hasidism: Between Ecstasy and Magic* (Albany, 1995), 72.

41. Zohar 3: 70b–71a.

42. On the Cave of Makhpelah as a passageway between the living and the dead, see Chapter 2, n. 10 below.

43. Moses Cordovero, *Or Yakar*, ed. Menachem Zev Ḥasida, vol. 8 (Jerusalem, 1985), 64.

44. This homophone is an ancient pun, found already in Midrash Rabbah Bereshit 20:12, and elaborated on in the Zohar 2:229b and the *Tikkunim*, e.g., *Hakdamah* 10b; *Tikkun* 59 (92b). A "garment" in kabbalistic terminology is an exterior that is grosser than the spiritual substance concealed "inside" it. Such concealment allows the finer substance to descend to a realm beneath its native station. The garment thus takes on a mediating role between realms that would otherwise be too removed from one another to be in contact. In an anthropological context, the Garment of the Soul allows for the relationship between the spiritual soul and the physical body. The garment shares in qualities associated with both of these, assuming a certain physicality while still remaining beyond the corporeal realm. On the body as the Garment of the Soul, see Zohar 1:20b. The body is the Garment of the Soul for the righteous, but not for the wicked, for whom the order is reversed. See Gershom Scholem, "The Paradisic Garb of Souls and the Origin of the Concept of *Ḥaluka de-Rabbanan*" (in Hebrew), *Tarbiẓ* 24 (1955): 290–306.

45. Cordovero, *Or Yakar*, 64.

46. Ibid.

47. Ibid.

48. See Zohar 3:70b. "And these *nefashot* of the *ẓaddikim* are present in this world, to defend the living. This is called *nefesh.* And this [*nefesh*] does not depart from this world, and remains present in this world to observe, to know, and to defend the generation." For Vital's elaboration on the zoharic passage here interpreted by

Cordovero, see Ḥayyim Vital, *Sha'ar Ruaḥ ha-Kodesh*, ed. Yehuda Zvi Brandwein, 15 vols., vol. 10, *Kitvei Rabenu ha-Ari ZT"L* (Jerusalem, 1988), 109b–10a (*Hakdamah* 5).

49. Cordovero, *Or Yakar*, 64.

50. Cordovero did not imagine that the Zohar itself was written by such great men of Spain less than three centuries before his birth. On the authorship and dating of the Zohar, see most recently Liebes, "How the Zohar Was Written" (in Hebrew).

51. Gravesite prostration has been the subject of a number of recent studies. See, e.g., Paul B. (Yosef) Fenton (Yanon), "Sufi Influences upon Safedian Kabbalah" (in Hebrew), *Maḥanayim* 6 (1993): 172; Pinchas Giller, "Recovering the Sanctity of the Galilee: The Veneration of Sacred Relics in Classical Kabbalah," *Journal of Jewish Thought and Philosophy* 4 (1994); Boaz Shoshan, *Popular Culture in Medieval Cairo, Cambridge Studies in Islamic Civilization*, ed. David Morgan (Cambridge, 1993), 21.

52. AR"I is the classic acronym for R. Isaac Luria, the initial "A" standing for "Ashkenazi" (as Jews of Ashkenazic descent were called in Sefardic lands) as well as "*Elohi*" (divine).

53. Avraham Azulai, *Ḥesed le-Avraham* (Jerusalem, [1996]), 141 (*Ma'ayan* 4 " '*Ein Ya'akov*" *Nahar* 24). Cited Bracha Sack, *Be-Sha'arei ha-Kabbalah shel Rabbi Moshe Cordovero* (Beer Sheva, 1995), 220 n. 32.

54. Scholem, *Kabbalah*, 76. For a more extensive treatment, see Lawrence Fine, "The Contemplative Practice of *Yiḥudim* in Lurianic Kabbalah," in *Jewish Spirituality II: From the Sixteenth-Century Revival to the Present*, World Spirituality: An Encylopedic History of the Religious Quest, ed. Arthur Green (New York, 1987).

55. Vital here cites Zohar *Aḥarei Mot*, the passage analyzed above.

56. Ḥayyim Vital, *Sha'ar ha-Yiḥudim* (Koretz, 1783), 3d.

57. Ḥayyim Vital, *Sefer ha-Ḥezyonot*, ed. A. Z. Aescoly (Jerusalem, 1954), 5, 16. The 1954 Aescoly edition remains the most reliable, based on the currently missing manuscript autograph. The copy made by Vital's grandson survives, and may be consulted. See Ḥayyim Vital, *Sefer ha-Ḥezyonot*, Cambridge-Trinity College F 12 43, Institute of Microfilmed Hebrew Manuscripts, # 12228. For an English translation of the Aescoly edition, see Morris M. Faierstein, trans., *Jewish Mystical Autobiographies: Book of Visions and Book of Secrets* (New York, 1999). On *Sefer ha-Ḥezyonot*, see Michal Oron, "Dream, Vision and Reality in Ḥayyim Vital's *Sefer ha-Ḥezyonot*" (in Hebrew), *Meḥkerei Yerushalayim be-Maḥshevet Yisrael*, ed. by Rachel Elior and Yehudah Liebes, 10 (1992); David Tamar, "Gleanings Regarding *Sefer ha-Ḥezyonot*" (in Hebrew), *Sinai* 46, no. 91 (1982): 92–96. See also Chapter 4 below.

58. Vital's writings on reincarnation were redacted by subsequent kabbalists (beginning with his son Samuel) into lengthy treatises, including *Sha'ar ha-Gilgulim* (Gate of Transmigrations), *Sefer ha-Gilgulim* (Book of Transmigrations), and *Meshivat Nafesh* (Restorer of the Soul). Editions include Ḥayyim Vital, *Sha'ar ha-Gilgulim* (Jerusalem, 1863); Ḥayyim Vital, *Sefer ha-Gilgulim* (Przemysl, 1875a; reprint, *Torat ha-Gilgul*, vol. 1. Jerusalem, 1982); Ḥayyim Vital, *Sha'ar ha-Gilgulim*, Radomsk ed. (Przemysl, 1875).

59. See, e.g., Zohar 1: 264b; 3: 47b; 54a–b.

60. Ḥayyim Vital, *Sha'ar ha-Gilgulim*, ed. Yehuda Zvi Brandwein, 15 vols., vol. 10, *Kitvei Rabbenu ha-Ari ZT"L* (Jerusalem, 1988), 60b.

61. Ancient Jewish concepts of Gehinnom may well have shaped the medieval Christian idea of purgatory. See Jacques Le Goff, *The Birth of Purgatory*, trans. Arthur Goldhammer (Chicago, 1984), 39ff. For a Jewish appropriation of the term *purgatory* to describe the nature of transmigration into animal bodies, see Ruderman, *Kabbalah, Magic, and Science: The Cultural Universe of a Sixteenth-Century Jewish Physician*, 135–37. On the Islamic *barzakh*, or limbo state between the material and spirit worlds, see Ragnar Eklund, *Life between Death and Resurrection according to Islam*, trans. Elsa Lundequist (Uppsala, 1941).

62. Mishna Eduyot 2, 10. See Saul Lieberman, "On Sins and Their Punishments," in *Texts and Studies* (New York, 1974); Saul Lieberman, "Some Aspects of After Life in Early Rabbinic Literature," in *Texts and Studies* (New York, 1974). The third chapter of *Seder 'Olam*, a talmudic-era midrashic-chronological work, asserts that the worst sinners do not leave Gehinnom after twelve months, but remain there forever. See Chaim Milikowsky, "Gehinnom and 'Sinners of Israel' in the Light of *Seder'Olam*" (in Hebrew), *Tarbiẓ* 55, no. 3 (1986): 311–44.

63. Lyndal Roper has written on such notions of the body. See Lyndal Roper, *Oedipus and the Devil: Witchcraft, Sexuality and Religion in Early Modern Europe* (London, 1994) 24.

64. See Elazar Azikri, *Sefer Ḥaredim* (Venice, 1601; reprint Jerusalem, 1990), Chapter 33. Cf. Abraham Galante, *Yeraḥ Yakar*, Jerusalem Ms. 8°493. 263b, 64a; Vital, *Sha'ar ha-Gilgulim*, Radomsk ed., 17a. Cf. Ronit Meroz, "From the Compilation of Ephraim Penzieri: The Ari's Homily in Jerusalem and the Intentions for Eating" (in Hebrew), in *Meḥkerei Yerushalayim be-Maḥshevet Yisrael*, ed. Rachel Elior and Yehudah Liebes, *Kabbalat ha-Ari* (Jerusalem, 1992), 237, 211–57. Galanti's text was published in Benayahu, *Toledot ha-Ari*, 111, 250 n. 2.

65. Moshe Idel, "R. Yehudah Ḥallewa and His *Ẓafnat Pa'aneaḥ*" (in Hebrew), in *Shalem: Studies in the History of the Jews in Ereẓ-Israel*, ed. Joseph Hacker, 4 (1984): 146 n. 66. Cf. R. J. Zwi Werblowsky, *Joseph Karo: Lawyer and Mystic*, 2nd ed. (Philadephia, 1977), 245. The significance of *gilgul* stories to the growing preoccupation with the doctrine in sixteenth-century Safed was touched upon as well by Hellner, "Transmigration of Souls in the Kabbalistic Writings of R. David ibn Zimra," 28, and Meroz, "From the Compilation of Ephraim Penzieri: The Ari's Homily in Jerusalem and the Intentions for Eating," 241.

66. The term *kavvanah* refers to consciously directed or guided thought. *Lekhaven*, its verbal form, literally means "to aim" or "to direct." In kabbalistic sources, a particular set of *kavvanot*, or "intentions," thus signifies something like a "guided meditation." These meditations are often charged with significant theurgic and magical power.

67. Here we may find the source of what would eventually be termed *soul food*.

68. On animal hearts, see Vital's *Ta'amei ha-Miẓvot*, pericope *'Ekev*. Cf. Azulai, *Ḥesed le-Avraham, Ma'ayan* 5, *Nahar* 32 ("The Secret of Slaughtering"). On water, see Vital, *Sha'ar ha-Yiḥudim*, 63a–b; Vital, *Sha'ar ha-Gilgulim*, 62b. See also Meroz, "From the Compilation of Ephraim Penzieri: The Ari's Homily in Jerusalem and the Intentions for Eating," 240. According to Vital, those who transmigrate into water are former murderers, spillers of blood (as well as those not careful to wash their hands ritually—no minor transgression in Vital's mind).

69. Cited in Meroz, "From the Compilation of Ephraim Penzieri: The Ari's Homily in Jerusalem and the Intentions for Eating," 240.

70. See, e.g., Solomon Buber, ed., *Midrash Tanḥuma* (Vilna, 1885), *Kedoshim* §9.

71. Azulai, *Ḥesed le-Avraham, Ma'ayan* 5, *Nahar* 24, 209.

72. See Meroz, "From the Compilation of Ephraim Penzieri: The Ari's Homily in Jerusalem and the Intentions for Eating,' 241. The fear of drinking fresh water was widespread—for avowedly naturalistic reasons—and longstanding, as attested to by rabbinic warnings of parasites in sources such as BT *Avodah Zarah* 12b.

73. For the account of Luria's possession by spirit of *tanna* R. Yannai, a good *'ibbur* that also speaks through/to him, see Vital, *Sha'ar ha-Gilgulim*, 126.

74. Ibid., *Hakdamah* 3, 16. For a thorough emic explication of *'ibbur* in Lurianic Kabbalah, see Menachem Kallus, "Pneumatic Mystical Possession and the Eschatology of the Soul in the Lurianic Qabbalah," in *Spirit Possession in Jewish Culture*, ed. M. Goldish (Detroit, 2003). I am grateful to my friend Menachem for sharing this article with me before its publication.

75. See Scholem, "Gilgul: The Transmigration of Souls," 225.

76. Gary Tomlinson, *Music in Renaissance Magic: Toward a Historiography of Others* (Chicago, 1993), 50–51.

77. Luria's ambivalent relationship to the Jewish (and Renaissance) magical tradition is discussed below.

78. On the unprecedented centrality of *gilgul* in the culture of this community in the early decades of the sixteenth century, see R. Elior, "The Doctrine of Transmigration in *Galya Raza*," in *Essential Papers on Kabbalah*, ed. Lawrence Fine (New York, 1995); Hellner, "Transmigration of Souls in the Kabbalistic Writings of R. David ibn Zimra"; Meroz, "From the Compilation of Ephraim Penzieri: The Ari's Homily in Jerusalem and the Intentions for Eating."

79. Yehuda Ḥallewa, *Zafnat Pa'neaḥ*, Ms. Dublin, Trinity College B. 5. 27, Institute of Microfilmed Hebrew Manuscripts, #16958. This unique manuscript was copied in 1628, as we know from the colophon on p. 245a.

80. Idel, "R. Yehudah Ḥallewa and His *Zafnat Pa'aneaḥ*," 123.

81. On the genre of ethical literature of sixteenth-century Safed to which this work belongs, see M. Pachter, "Sifrut ha-Derush ve-ha-Mussar shel Ḥakhmei Ẓfat be-Meah ha–16 u-Ma'arekhet Ra'ayonoteha ha-'Ikariim" (Homiletic and Ethical Literature of Safed in the Sixteenth Century) (Ph.D. diss., Hebrew University of Jerusalem, 1976).

82. See Idel, "R. Yehudah Ḥallewa and His *Ẓafnat Pa'aneaḥ*," 124.

83. This story was retold by Vital in his *Sefer ha-Ḥezyonot* in 1577. Vital's only significant addition to Ḥallewa's cow story involves the reparation of the cow's soul through eating. (Ibid., 127.) Nevertheless, this is not a Lurianic innovation; see Louis Jacobs, "Eating as an Act of Worship in Hassidic Thought," in *Studies in Jewish Religious and Intellectual History Presented to Alexander Altmann on the Occasion of His Seventieth Birthday*, ed. Siegfried Stein and Raphael Loewe (University, Ala., 1979), 157–66; S. Pines, "Shi'ite Terms and Conceptions in Judah Halevi's *Kuzari*" (in Hebrew), *Jerusalem Studies in Arabic and Islam* 2 (1989): 245–46.

84. *Encyclopedia Judaica,* s.v., "Joseph Della Reina." See also Meir Benayahu, "Shlomo Navaro: Actual Writer of *Ma'aseh Nora me-Rabi Yosef Della Reina*?" (in Hebrew), *Tarbiẓ* 51 (1982); Idel, "Investigations in the Methodology of the Author of *Sefer ha-Meshiv*"; Idel, "R. Yehudah Ḥallewa and His *Zafnat Pa'aneaḥ*."

85. Ḥallewa, *Zafnat Pa'aneaḥ,* 143b–45a. Cited in Moshe Idel, "Investigations in the Methodology of the Author of *Sefer ha-Meshiv*" (in Hebrew), *Sefunot* 2, no. 17 (1983a): 224. My translation reflects minor corrections to Idel's text on the basis of my examination of the manuscript.

86. On this early fourteenth-century Spanish Kabbalist, see the bibliography in nn. 4–5 above.

87. Hallamish, ed., *A Kabbalistic Commentary of Yoseph ben Shalom Ashkenazi,* 111.

88. See Chapter 4 below.

89. On Zacuto, the seventeenth-century rabbinic mystic and baroque author, see Robert Bonfil, "Change in the Cultural Patterns of a Jewish Society in Crisis: Italian Jewry at the Close of the Sixteenth Century," *Jewish History* 3, no. 2 (1988): 11–30; Devorah Bregman, "Sonnet Sequences in Moshe Zacut's *Yesod 'Olam*" (in Hebrew), *Meḥkerei Yerushalayim be-Sifrut* 9 (1986): 301–12; Y. Melkman, "Mozes Zacuto en Zijn Familie," *Studia Rosenthaliana* 3, no. 2 (1969): 145–55; David B. Ruderman, "The Language of Science as the Language of Faith: An Aspect of Italian Jewish Thought in the Seventeenth and Eighteenth Centuries," in *Studies on the History of the Jews in the Middle Ages and Renaissance Period,* Shlomo Simonshon Jubilee Volume, Harvard Judaic Texts and Studies (Tel Aviv, 1993). He is also treated at some length Chapter 3 below.

90. On the term *maggid,* see S. Pines, "Le *sefer ha-Tamar* et les *Maggidim* des Kabbalistes," in *Hommage à Georges Vajda—Études d'histoire et de pensée juives,* ed. Gérard Nahon and Charles Touati (Louvain, 1980). Pines notes the phenomenological similarity between the *ruḥaniyut* (efflux) of stars moving a prophet's lips and kabbalistic maggidism, 360–63; Lawrence Fine, "Maggidic Revelation in the Teachings of Isaac Luria," in *Mystics, Philosophers and Politicians: Essays in Jewish Intellectual History in Honour of A. Altmann,* ed. J. Reinharz and D. Swetschinski (Durham, N.C., 1982).

91. Idel, "Investigations in the Methodology of the Author of *Sefer ha-Meshiv,*" 201. Karo (1488–1575) was the author of the *Shulḥan Arukh* (The Ordered Table), the standard code of Jewish law. The classic study is Werblowsky, *Joseph Karo: Lawyer and Mystic.*

92. Idel, "Jewish Magic from the Renaissance Period to Early Hasidism," in *Religion, Science, and Magic, in Concert and Conflict,* edited by Jacob Neusner, Ernest S. Frerichs, and Paul Virgil McCracken Flesher (New York, 1989) 107–8. Idel's felicitous formulation was preceded by observations similar to those of Gershom Scholem. See Gershom Scholem, *Sabbatai Sevi, the Mystical Messiah, 1626–1676,* rev. and aug. translation of the Hebrew ed., Bollingen Series, trans. R. J. Zwi Werblowsky (Princeton, N.J., 1973), 82. Cf. Gershom Scholem, "New Sources on R. Joseph Ashkenazi, the 'Tanna' of Safed" (in Hebrew), *Tarbiẓ* 28 (1958–59): 61–62; Werblowsky, *Joseph Karo: Lawyer and Mystic,* 283. For an analysis of the categories *dybbuk* and *maggid* from an

ethnopsychiatric perspective, see Yoram Bilu, "*Dybbuk* and *Maggid*: Two Cultural Patterns of Altered Consciousness in Judaism," *AJS Review* 21 no. 2 (1996): 341–66.

93. Idel, "Jewish Magic from the Renaissance Period to Early Hasidism," 108. Cf. Idel, "Investigations in the Methodology of the Author of *Sefer ha-Meshiv*," 224–25; Idel, "R. Yehudah Ḥallewa and His *Zafnat Pa'aneah*," 127.

94. Hayyim Joseph David Azulai and Isaac Benjacob, *Sifre Shem ha-Gedolim: Va'ad la-Ḥakhamim* (Vilna, 1852), §121.

95. The feminine nature of the *Shekhina* (root *S.Kh.N.*, "dwell"), or indwelling Divine presence, was emphasized by the kabbalists. See Gershom Scholem, *Major Trends in Jewish Mysticism*, 3rd Rev. ed. (New York, 1961), 229–35.

96. Shlomo ben David Gabbai, ed., *Ma'aseh Nissim shel ha-Ari Z"L (Shivḥei ha-Ari), Meirat 'Ainayim* (Constantinople, 1666), 1b. See Ḥayyim Vital, *Sha'arei Kedusha* (Jerusalem, 1985), 99. On Elijah revelations, see Gershom Scholem, "*Sidrei de-Shimushei Raba*," *Tarbiẓ* 16 (1945): 196–209; Gershom Scholem, *Origins of the Kabbalah*, trans. Allan Arkush (Philadelphia, 1987); Elliot R. Wolfson, "Weeping, Death, and Spiritual Ascent in Sixteenth-Century Jewish Mysticism," in *Death, Ecstasy and Other-Worldly Journeys*, ed. J. Collins and M. Fishbane (Albany, N.Y., 1995), 212–14.

97. Gabbai, ed., *Ma'aseh Nissim shel ha-Ari Z"L (Shivḥei ha-Ari)*, 1b.

98. Moshe Sluhovsky has studied cases of spirit possession in cases in sixteenth-century France in which the possessed initially identified their possessing agent as "a messenger who reappeared from the dead to demand stricter obedience by family members of religious precepts." See Moshe Sluhovsky, "A Divine Apparition or Demonic Possession? Female Agency and Church Authority in Demonic Possession in Sixteenth-Century France." *Sixteenth Century Journal* 27, no. 4 (1995): 1036–52.

99. Christian, *Apparitions in Late Medieval and Renaissance Spain*, 6–7.

100. Castañega was a Franciscan friar of Burgos and the Basque country, and author of *Tratado de las supersticiones y hechicerías* (Treatise of Superstitions and Sorcieries) (Logroño, 1529). Ciruelo was professor of Thomistic theology at the University of Alcalá. A Hebrew scholar and mystic of Converso origin, he published his *Reprobación de las supersticiones y hechicerías* (Reprobation of Superstitions and Sorceries) in 1530. This work is available in English as Pedro Ciruelo, *A Treatise Reproving all Superstitions and Forms of Witchcraft Very Necessary and Useful for all Good Christians Zealous for Their Salvation*, ed. W. Pearson D'Orsay, trans. E. A. Maio and W. Pearson D'Orsay (London, 1977). See Lu Ann Homza, *Religious Authority in the Spanish Renaissance* (Baltimore, 2000). I am grateful to Prof. Homza for sharing Chapter 4, "Bewitching the Sheep," with me before its publication. I also benefited from her unpublished lecture, "Theologians and the Possessed in Early Modern Spain: Paradigms and Paradoxes," presented at the annual conference of the American Historical Association, 1995.

101. Castañega, *Tratado de las supersticiones y hechicerías* (Treatise of superstitions and sorcieries), 68–69. The characterizations here are indebted to Homza's work.

102. A street prophet known as *el bachiller Marquillos* claimed to be inspired by the Holy Spirit and enjoyed a large following during the 1449 anticonverso riots in

Toledo. See Richard L. Kagan, "Politics, Prophecy, and the Inquisition in Late Sixteenth-Century Spain," in *Cultural Encounters: The Impact of the Inquisition in Spain and the New World*, ed. Mary Elizabeth Perry and Anne J. Cruz (Berkeley and Los Angeles, 1991), 107.

103. Ḥaim Beinart's studies are noteworthy. See Ḥaim Beinart, "A Prophesying Movement in Cordova in 1499–1502" (in Hebrew), *Ẓion* 44 (1980): 190–220; Ḥaim Beinart, "The Prophetess Inés and her Movement in Puebla de Alcocer and in Talarrubias" (in Hebrew), *Tarbiẓ* 51 (1982): 633–58; Ḥaim Beinart, "The Prophetess Inés and Her Movement in Her Hometown, Herrera" (in Hebrew), in *Studies in Jewish Mysticism, Philosophy, and Ethical Literature Presented to Isaiah Tishby on His Seventy-fifth Birthday* (Jerusalem, 1986), 459–506; Ḥaim Beinart, "The Conversos of Halia and the Movement of the Prophetess Ines" (in Hebrew), *Ẓion* 53 (1988): 31–52.

104. See the characteristic remarks of Scholem: "This shocking of the hearts after this episode (the expulsion) and the meditations of the sensitive souls gave birth to the phenomenon of *maggidim*, and from this standpoint there is a psychological resemblance between what happened in that generation and the similar revelations in the generation after the Sabbatian shock, when, once again, the voices of *maggidim* broke out from the depths of souls." Gershom Scholem, "The *Maggid* of R. Yosef Taitazak [Taytaczack] and the Revelations Attributed to Him" (in Hebrew), in *Sefunoth* (The Book of Greek Jewry—1), ed. Meir Benayahu (Jerusalem, 1971–78), 89. Cf. "The doctrine of *gilgul* had come to express in a new and forcible way the reality of Exile." Scholem, *Major Trends in Jewish Mysticism*, 281. Cf. Scholem, *Sabbatai Sevi, the Mystical Messiah, 1626–1676*, 51ff.

It should also be noted that Scholem could also cast *gilgul*—and exile—in a positive light. Thus exile is a mission to be embraced by Israel allowing it "to uplift the fallen sparks from all their various locations." Scholem, *Major Trends in Jewish Mysticism*, 284. Is this the same *gilgul* that articulates the "tragic destiny of the whole people" going through "the horrors of Exile?" Scholem, *Major Trends in Jewish Mysticism*, 250. Cf. Scholem, *Sabbatai Sevi, the Mystical Messiah, 1626–1676*, 46.

## *Chapter 2*

This chapter is an expanded and updated version of J. H. Chajes, "City of the Dead: Spirit Possession in Sixteenth-Century Safed," in *Spirit Possession in Judaism: Cases and Contexts from the Middle Ages to the Present*, ed. Matt Goldish (Detroit: Wayne State University Press, 2003), 124–58.

1. Vital, *Sha'ar ha-Gilgulim* (Jerusalem, 1967), 59a. See also the material in Meir Benayahu, *Toledot ha-Ari*, 236–37.

2. Vital emphases the positive role played by the sacred imagination in cultivating mystical experience. See Ḥayyim Vital, *Sha'arei Kedusha* (Jerusalem, 1985), 89–90. Nevertheless, here he emphasizes the nonimaginary nature of Luria's visions. Cf. Vital, *Sha'ar ha-Gilgulim*, 117b.

3. On the location of the Jewish quarter of sixteenth-century Safed, see Abraham David, *To Come to the Land: Immigration and Settlement in Sixteenth-Century Eretz-Israel*, trans. Dena Ordan (Tuscaloosa, 1999), 95–97.

4. See Meir Benayahu, "Devotional Practices of the Kabbalists of Safed in Meron" (in Hebrew), in *Sefer Ẓfat* (*Sefunot* 6), ed. Meir Benayahu and Y. Ben Zvi (Jerusalem, 1962); Pinchas Giller, "Recovering the Sanctity of the Galilee: The Veneration of Sacred Relics in Classical Kabbalah," *Journal of Jewish Thought and Philosophy* 4 (1994): 147–69. *Sha'ar ha-Gilgulim* concludes with a kind of traveler's guide to the tombs of Safed and its environs, including examples of tombs identified (or reidentified) by Luria. See Vital, *Sha'ar ha-Gilgulim*, 181a–85b. Samuel Vital, Ḥayyim's son and the redactor-editor of *Sha'ar ha-Gilgulim*, saw fit to place his account of the possession of Esther Weiser as its "epilogue," just after this excursus on the dead of the Galilee. See Appendix, Case 10.

5. Carlos M. N. Eire, *From Madrid to Purgatory: The Art and Craft of Dying in Sixteenth-Century Spain* (Cambridge, 1995), 518–19.

6. Alsheikh (c. 1507, Adrianople or Salonika–1597, Damascus) ordained Vital in 1590. Notwithstanding his desire to study Kabbalah with Luria nearly twenty years earlier, Alsheikh—like his own teacher, R. Joseph Karo—was not accepted as a student by the master. On this matter, see Vital's account in Meir Benayahu, *Yosef Beḥiri: Maran Rabi Yosef Karo* (Joseph, My Chosen: Our Master Rabbi Joseph Karo) (Jerusalem, 1991), 233–55; David Tamar, "On the Book *Toledot ha-Ari*" (in Hebrew), in *Meḥkarim be-Toledot ha-Yehudim be-Ereẓ Yisrael u'be-Italia* (Studies in the History of the Jews in the Land of Israel and in Italy) (Jerusalem, 1986), 176–77; Vital, *Sefer ha-Ḥezyonot*, 8.

7. Cited from Mordechai Pachter, " 'Terrible Vision' by R. Moses Alsheikh" (in Hebrew), in *From Safed's Hidden Treasures: Studies and Texts Concerning the History of Safed and Its Sages in the Sixteenth Century* (Jerusalem, 1994), 112–13.

8. For recent treatments and bibliography, see Bruce Gordon and Peter Marshall, *The Place of the Dead in Late Medieval and Early Modern Europe* (Cambridge, 2000).

9. Safed's numerical value is 21 if one drops the zeros from each of its letters (*mispar katan*). Thus Ẓ=90, P=80, Th=400, which gives us 9+8+4=21. Adding the entire word itself (the *kollel*) brings us to 22.

10. Now simply 90+80+400=570. Azulai explains earlier in this chapter the significance of the word *TK'A* (literally "pitch" as in pitching a tent, as in Gen. 31:25) as alluding to the Cave of Makhpelah, the passageway to the Garden of Eden given its numerical equivalence to *'over le-soḥer* (lit. "current money with the merchant"). This latter phrase was mystically interpreted in earlier kabbalistic literature as "passage to the supernal worlds." See, e.g., Zohar 1:123b and 141a, 3:128b.

11. The Cave of Makhpelah, the first and foremost grave in the Bible (Gen. 23), was the resting place of the Patriarchs and Matriarchs. Located in Hebron, mystical tradition held that this cave served as the entrance to the Garden of Eden. See, e.g., Zohar 1:127a, 219a, and 248b and the discussion of R. Isaiah Horowitz in *Shnei Luḥot ha-Brit* (Two Tablets of the Covenant), Genesis, pericope "The Life of Sarah," *Torah Or* 1.

12. Avraham Azulai, *Ḥesed le-Avraham* (Jerusalem, [1996]), 115–16.

13. On the especially intense link between spiritual ecstasy and death in early modern Spain, see Eire, *From Madrid to Purgatory: The Art and Craft of Dying in Sixteenth-Century Spain*, 6–7, 396–98, 411–12.

14. Karo was inspired by the martyrdom of Shlomo Molcho. On Karo's death wish, see Joseph Karo, *Maggid Mesharim* (Amsterdam: 1708), 65a; R. J. Zwi Werblowsky, *Joseph Karo: Lawyer and Mystic*, 2nd ed. (Philadelphia, 1977), 98–99. On "martyrological devotion during prayer" from the thirteenth to the nineteenth century, see Michael Fishbane, "The Imagination of Death in Jewish Spirituality," in *Death, Ecstasy and Other-Worldly Journeys*, ed. J. Collins and M. Fishbane (Albany, 1995). Luria's "daring" amplification of death meditations in worship is discussed on pp. 199–202. Fishbane's full treatment of the subject may be found in Michael Fishbane, *The Kiss of God: Spiritual and Mystical Death in Judaism* (Seattle, 1993). See also Elliot R. Wolfson, "Weeping, Death, and Spiritual Ascent in Sixteenth-Century Jewish Mysticism," in *Death, Ecstasy and Other-Worldly Journeys*, ed. J. Collins and M. Fishbane (Albany, 1996), 230–31.

On the phenomenon of apparitions, see William A. Christian, Jr., *Apparitions in Late Medieval and Renaissance Spain* (Princeton, 1981); Carlos María Staehlin, *Apariciones* (Madrid, 1954).

15. Another Safedian who had frequent contact with the dead was R. Lapidot Ashkenazi. See Vital, *Sefer ha-Ḥezyonot*, 5. On this figure and the stories associated with him, see Moshe Idel, "R. Yehudah Ḥallewa and His *Ẓafnat Pa'aneaḥ*" (in Hebrew), in *Shalem: Studies in the History of the Jews in Erez-Israel*, ed. Joseph Hacker, 4 (1984): 145–48.

16. See S. Aviẓur, "Safed—Center of the Manufacture of Woven Woolens in the Fifteenth Century" (in Hebrew), *Sefunot* 6 (1962): 43–69. For a poetic introduction to the superabundance of rabbinic talent that gathered in sixteenth-century Safed, see the classic essay by S. Schechter, "Safed in the Sixteenth Century: A City of Legists and Mystics," in *Studies in Judaism*, 2nd ser. (Philadelphia, 1908).

17. See Abraham David, "Demographic Changes in the Safed Jewish Community of the Sixteenth Century," in *Occident and Orient: A Tribute to the Memory of Alexander Scheiber*, ed. Robert Dan (Budapest and Leiden, 1988); Abraham David, "The Spanish Exiles in the Holy Land," in *The Sephardi Legacy*, ed. Haim Beinart (Jerusalem, 1992); Joseph Hacker, "The Relationship and Immigration of Spanish Jews to the Land of Israel" (in Hebrew), *Katedra* 36 (1985): 3–34; Bernard Lewis, *Notes and Documents from the Turkish Archives: A Contribution to the History of the Jews in the Ottoman Empire* (Jerusalem, 1952), 5–7. For a critical appraisal of the demographic conclusions based on these sources, see Joseph Hacker, "The Payment of *Djizya* by Scholars in Palestine in the Sixteenth Century" (in Hebrew), in *Shalem: Studies in the History of the Jews in Erez-Israel*, ed. Joseph Hacker (Jerusalem, 1984); Joseph Hacker, "Romaniyot Jews in Sixteenth-Century Safed: A Chapter in the History of Support for the Jews of Erez Yisrael by Communities in the Ottoman Empire" (in Hebrew), in *Shalem: Studies in the History of the Jews in Erez-Israel*, ed. Joseph Hacker (Jerusalem, 2002), 133–50.

18. See Abraham David, "Safed, foyer de retour au judaïsme de 'conversos' au XVIe siècle," *Revue des études juives* 146, no. 1/2 (1986): 63–83.

19. Giller, "Recovering the Sanctity of the Galilee: The Veneration of Sacred Relics in Classical Kabbalah," 155.

20. Appendix, Case 3. Visitations of the dead in dreams were not unknown. See, e.g., Elijah de Vidas, *Reshit Ḥokhmah ha-Shalem*, ed. Chaim Waldman, 3 vols., vol. 1 (Jerusalem, 1984), 471 (Gate of Fear 12:49, Gate of Love 6:35).

21. See Yehuda Ḥallewa, *Ẓafnat Pa'aneaḥ;* ms. Dublin, Trinity College B. 5. 27, Institute of Microfilmed Hebrew Manuscripts #16958; Vital, *Sefer ha-Ḥezyonot.* The Damascus case features prominently in Chapter 4 below.

22. See Ya'aqov Ẓemaḥ, *Meshivat Nafesh*, London Montefiore Library, 342, Institute of Hebrew Microfilmed Manuscripts # 05286. Cf. other seventeenth-century manuscripts: Oxford, Bodleian Ms. opp. 121 / Institute of Microfilmed Hebrew Manuscripts # 18799, Moscow, Russian State Library Ms. Günzburg 696 / Institute of Microfilmed Hebrew Manuscripts # 47870; Ya'aqov Ẓemaḥ, *Ronu le-Ya'akov*, Ms. Bodleian 1870 / Institute of Hebrew Microfilmed Manuscripts # 18805. Cf. Ms. Cincinnati 544, Seventeenth Century Italian / Institute of Microfilmed Hebrew Manuscripts # 19469, Ms. Machon Ben-Zvi 203 / Institute of Microfilmed Hebrew Manuscripts # 26559. *Divrei Yosef* is now available in a scientific edition. See Shimon Shtober, ed., *Sefer Divrei Yosef by Yosef ben Yitzhak Sambari* (Jerusalem, 1994).

23. Joseph Dan has suggested that the case of *dybbuk* possession in ibn Yaḥia's 1586 work *Shalshelet ha-Kabbalah* is the result of Safedian influence. See Joseph Dan, "The Case of the Spirit and the She-Demon" (in Hebrew), *Ha-Sifrut* 18–19 (1974): 75. Though this work was published decades before the Safedian cases were published for the first time, oral reports and broadsheets certainly found their way to Italy well before, as we shall soon discuss. Given the contemporary European proliferation of spirit possession, however, it would seem to me that it is not necessary to posit Safedian influence to account for the case in ibn Yaḥia. The account is reproduced in full as Case 8 in the Appendix.

24. See Moses Gaster, ed., *Maaseh Book*, vol. 1 (Philadelphia, 1934), 301–3.

25. A complete list of these works and the accounts they contain may be found in Appendix 1 of J. H. Chajes, "Spirit Possession and the Construction of Early Modern Jewish Religiosity" (Ph.D. diss., Yale University, 1999).

26. See Joseph Dan, "Towards the History of Hagiographical Literature" (in Hebrew), *Meḥkerei Yerushalayim be-Folklor Yehudi*, 1 (1981): 82–100; Joseph Dan, "Hagiographic Literature: East and West" (in Hebrew), *Pe'amim* 26 (1986): 77–86.

27. The gravity of failing to don *tefillin* is noted already in BT *Rosh ha-Shanah.* 17a.

28. For the full text of this case in English, see the Appendix, Case 3 Falcon was a student of Luria's, who immigrated to the Land of Israel from Turkey. On Falcon's relation to the Lurianic circle, see David Tamar, "On the Confraternities of Safed" (in Hebrew), in *Meḥkarim be-Toledot ha-Yehudim be-Ereẓ Yisrael u'be-Italia* (Studies in the History of the Jews in the Land of Israel and in Italy) (Jerusalem, 1986b). Vital discusses Falcon's relationship to Luria and the other members of their circle in Vital, *Sha'ar ha-Gilgulim*, 172a-b.

29. On the publication of this story as a broadsheet, see Benayahu, *Toledot ha-Ari*, 47 and 104 n. 6. It is possible, though unlikely, that the printing could have been done in Safed, considering the earliest printing press in Safed—and in the entire

region—dates back to 1577. See A. Yaari, *Ha-Defus ha-'Ivri be-Arẓot ha-Mizraḥ* (Hebrew printing in the East), 2 vols., vol. 1 (Jerusalem, 1936), 10.

30. See Gedalia Ibn Yaḥia, *Shalshelet ha-Kabbalah* (Venice, 1586), 204.

31. This centrality was acknowledged by world Jewry. As Pachter notes, "the recognition of the centrality of Safed became one of the unquestioned givens of the period." See Pachter, " 'Terrible Vision' by R. Moses Alsheikh" (in Hebrew), 76 n. 36. On the contemporary propagandistic writing of R. Shlomo Alkabetz (c. 1505 Salonika–1584 Safed) on behalf of Safed, see Mordechai Pachter, "The Parting Sermon of R. Shlomo Alkabetz in Salonika" (in Hebrew), in *From Safed's Hidden Treasures: Studies and Texts Concerning the History of Safed and its Sages in the Sixteenth Century* (Jerusalem, 1994). Alkabetz signed Falcon's account as a witness.

32. See Mary Douglas, *Natural Symbols: Explorations in Cosmology* (London, 1970); S. Nadel, "A Study of Shamanism in the Nuba Hills," *Journal of the Royal Anthropological Institute*, in *Reader in Comparative Religion: An Anthropological Approach*, ed. William Armand and Evon Zartman Vogt (Evanston, Ill., 1958), 464–79. This is the approach generally advocated in I. M. Lewis, *Ecstatic Religion: A Study of Shamanism and Spirit Possession*, 2nd ed. (London, 1989).

33. Another sage of Safed, whose name also appears alongside those of Joseph Karo and Moshe Trani in a *halakhic* responsum from 1560.

34. Some versions read "more than one hundred," others "nearly one hundred." Accounts of the other Safed exorcisms of the early 1570s also stress the large numbers of people who assembled to observe the proceedings.

35. Michelde Certeau, "Discourse Disturbed," in *The Writing of History* (Paris, 1970), 255–56.

36. H. C. Erik Midelfort, "The Devil and the German People: Reflections on the Popularity of Demon Possession in Sixteenth-Century Germany," in *Religion and Culture in the Reformation*, vol. 11 of *Sixteenth Century Essays and Studies*, ed. Steve Ozment (Kirksville, 1989), 119.

37. I address the problem of agency primarily in Chapter 4 below.

38. Shtober, ed., *Sefer Divrei Yosef by Yosef ben Yitzhak Sambari*, 319.

39. Menasseh ben Israel, *Nishmat Ḥayyim* (Amsterdam, 1651), III 10, 109a–11a. On such bowdlerization by editors seeking to remove "objectionable or offensive references to living or revered personalities" see Werblowsky, *Joseph Karo: Lawyer and Mystic*, 31.

40. Ẓarfati is a surname given to Jews of French origin. Well-known families by this name lived in Italy, Morocco, and the Ottoman empire beginning in the late fifteenth-century. Our Ẓarfatis have connections in Salonika, where the young woman's husband is away on business. On the Saloniki branch of the family, see Joseph Hacker, "Jewish Society in Salonica and Its Environs in the Fifteenth and Sixteenth Centuries: A Chapter in the History of Jewish Society in the Ottoman Empire and Its Relation to the Authorities" (Ph.D. diss., Hebrew University, 1978).

The Italian branch included a number of figures by the name of Joseph and Samuel, the names that figure in this possession case. On conversions to Christianity in the Italian Ẓarfati family in the mid-sixteenth century, see Renata Segre,

"Sephardic Refugees in Ferrara: Two Notable Families," in *Crisis and Creativity in the Sephardic World, 1391–1648*, ed. Benjamin R. Gampel (New York, 1997), 167. Joseph Ẓarfati (Sarfati), a rabbi in Fez in the early sixteenth century, converted to Christianity and actively preached against Jews and Judaism under the auspices of his godfather, Pope Julius III (1550–55). This Joseph Ẓarfati, whose vehemently antisemitic sermons were heard by Michel de Montaigne, was an instigator of the condemnation of the Talmud and its subsequent burning in Rome in 1553. See *Encyclopedia Judaica*, s.v. "Sarfati (Ẓarefati, Sarfatti)."

41. See Cecil Roth, "The Religion of the Marranos," in *A History of the Marranos* (New York, 1992), 186–88.

42. According to Menasseh ben Israel's version, he left one son, two divorcees, and a widow. This reading accords better with the expression "from the third one, he passed away," which seems to express that he left her a widow, rather than a divorcee. It also makes the spirit's mention of her husband more intelligible. Then again, *lexio difficilis* could give Sambari's text the nod.

43. The name indicates that the man's family was of Portuguese origin, from the town of Leiria.

44. This synagogue was founded around 1525 and led by R. Moses Trani for some fifty years.

45. Menasseh ben Israel's version has the somewhat more generic "he would speak against the Torah of Moses our teacher, of blessed memory."

46. The most significant studies of this high skepticism of the sixteenth century are Richard H. Popkin, *The History of Scepticism from Erasmus to Spinoza*, rev. and expanded ed. (Berkeley and Los Angeles, 1979), and M. Burnyeat, ed., *The Skeptical Tradition* (Berkeley and Los Angeles, 1983).

47. Lucien Febvre, *The Problem of Unbelief in the Sixteenth Century: The Religion of Rabelais*, trans. Beatrice Gottlieb (Cambridge, Mass., 1982). See the criticism of this position in Alan Charles Kors, *Atheism in France, 1650–1729*. vol. 1, *The Orthodox Sources of Disbelief* (Princeton, N.J., 1990), 8–9; José Luis Sánchez Lora, *Mujeres, conventos y formas de la religiosidad barroca* (Madrid, 1988), 217. A trailblazing study of popular skepticism in the early modern period is Carlo Ginzburg, *The Cheese and the Worms*, trans. John Tedeschi and Anne Tedeschi (Baltimore, 1980).

48. See the discussion in Yirmiyahu Yovel, *Spinoza and Other Heretics: The Marrano of Reason* (Princeton, N.J., 1989), 62. See also the recent contributions of J. Faur, *In the Shadow of History: Jews and Conversos at the Dawn of Modernity* (Albany, 1992); Yosef Kaplan, *From Christianity to Judaism: The Story of Isaac Orobio de Castro*, trans. Raphael Loewe, ed. Albert H. Friedlander, Louis Jacobs, and Vivian D. Lipman, (Oxford, 1989), 319–22; David B. Ruderman, *Jewish Thought and Scientific Discovery in Early Modern Europe* (New Haven, Conn., 1995), 153–84, 276–80. Skepticism is discussed at greater length in Chapter 5 below.

49. This example of xenoglossia was examined in R. Patai, "Exorcism and Xenoglossia Among the Safed Kabbalists," *Journal of American Folklore* 91 (1978): 823–35. Patai's rather far-reaching conclusion: "Given the skeptical frame of mind of the exorcists as [to] the identity of the spirit, one must assume that the spirit's display of mastery of the three languages was sufficient to convince them that it was indeed

the spirit who was speaking because it exceeded by far the rudimentary knowledge the woman could have had. That is to say, the account as it stands must be taken as prima facie evidence of an authentic multiple xenoglossia." (Ibid., 827–28.)

50. See R. C. Finucane, *Appearances of the Dead: A Cultural History of Ghosts* (London, 1982), 84.

51. Ruth Lamdan has argued that adultery became quite widespread in the Jewish communities of Palestine and Egypt of the sixteenth century. See Ruth Lamdan, "Deviations from Norms of Moral Behavior in the Jewish Society of Ereẓ Israel and Egypt in the Sixteenth Century" (in Hebrew), in *Sexuality and the Family in History*, ed. Israel Bartal and Isaiah Gafni (Jerusalem, 1998).

52. See Edward Muir, *Ritual in Early Modern Europe*, New Approaches to European History: 11 (Cambridge, 1997), 37.

53. See, e.g., Ḥayyim Joseph David Azulai, *She'elot u'Teshuvot Ḥayyim Shaal*, 1 §53. The *Ḥida* cites responsum §117 of the *Maharam mi-Lublin* (R. Meir ben Gedaliah of Lublin [1558–1616], Responsa *Manhir 'Einei Ḥakhamim* [Venice, 1618]) to the same question. These reponsa also treat male intercourse with female spirits, which is a less halakhically problematic phenomenon. See H. J. Zimmels, *Magicians, Theologicans, and Doctors: Studies in Folk-Medicine and Folk-Lore as Reflected in Rabbinical Responsa (Twelfth–Nineteenth Centuries)* (New York, 1952), 82. References to parallel discussions in Islamic legal literature may be found in Abu Ameenah Bilal Philips, *The Exorcist Tradition in Islam* (Sharjah, 1997). See also the relevant entries in the *Encyclopedia of Islam*, e.g., " 'Ifrit." and "Djinn."

Jewish mystical literature is replete with discussions and stories of incubi and succubi. See, e.g., Zohar 3:276a; *'Arba Meot Shekel Kesef*, 252; Shlomo ben David Gabbai, ed., *Ma'aseh Nissim shel ha-Ari Z"L (Shivḥei ha-Ari), Meirat 'Ainayim* (Constantinople, 1666), 3b; Ibn Yaḥia, *Shalshelet ha-Kabbalah*, 195.

54. Although she may simply have been menstruating, it is also possible that the woman hemorrhaged vaginally in the course of her violent seizures. St. Teresa of Avila hemorrhaged vaginally shortly before her death, leading some to suspect that she may have had epilepsy. See Marcella Biró Barton, "Saint Teresa of Avila. Did She Have Epilepsy?" *Catholic Historical Review* 68 (1982): 581–98; Eire, *From Madrid to Purgatory: The Art and Craft of Dying in Sixteenth-Century Spain*, 404 n. 17.

55. The expression of resignation to the possibility of destruction from Esther 4:16 follows her declaration of determination to come before the king in violation of the law.

56. This analysis of the cultural function of spirit possession is based on Finucane, *Appearances of the Dead: A Cultural History of Ghosts*, 85–86. Eire made use of Finucane's categories in his analysis of St. Teresa's apparitions. See Eire, *From Madrid to Purgatory: The Art and Craft of Dying in Sixteenth-Century Spain*, 475.

57. Midelfort, "The Devil and the German People: Reflections on the Popularity of Demon Possession in Sixteenth-Century Germany," 118.

58. For the full text of this case in English, see the Appendix, Case 4.

59. The status of the *'agunah* and the requirement to rule legally on her behalf are discussed in Maimonides, Mishnah Torah, Laws of Divorce, Ch. 13, §28. Earlier rabbinic discussions of the status may be found in the Jerusalem Talmud *Gittin* 20a

and BT *Babba Kamma* 80a and Rashi and Tosaphot there. On the *'agunah* problem and young brides in sixteenth-century Egypt, Syria, and Palestine, see Ruth Lamdan, "Child Marriage in Jewish Society in the Eastern Mediterranean during the Sixteenth Century," *Mediterranean Historical Review* 11 (1996): 49–50.

60. Cf. Rashi on Lev. 20:10: " 'The adulterer and the adulteress shall surely be put to death.' All death [penalties] mentioned without specification in the Torah are carried out by strangulation." See also BT *Ketubot* 30a–b. Cf. BT *Sanhedrin* 37b; Numbers Rabbah, XIV §6.

61. See Lamdan, "Deviations from Norms of Moral Behavior in the Jewish Society of Eretz Israel and Egypt in the Sixteenth Century."

62. Yoram Bilu, "The Taming of the Deviants and Beyond: An Analysis of *Dibbuk* Possession and Exorcism in Judaism," in *The Psychoanalytic Study of Society*, ed. Bryce Boyer and Simon A. Grolnick (Hillsdale, 1985).

63. For the text of these cases in English, see the Appendix, Cases 5 and 7.

64. Appendix, Case 6.

65. Naftali ben Jacob Bacharach, *'Emek ha-Melekh* (Amsterdam, 1648). On this work, see Yehudah Liebes, "Towards a Study of the Author of '*Emek ha-Melekh:* His Personality, Writings, and Kabbalah" (in Hebrew), *Jerusalem Studies in Jewish Thought* 11 (1993b): 101–37.

66. Vital, *Sefer ha-Ḥezyonot,* 36, §25. On the private nature of this work, see Oron, "Dream, Vision and Reality in Ḥayyim Vital's *Sefer ha-Ḥezyonot*" (in Hebrew), *Mehkenei Yerushalayim be-Maḥshevet Yisrael* 10 (1992): 299–309. Cf. Benayahu, *Toledot ha-Ari,* 99.

67. On this technique, see Mark Verman and Shulamit H. Adler, "Path Jumping in the Jewish Magical Tradition," *Jewish Studies Quarterly* 1 (1993–94): 131–48. The technique is also part of the Islamic magical tradition. See the references in Gerrit Bos, "Moshe Mizrachi on Popular Science in Seventeenth Century Syria-Palestine," *Jewish Studies Quarterly* 3 (1996): 261 n. 68.

68. For the account in translation, see Case 5 of the Appendix. A didactic prologue introduces the account in Bacharach's *'Emek ha-Melekh,* but not the accounts in the earlier *Ta'alumot Ḥokhmah* or in Sambari's manuscript.

69. The more sympathetic portrayal may be found in *'Emek ha-Melekh* and *Ta'alumot Ḥokhmah.* Sambari adheres more strictly to a problematized portrayal of the situation. For a synoptic edition of these accounts in Hebrew, see Appendix 2 of Chajes, "Spirit Possession and the Construction of Early Modern Jewish Religiosity."

70. Sources differ as to the identity of this sage, owing to the probability that the earliest written source of the account provided no more than his initials. As it would happen, these initials were shared by a number of leading rabbinic figures in Safed in 1571, including Isaac Luria (Ashkenazi), Joseph Ashkenazi, Joseph Arzin, Isaac Arḥa, Joseph Alton, Jacob Altaraẓ, Israel Auri, and Judah Ashkenazi. According to Meir Benayahu, Joseph Ashkenazi is correct here, whereas David Tamar argues for Joseph Arzin. See Benayahu, *Toledot ha-Ari,* 46; Tamar, "On the Book *Toledot ha-Ari,*" 191.

71. A comparative morphological analysis of Lurianic exorcism technique will follow in Chapter 3 below.

72. Vital, *Sefer ha-Ḥezyonot,* 36. In a similar vein, Vital describes elsewhere in his

journal a consultation with sorcerers who engaged in divinatory practices involving the adjuration of demons. The sorcerers were unable to proceed because the demons were reluctant to appear in Vital's presence. See, e.g., Vital, *Sefer ha-Ḥezyonot*, 11–16.

73. See Vital, *Sefer ha-Ḥezyonot*, 1–13. The visionary women surrounding Vital are the subject of Chapter 4 below.

74. See Vital, *Sha'ar ha-Gilgulim*, 139b–40b. Vital discusses the complications of male-souled females in pregnancy and birth in Vital, *Sha'ar ha-Gilgulim*, 33a–35b.

75. See Vital, *Sha'ar ha-Gilgulim*, 128b, 32b, 33b. Cf. Vital, *Sha'ar ha-Gilgulim* (Radomsk ed.), 33c; Vital, *Sefer ha-Ḥezyonot*, 238. In the case of the possessed *woman* of Safed (Appendix, Case 7), Vital writes that Luria sent him to perform exorcisms specifically because of his Cainic descent. This will be discussed in Chapter 3 below.

76. Although medieval Jewish legal sources did not generally forbid nonlibidinous touching between the sexes, pietistic works tended to amplify such prohibitions or to upgrade their status from rabbinic to biblically mandated. Medical care in which the doctor was male and the patient female was one area where touching was almost universally accepted. Because treating the possessed was, at least in part, a healing intervention, there would be scant reason to object to physical contact between the exorcist and the possessed on the grounds of modesty alone. Relevant sources on these issues include Maimonides' *Mishna Torah*, Laws of Matriomony, Ch. 23; Joseph Karo, *Beit Yoseph 'al ha-Tur, Yoreh De'ah*, §195. A particularly stringent view may be found in the writings of the thirteenth-century Geronese Rabbenu Yonah. See his *Sha'arei Teshuva* (Gates of Repentance), III 90.

77. In the parallel case, the spirit anticipates Vital's arrival prophetically, questions Vital's capacity to evict him from his abode in the woman's body, but then greets Vital with great respect upon his entry.

78. The circumstances of the spirit's death are presented after a dialogue between Vital and the spirit over the meaning a rabbinic passage (Mishna *Eduyot* 2, 10). See above and the Appendix, Case 4. This close parallel with the account of the young man discussed above probably, though not necessarily, indicates literary dependence of one account on the other.

79. Until 1622, a Portuguese outpost at the mouth of the Persian Gulf. My thanks to Professor Geoffrey Parker for assisting me with this identification.

80. Benayahu located a reference to this episode in Abraham Galante's commentary on the Zohar, *Yeraḥ Yakar* (Ms. Jerusalem 8°493, 263b). See Benayahu, *Toledot ha-Ari*, 101.

81. The motif of a doe struggling with a painful delivery appears in Jewish mystical literature in an esoteric eschatological context. Although it seems unlikely that the account under consideration was fashioned with such an association in mind, it is an interesting possibility to consider. On the mystical parable, see Yehuda Liebes, "Two Fawns of a Doe: The Secret Homily of the AR"I Delivered before His Death," in *Meḥkerei Yerushalayim be-Maḥshevet Yisrael*, ed. Rachel Elior and Yehudah Liebes, *Kabbalat ha-Ari* (Jerusalem, 1992).

82. See Lewis, *Notes and Documents from the Turkish Archives: A Contribution to the History of the Jews in the Ottoman Empire*, 8.

83. Given what we know of Vital's own frequenting of Muslim wonder-workers,

this astonishment seems either disingenuous or a literary embellishment by someone unfamiliar (or uncomfortable) with Vital's openness in these matters. The entire passage of the account relating to the possession of the Kohen in Nablus is absent from Sambari's version, which has the doe wandering "crazily" until arriving in Safed and the spirit vacating the doe for the widow, who was among a crowd of people observing the strange behavior of the suffering doe.

84. Adjurations to demonic forces may be found in numerous works, including, e.g., Joseph Tirshom, *Shushan Yesod ha-'Olam*, Sassoon 290/Institute of Microfilmed Hebrew Manuscripts #39891; Moshe Zacuto and Abraham Alnakar, *Shorshei ha-Shemot*, 2 vols., vol. 1 (Jerusalem, 1995). These works will be discussed below.

85. See Léon (Pierre de Bérulle) D'Alexis, *Traicté des Energumènes, suivy d'un Discours sur la possession de Marthe Brossier, contre les calomnies d'un Médecin de Paris* (Troyes, 1599), fol. 38–39. Cited H. C. Lea, *Materials Toward a History of Witchcraft*, ed. Arthur C. Howland, 3 vols., vol. 3. (Philadelphia, 1939), 1062. On this image, see R. J. Zwi Werblowsky, "Ape and Essence," in *Ex Orde Religionum (Geo Widengren Festschrift)* (Leiden, 1972).

86. See Midelfort, "The Devil and the German People: Reflections on the Popularity of Demon Possession in Sixteenth-Century Germany," 112.

87. Moses Cordovero, "*Drishot be-'Inyanei ha-Malakhim me-ha-RM"K*," in *Malakhei 'Elyon*, ed. R. Margalioth (Jerusalem, 1945); *Or Yakar* vol. 17, Jerusalem, 1989). Translation from Werblowsky, *Joseph Karo: Lawyer and Mystic*, 81. Cf. Gershom Scholem, "The *Maggid* of R. Yosef Taitazak [Taytaczack] and the Revelations Attributed to Him" (in Hebrew), in *Sefunoth.* (The book of Greek Jewry—1), ed. Meir Benayahu (Jerusalem, 1971–78), 71–72. See also Chapter 1 above.

88. See Appendix, Case 3.

89. The wording here indicates that although Satan did not possess the woman upon her "invitation," the disembodied soul received "permission" to possess her, ostensibly from Satan. This would imply a belief that Satan oversaw the peregrinations of disembodied souls. The important early sixteenth-century kabbalistic work *Galya Raza* maintained a broader conception of this idea, namely that Satan and the *Sitra Aḥra* oversaw the entire realm of transmigration. See R. Elior, "The Doctrine of Transmigration in *Galya Raza*," in *Essential Papers on Kabbalah*, ed. Lawrence Fine (New York, 1995).

90. See, e.g., the discussions in BT *Sanhedrin* 45b ff., where the death penalty applied to blasphemers, witches, and idolators is discussed in a single Mishnaic passage. See also the remarks by Israel Ta-Shma, "Notes to 'Hymns from Qumran' " (in Hebrew), *Tarbiẓ* 55, no. 3 (1986): 440–42; Joshua Trachtenberg, *Jewish Magic and Superstition: A Study in Folk Religion*, (New York, 1939), 58–59; Eli Yasif, *Sippur ha-'Am ha-'Ivri* (Jerusalem and Beer Sheva, 1994), 394.

91. See David D. Hall, "A World of Wonders: The Mentality of the Supernatural in Seventeenth-Century New England," in *Seventeenth-Century New England*, ed. David D. Hall and David Grayson Allen (Charlottesville, 1984), 246.

92. Maureen Flynn, "Blasphemy and the Play of Anger in Sixteenth-Century Spain," *Past & Present* 149 (November 1995): 29–57.

93. Jean-Pierre Dedieu, "Les causes de foi de l'Inquisition de Tolede (1483–1820)," *Melanges de la Casa de Velazquez*, 14 (1978): 148ff.

94. See, e.g., Zohar 2:267b; cf. Menasseh ben Israel's discussion of this matter in *Nishmat Ḥayyim* III 27, 268.

95. Psalms 113–118, which are included in the liturgy on special occasions to express thanksgiving and joy. On Passover night and its rituals, see E. D. Goldschmidt, ed., *The Passover Haggadah: Its Source and History* (Jerusalem, 1969).

96. Although he managed to bring about the spirit's expulsion, Vital was unable to rectify the spirit, who was consigned to his torments until the last bastard whom he had fathered died. The irrevocability of the spirit's punishment and Vital's inability to assist in his rectification brought "the many assembled" to tears and repentance.

97. The frequent lack of *mezuzot* among medieval Jews is noted in Elliott Horowitz, "The Way We Were: 'Jewish Life in the Middle Ages,' " *Jewish History* 1, no. 1 (1986).

98. Although some rabbinic authorities made earnest efforts to mitigate the view that the mezuzah was an amulet, this perception, already explicit in talmudic literature (e.g., Jerusalem Talmud *Peah* 1:1, 15d; BT *Avodah Zarah*, 11a), remained dominant. For a critique of this view, see Maimonides, *Mishnah Torah, Hilkhot Tefillin*, 5 §4.

99. On this work, see Robert Brody, *The Geonim of Babylonia and the Shaping of Medieval Jewish Culture* (New Haven, Conn., 1998), 202–15.

100. See *Sheiltot* on the weekly portion *Ekev*, and the comments of Z. H. Chajes in Z. H. Chajes, "Demons, Witchcraft, Incantations, Dreams, and Planetary Influences, Medical Prescriptions, and Curative Methods in the Aggadah (Including also References to Additions in the Gemara by the Saboraim)," in *The Student's Guide Through the Talmud* (London, 1952), 236.

101. Midelfort, "The Devil and the German People: Reflections on the Popularity of Demon Possession in Sixteenth-Century Germany," 118.

102. See Chapter 2 for Scholem's remarks to this effect, cited from Gershom Scholem, *Sabbatai Sevi, the Mystical Messiah, 1626–1676*, rev. and aug. translation of the Hebrew ed., trans. R. J. Zwi Werblowsky (Princeton, 1973), 19. For an introduction to the mystical pietism of sixteenth-century Safed, see Lawrence Fine, ed., *Safed Spirituality: Rules of Mystical Piety, the Beginning of Wisdom* (New York, 1984).

103. Scholem, *Sabbatai Sevi, The Mystical Messiah, 1626–1676*, 19.

104. Joseph Dan, "Rabbi Joseph Karo: Halakhist and Mystic" (in Hebrew), *Tarbiẓ* 33 (1964): 89–96, esp. p. 93. Dan is here summarizing the argument made in Jacob Katz, "The Ordination Controversy between R. Jacob Berab and R. Levi b. Ḥabib" (in Hebrew), *Ẓion* 16 (1951): 28–45. In the lines that follow those quoted, Dan notes that even more astounding than the audacity of the megalomaniacal aspirations of individuals (e.g., Karo and Vital), is the fact their aspirations—nonmessianic, at least—were realized. Safed and its rabbis indeed became the font of legal and mystical teaching for the entire Jewish world.

M. Pachter's studies also provide generous evidence of Safed's pietistic aspirations, while asserting the relative marginality of the circle of Luria within the larger Jewish population. See, for example, the many synagogues and study halls noted in Pachter, " 'Terrible Vision' by R. Moses Alsheikh" (in Hebrew) 76–77. On Luria and the larger community of Safed, see Mordechai Pachter, "The Eulogy of R. Samuel Uzeda upon the Death of the AR"I," in *From Safed's Hidden Treasures: Studies and Texts Concerning the History of Safed and Its Sages in the Sixteenth Century* (Jerusalem, 1994).

## *Chapter 3*

1. Julio Caro Baroja, *The World of the Witches*, trans. O. N. V. Glendinning (Chicago, 1964), 134.

2 See Nancy Caciola, "Discerning Spirits: Sanctity and Possession in the Later Middle Ages" (Ph.D. diss., University of Michigan, 1994); Nancy Caciola, "Wraiths, Revenants, and Ritual in Medieval Culture," *Past and Present* 152 (1996): 3–45. On the subject of ritual more generally in the early modern period, see Edward Muir, *Ritual in Early Modern Europe: New Approaches to European History* (Cambridge, 1997).

The exorcism rite from the *Rituale Romanum* has been published in English by the Catholic Church. See *The Roman Ritual*, trans. Philip T. Weller (Milwaukee, 1964).

3. See Flavius Josephus, *The Complete Works of Flavius-Josephus, the Celebrated Jewish Historian; Comprising the History and Antiquities of the Jews, with the Destruction of Jerusalem by the Romans. With His autobiography*, trans. William Whiston (Chicago, 1900), Antiquities, vi. 8, §2.

4. See Jonathan Z. Smith, *Map Is Not Territory: Studies in the History of Religions* (Leiden, 1978). A synthetic overview may be found in Naomi Janowitz, *Magic in the Roman World: Pagans, Jews and Christians* (London, 2001), 27–46.

5. On exorcism in the New Testament, see Henry Ansgar Kelly, *The Devil, Demonology, and Witchcraft: The Development of Christian Beliefs in Evil Spirits*, rev. ed. (Garden City, 1974); Morton Smith, *Jesus the Magician* (New York, 1978); Graham H. Twelftree, *Jesus the Exorcist: A Contribution to the Study of the Historical Jesus* (Tübingen, 1993).

The apocryphal Book of Tobit (composed approx. third century B.C.E.) also contains an exorcism account that calls for the use of fumigated fish intestines to expel demons. R. Kotansky has suggested that the story "reflects in its ritual instruction and overall diction a dependence upon magico-medical handbooks, much like those preserved in the later magical papyri." Roy Kotansky, "Greek Exorcistic Amulets," in *Ancient Magic and Ritual Power*, ed. Marvin Meyer and Paul Mirecki, Religions in the Graeco-Roman World (Leiden, 1995), 258–59.

Exorcism in Qumran has been treated in R. H. Eisenman and M. Wise, *The Dead Sea Scrolls Uncovered* (Shaftesbury, 1992); Bilha Nitzan, "Hymns from Qumran 'to Frighten and to Terrify' Evil Ghosts" (in Hebrew), *Tarbiẓ* 55, no. 1 (1985): 19–46.

6. See Meir Bar-Ilan, "Exorcism of Demons by Rabbis: On the Involvment of Talmudic Sages in Magic" (in Hebrew), *Da'at* 34 (1994): 61–77. On rabbinic-era magic more generally, see P. S. Alexander, "Incantations and Books of Magic," in *Emil*

*Schürer, The History of the Jewish People in the Age of Jesus Christ,* ed. G. Vermes, F. Millar, M. Goodman, and M. Black (Edinburgh, 1986); L. Blau, *Das altjüdische Zauberwesen* (Budapest, 1898); Jacob Neusner, *The Wonder Working Lawyers of Babylonia* (Lanham, 1987); Peter Schäfer, "Jewish Magic Literature in Late Antiquity and Early Middle Ages," *Journal of Jewish Studies* 41 (1990): 75–91; Michael D. Swartz, *Scholastic Magic: Ritual and Revelation in Early Jewish Mysticism* (Princeton, N.J., 1997). See also the bibliographic essay "On Transforming and Replicating Nature: The Place of Magic in Ancient Judaism" in David Ruderman, *Jewish Thought and Scientific Discovery in Early Modern Europe* (New Haven, Conn., 1995), 14–53.

7. D. Mandeboim, ed., *Pesikta de Rav Kahana* (New York, 1962), 1:74.

8. Bar-Ilan, "Exorcism of Demons by Rabbis: On the Involvment of Talmudic Sages in Magic," 18–19 and n. 11.

9. See B. M. Boxer, "Wonder-Working and the Rabbinic Tradition: The Case of Hanina ben Dosa," *Journal for the Study of Judaism* 16 (1985): 45–92.

10. "R. Yehudah be-Rabi Kalonymus me-Shapira," in *Yeḥusei Tenaim ve-Amoraim,* ed. Y. L. Hakohen Maimon (Jerusalem, 1962), 438. This story survives only in a twelfth-century Ashkenazic work, but Bar-Ilan argues that it is most probably an authentic rabbinic-era source. See Bar-Ilan, "Exorcism of Demons by Rabbis: On the Involvment of Talmudic Sages in Magic," 19–20. The medieval source also accords very well with another Talmudic source [BT *Pesaḥim* 112b] in which R. Ḥanina encounters the queen of the demons, Igrat bat Maḥlat, and decrees upon her that she flee from any inhabited locale.

11. See BT *Me'ilah* 17a-b, and W. Bacher, "La Legende de L'Exorcisme D'un Demon par Simon B. Yohai," *Revue des études juives* 35 (1897): 285–87.

12. Adolph Jellinek, ed., *Bet ha-Midrasch,* 3rd ed., 2 vols., vol. 2 (Jerusalem, 1967), 128–30.

13. *Antiquitates Judaicae* 8.42–49. On the work on healing hidden by Hezekiah, see the *Baraitha* in BT *Pesaḥim* 56a. See also Dennis C. Duling, "The Elazar Miracle and Solomon's Magical Wisdom in Flavius Josephus's Antiquitates Judaicae 8:42–49," *HTR* 78 (1985): 1–25.

14. See *De Bello Judaico,* vii.6 §3, cited in *The Jewish Encyclopedia,* s.v. "Demonology."

15. Flavius Josephus, *Kadmoniot ha-Yehudim,* trans. A. Shalit (Jerusalem, 1976), 125. Shalit's identification is disputed by M. Bar-Ilan in Bar-Ilan, "Exorcism of Demons by Rabbis: On the Involvment of Talmudic Sages in Magic," 18. Cf. the discussion of this passage in Duling, "The Elazar Miracle and Solomon's Magical Wisdom in Flavius Josephus's *Antiquitates Judaicae* 8:42–49"; Nitzan, "Hymns from Qumran 'to Frighten and to Terrify' Evil Ghosts," 42.

16. See Janowitz, *Magic in the Roman World: Pagans, Jews and Christians,* 25–26.

17. Origen, *Contra Celsum,* trans. Henry Chadwick (Cambridge: Cambridge University Press, 1965), IV 33, 209. Origen took pains to argue that Christian exorcism was itself not magical. See Origen, "Against Celsus," I: 24–25 and R. Bardy, "Origène et la Magie," *Revue des Sciences Religieuses* 18 (1928): 126–42.

18. Origen, *Contra Celesum,* IV 34, 210.

19. See Marcel Simon, *Verus Israel: A Study of the Relations between Christians*

*and Jews in the Roman Empire (135–425)*, trans. H. McKeating (Oxford, 1986), 339–68 (quotation on 40); Kotansky, "Greek Exorcistic Amulets," 246. On the cultural contacts between the ancient Near East and Greece generally, see W. Burkert, *The Orientalizing Revolution: Near Eastern Influence on Greek Culture in the Early Archaic Age*, trans. M. E. Pinder and W. Burkert (Cambridge, 1992), 55–72 (on exorcism).

20. On the *PGM*, see Hans Dieter Betz, ed., *The Greek Magical Papyri in Translation, Including the Demotic Spells* (Chicago, 1986).

21. See Hans Dieter Betz, "Jewish Magic in the Greek Magical Papyri," in *Envisioning Magic*, ed. Peter Schäfer and Hans G. Kippenberg (Leiden, 1997).

22. A legendary magician from Egypt.

23. *PGM* IV 3007–86, in Betz, ed., *The Greek Magical Papyri in Translation, Including the Demotic Spells*, 96–97. This text is analyzed in Adolf Deissmann, *Light from the Ancient East: The New Testament Illustrated by Recently Discovered Texts of the Graeco-Roman World*, trans. Lionel R. M. Strachan (London, 1927), 256–64; Janowitz, *Magic in the Roman World: Pagans, Jews and Christians*, 41–43; W. L. Knox, "Jewish Liturgical Exorcism," *Harvard Theological Review* 31, no. 3 (1938): 191–203; Simon, *Verus Israel: A Study of the Relations Between Christians and Jews in the Roman Empire (135–425)*, 349–51; Daniel Sperber, "Some Rabbinic Themes in Magical Papyri," *Journal for the Study of Judaism* 16 (1985): 95–99.

24. Jews were not entirely averse to being treated by Christian healers who used the name of Jesus. Fourteenth-century R. Menachem ben Meir of Speyer apparently believed that such usage should be permissable because the sounds rather than the names accounted for the effectiveness of the treatment. See Joshua Trachtenberg, *Jewish Magic and Superstition: A Study in Folk Religion* (New York, 1939), 200. Claudia Rohrbacher-Sticker, "From Sense to Nonsense, from Incantation Prayer to Magical Spell," *Jewish Studies Quarterly* 3, no. 1 (1996): 27.

25. Herbal exorcism techniques appear in the story in Josephus above. See C. Bonner, "The Technique of Exorcism," *Harvard Theological Review* 36 (1943): p. 47.

26. See Meir Bar-Ilan, "Writing a *Sefer Torah, Tefilin,* and *Mezuzah* on Deer Skin" (in Hebrew), *Beit Mikrah* 30, no. 102 (1985): 375–81. The Church Council of Laodicaea (c. 360) condemned *tefillin* precisely on the grounds that they were magical accoutrements. See Simon, *Verus Israel: A Study of the Relations Between Christians and Jews in the Roman Empire (135–425)*, 361, 364.

27. Michelde Certeau, "Discourse Disturbed," in *The Writing of History* (New York, 1988), 246–47 55–56.

28. See David Frankfurter, "Narrating Power; The Theory and Practice of the Magical *Historiola* in Ritual Spells," in *Ancient Magic and Ritual Power*, ed. Marvin W. Meyer and Paul Allan Mirecki (Leiden, 1995).

29. See the *Metamorphoses* of Apuleius, I. 19. 62; BT *Sanhedrin* 67b; *Berakhot* 51a. Additional references may be found in Trachtenberg, *Jewish Magic and Superstition: A Study in Folk Religion*, 298, n. 11. See also Knox, "Jewish Liturgical Exorcism," 195. "The God who drowned the king of Egypt and the Egyptians in the Red Sea" is cited by Origen as one of the "formulae which are often used to overcome daemons or certain evil powers" in Origen, "Against Celsus," IV 34, 210. Islamic amulets against

demons also mention the parting of the sea. See, e.g., the amulet in *Kitab Mujaribat* by Sheikh Ahmed Al Dirbi. This amulet is translated in Samuel M. Zwemer, "The Familiar Spirit or *Qarina*," in *Studies in Popular Islam: A Collection of Papers Dealing with the Superstitions and Beliefs of the Common People* (London and New York, 1939), 63–64. Cf. Ignaz Goldziher, "Wasser als Dämonen abwehrendes Mittle," *Archiv für Religionswissenschaft* 13 (1910): 20–46.

A tale in the Dialogue of Caesarius of Heisterbach involves the crossing of the Rhine River to cure a demonic ailment:

> She was made so demented and was so out of her senses, as much from grief as from diabolic influence, that she used to put little worms . . . into her mouth and eat them. The father was saddened, and he sent her across the Rhine, hoping that the change of air would do her good, and that she might be liberated from the incubus demon through the interposition of the river. After the girl was sent across, the demon appeared to the priest and said in shouting words, "Wicked priest, why have you stolen my wife from me?" (*Dial.* I: 121; cited in Caciola, "Discerning Spirits: Sanctity and Possession in the Later Middle Ages," 198)

Parallels between the tales of Caesarius of Heisterbach and medieval Jewish folklore are adduced in Eli Yasif, *Sippur ha-'Am ha-'Ivri* (Jerusalem and Beer Sheva, 1994), 386–99.

Sixteenth-century Catholic exorcism manuals include warnings against sending the possessed through rivers: "Put aside the superstition that the ignorant hold, to send [possessed persons] to running rivers." Caciola, "Discerning Spirits: Sanctity and Possession in the Later Middle Ages," 188–89. My interpretation here differs, however, from Caciola's.

30. Ioan P. Couliano, *Eros and Magic in the Renaissance* (Chicago, 1987), 117.

31. Baroja, *The World of the Witches*, 134. Celestina was the witchlike protagonist of the great masterpiece of late fifteenth-century literature known as *La Celestina.*

32. See, e.g., Joseph Naveh, *'Al Ḥeres ve-Gomeh* (On Pottery and Papyrus) (Jerusalem, 1992), 159; Joseph Naveh and Shaul Shaked, *Amulets and Magic Bowls: Aramaic Incantations of Late Antiquity*, 2nd corrected ed. (Jerusalem, 1987), 88. Seventeenth-century (primarily) Hebrew magical manuscripts, to be discussed below, also include techniques identical to ones discovered in the Cairo Geniza as well as in Heikhalot literature. See Gerrit Bos, "Moshe Mizrachi on Popular Science in Seventeenth Century Syria-Palestine," *Jewish Studies Quarterly* 3 (1996): 259, nn. 52 and 53. Bos also notes parallel procedures in twelfth-century Arabic magic.

33. See, e.g., the manuscripts cited in Richard Kieckhefer, *Magic in the Middle Ages* (Cambridge, 1990), 73, 85, 159. Regarding the name *AGLA*, H. Zafrani writes, "Il semble que ce fameux Nom fut plus ouvent utilisé par les magiciens chrétiens que par les fabricants juifs d'amulettes." Haïm Zafrani, *Kabbale, vie mystique et magie* (Paris, 1986), 394. Cf. Trachtenberg, *Jewish Magic and Superstition: A Study in Folk Religion*, 262. For other examples of Christian use of Hebrew in amulets, see T. Schrire, *Hebrew Amulets: Their Decipherment and Interpretation* (London, 1966), 69–72.

34. *Tratado*, 64. Cited in LuAnn Homza, *Religious Authority in the Spanish Renaissance* (Baltimore, 2000), 199.

35. This critique is discussed at length in Simon, *Verus Israel: A Study of the Relations Between Christians and Jews in the Roman Empire (135–425)*, 339–68.

36. Daniel Defoe, *A System of Magick; or, A History of the Black Art. Being an Historical Account of Mankind's Most Early Dealings with the Devil; and How the Acquaintance of Both Sides First Began* (London, 1727), 402. Defoe has been discussed recently in Ian Bostridge, *Witchcraft and Its Transformations, c.1650–c.1750*, Oxford Historical Monographs (Oxford, 1997), 111–38.

37. Samuel M. Zwemer, *The Influence of Animism on Islam: An Account of Popular Superstitions* (London, 1920), 192.

38. Joseph Tirshom, *Shushan Yesod ha-'Olam*, Sasson 290 (Institute for Microfilmed Hebrew Manuscripts # 39891). The description of the manuscript and the author that follows is based on Meir Benayahu, "The Book 'Shoshan Yesod ha-'Olam' by Rabbi Joseph Tirshom (MS Sassoon 290)" (in Hebrew), in *Temirin*, ed. Israel Weinstock (Jerusalem, 1972). For a recent study based on the manuscript, see Rohrbacher-Sticker, "From Sense to Nonsense, from Incantation Prayer to Magical Spell." The odd name of this work may be the result of its having been formulated to equal the numerical value of the author's name: Joseph ben Elijah Tirshom. (Noted by Weinstock in Benayahu, "The Book 'Shoshan Yesod ha-'Olam' by Rabbi Joseph Tirshom (MS Sassoon 290)," 188 n. 5.) The first word may be rendered as *Shushan* (the city) or *Shoshan* (lily). Cf. Gershom Scholem, *Kabbalah* (New York, 1974), 324.

39. Benayahu, "The Book 'Shoshan Yesod ha-'Olam' by Rabbi Joseph Tirshom (MS Sassoon 290)," 201.

40. Ibid., 202–4. *Ḥarba de-Moshe* (The Sword of Moses), *Sefer ha-Kasdim* (The Book of the Chaldeans), and *Sefer ha-Razim* (The Book of the Mysteries) are among the works Tirshom copied into the manuscript. The first has recently been published in a scientific edition. See Yuval Harrari, *Ḥarba de-Moshe* (Jerusalem, 1997). To get an impression of the material in English, Moses Gaster's century-old editions may still be consulted. See Moses Gaster, *The Sword of Moses: An Ancient Book of Magic from a Unique Manuscript* (London, 1896); Moses Gaster, "The Wisdom of the Chaldeans: An Old Hebrew Astrological Text," in *Studies and Texts* (London, 1925–28). For *Sefer ha-Razim*, see Mordechai Margaliyot, ed., *Sefer ha-Razim* (Jerusalem, 1966). For an English edition, see Michael A. Morgan, ed., *Sefer ha-Razim* (Book of the Mysteries) (Chico, Calif., 1983).

41. Benayahu, "The Book 'Shoshan Yesod ha-'Olam' by Rabbi Joseph Tirshom (MS Sassoon 290)," 200 n. 41.

42. Ibid., 206.

43. On Ẓemaḥ, see Gershom Scholem, "On the Biography and Literary Activity of the Kabbalist R. Jacob Ẓemaḥ" (in Hebrew), *Qiryat Sefer* 26 (1950): 185–94. The classic study on Sevi is Gershom Scholem, *Sabbatai Sevi, the Mystical Messiah, 1626–1676*, rev. and aug. translation, trans. R. J. Zwi Werblowsky (Princeton, N.J., 1973).

44. Benayahu, "The Book 'Shoshan Yesod ha-'Olam' by Rabbi Joseph Tirshom (MS Sassoon 290)," 194.

45. Certain Psalms have a long history of magical use. Psalm 91, referred to in BT *Shavuot* 15b as "the song of evil spirits"(*shir shel pega'im*), was perhaps the most

common medieval antidemonic Psalm. See Trachtenberg, *Jewish Magic and Superstition: A Study in Folk Religion*, 112–13 n. 25; Meir Benayahu, *Sefer Zikaron: Ma'amadot ve-Moshavot* (Studies in Memory of the Rishon Le-Zion R. Yiẓḥak Nissim), vol. 6 (Jersualem, 1985); Gershom Scholem, " 'Havdalah d'Rebbe 'Akiva'—Source for the Jewish Magical Tradition in the Gaonic Period" (in Hebrew), *Tarbiẓ* 50 (1980–81): 243–81. The antidemonic use of this Psalm is already to be found in Qumran literature. See n. 5 above. This Psalm is also quoted by Satan in Matt. 4:6 in his attempt to convince Jesus to jump from the roof of the temple and fly. The magical use of this Psalm is implicitly discredited by association with the devil. See Smith, *Jesus the Magician*, 105.

Psalm 91 recited forward and backward, is used in a procedure recommended by Vital in his magical and alchemical manuscript (Ms. Musayoff 219) to cure someone who has been injured by a demon. See Gerrit Bos, "Ḥayyim Vital's 'Practical Kabbalah and Alchemy': A Seventeenth Century Book of Secrets," *The Journal of Jewish Thought and Philosophy* 4 (1994): 74. We will also find it prescribed by the seventeenth-century R. Moses Zacuto in one of his exorcism procedures discussed below.

Psalms played a central role in Catholic exorcisms as well. See the many Psalms in the *Rituale Romanum* and in the ceremonies in Adolf Franz, *Die Kirchlichen Benediktionen im Mittelalter* (Freiburg im Breisgau, 1909), II, 586–615.

46. See Sassoon Ms. 290, §493. Date palms were considered popular abodes for pernicious spirits, so this formula may be based on an attractive-sympathetic principle.

47. Sassoon Ms. 290, §265 (125); Benayahu, "The Book 'Shoshan Yesod ha-'Olam' by Rabbi Joseph Tirshom (Sassoon Ms. 290)," 222. Sources from Sophocles, Philostratus, the New Testament, and the Greek Magical Papyri routinely conflate natural illnesses, such as fevers, with demonic possession. See Sophocles, *Philoctetes* 758ff.; Philostratus, *Life* IV.10; Mark 1.31; Luke 4.38ff.; *PGM* XIV.25ff. See also the discussion in Smith, *Jesus the Magician*, 106–7, 95–96.

48. Benayahu, "The Book 'Shoshan Yesod ha-'Olam' by Rabbi Joseph Tirshom (Sassoon Ms. 290)," 230; Tirshom, *Shushan Yesod ha-'Olam*, §481. Cf. Moshe Zacuto, *Sefer ha-Shemot* (MS facimile) (Jerusalem, 1987), 10b; Moshe Zacuto and Abraham Alnakar, *Shorshei ha-Shemot*, 2 vols., vol 1, (A:148:1), 52. On this work, see below, and Gershom Scholem, *Kitvei Yad be-Kabbalah*, ed. B. Joel, vol. 1, *Kitvei ha-Yad Ha-'Ivriim: ha-Nimẓaim be-Vait ha-Sefarim ha-Leumi ve-ha-Universitai be-Yerushalayim* (Jerusalem, 1930), 54; Scholem, *Kabbalah*, 186; Zafrani, *Kabbale, vie mystique et magie*, 405. Portions of the work were translated into French and appeared in Moïse Schwab, *Le Ms. 1380 du Fonds hébreu* (Paris, 1899).

49. Cf. *Tikkunei ha-Zohar, Tikkun* 60 (93a).

50. The expansion (*millui*) of the tetragrammaton associated with the angelic dimension, or "World of *Yeẓirah*," in medieval kabbalah.

51. Tirshom, *Shushan Yesod ha-'Olam*, §511, 225–26.

52. On natural and demonic magic, see Stuart Clark, *Thinking with Demons: The Idea of Witchcraft in Early Modern Europe* (Oxford, 1997), 214–50; Kieckhefer, *Magic in the Middle Ages*, 8–17.

53. Certeau has written extensively of the theatrical elements of spirit possession. "Possession is the scene of a play, while sorcery is a conflict. . . . In this respect,

possession is a phenomenon parallel to the creation of theater in the sixteenth and seventeenth centuries." Certeau, "Discourse Disturbed," 245–46. This subject is treated at length in Michel de Certeau, *La Possession de Loudun* Collection Archive Series, vol. 37, (Paris, 1970). The analysis of possession and exorcism in terms of theater has also been undertaken by anthropologists. See Bruce Kapferer, *A Celebration of Demons: Exorcism and the Aesthetics of Healing in Sri Lanka* (Bloomington, Ind., 1983).

54. Because of its harsh condemnation of idols and "vanity"—the latter having in Hebrew the same numerical value (*mispar katan*) as Jesus (316)—the prayer was repeatedly censured by the Inquisition. See Abraham E. Millgram, *Jewish Worship* (Philadelphia, 1971), 455–57.

55. On this technique, see Blau, *Das altjüdische Zauberwesen*, 85, 148–49; Joseph Naveh and Shaul Shaked, *Magic Spells and Forumulae: Aramaic Incantations of Late Antiquity* (Jerusalem, 1993), 27; Trachtenberg, *Jewish Magic and Superstition: A Study in Folk Religion*, 116.

56. See Jean Bodin, *On the Demon-Mania of Witches*, abr. ed., trans. Randy A. Scott, ed. Jonathan L. Pearl (Toronto, 1995), 97. Bodin's assertion seems to be borne out by the mention of such techniques in mid-sixteenth-century trials against magical healers in Italy, many of whom were accused of reciting the Pater Noster backward (*all'roversa overo indietro*). See Mary Rose O'Neil, "Discerning Superstition: Popular Errors and Orthodox Response in Late Sixteenth Century Italy" (Ph.D. diss., Stanford University, 1981), 62, 119.

57. The technique could also be applied in mystical contemplation. Of its use in this context, Gershom Scholem wrote, "Permutations of the letters of holy names, forward and backwards, are the secret of the supernal motion of the divine world, and there is in them also something of the secret of the motion of the spheres." See Scholem, "The *Maggid* of R. Yosef Taitazak [Taytaczack] and the Revelations Attributed to Him" (in Hebrew), in *Sefunoth* (The Book of Greek Jewry—1), ed. Meir Benayahu (Jerusalem, 1971–78), 87.

58. Yizhak Bar Sheshet, *She'elot u-Teshuvot Rabbenu Yiẓḥak Bar Sheshet* (Jerusalem, 1993), §92.

59. For the prescription of fumigations in exorcism manuals, see *Thesaurus Exorcismorum* (Cologne, 1626), 417.

60. Cited in H. C. Lea, *Materials Toward a History of Witchcraft*, ed. Arthur C. Howland, 3 vols., vol. 3, 1054, 1061.

61. Lynn Thorndike, *A History of Magic and Experimental Science*, 8 vols., vol. 8 (New York, 1923–58), 547.

62. D. P. Walker, *Unclean Spirits: Possession and Exorcism in France and England in the Late Sixteenth and Early Seventeenth Centuries* (Philadelphia, 1981), 46.

63. On the *sliḥot* penitential liturgy, see Millgram, *Jewish Worship*, 226–31.

64. See Lea, *Materials Toward a History of Witchcraft*, vol. 2, 1054; Thorndike, *A History of Magic and Experimental Science*, 557.

65. Such suggestive manipulation of the woman's body by these exorcists is striking, though it pales besides reports like those surrounding Puritan diviner Cotton Mather, who exposed and fondled the breasts of demoniacs, including a seventeen-year-old at Salem. See M. Wynn Thomas, "Cotton Mather's *Wonders of the Invisible*

*World*: Some Metamorphoses of Salem Witchcraft," in *The Damned Art: Essays in the Literature of Witchcraft* (London, 1977), 206.

66. Rapid "repossession" was a common phenomenon. Barthélemy Perdoux, an early seventeenth-century French doctor, described it in his *De Morbis Animi* of 1639. His explanations are discussed in Sarah Ferber, "The Demonic Possession of Marthe Brossier, France 1598–1600," in *No Gods Except Me: Orthodoxy and Religious Practice in Europe, 1200–1600*, ed. Charles Zika (Melbourne, 1991), 63.

67. The case, discussed above, is reproduced in the Appendix, Case 7.

68. The rationale for Luria's decision will be spelled out in our analysis below.

69. Vital, *Sha'ar Ruaḥ ha-Kodesh*, 90b. Luria's new approach to exorcism is noted en passant in the accounts of the cases in which he was involved in 1571 and 1572. The technical details of the new techniques may be found in various recensions of Vital's writings, including *Sha'ar Ruaḥ ha-Kodesh* (Gate of the Holy Spirit), *Sha'ar ha-Yiḥudim* (Gate of the Unifications), and *Ronu le-Ya'akov* (Rejoice for Jacob).

*Sha'ar Ruaḥ ha-Kodesh* was redacted by Vital's son Shmuel, whereas *Sha'ar ha-Yiḥudim* (based on material common to *Sha'ar Ruaḥ ha-Kodesh)* and *Ronu le-Ya'akov* (based on material common to *Sha'ar ha-Gilgulim*, another Shmuel Vital redaction) were redacted by Jacob Ẓemaḥ. Later works presenting Luria's exorcism procedures are simply copies or abridgements of these presentations. See, e.g., Emanuel Ḥiriki, *Mishnat Ḥasidim* (Amsterdam, 1727), 110a.

70. *Kofeh*, as in the famous use of BT *Nedarim* 20b, "as if overcome by a *shed*."

71. The choreography of the ritual is somewhat clearer in the version of this technique preserved in *Sha'ar ha-Yiḥudim*. The exorcist is positioned behind the possessed in a sort of rear-embrace, gripping his or her wrists while intoning phrases into his or her right ear: "And I, Ḥayyim, would practice and tried a number of times to hold the right and left arm[s] at the place of the pulse, for there is the *Ruaḥ*. From this position, I would say that verse in his right ear, forward and backward." See Vital, *Sha'ar ha-Yiḥudim*, 16a.

72. It is instructive to compare this to the version preserved in the *Sha'ar ha-Yiḥudim:*

> Behold, you already know that there is no wicked man before whom is not to be found a court and guards who punish him according to his deeds, and a *satan* who tyrannizes him to destroy wrongdoing and sin. And King David prayed with regard to his enemies, "Appoint over him a wicked man. . . ." and the intention is that the Blessed Holy One should punish [also a meaning of *lifkod*, "appoint"] those who despise Him with a wicked man who will pentrate and become impregnated [*yit'abber*] in him, like those spirits who wander in the world and enter the body of a man. And the sign is that in that place a buldge appears in the body of a person, like an egg, and the spirit afflicts the person and compulsion and different sorts of suffering. And this is the secret of "Appoint over him a wicked man." Now each and every day, this wicked man must be judged according to his deeds and must depart from that body to be judged in Gehinnom. He then leaves a *satan* and a *shed* in his place to hold the place so that he might be able to return again. This is the secret of "And the *satan* will stand on his right," that the *satan* will hold his place. And behold this verse, which is itself a curse, is the remedy [*segulah*] and *yiḥud* to expell a *Ruaḥ ra'ah* from the body of a person, for the Blessed Holy One, that which he uses to crush, he uses to heal.

73. I have located this in only one other context: in the *yiḥud* against plague adduced in *Sha'ar ha-Yiḥudim.* Possibly borne of kabbalistic-numerological considerations, the name may be broken down into SG (63—the expansion of YHVH in the World of *Briah* [Creation]) and ZGIEL (52—the expansion of YHVH in the World of *'Asiyah* [Action]). Although this explanation is offered in one edition of the *yiḥud,* the numbers only work if one adds one for the word itself, a common tactic known as "adding the *kollel*" in the lingo of *gematria.* The name is very similar to the better-known ZGZGEL and SGNZGEL, about which one can find rich associations in Reuben Margalioth, *Malakhei 'Elyon* (Jerusalem, 1945).

74. That one goal of exorcism is to assist the possessing spirit to reincarnate normally is stated explicitly in Vital, *Sha'ar ha-Gilgulim,* 60b.

75. On the history of the relationship between epilepsy and possession, see Owsei Temkin, *The Falling Sickness,* 2nd ed. (Baltimore, 1971), 86ff, 138ff; Walker, *Unclean Spirits: Possession and Exorcism in France and England in the Late Sixteenth and Early Seventeenth Centuries,* 11. For a sustained examination of the early modern attempts to delineate clearly between possession, madness, epilepsy, witchcraft, and so on, see Robert Mandrou, *Magistrats et sorciers en France au XVII$^{e}$ siècle: Une analyse de psychologie historique* (Paris, 1968). A list of Jewish sources associating epilepsy and possession may be found in Benayahu, *Toledot ha-Ari,* 295 n. 6.

76. Vital, *Sha'ar ha-Yiḥudim,* 16a. Cf. Vital, *Sha'ar ha-Gilgulim,* 24b.

77. See Benayahu, *Toledot ha-Ari* (Studies and texts), 190, 253, 295 n. 7.

78. On scientific views regarding blood and circulation in this period, see Jerome J. Bylebyl, "Disputation and Description in the Renaissance Pulse Controversy," in *The Medical Renaissance of the Sixteenth Century,* ed. A. Wear, R. K. French, and Iain M. Lonie (Cambridge, 1985); Karl Eduard Rothschuh, "Von der Viersäftelehre zur Korpuskeltheorie des Blutes," in *Einführung in die Geschichte der Hämatologie,* ed. Karl G. Boroviczeny, et al. (Stuttgart, 1974); Heinrich Schipperges, "Blut in Altertum und Mittelalter," in *Einführung in die Geschichte der Hämatologie,* ed. K. Boroviczeny, et al. (Stuttgart, 1974); Andrew Wear, "Medicine in Early Modern Europe, 1500–1700," in *The Western Medical Tradition: 800 B.C.–1800 A.D,* ed. Lawrence I. Conrad, et al. (Cambridge, 1995), 325–40.

79. Ḥayyim Vital, *Adam Yashar* (Jerusalem, Ahavat Shalom, 1994), 42b; Ḥayyim Vital, *Eẓ Ḥayyim,* ed. Yehuda Zvi Brandwein, 15 vols., vol. 2, *Kitvei Rabbenu Ha-Ari ZT"L* (Jerusalem, 1988), Gate 40, §12 pp. 285–86. I have adopted variants from Etẓ Ḥayyim.

80. Vital, *Sha'ar Ruaḥ ha-Kodesh,* 14.

81. For a recent work presenting classical rabbinic and kabbalistic Jewish concepts of anatomy and physiology, see Moshe Yair Weinstock, *Mareh ha-Adam* (Jerusalem, 1995).

82. Stanley Tambiah, "The Magical Power of Words," in *Culture, Thought, and Social Action: An Anthropological Perspective* (Cambridge, Mass. 1985), 20–21. Rebecca Lesses has written in a similar vein that divine or angelic language allows "the human being . . . [to] utter words in the adjuration that he does not understand. In the context of the adjuration it is not important that he comprehend them. What is impor-

tant is that the angel understands and obeys the words." See Rebecca M. Lesses, "The Adjuration of the Prince of the Presence: Performative Utterance in a Jewish Ritual," in *Ancient Magic and Ritual Power*, ed. Marvin Meyer and Paul Mirecki (Leiden, 1995). Cf. Patricia Cox Miller, "In Praise of Nonsense," in *Classical Mediterranean Spirituality*, ed. A. H. Armstrong (London, 1986).

83. See Rohrbacher-Sticker, "From Sense to Nonsense, from Incantation Prayer to Magical Spell," 24–28.

84. The word *spell* is itself related to speech, etymologically related to the German *spiel*; *incantation*, similarly derives from the Latin *incantare*, to chant or to sing. On the Hebrew "whisper" (*laḥash*), see, e.g., Eccles. 10:11; BT *Sanhedrin* 90a.

85. Islamic demonology had its own image of the *shaytan* who accompanied men in all their activities. See the extensive examples adduced in Zwemer, "The Familiar Spirit or *Qarina*." More recent literature is cited in *The Encyclopedia of Islam, New Edition*, s.v. "Shaytan."

86. Vital, *Sha'ar ha-Yiḥudim*, 16a.

87. Of course the notion that God "employs the same means in inflicting pain and in curing it" has many precedents in rabbinic *midrashim*. For bibliographical information on this topic, see Louis Ginzberg, *Notes to Volumes III and IV: From Moses in the Wilderness to Esther*, trans. Henrietta Szold, 7 vols., vol. 6, *The Legends of the Jews* (Philadelphia, 1968), 14–15.

88. To heal the wound inflicted upon the victim's body, the inflicting weapon would be covered with a special ointment that was supposed to "assist the vital spirits of the congealed blood to reunite with the victim's body." See Keith Thomas, *Religion and the Decline of Magic* (New York, 1971), 190–91.

89. Abraham Hammawi, *Davek me-Aḥ* (Livorno, 1875).

90. The similarities include the use of the names *KR'A STN, MTTRON* with its permutations, *SGZGIEL, ILI*, and the use of Psalm 109:6.

91. Vital, *Sha'ar ha-Yiḥudim*.

92. Mashe Hallamish, ed., *A Kabbalistic Commentary of Yoseph ben Shalom Ashkenazi* (Jerusalem, 1985), 137.

93. See Michel Foucault, *The Order of Things: An Archaeology of the Human Sciences* (New York, 1970), 17–45. Cf. David Ruderman's interesting application of this insight in his discussion of the epistemology of sixteenth-century Jewish savant Abraham Yagel in David Ruderman, *Kabbalah, Magic, and Science: The Cultural Universe of a Sixteenth-Century Jewish Physician*, (Cambridge, 1988), 69.

94. Incidentally, this lineage did not prevent Luria and Vital from getting along. On the contrary, according to Luria, Cain and Abel have repeatedly reincarnated in contexts that facilitate their reconciliation and mutual rectification. E.g., Cain/Yitro gives Abel/Moses his daughter, herself a reincarnation of the twin over which Cain killed Abel. See Ḥayyim Vital, *Likkutei Torah*, ed. Yehuda Zvi Brandwein, 15 vols.,vol. 11, *Kitvei Rabbenu Ha-Ari ZT"L* (Jerusalem, 1988), pericope "Yitro," 145.

On Vital's "descent" from Cain, see Gershom Scholem, "Gilgul: The Transmigration of Souls," in *On the Mystical Shape of the Godhead*, ed. Jonathan Chipman (New York, 1991), 235–36. Among the primary sources, see Vital, *Sha'ar ha-Gilgulim*,

28, 30, 37, 77–78, 81, 83–84, 92–94, 100–104, 12, 29, 33, 52–64. Cf. Vital, *Sefer ha-Ḥezyonot*, 83, 142–44, 52.

95. On evil and Lurianic theosophy, see Isaiah Tishby, *Torat ha-Ra ve-ha-Kelipah be-Kabbalat ha-Ari*, new ed. (Jerusalem, 1984).

96. See *The Encyclopedia of Religion*, s.v., "Exorcism."

97. Kabbalistic sources distinguish between *Adam ha-Rishon* (the First Adam) and *Adam Kadmon* (Primordial Adam). The former is the Adam of Genesis, whereas the latter is the primordial anthropos, i.e., the divine being itself.

98. *Gevurah* (severity) is the fifth of the 10 Sefirot, or divine emanations/attributes, according to theosophical kabbalistic sources.

99. See the Appendix, Case 7.

100. Hiriki, *Mishnat Ḥasidim*, 110a.

101. *New Catholic Encyclopedia*, s.v. "Exorcist: In the Church" (Washington, 1967). See also Ferber, "The Demonic Possession of Marthe Brossier, France 1598–1600," 62–63.

102. Cited in *The Encyclopedia of Witchcraft and Demonology*, 181.

103. Alan Charles Kors and Edward Peters, eds., *Witchcraft in Europe, 1100–1700: A Documentary Study* (Philadelphia, 1972), 263–64. I am grateful to Prof. Peters for bringing this passage to my attention.

104. The "feeling" of Surin that he was possessed by a second soul, deprived of its body, is a further indication of the contradiction between the *experience* of the possessed and the *theological possibilities* offered by the Church discussed above.

105. Vital, *Sha'ar ha-Yiḥudim*, 5a.

106. Zacuto and Alnakar, *Shorshei ha-Shemot*, vol. 1, 170.

107. This story was published originally in Gedalia Ibn Yaḥia, *Shalshelet ha-Kabbalah* (Venice, 1546), 86b. It would later appear in works by Menasseh ben Israel, Eliezer Ashkenazi, Gedalia ibn Yaḥia, and Abraham Yagel. On Yagel, see Ruderman, *Kabbalah, Magic, and Science: The Cultural Universe of a Sixteenth-Century Jewish Physician*, 188 n. 4. For the full account in English, see the Appendix, Case 8.

108. Elijah de Vidas, *Reshit Ḥokhmah ha-Shalem*, 3 vols., vol. 1 (Jerusalem, 1984), 238 (*Sha'ar ha-Yirah* §49).

109. "Good" possession was rejected by Christian theorists, who preferred to view such cases as deceptions—the devil disguised as an angel of light. Individuals who believed themselves to be possessed by a divine, holy spirit, were subjected to lengthy interrogations designed invariably to promote an "admission" that, in fact, a devil and not an angel was at work. See Walker, *Unclean Spirits: Possession and Exorcism in France and England in the Late Sixteenth and Early Seventeenth Centuries*, 22, 55–56. For a case of the transformation of good witches into evil witches, see the classic study by Carlo Ginzburg, *The Night Battles: Witchcraft and Agrarian Cults in the Sixteenth and Seventeenth Centuries*, trans. John and Anne Tedeschi (Baltimore, 1983). During the Interregnum in England, however, good possession became viable and popular. See Christopher Hill, *The World Turned Upside Down* (London, 1972), 223–30.

110. Walker, *Unclean Spirits: Possession and Exorcism in France and England in the Late Sixteenth and Early Seventeenth Centuries*, 8.

111. Cited in Lea, *Materials Toward a History of Witchcraft*, vol. 2, 1051. Lea cites a

similar warning in the *Practica of Exorcists* by Valerio Polidoro of Padua. There the exorcist is warned "to beware of curious digressions and not to repose too much trust in the demon's replies, in fact to shut him off if he volunteers too much information and seems fraudulent."

112. On naming, see above and ibid., vol. 3, 1061; Thorndike, *A History of Magic and Experimental Science*, 557.

113. This exorcistic connotation is explicit in Rashi's comments upon the passage in BT *Rosh ha-Shana* 28a. See Bar-Ilan, "Exorcism of Demons by Rabbis: On the Involvment of Talmudic Sages in Magic," 28 n. 40.

114. C. Lévi-Strauss, "Symbolic Efficacity," in *Structural Anthropology* (New York, 1963). For a historical anthropological application of the concept, see Peter Burke, "Rituals of Healing in Early Modern Italy," in *The Historical Anthropology of Early Modern Italy: Essays on Perception and Communication* (Cambridge, 1987).

115. Walker, *Unclean Spirits: Possession and Exorcism in France and England in the Late Sixteenth and Early Seventeenth Centuries*, 29.

116. Valerio Polidoro, "Practica exorcistarum ad daemones et maleficia de Christi fidelibus pellendom," in *Thesaurus Exorcismorum (Cologne, 1626)* (Padua, 1582), 167–69.

117. The secret of the forty-two-lettered name was an esoteric tradition already in talmudic times (see BT *Kiddushin* 71a). The name was known and discussed in a responsum of Ḥai Gaon (969–1038) (*Oẓar ha-Geonim, Ḥagigah*, 23). In the thirteenth century, the name was expanded as an acrostic into a prayer hymn by Spanish Kabbalists. On the name, see L. H. Schiffman, "A Forty-two Letter Divine Name in the Aramaic Magic Bowls," *Bulletin of the Institute for Jewish Studies* 1 (1973): 97–1–102; Yakov Urbach, "On the Matter of the 42–Lettered Name" (in Hebrew), *Ma'anayim* 6 (1993): 238–40. On *KR'A STN*, see Zohar 2:160a; *Tikkunei ha-Zohar, Tikkun* 4; Moses Cordovero, *Pardes Rimonim* (Munkacz, 1906; reprint Jerusalem, 1962), 102c–3b.

118. The association between *Shva* and *Gevurah* dates back to the *Tikkunei ha-Zohar, Tikkunim* 5, 19, and 69. See Jacob Zvi Juelich, *Kehilat Ya'akov* (Lvov, 1869; reprint, Jerusalem, 1971), s.v. *"shva"*; Eliyahu Peretz, *Ma'alot ha-Zohar: Mafteaḥ Shemot ha-Sefirot* (Jerusalem, 1987), s.v. *"shva."*

119. *A"T B"Sh* is a form of *temurah*, or "interchange of letters according to certain systematic rules." Gershom Scholem, *Major Trends in Jewish Mysticism*, 3rd rev. ed. (New York, 1961), 100. In *A"T B"Sh*, the first letter of the alphabet becomes the last, the second, the penultimate, usw. The sestet *DGZBNT* is *KR'A STN* via *A"T B"Sh*. The *K* of *KR'A*, the fourth from the end of the Hebrew alphabet, becomes the *D* of *DGZBNT*, usw.

120. "*Eleh Toledot Yiẓḥak*," in Benayahu, *Toledot ha-Ari* (Studies and Texts), 251. Another fascinating example of custom-made exorcism technique is the self-exorcism Luria designed for his disciple Yehudah Mishan preserved in Vital, *Sha'ar Ruaḥ ha-Kodesh*, 107a–b. An English translation may be found in my dissertation, J. H. Chajes, "Spirit Possession and the Construction of Early Modern Jewish Religiosity" (Ph.D. diss., Yale University, 1999), 120–22.

121. See Scholem, "Gilgul: The Transmigration of Souls," 230–31. Cf. Foucault, *The Order of Things: An Archaeology of the Human Sciences*, 25–30.

122. See L. Fine, "The Art of Metoposcopy: A Study in Isaac Luria's Charismatic Knowledge," *AJS Review* 11 (1986): 79–101. I hope to treat the issue of "somatic exegesis" in more depth elsewhere. For pre-Lurianic examples, see Moshe Idel, "Gazing at the Head in Ashkenazi Hasidism," *Journal of Jewish Thought and Philosophy* 6, no. 2 (1997): 265–300. I thank Prof. Idel for sharing an early typescript of this article with me.

123. Vital, *Sha'ar ha-Gilgulim*, 48b. For examples of Luria's sefirotic exegesis of human beings, see, e.g., Vital, *Sha'ar ha-Gilgulim*, 133b, 67a. More theoretical treatment may be found, for example, in Vital, *Adam Yashar*, 29–36.

124. See Vital, *Sha'ar Ruaḥ ha-Kodesh*, 41–42. On the personal nature of Luria's teaching, see Yehudah Liebes, "New Directions in the Study of Kabbalah" (in Hebrew), *Pe'amim* 50 (1992).

125. Yuval Harrari has recently suggested that Wittgenstein's notion of "family resemblance" be employed by scholars vexed by the problem of defining magic in opposition to religion. Though his argument has a certain circularity—texts are magical to the extent that they display more of the characteristic features of known magical texts—it is well worth considering for an etic perspective of magic. See Yuval Harrari, "Magic Witchcraft and Adjurations: Methodological Reflections Toward a Renewed Definition of Ancient Jewish Magic" (in Hebrew), *Da'at* 48 (2002): 33–56. From an emic standpoint, it is clear that magic is understood in nearly all Jewish sources, biblical and rabbinic, as forbidden as a form of *'avodah zarah*, or alien worship: an inverted reflection of the licit religion of Israel. *Kabbalah ma'asit*, while obviously magical by any etic definition of the term, would not be considered magic from within the tradition. Objection to it, as we find in the case of the AR"I, may be based on factors such as the lack of purity of the adept, or suspicions regarding the reliability of the manuscript readings, but not, strictly speaking, on the basis of its being "magical." Harrari's article includes a fine summary of the history of scholarly definitions of magic. For an English discussion, see Kieckhefer, *Magic in the Middle Ages*, 8–17. On magic as antinormative praxis, see H. S. Versnel, "Some Reflections on the Relationship Magic-Religion," *Numen* 38 (1991): 177–97, esp. 182–84.

126. Gary Tomlinson, *Music in Renaissance Magic: Toward a Historiography of Others* (Chicago, 1993), 44.

127. A translation of the complete account may be found in the Appendix, Case 10.

128. This unusual usage probably connotes a master of prayer, from the root *PLL*. It can also imply judgment or wisdom. I have found no Arabic or Turkish cognates that would account for the term here.

129. Ibn Yaḥia's interrogation, which does not include an account of any exorcism, is translated in the Appendix, Case 8.

130. Various aspects of Zacuto's background and wide-ranging literary production are treated in Abba Apfelbaum, *Moshe Zacut: Ḥayyav, Sefarav, Shitato ha-Kabbalit* (Lvov, 1926); Robert Bonfil, "Change in the Cultural Patterns of a Jewish Society in Crisis: Italian Jewry at the Close of the Sixteenth Century," Jewish History 3, no. 2 (1988): 11–30; Devorah Bregman, "Sonnet Sequences in Moshe Zacut's *Yesod 'Olam* (in Hebrew)," *Meḥkerei Yerushalayim be-Sifrut* 9 (1986): 301–12; Y. Melkman, "Mozes Zacuto en Zijn Familie, *Studia Rosenthaliana* 3, no. 2 (169): 145–55;" David B. Ruder-

man, "The Language of Science as the Language of Faith: An Aspect of Italian Jewish Thought in the Seventeenth and Eighteenth Centuries," in *Studies of the History of the Jews in the Middle Ages and Renaissance Period*, Shlomo Simonston Jubilee Volume, Harvard Judaic Texts and Studies (Tel Aviv, 1993).

131. Moshe Zacuto, *Iggerot ha-Remez* (Livorno, 1780), 2a–b. Bacchi was an accomplished kabbalist and the head of the rabbinical court of Casale. In 1666 he was sent by the Jewish community of Casale to visit Sabbatai Ẓevi, whom he supported until Ẓevi's apostasy. See Gershom Scholem, *Meḥkerei Shabtaut* (Researches in Sabbateanism), ed. Yehudah Liebes (Jerusalem, 1991), 494, 511. Judging from Zacuto's response, the case of the possessed woman was part of the middle of the Bacchi's query, the first part being devoted to bibliographical questions pertaining to the various editions of the Zohar, and the last part being devoted to the kabbalistic-halakhic question of the permissibility of taking a haircut in preparation for a circumcision occurring in the '*Omer* mourning period between Passover and Shavu'ot.

132. The name *KhH"Th* is used in the Lurianic exorcism technique known as "*Yiḥud* (Unification) Three" and may be found in Vital, *Sha'ar Ruaḥ ha-Kodesh*, 91a. This magical name is the eighth triplet in the seventy-two lettered divine name. This triplet has a long history of magical uses in kabbalistic sources. These sources suggest, among other things, that this name was used by Moses to slay the Egyptian (Exod. 2:12) and to split the Red Sea (Exod. 2:14). See Zacuto and Alnakar, *Shorshei ha-Shemot*, vol. 1, 246 (§175, 8) and 141. Like other names and verses used in Lurianic exorcism rituals, this name was also used to combat the plague. See Ḥayyim Vital, *Sefer Pri Eẓ Ḥayyim*, ed. Yehuda Zvi Brandwein, 15 vols., vols. 13–14, *Kitvei Rabbenu Ha-Ari ZT"L* (Jerusalem, 1988).

133. Benjamin Kohen of Reggio was a leader of the Italian Sabbatians. See Scholem, *Sabbatai Sevi, the Mystical Messiah, 1626–1676*, 578 n. 284, 926. Cf. Scholem, *Kabbalah*, 449–50. His Sabbatian notes may be found in Ms. Moscow-Günzburg 517, *The Mystery of the Faith of Our Lord.*

134. T. Browne, *Sir Thomas Browne: Selected Writings*, ed. G. Keynes (Chicago, 1968), vol. 2. 44. Cited in Clark, *Thinking with Demons: The Idea of Witchcraft in Early Modern Europe*, 394.

135. See, e.g., Sydney Anglo, "Melancholia and Witchcraft: The Debate between Wier, Bodin, and Scot," in *Folie et déraison à la Renaissance* (Brussels, 1976); Ruderman, *Kabbalah, Magic, and Science: The Cultural Universe of a Sixteenth-Century Jewish Physician*, 43; Walker, *Unclean Spirits: Possession and Exorcism in France and England in the Late Sixteenth and Early Seventeenth Centuries*, 9–10. See also above, n. 75.

136. See Harrari, *Ḥarba de-Moshe*, 37. Cf. Benayahu, "The Book 'Shoshan Yesod ha-'Olam' by Rabbi Joseph Tirshom (MS Sassoon 290)," 197 n. 30, 220; Gaster, "The Wisdom of the Chaldeans: An Old Hebrew Astrological Text," 347–51. See also Zacuto and Alnakar, *Shorshei ha-Shemot*, vol. 1, 161 (§17.2).

137. Zacuto and Alnakar, *Shorshei ha-Shemot*, vol. 1, 47 (§138.10).

138. See Tirshom, *Shushan Yesod ha-'Olam*, §629, 266. Comparable pairings between bad thoughts and demonic afflictions are found in §265 (see below); §641, §1186. Cf. Benayahu, "The Book 'Shoshan Yesod ha-'Olam' by Rabbi Joseph Tirshom (Sassoon Ms. 290)," 236.

139. The lack of a sensitivity to culture and its role in illness plagues contemporary mental health professionals no less than it does psychohistorians. For trenchant critiques of psychiatry on this issue, see B. J. Good, *Medicine, Rationality and Experience: An Anthropological Perspective* (Cambridge, 1994); Sushrut Jadhav, "The Ghostbusters of Psychiatry," *The Lancet* 345, no. 8953 (1995): 808–11.

140. This sign of possession was mentioned by Jean Bodin in his description of the possession of the Jewish converts in Rome. See Jean Bodin, *De la Démonomanie des sorciers* (Paris, 1580), II, §3; Bodin, *On the Demon-Mania of Witches*, 109. I hope to discuss the Bodin material in a separate study.

141. Girolamo Menghi, *Compendio dell'Arte Essorcistica* (Bologna, 1580). On Menghi and his works, see Clark, *Thinking with Demons*, 389–90. Cf. Burke, "Rituals of Healing in Early Modern Italy," 258 n. 11; O'Neil, "Discerning Superstition: Popular Errors and Orthodox Response in Late Sixteenth Century Italy," esp. 304ff; Mary Rose O'Neil, "*Sacerdote ovvero strione*: Ecclesiastical and Superstitious Remedies in Sixteenth-Century Italy," in *Understanding Popular Culture: Europe from the Middle Ages to the Nineteenth Century*, ed. Steven Kaplan (Berlin, 1984). Prof. Armando Maggi was kind enough to send me an illuminating chapter of a forthcoming work on Menghi, for which I thank him.

142. Polidoro, "Practica exorcistarum ad daemones et maleficia de Christi fidelibus pellendom." Cited in Lea, *Materials Toward a History of Witchcraft*, vol. 3, 1057. Maximilian van Eynatten, in his *Manuale* of 1648, provides a similar list of symptoms, as well as strong cautions to not rashly assume "that any one is possessed or bewitched, but carefully to weigh all indications and circumstances." The symptoms he adumbrated include that

> the disease comes on suddenly, and not gradually as natural ones do; the patient's eyes are pinched; the skin, especially of the face, is yellow or ashen; the humors are dried up and there is extraordinary emaciation, all the members seem to be tied or constricted, especially the heart and mouth; there seems to be a lump at the orifice of the stomach or one passing up and down the throat; needle-pricks are felt in the heart and other places; sometimes the heart is as if corroded, or the kidneys are lacerated, or there are convulsions and epileptic seizures; they often are scarce able to look a priest in the face and the whites of the eyes are changed in various ways.

See Lea, *Materials Toward a History of Witchcraft*, 1063. The works of Van Eynatten were collected in the 1,232–page work *Thesaurus Exorcismorum* along with Polidoro's above and their demonological-exorcism authorities, such as Zacharias Vicecomes, and Pietro Antonia Stampa. See Robbins, *The Encyclopedia of Witchcraft and Demonology*, 185ff.

143. See, for example, the excerpt from T. Sanchez's *In Praecepta Decalogi* in Lea, *Materials Toward a History of Witchcraft*, vol. 3, 1053. Cf. R. Patai, "Exorcism and Xenoglossia Among the Safed Kabbalists," *Journal of American Folklore* 91 (1978): 823–35. In the anthropological literature, see Felicitas D. Goodman, *Speaking in Tongues: A Cross-Cultural Study of Glossolalia* (Chicago, 1972); L. Carlyle May, "A Survey of Glossolalia and Related Phenomena in Non-Christian Religions," *American Anthropologist* 58 (1956): 75, 77, 83–86.

144. Menasseh ben Israel, *Nishmat Ḥayyim* (Amsterdam, 1651), 110a.

145. Zacuto writes that the amulets he gave R. Benjamin Kohen were prepared according to the directives of the Rav. Presumably, he means Luria here, as earlier in the letter. If this is the case, it probably indicates that he saw amulets prepared in accordance with the AR"I's *yiḥud* that he assumed were authentic. Magical material associated with Luria was included in Sarugian manuscripts in circulation in Italy during Zacuto's lifetime. Nevertheless, Zacuto goes beyond the AR"I's original exorcism prescriptions and, as will become clear below, devoted himself to collecting and employing magical formulas patently at odds with the AR"I's position (and well beyond the limited Sarugian material). The 1651 manuscript of *Sha'ar ha-Yiḥudim*, executed in Cracow by R. Meir Poppers, includes amulets and magical diagrams, but these do not appear in earlier manuscripts.

146. Vital, *Sha'ar Ruaḥ ha-Kodesh*. 41. This stringent position recalls that of R. Judah the Pious (c. 1150–1217) as recorded in his *Sefer Ḥasidim*. See Margalioth, ed., *Sefer Ḥasidim*, e.g., §205 and Margoliot's notes there and index, s.v. *"kheshafim ve-hashba'ot."* See also Dan, "Demonological Stories from the Writings of R. Judah the Pious." For exceptions, however, see, e.g., Margalioth, ed., *Sefer Ḥasidim*, §247. See also the important new work of Ephraim Kanarfogel, *Peering through the Lattices: Mystical, Magical, and Pietistic Dimensions in the Tosafist Period* (Detroit, 1999), 210–14.

147. See Bonfil, "Change in the Cultural Patterns of a Jewish Society in Crisis: Italian Jewry at the Close of the Sixteenth Century," 20–21. Devorah Bregman has shown that Zacuto's *Yesod 'Olam* (Foundation of the world) is a series of sonnets that exemplifies the poetics of the baroque. See Bregman, "Sonnet Sequences in Moshe Zacut's *Yesod 'Olam*." David Ruderman characterized Zacuto as a "pure or mythical kabbalist" who was nevertheless active in areas other than kabbalah, including literature, theater, and science. See Ruderman, "The Language of Science as the Language of Faith: An Aspect of Italian Jewish Thought in the Seventeenth and Eighteenth Centuries." For a discussion of the baroque sensibility, with extensive bibliographical references, see David B. Ruderman, ed., *A Valley of Vision: The Heavenly Journey of Abraham ben Hananiah Yagel* (Philadelphia, 1990), 63–68.

148. In responsum §8 of *Iggerot ha-Remez*, Zacuto discusses the conservative nature of his fidelity to Lurianism.

149. See Bos, "Hayyim Vital's 'Practical Kabbalah and Alchemy': A Seventeenth Century Book of Secrets."

150. The autograph of this manuscript is extant. See Moshe Zacuto, *Sefer ha-Sodot sh'Kibbalti mi-Rabbotai* (The book of secrets I received from my masters), MS Günzburg 1448. Institute of Microfilmed Hebrew Manuscripts # 48570, 28b.

151. So assumed Benayahu, *Toledot ha-Ari*, 291. An example of Luria's chastisement of Vital for having wasted precious time on alchemical pursuits may be found in Vital, *Sha'ar ha-Gilgulim*, 182b. Vital's relationship with Luria is treated in Ronit Meroz, "Faithful Transmission versus Innovation: Luria and His Disciples," in *Gershom Scholem's Major Trends in Jewish Mysticism 50 Years After: Proceedings of the Sixth International Conference on the History of Jewish Mysticism*, ed. Peter Schäfer and Joseph Dan (Tübingen, 1993).

152. See Zacuto's *Mikdash ha-Shem* in Shalom Buzaglo, *Mikdash Melekh*, abr. (complete in manuscripts) ed., 2 vols. (Amsterdam, 1750; reprint, 1973).

153. See the extensive treatment of this topic in H. J. Zimmels, *Magicians, Theologicans, and Doctors: Studies in Folk-Medicine and Folk-Lore as Reflected in Rabbinical Responsa (Twelfth–Nineteenth Centuries)* (New York, 1952).

154. Corpus Juris Civilis, codex 9, title 18[a]. Cited in Norman Cohn, *Europe's Inner Demons: An Enquiry Inspired by the Great Witch-Hunt* (New York, 1975), 156.

155. Heinrich Kramer and James Sprenger, *The Malleus Maleficarum*, ed. Montague Summers (New York, 1971), II 2, 156.

156. See Wolfgang Behringer, *Shaman of Oberstdorf: Chonrad Stoeckhlin and the Phantoms of the Night*, trans. H. C. Erik Midelfort (Charlottesville, Va., 1998), 84; E. W. Monter, *Witchcraft in France and Switzerland* (Ithaca, N.Y., 1976), 167ff.

157. Burke, "Rituals of Healing in Early Modern Italy," 208. Cf. Michael MacDonald, *Mystical Bedlam: Madness, Anxiety, and Healing in Seventeenth-Century England* (Cambridge, 1981). MacDonald uses the term *therapeutic eclecticism* to describe this attitude. See also Thomas, *Religion and the Decline of Magic*, 151–58; C. Webster, ed., *Health, Medicine, and Mortality in the Sixteenth Century* (Cambridge, 1979).

For discussions focusing upon Jewish culture, see Immanuel Etkes, "The Role of Magic and *Ba'alei-Shem* in Ashkenazic Society in the Late Seventeenth and Early Eighteenth Centuries" (in Hebrew), *Ẓion* 60, no. 1 (1995): 77; Ruderman, *Kabbalah, Magic, and Science: The Cultural Universe of a Sixteenth-Century Jewish Physician*, 25–42.

158. For Ḥayyim, see Vital, *Sefer ha-Ḥezyonot*, 12, 13, 16, 18. For Samuel, see the Appendix, Case 10

159. See ben Israel, *Nishmat Ḥayyim*, 120a (III 14); Gedalyah Nigal, *Sippurei Dybbuk be-Sifrut Yisrael* (Dybbuk Stories in Jewish Literature), 2nd ed. (Jerusalem, 1994), 76.

160. Cited by G. Bousquet, *L'authentique tradition musulmane* (Paris, 1964), 301 n. 104; *The Encyclopedia of Islam, New Edition*, s.v. "Ruḳya,"

161. See Sara Zfatman-Biller, " 'Tale of an Exorcism in Koretz'—A New Stage in the Development of a Folk-Literary Genre" (in Hebrew), *Jerusalem Studies in Jewish Folklore* 2 (1982): 36.

162. Moshe Rosman, *Founder of Hasidism: A Quest for the Historical Ba'al Shem Tov* (Berkeley and Los Angeles, 1996), 57.

163. Solomon Luria, *She'elot u'Teshuvot Maharshal* (Jerusalem, 1969), §3. Another fascinating source on this topic is the responsum of the seventeenth-century Italian rabbi Samuel Aboab (1610–94), which treats the permissability of consulting priests on behalf of the possessed given the invocation of idols by the priests. Aboab prohibited this, but noted that it was a widespread phenomenon. See Samuel ben Abraham Aboab, *Devar Shmuel* (Venice, 1702); Zimmels, *Magicians, Theologicans, and Doctors: Studies in Folk-Medicine and Folk-Lore as Reflected in Rabbinical Responsa (Twelfth–Nineteenth Centuries)*, 34, 193 n. 81.

164. See Lev. 20:27 and Deut. 18:11. Deuteronomy explicitly labels these forms of magic as "abominations of those [Canaanite] nations" (Deut. 18:9).

165. As Maharshal notes, Maimonides, in chapter 11 §7 of his laws of idolatry

wrote that sorcerers and their clients are only to be flogged rather than suffer the biblically mandated consequences.

166. See, e.g., comments to this effect in Moshe Idel, *Kabbalah: New Perspectives* (New Haven, Conn., 1988), 268–69.

167. Karo, Luria's Safedian contemporary, presents many of the same sources in his discussion of these issues (*Beit Yosef* 179 §16). Karo, however, concludes his survey of opinions on a conservative note by citing the Zohar's strong aversion to consulting sorcerers, even in the case of illness.

See also the responsa of R. David ibn Zimra, R. Isaac Luria's teacher, which deal with these and related questions. David ibn Zimra, *She'elot u'Teshuvot RaDBaZ* (New York, 1967), I §485, III §05, V §15. Cf. Asher Ziv, ed., *She'elot u-Teshuvot ha-Rama, le-Rabenu Mosheh Isarles* (Jerusalem, 1970), I §485, III §05, V §15.

168. Solomon ben Joseph Ganzfried, *Kiẓur Shulḥan 'Arukh* (Jerusalem, 1963), §166.5.

169. This principle is adduced in many rabbinic sources, including BT *Shabbat* 66a–67a; *Ḥulin* 77b; *Bava Meẓiah* 27b; and JT *Shabbat* 6.9. The "ways of the Amorites" was a rabbinic shorthand for prohibited magic, many of them being common practices in the Greco-Roman world. J. Goldin thus suggested that "Amorite" might have been a metathesis for "Romai." See Judah Goldin, "The Magic of Magic and Superstition," in *Aspects of Religious Propaganda in Judaism and Early Christianity*, ed. Elizabeth Schussler Fiarenza (Notre Dame, Ind., 1976), 117. Giuseppe Veltri's recent work compares these practices in detail to anti-magical legislation in antiquity. See, e.g., Veltri, "The 'Other' Physicians: The Amorites of the Rabbis and the Magi of Pliny," *Korot* 13 (1998–99): 37–54. For a summary of scholarly views, see Janowitz, *Magic in the Roman World: Pagans, Jews and Christians*, 23–25. For the reception of this principle in Jewish law, see the responsa of RaShBa, R. Solomon ben Abraham Adret (Spain, c. 1235–c. 1310), §443 and 454, and the glosses of Z. H. Chajes on *Bava Meẓiah* 27b. See also my comments above, n. 125.

170. See Moses Maimonides, *The Guide of the Perplexed*, trans. Shlomo Pines (Chicago, 1963), 544 (III 37). On the antimagical posture of Maimonides, see Y. T. Langermann, "Maimonides' Repudiation of Astrology," *Maimonidean Studies* 2 (1991): 123–58.

171. See H. C. Erik Midelfort, "Catholic and Lutheran Reactions to Demon Possession in the Late Seventeenth Century: Two Case Histories," *Daphnis* 15 (1986): 623–48.

172. On the early modern crisis of rabbinic authority, see Shalom Rosenberg, "Emunat Ḥakhamim," in *Jewish Thought in the Seventeenth Century* Harvard Judaic Texts and Studies, ed. Isadore Twersky and Bernard Septimus, (Cambridge, Mass., 1987).

173. Cf. the reformation-style rabbinic attempts to control behaviors in Renaissance Italy discussed in Elliott Horowitz, "The Eve of the Circumcision: A Chapter in the History of Jewish Nightlife," *Journal of Social History* 23 (1989).

## Chapter 4

This chapter is a revised and expanded version of J. H. Chajes, "In a Different Voice: The Non-Kabbalistic Women's Mysticism of Early Modern Jewish Culture" (in Hebrew), *Ẓion* 67, no. 2 (2002): 139–62.

1. Caroline Walker Bynum, *Jesus as Mother: Studies in the Spirituality of the High Middle Ages* (Berkeley and Los Angeles, 1982), 4. See also Daniel Bornstein's introductory essay in Daniel Bornstein and Roberto Rusconi, eds., *Women and Religion in Medieval and Renaissance Italy*, trans. Margery J. Schneider (Chicago, 1996), 22 n. 42.

2. Gabriella Zarri, *La Sante Vive: Cultura e religiosita femininte nella prima eta moderna* (Torino, 1990); Gabriella Zarri, "Living Saints: A Typology of Female Sanctity in the Early Sixteenth Century," in *Women and Religion in Medieval and Renaissance Italy*, ed. Daniel Bornstein and Roberto Rusconi, trans. Margery J. Schneider (Chicago, 1996).

3. Geraldine McKendrick and Angus MacKay, "Visionaries and Affective Spirituality during the First Half of the Sixteenth Century," in *Cultural Encounters: The Impact of the Inquisition in Spain and the New World*, ed. Mary Elizabeth Perry and Anne J. Cruz (Berkeley and Los Angeles, 1991); Alison Weber, "Between Ecstasy and Exorcism: Religious Negotiation in Sixteenth-Century Spain," *Journal of Medieval and Renaissance Studies* 23, no. 2 (1993): 221–34.

4. Rudolph Bell, *Holy Anorexia* (Chicago, 1985); Caroline Walker Bynum, *Holy Feast and Holy Fast: The Religious Significance of Food to Medieval Women* (Berkeley and Los Angeles, 1987).

5. See, e.g., Weber, "Between Ecstasy and Exorcism: Religious Negotiation in Sixteenth-Century Spain," 222.

6. In the words of the fourteenth-century Fransciscan Nicolás de Lyra, they were *illuminatae mentis* (made lucid by special grace). See McKendrick and MacKay, "Visionaries and Affective Spirituality during the First Half of the Sixteenth Century," 98. Cf. Phyllis Mack, *Visionary Women: Ecstatic Prophecy in Seventeenth-Century England* (Berkeley and Los Angeles, 1992), 32–34.

7. See, e.g., J. Imirizaldu, *Monjas y beatas embaucadoras* (Madrid, 1977); Mary Elizabeth Perry, *Gender and Disorder in Early Modern Seville* (Princeton, 1990); Zarri, "Living Saints: A Typology of Female Sanctity in the Early Sixteenth Century."

8. See Jodi Bilinkoff, "Charisma and Controversy: The Case of María de Santo Domingo," *Archivo Dominicano* 10 (1989): 55–66; Jodi Bilinkoff, "A Spanish Prophetess and Her Patrons: The Case of María de Santo Domingo," *Sixteenth Century Journal* 23 (1992): 21–34; J. W. Coakley, "Female Saints and Male Confidants in Medieval Dominican Hagiography," *Images of Sainthood in Medieval and Renaissance Europe, Conference at Barnard College* (paper presented at the conference on Images of Sainthood in Medieval Renaissance Europe, Barnard College, New York, 1987); Romana Guarnieri, "Nec Domina Nec Ancilla, Sed Socia': Three Cases of Spiritual Guidance Between the Sixteenth and Seventeenth Centuries," in *Women and Men in Spiritual Culture, XIV–XVII Centuries: A Meeting of South and North*, ed. Elisja Schulte van Kessel (The Hague, 1986).

9. Nancy Caciola, "Discerning Spirits: Sanctity and Possession in the Later Middle Ages"(Ph.D, diss., University of Michigan, 1994); Moshe Sluhovsky, "A Divine Apparition or Demonic Possession? Female Agency and Church Authority in Demonic Possession in Sixteenth-Century France," *Sixteenth Century Journal* 27, no. 4 (1995): 1036–52; Cf. Mack, *Visionary Women: Ecstatic Prophecy in Seventeenth-Century England*, 50–58, 75–86.

10. On Magdalena de la Cruz, see, e.g., Imirizaldu, *Monjas y beatas embaucadoras;* McKendrick and MacKay, "Visionaries and Affective Spirituality during the First Half of the Sixteenth Century." On Jeane des Anges, see Michel de Certeau, *La Possession de Loudun*, Collection Archive Series, vol. 37 (Paris, 1970).

11. See Tommaso Caffarini, Le opere di S. Caterina da Siena (Rome, 1866); Antonio Volpato, "Tra sante profetesse e santi dottori: Caterina da Siena," in *Women and Men in Spiritual Culture, XIV–XVII Centuries: A Meeting of South and North*, ed. Elisja Schulte van Kessel (The Hague, 1986).

12. On the relationship between these categories, see Gábor Klaniczay, "Hungary: The Accusations and the Universe of Popular Magic," in *Early Modern European Witchcraft: Centres and Peripheries*, ed. Bengt Ankarloo and Gustav Henningsen (Oxford, 1990), 240–41. On symbolic inversion in witchcraft beliefs, see Stuart Clark, "Inversion, Misrule, and the Meaning of Witchcraft," *Past and Present* 87 (1980): 98–127. Clark expands this approach in Part 1 of his recent work, Stuart Clark, *Thinking with Demons: The Idea of Witchcraft in Early Modern Europe* (Oxford, 1997). See also Richard Kieckhefer, "The Holy and the Unholy: Sainthood, Witchcraft, and Magic in Late Medieval Europe," *Journal of Medieval and Renaissance Studies* 24, no. 3 (1994): 355–85.

13. Y. Baer, "The Messianic Movement in Spain in the Period of the Expulsion" (in Hebrew), *Ẓion* 5 (1930): 61–77, 61.

14. Fritz Baer, *Die Juden in christlichen Spanien*, vol. 1, pt. 2, Inquisitionsakten, no. 423. (Berlin, 1936); Baer, "The Messianic Movement in Spain in the Period of the Expulsion," 66–67.

15. See Ḥaim Beinart, "A Prophesying Movement in Cordova in 1499–1502" (in Hebrew), *Ẓion* (Y. Baer Memorial Volume) 44 (1980): 190–220; Ḥaim Beinart, "The Prophetess Inés and Her Movement in Puebla de Alcocer and in Talarrubias"; Ḥaim Beinart, "Conversos of Chillón and Siruela and the Prophecies of Mari Gómez and Inés, the Daughter of Juan Esteban," *Ẓion* 48 (1983): 241–72; Ḥaim Beinart, "The Prophetess Inés and her Movement in her Hometown, Herrera" (in Hebrew). In *Studies in Jewish Mysticism, Philosophy, and Ethical Literature Presented to Isaiah Tishby on His Seventy-Fifth Birthday* (Jerusalem, 1986). Ḥaim Beinart, "The Conversos of Halia and the Movement of the Prophetess Ines" (in Hebrew), *Ẓion* 53 (1988): 31–52.; Ḥaim Beinart, "The Prophetess of Extremadura: Inés of Herrera del Duque," in *Women in the Inquisition: Spain and the New World*, ed. Mary Giles (Baltimore, 1999).

16. See, however, the brief yet perceptive treatment in Yirmiyahu Yovel, *Spinoza and Other Heretics: The Marrano of Reason* (Princeton, N.J., 1989), 22.

17. Beinart, "The Prophetess Inés and Her Movement in Her Hometown, Herrera," 495.

18. On the ideological history of Israeli historiography, see the various essays collected in Gulie Arad, Dan Diner, and Saul Friedlander, eds., *Israeli Historiography Revisited*, vol. 7, *History and Memory* (1995).

19. Gershom Scholem, *Major Trends in Jewish Mysticism*, 3rd rev. ed. (New York, 1961), 37.

20. Scholem's dismissive treatment of the female prophets in Sabbatianism shows how he dealt with female mystics when directly confronted with them. See Gershom Scholem, *Sabbatai Sevi, the Mystical Messiah, 1626–1676*, rev. and aug. translation of the Hebrew ed., Bolligen Series, trans. R. J. Zwi Werblowsky (Princeton, N.J., 1973), 403–5. Ada Rapoport-Albert touches upon this issue in Ada Rapoport-Albert, "On the Position of Women in Sabbatianism" (in Hebrew), in *The Sabbatian Movement and its Aftermath: Messianism, Sabbatianism and Frankism*, ed. Rachel Elior, *Jerusalem Studies in Jewish Thought, Volume 16* (Jerusalem, 2001), 146–47 no. 6.

Many of Chava Weissler's important studies on female piety, which treat later seventeenth- and eighteenth-century Ashkenazic Jewish culture, explore the extent of the kabbalistic knowledge of Jewish women, implicitly making textual knowledge the measure of their mystical lives. See Chava Weissler, *Voices of the Matriarchs: Listening to the Prayers of Early Modern Jewish Women* (Boston, 1998). See also the discussion in J. H. Chajes, "Review of *Voices of the Matriarchs: Listening to the Prayers of Early Modern Jewish Women*, by Chava Weissler. Boston: Beacon Press, 1998," *Jewish Quarterly Review* 92, nos. 1–2 (2001).

21. The many studies of Moshe Idel have been largely devoted to treating these dimensions of Jewish mysticism. The revisionist juggernaut is Moshe Idel, *Kabbalah: New Perspectives* (New Haven, Conn., 1988). A comprehensive bibliography, though already out-of-date at the time of publication, may be found in Daniel Abrams, ed., *Reshimat ha-Ketavim shel Profesor Moshe Idel: Hoẓaah Meyuḥedet Bi-Melot Lo Ḥamishim Shanah* (Bibliography of the Writings of Professor Moshe Idel) (Los Angeles, 1997). This phenomenological revision notwithstanding, Idel has not devoted a study to women's mysticism in particular.

22. Elliot R. Wolfson's works on gender and kabbalah are the most significant contribution to this field. See, e.g., the essays collected in his *Circle in the Square: Studies in the Use of Gender in Kabbalistic Symbolism* (Albany, N.Y., 1995). In another essay, Wolfson notes that "the literary evidence attests that women did have visionary experiences that should qualify as mystical in nature. Thus, e.g., we find that such visions are attributed to women in Ḥayyim Vital's diary, *Sefer ha-Ḥezyonot*." Elliot R. Wolfson, "Woman—The Feminine as Other in Theosophic Kabbalah: Some Philosophical Observations on the Divine Androgyne," in *The Other in Jewish Thought and History: Constructions of Jewish Culture and Identity*, ed. Laurence J. Silberstein and Robert L. Cohn (New York, 1994), 194 n. 15. See also Arthur Green, "Bride, Spouse, Daughter: Images of the Feminine in Classical Jewish Sources," in *On Being a Jewish Feminist: A Reader*, ed. S. Heschel (New York, 1983); Reuven Kimmelman, "An Introduction to '*Lekha Dodi*' and '*Kabbalat Shabbat*'," *Meḥkerei Yerushalayim be-Maḥshevet Yisrael* (Semoneta Memorial Volume), ed. Aviezer Ravitzky, 14 (1998): 395 n. 15.

23. See Caroline Walker Bynum, "The Complexity of Symbols," in *Gender and Religion: On the Complexity of Symbols*, ed. Caroline Walker Bynum, Stevan Harrell,

and Paula Richman (Boston, 1986). Cf. T. Fishman, "A Kabbalistic Perspective on Gender-Specific Commandments: On the Interplay of Symbols and Society," *AJS Review* 17 (1992): 199–245.

24. My suggestions here follow those of Carol Gilligan regarding the development of psychological theory. Gilligan has noted that psychology has persistently based its notions of development upon the observation of men's lives and has therefore systematically misunderstood women. See Carol Gilligan, *In a Different Voice: Psychological Theory and Women's Development* (Cambridge, Mass., 1993). Caroline Walker Bynum has also noted that "the work of traditional medievalists has tended to use male religiosity as a model." See Caroline Walker Bynum, "Religious Women in the Later Middle Ages," in *Christian Spirituality: High Middle Ages and Reformation*, ed. Jill Raitt, John Meyendorff, and Bernard McGinn (New York, 1988), 137.

25. There were, of course, exceptions. One such woman was the grandmother of R. Aaron Berakhia of Modena, Fioretta. According to her grandson, whom she raised, Fioretta was fluent in Bible, Mishna, medieval decisors and, "to her capacity" the Zohar. See his introduction to Aaron Berakhia, *Ashmorat ha-Boker* (The Morning Watch) (Mantua, 1724), 3a. Fioretta was also the aunt of R. Leon Modena and is mentioned in his autobiography. See Leon Modena, "The Autobiography of a Seventeenth-Century Venetian Rabbi," ed. Mark R. Cohen, Theodore K. Rabb, Howard E. Adelman, and Natalie Zemon Davis (Princeton, N.J., 1988). Fioretta is among the many learned women whose accomplishments were surveyed in Shlomo Ashkenazi, *Nashim Lamdaniot: Sekirah Historit* (Learned Women: A Historical Survey) (Tel Aviv, 1942). We might also mention Rebecca bas Meir Tiktiner, whose Yiddish religious-ethic work *Meineket Rivkah* was published in Prague in 1609—the very year of the unusual possession case to be discussed below. This work is noted briefly in Natalie Zemon Davis, *Women on the Margins: Three Seventeenth-Century Lives* (Cambridge, Mass., 1995), 59–60. See 257 n. 12 for further bibliography.

A fascinating example of a woman's participation in the textual culture of Jewish mysticiam (with a twist) may be found in the relationship between William Postel and Johanna, the virgin of Venice. In addition to her centrality in his eschatalogical expectations, Postel claimed that Johanna had revealed to him the secrets of the Zohar, notwithstanding her ignorance of the requisite languages for its study. See Moshe Idel, *Messianic Mystics* (New Haven, Conn., 1999), 155 and bibliographical references on 381 n. 3.

26. In her recent work on women in Sabbatianism, Prof. Ada Rapoport-Albert discussed several of the women of *Sefer ha-Ḥezyonot*. Ada and I are in substantial agreement regarding the historical contextualization of these women.

27. On Vital, see Chapter 1, n. 14. Vital wrote and assembled the autobiographical notes that comprise *Sefer ha-Ḥezyonot* in Damascus between 1609–12. See Gershom Scholem, *Kabbalah* (New York, 1974), 444.

28. *Sefer ha-Ḥezyonot* was one of three mystical journals authored by sixteenth-century Safedian Kabbalists, the other two being R. Elazar Azikri's *Millei di-Shemaya* and Joseph Karo's *Maggid Mesharim*. Moshe Idel has suggested that the simultaneous emergence of these subjective works signals the new subjective orientation of sixteenth-century kabbalah. See Moshe Idel, "On Mobility, Individuals and Groups:

Prolegomenon for a Sociological Approach to Sixteenth-Century Kabbalah," *Kabbalah: Journal for the Study of Jewish Mystical Texts* 3 (1998): 145–73.

29. See Michal Oron, "Dream, Vision and Reality in Ḥayyim Vital's *Sefer ha-Ḥezyonot*" (in Hebrew), *Meḥkerei Yerushalayim be-Maḥshevet Yisrael*, ed. Rachel Elior and Yehudah Liebes, 10 (1992): 229–309 Cf. Meir Benayahu, *Toledot ha-Ari* (Jerusalem, 1967), 99.

30. Vital, *Sefer ha-Ḥezyonot*, 3–4.

31. Lecanomancy seems to have been a form of divination practiced predominantly by women, though a number of men mentioned in *Sefer ha-Ḥezyonot* are noted for their divinatory abilities, clairvoyance, and ability to contact the spirits of the dead. See for example pp. 1 §2; 2, §4, and 5 §9. On this technique in the history of Jewish magic, and its origins and parallels, see S. Daiches, *Babylonian Oil Magic in the Talmud and in Later Jewish Literature* (London, 1913); Joseph Dan, "The Princes of Thumb and Cup" (in Hebrew), *Tarbiẓ* 32 no. 4 (1963): 359–69.

32. See Vital, *Sefer ha-Ḥezyonot*, 122.

33. Mira was the sister of R. S. Ḥayyati. Ḥayyati's dreams were recorded by Vital, as were those of his wife, Marḥava, and his sister Mira. See *Sefer ha-Ḥezyonot*, 110–120. On Mira's dream implicating Jacob Abulafia in the moral decline of Damascus and the plague that struck the city that week, see p. 113. On the missions imposed upon her by her dreams, see p. 114. On her divinatory expertise and Vital's consultation, see p. 120. Another consultation in 1565 with an unnamed woman expert in lecanomancy (oil-water divination) is recorded on p. 3.

34. See Francisco Bethencourt, "Portugal: A Scrupulous Inquisition," in *Early Modern European Witchcraft: Centres and Peripheries*, ed. Bengt Ankarloo and Gustav Henningsen (Oxford, 1990), 411–14. See María Helena Sánchez Ortega, "Sorcery and Eroticism in Love Magic," in *Cultural Encounters: The Impact of the Inquisition in Spain and the New World*, ed. Mary Elizabeth Perry and Anne J. Cruz (Berkeley and Los Angeles, 1991). On this "Mediterranean image" of the witch, as distinct from the image of witches as harm-inflicting, child-eating, orgiastic coven members, see Julio Caro Baroja, *The World of the Witches*, trans. O. N. V. Glendinning (Chicago, 1964). Lu Ann Homza notes the rather more complex picture of the witch image in Spain in Lu Ann Homza, *Religious Authority in the Spanish Renaissance* (Baltimore, 2000), 180–81. See also Guido Ruggiero's treatment of the "Women Priests of Latisana" in Guido Ruggiero, *Binding Passions: Tales of Magic, Marriage, and Power at the End of the Renaissance* (Oxford, 1993), 149–69.

Love magic also figures prominantly in magical writings written with male practioners in mind, including Sassoon Ms. 290. See the discussion in Ruth Lamdan, *'Am Bifnei 'Aẓman* (A Separate People: Jewish Women in Palestine, Syria and Egypt in the Sixteenth Century) (Tel Aviv, 1996), 61–62, 66 n. 4.

35. Vital, *Sefer ha-Ḥezyonot*, 10–11.

36. On Vital's attitude towards women and sexuality more generally, see David Biale, "Sexuality and Spirituality in the Kabbalah," in *Eros and the Jews: From Biblical Israel to Contemporary America* (New York, 1992), 115–16; Lawrence Fine, "Purifying the Body in the Name of the Soul: The Problem of the Body in Sixteenth-Century

Kabbalah," in *People of the Body: Jews and Judaism from an Embodied Perspective*, ed. Howard Eilberg-Schwartz (Albany, N.Y., 1992).

37. Simon Shtober, ed., *Sefer Divrei Yosef by Yosef ben Yiẓḥak Sambari* (Jerusalem, 1994), 364–66.

38. On the hierarchy of revelatory agents, see, e.g., Ḥayyim Vital, *Sha'arei Kedusha* (Jerusalem, 1985), 99. Francesa's maggid is noted by Yoram Bilu, "Dybbuk and Maggid: Two Cultural Patterns of Altered Consciousness in Judaism," *AJS Review* 21, no. 2 (1996): 362 n. 72. See also Chapter 1 above.

39. Sambari's decision to include these accounts may have derived from his Sabbatian proclivities. The proliferation of maggidism among Sabbatian women might have also led him to introduce that terminology into an earlier account. I thank Dr. Avraham Elkayam for bringing this possibility to my attention.

40. Shtober, ed., *Sefer Divrei Yosef by Yosef ben Yiẓḥak Sambari*, 364–65.

41. Ibid., 365–66.

42. Ibid.

43. Ibid., 366 n. 226. Cf. H. Z. Hirschberg, "The Author of *Divrey Yosef* and His Attitude Toward the Duty of Settling in Ereẓ Israel" (in Hebrew), in *Sefer Shazar* (Jerusalem, 1971).

44. See the Appendix, Case 9

45. This type of religious development has been studied by the anthropologist I. M. Lewis. See his *Religion in Context: Cults and Charisma* (Cambridge, 1986) and *Ecstatic Religion: A Study of Shamanism and Spirit Possession* (Harmondsworth, 1971), 57–60. Cf. Joseph Klaits, *Servants of Satan: The Age of the Witch Hunts* (Bloomington, Ind., 1985), 118–19.

On Elizabeth de Ranfaing, see Robert Mandrou, *Magistrats et sorciers en France au XVII^e siècle: Une analyse de psychologie historique* (Paris, 1968). The character of Jeanne des Anges is analyzed in Certeau, *La Possession de Loudun;* Aldous Huxley, *The Devils of Loudun* (London, 1952). On women evolving from demoniacs to spiritual leaders, see also I. Maclean, *The Renaissance Notion of Woman* (Cambridge, 1980), 21.

46. See Esther Pressel, "Disturbances in the Apostolic Church: A Trance-based Upheaval in Yucatan," in *Trance, Healing, and Hallucination; Three Field Studies in Religious Experience* (New York, 1974). Cited in *The Encyclopedia of Religion*, s.v. "Spirit Possession."

T. K. Oesterreich proposed to distinguish possession from mediumistic trance on the basis of the nature of the experience: voluntary or involuntary/spontaneous or artificial. A further refinement of this distinction can be found in the work of the anthropologist Raymond Firth, who in his *Tikopia Ritual and Belief*, distinguished between *spirit possession*, *spirit mediumship*, and *shamanism* on the basis of extent to which the possessed (the "host") controls the spirit. In *spirit possession*, the spirit is regarded by the victim and other members of her society as controlling the possessed—this usually on the basis of abnormal behaviors manifested by her. *Spirit mediumship* refers to a scenario in which the possessed is able to control these abnormal behaviors as a means of communication with the spirits. For the phenomenon to be considered true mediumship, the possessed must be able to communicate with the spirits regularly and intelligibly. According to Firth, *shamanism* refers to the phenomenon of actually controlling the spirits. Anav would seem to fit most aptly into the second category, though her initial possession was certainly of the involuntary, spontanious variety and in Firth's terms, *spirit possession* rather than *mediumship.* See *The Encyclopedia of Religion,* s.v. "Spirit Possession"; Raymond Firth, *Tikopia Ritual and Belief* (London, 1967); T. K. Oesterreich, *Possession Demoniacal and Other—Among Primitive Races in Antiquity, the Middle Ages and Modern Times* (New York, 1930).

47. Indeed, Anav takes it upon herself to become "repossessed" in the course of her mediumship, as we shall see directly.

48. Erika Bourguignon's work provides extensive analysis of these patterns, based upon synthetic collation of anthropological findings from around the world. See Bourguignon, "World Distribution and Patterns of Possession States"; Erika Bourguignon, *Possession* (San Francisco, 1976).

49. See Yoram Bilu, "The Girl Who Wanted to be Her Father," *Journal of Psychoanalytic Anthropology* (1987).

50. The phrase appears in *Ronu le-Ya'akov.*

51. See Peter Burke, "Rituals of Healing in Early Modern Italy," in *The Historical Anthropology of Early Modern Italy: Essays on Perception and Communication* (Cambridge, 1987), 212.

52. On the possession-related dangers associated with eating, see Chapter 1 above.

53. In an article under preparation, I discuss the transformation of memoir to popular story in some detail.

54. For the full text, see the Appendix, Cases 9ff.

55. Vital, *Sefer ha-Ḥezyonot,* 27–28.

56. Ibid., 29.

57. Vital was possessed in 1571 by the rabbinic figure Abbaye (278–338 C.E.), as he notes in Vital, *Sefer ha-Ḥezyonot,* §8, p. 5. On the identity of the terms *house* and *body,* see, e.g., Zohar 2:142a.

58. My thanks to Dr. Menachem Kallus for seaching his computerized database while I waited.

59. Vital, *Sefer ha-Ḥezyonot.*

60. Abulafia was the grandson of Jacob Berab and was also one of eight scholars who received rabbinic ordination from Berab in Safed. He was also a student of Solomon Absaban. Like Vital, Abulafia spent time serving as a rabbi in Safed before becoming rabbi of the Spanish congregation in Damascus (Vital served as the rabbi of the Sicilian community in Damascus for a time himself).

61. A man by the name of Joshua Altif dreams of a pogrom against the Jews of Damascus, for which Abulafia is responsible. See *Sefer ha-Ḥezyonot,* 123–24. For a memorable, if somewhat fictionalized, portrait of Grandier, see Huxley, *The Devils of Loudun.*

62. Richard Kieckhefer has described the late medieval and early modern necromancers as the exceptional class of religious figures who fused the saint/witch di-

chotomy in their own self-consciousness and in the eyes of their societies. See Richard Kieckhefer, *Forbidden Rites: A Necromancer's Manual of the Fifteenth Century* (University Park, Pa., 1998).

63. See Chapter 1, n. 105.

64. For a discussion of the vividly colorful clothing of Ottoman women of all religions and socioeconomic levels, specificially noting the *firengi*, see Yvonne J. Seng, "Invisible Women: Residents of Early Sixteenth-Century Istanbul," in *Women in the Medieval Islamic World: Power, Patronage, and Piety*, ed. Gavin Hambly (New York, 1998), 263.

65. Vital, *Sefer ha-Ḥezyonot*, 32–33.

66. R. J. Zwi Werblowsky, *Joseph Karo: Lawyer and Mystic*, 2nd ed. (Philadelphia, 1977), 58. For a recent summary treatment of his biography, see Meir Benayahu, "Rabbi Israel Najara" (in Hebrew), *Asufot* 4 (1990): 203–84.

67. On Vital's criticism of Najara, see Benayahu, "Rabbi Israel Najara," 227–31.

68. For a similar criticism leveled in 1612 by a Genoese patrician (Marcello Doria) against his wife, see Peter Burke, *The Historical Anthropology of Early Modern Italy: Essays on Perception and Communication* (Cambridge, 1987), 22.

69. The term *'artilain* is used in kabbalistic works to denote "naked" or bodiless souls. Without embodiment, they cannot be rectified. See *Tikkunei ha-Zohar, tikkun* 6, 23b (*Sulam* §62); Moses Cordovero, "*Shemu'ah be-'Inyan ha-Gilgul*," in *Or Yakar* (Jerusalem, 1991), 79.

70. Cf. the attempt to rehabilitate Najara from these charges in *Ḥemdat Yamim* and *Toledot ha-Ari*, discussed in Benayahu, "Rabbi Israel Najara," 227–28.

71. See the parallel passages of this case in the Appendix, Case 9—Alternative Version.

72. During this period, the three weeks before the ninth of Av, the anniversary of the destruction of the Temples, joyous gatherings are prohibited. During the final nine days of the period, all meat and wine consumption is forbidden (except on the Sabbath).

73. Vital, *Sefer ha-Ḥezyonot*, 34. These elder and younger brothers have been identified by Tova Beeri as Moshe and Levi, respectively. See Tova Beeri, "R. Levi—An Unknown Son of R. Israel Najara—and his *Piyyutim*" (in Hebrew), *Tarbiẓ* 64 no. 2 (1995): 278. This identification is probably correct, though her discussion of the passage in *Sefer ha-Ḥezyonot* displays suprisingly careless reading. (She is under the impression that the spirit appeared to Vital in a dream and is totally unaware of the daughter of R. Raphael Anav.)

74. Ḥasidism here is to be taken in its pre-Beshtian sense of ascetic piety, as in medieval German Ḥasidism.

75. Mack, *Visionary Women: Ecstatic Prophecy in Seventeenth-Century England*, 120. See also in this context Mack's illuminating treatment of "Ecstasy and Self-Transcendence" in chapter 4 of that work, pp. 127–64.

76 .The Anav case is, of course, exceptional, with its "evil spirit of a sage."

77. D. P. Walker, *Unclean Spirits: Possession and Exorcism in France and England in the Late Sixteenth and Early Seventeenth Centuries* (Philadelphia, 1981), 24, 76–77.

78. Midelfort regards this phenomenon as an indicator of the power of popular culture over the essentially "unregulated" syndrome of possession. (It was "unregulated" in the sense that it was never illegal to be possessed, as opposed to practicing witchcraft, which therefore became "defined, prosecuted, and routinized by the literate magisterial classes of Europe.") Whereas the learned theorists might emphasize God's willingness to allow the Devil to possess in order to demonstrate the power of the sacraments, they could never imagine the "victims" of possession adopting its symptoms as an idiom for the expression of their most pious and irreverent ideas at the same time. See H. C. Erik Midelfort, "The Devil and the German People: Reflections on the Popularity of Demon Possession in Sixteenth-Century Germany," in *Religion and Culture in the Renaissance and Reformation*, vol. 11 of *Sixteenth Century Essays and Studies*, ed. Steve Ozment (Kirksville, 1989), 111–13.

79. On the assumption of male behaviors and functionalist theory, see below.

80. See Joseph Hacker, "The Payment of *Djizya* by Scholars in Palestine in the Sixteenth Century" (in Hebrew), in *Shalem: Studies in the History of the Jews in Ereẓ-Israel*, ed. Joseph Hacker (Jerusalem, 1984), 68–70, 103. For further biographical information on Aberlin, albeit embedded in an inaccurate presentation of the tax crisis, see Meir Benayahu, "The Tax Concession Enjoyed by the Scholars of Safed" (in Hebrew), in *Sefer Ẓfat*, ed. Meir Benayahu and Y. Ben Zvi (Jerusalem, 1963).

81. See Vital, *Sha'ar ha-Gilgulim* (Radomsk ed.) (Przemysl, 1875b), II, 10a. Cf. Vital, *Sefer ha-Ḥezyonot*, 252. Cf. Num. 32:41; BT *Baba Batra* 121b.

82. See Vital, *Sefer ha-Ḥezyonot*, 6–7. On Yehudah Mishan, see Gershom Scholem, "A Document by the Disciples of Isaac Luria" (in Hebrew), *Ẓion*, n.s., 5 (1940): 136. For a discussion of the self-exorcism prescribed by Luria for Mishan, see J. H. Chajes, "Spirit Possession and the Construction of Early Modern Jewish Religiosity" (Ph.D. diss., Yale University, 1999), 120–22.

83. In 1590, Rachel found Moses Alsheikh upset and asked him why. He explained that his request to learn kabbalah with Luria and Vital had been rejected by them. On Alsheikh, see Chapter 2, n. 6. Rachel's encounter with him may be found in Vital, *Sefer ha-Ḥezyonot*, §16, p. 8. D. Tamar argues that the *ḥatzer* was in Safed (on the basis of Vital, *Sefer ha-Ḥezyonot*, §12, 89. Meir Benayahu claims that it was in Jerusalem (on the basis of Vital, *Sefer ha-Ḥezyonot*, §15, 89. See Meri Benayahu, "R. Ḥayyim Vital in Jerusalem" (in Hebrew), *Sinai*, 30 (1952): 65; David Tamar, "The Greatness and Wisdom of Rabbi Ḥaim Vital," in vol. 2, *Jubile Volume in Honor of Moreinu Hagaon Rabbi Joseph B. Soloveitchik*, ed. Shaul Israeli, Norman Lamm, and Yitzchak Raphael (Jerusalem and New York, 1984), p. 1302 n. 26.

84. See Chapter 1, n. 69 above.

85. Vital, *Sefer ha-Ḥezyonot*, 117.

86. Ibid., pp. 6–7. Rachel's vision is noted by E. Wolfson in the context of a treatment of ecstatic experiences in sixteenth-century mysticism—in this case, not Rachel's, but Vital's (i.e., the *derashah* as "an occasion for revelatory experience.") See Elliot R. Wolfson, "Weeping, Death, and Spiritual Ascent in Sixteenth-Century Jewish Mysticism," in *Death, Ecstasy and Other-Worldy Journeys*, ed. J. Collins and M. Fishbane (Albany, 1995), 214 and 238 n. 30.

87. See, e.g., Bilinkoff, "A Spanish Prophetess and Her Patrons: The Case of María de Santo Domingo."

88. *Sefer ha-Ḥezyonot*, 89.

89. See for example the austere recommendation to avoid eating meat, proffered by Joseph Karo. See Joseph Karo, *Maggid Mesharim*, ed. Yeḥiel Avraham Bar Lev (Petaḥ Tikwah, 1990), 1.

90. The passage on Antoninus and Rabbi Judah the Prince in BT *Avodah Zarah* 11a to which Vital's statement regarding the ever-present radishes and lettuce on his table alludes, is part of an extended passage on the exceptionally good "brotherly" relations between these two scions of Esau and Jacob. There is thus a thematic link, albeit inverted in import, between this passage and Obad. 1:18. One is tempted to see in this dream both the conversionary *and* vengeful messianic scenarios of Israel Yuval, "Revenge and Curse, Blood and Libel" (in Hebrew), *Ẓion* no. 58 (1993): 33–90.

The biblical and rabbinic allusions in this dream are sufficiently rich (and obscure) to make one wonder to what extent Vital has "retold" Rachel's reported dream. On this problem, see chapter 2, n. 36 above.

91. Vital, *Sefer ha-Ḥezyonot*, 109.

92. On possession and sexual deprivation, see M. E. Spiro, *Burmese Supernaturalism* (Englewood Cliffs, 1967).

93. On women "using" the idiom of possession, see Allison P. Coudert, "The Myth of the Improved Status of Protestant Women: The Case of the Witchcraze," in *The Politics of Gender in Early Modern Europe*, ed. Jean R. Brink, Allison P. Coudert, and Maryanne C. Horowitz, *Sixteenth Century Essays and Studies*, vol. 12 (Kirksville, Mo., 1989); Anita M. Walker and Edmund H. Dickerman, " 'A Woman under the Influence': A Case of Alleged Possession in Sixteenth-Century France," *Sixteenth Century Journal* 22 (1991): 535–54. On preaching demoniacs, see Midelfort, "The Devil and the German People: Reflections on the Popularity of Demon Possession in Sixteenth-Century Germany," 113–14. The case of Marthe Brossier is an excellent example of this phenomenon, from late sixteenth-century France. On this case, see Sarah Ferber, "The Demonic Possession of Marthe Brossier, France 1598–1600," in *No Gods Except Me: Orthodoxy and Religious Practice in Europe, 1200–1600*, ed. Charles Zika (Melbourne, 1991); Mandrou, *Magistrats et sorciers en France au XVII^e siècle: Une analyse de psychologie historique*, 163–79; Walker, *Unclean Spirits: Possession and Exorcism in France and England in the Late Sixteenth and Early Seventeenth Centuries*, 33–42.

94. I. M. Lewis, "A Structural Approach to Witchcraft and Spirit-Possession," in *Witchcraft Confessions and Accusations*, ed. Mary Douglas (London, 1970), 307 n. 2. See also I. M. Lewis, "Spirit Possession and Deprivation Cults," *Man* 1 (1966): 307–29; Lewis, *Ecstatic Religion: A Study of Shamanism and Spirit Possession*. (Lewis toned down this thesis somewhat I. M. Lewis, *Religion in Context: Cults and Charisma*; I. M. Lewis, *Ecstatic Religion: A Study of Shamanism and Spirit Possession*, 2nd ed. (London, 1989). Cf. C. Harris, "Possession Hysteria in a Kenyan Tribe," *American Anthropologist* 59, no. 6 (1957): 1046–66.

95. Walker, *Unclean Spirits: Possession and Exorcism in France and England in the Late Sixteenth and Early Seventeenth Centuries*, 76.

96. P. J. Wilson, "Status Ambiguity and Spirit Possession," *Man*, n.s., 2, no. 3 (1967): 366–78.

97. Sluhovsky, "A Divine Apparition or Demonic Possession? Female Agency and Church Authority in Demonic Possession in Sixteenth-Century France."

98. Janice Boddy, *Wombs and Alien Spirits* (Madison, 1989), 146. Yoram Bilu has made a similar argument in Yoram Bilu, "The Taming of the Deviants and Beyond: An Analysis of *Dibbuk* Possession and Exorcism in Judaism," in *Psychoanalytic Study of Society*, ed. L. Bryce Boyer and Simon A. Grolnick (Hillsdale, 1985).

99. Susan Starr Sered, *Priestess, Mother, Sacred Sister: Religions Dominated by Women* (New York, 1994), 65. As for female "prophets," and the common historiographical assumption that "visionary women were pursuing a covert strategy of self-assertion," Phyllis Mack has argued that "the ground of women's authority as spiritual leaders was their achievement of complete self-transcendence, surely a very different subjective experience from that of the modern social activist or career woman." Mack, *Visionary Women: Ecstatic Prophecy in Seventeenth-Century England*, 5.

100. On the rapid growth of Safed, and the cultural hegemony quickly attained by the Sephardic immigrants, see Chapter 2, n. 17, above.

101. See, for now, Madeline C. Zilfi, ed., *Women in the Ottoman Empire: Middle Easter Women in the Early Modern Era* (Leiden, 1997). None of the essays in this collection treats women's religiosity directly.

102. Fioretta, mentioned in note 25 above, was one such widow to make her way to the Land of Israel in 1585 at the age of 75 (dying shortly thereafter). See Berakhia, *Ashmorat ha-Boker* (The Morning Watch), 3a. Bilah Falk , the wife of R. Joshua Falk of Lvov (1550–1614), a scholar who published *halakhic*, astronomical, and kabbalistic works, emigrated to Jerusalem upon her husband's death. Bilah's daily fasts and unwillingness to eat meat during the night were noted by her son, R. Yosef Yozpa, in his introduction to his commentary *Drisha* on the *Tur* (*Yoreh De'ah* II) (Lublin, 1635). R. Yosef Yozpa's wife took her mother-in-law's example and emigrated to Jerusalem to live out the end of her life in pietistic devotion. Other such women include Ḥavah Bacharach (1585–1652), the grandmother of R. Yair Ḥayyim Bacharach. See references in Ashkenazi, *Nashim Lamdaniot: Sekirah Historit* (Learned Women: A Historical Survey), 45–49. Cf. Cheryl Tallan, "Medieval Jewish Widows: Their Control of Resources," *Jewish History* 5, no. 1 (1990): 63–74. Glückel of Hameln considered emigration to the Holy Land as a widow. See Glückel of Hameln, ed., *The Life of Glückel of Hameln, 1646–1724*, ed. Beth-Zion Abrahams (London, 1962), 149. Glückel's widowhood has been discussed recently in Davis, *Women on the Margins: Three Seventeenth-Century Lives.*

103. Thus, in the period of the Inés prophecies, one of the prophetesses in the Cordovan household (the maid) was regarded as possessed "que la tomaba un espiritu" by the "Old" Christians, whereas the conversos regarded her as a prophet. This maid converted to Judaism and spit on icons of Jesus brought to her to bring her to her senses. See Beinart, "A Prophesying Movement in Cordova in 1499–1502," 193.

## Chapter 5

1. A. B. Grosart, ed., *The Complete Poems of Dr. Henry More* (1878; repr. New York, 1967) 21. Cited in Jan van den Berg, "Menasseh ben Israel, Henry More, and Johannes Hoornbeeck on the Pre-existence of the Soul," in *Menasseh ben Israel and His World*, ed. Yosef Kaplan, Henry Méchoulan, and Richard Popkin (Leiden, 1989), 103.

2. Here we chiefly except the works of Johann Weyer and Reginald Scot.

3. Although the text was originally published in 1651 in Amsterdam, the references here are to the Jerusalem 1995 edition.

4. I refer to C. O. Parsons, "Glanvill's Witch Book and Its Influence (Introduction to Joseph Glanvill's *Saducismus triumphatus*: or, Full and Plain Evidence Concerning Witches and Apparitions)" (Gainesville, 1966).

5. See Gedalyah Nigal, *Sippurei Dybbuk be-Sifrut Yisrael* (Dybbuk Stories in Jewish Literature), 2nd ed. (Jerusalem, 1994). On the provenance and reliability of the transcriptions of these stories in Nigal's collection, see J. H. Chajes, Review of *Dibbuk Stories in Jewish Literature*, by Gedalyah Nigal, *Kabbalah: Journal for the Study of Jewish Mystical Texts*, 1 (1996): 288–93.

6. For biographical and bibliographical information, see J. H. Coppenhagen, *Menasseh ben Israel: Manuel Dias Soeiro, 1604–1657: A Bibliography* (Jerusalem, 1990); Menachem Dorman, *Menasseh ben Israel* (Ha-Kibbuẓ ha-Meuḥad, 1989); Yosef Kaplan, Henry Méchoulan, and R. H. Popkin, eds., *Menasseh ben Israel and His World* (Leiden, 1989); Henry Méchoulan, "Menasseh ben Israel" (in Hebrew), in *Moreshet Sepharad: The Sephardi Legacy*, ed. Ḥaim Beinart (Jerusalem, 1992); Cecil Roth, *A Life of Menasseh ben Israel* (Philadelphia, 1945).

7. Menasseh's place of birth is uncertain. His parents were from Lisbon, though Menasseh may have been born shortly after their departure from Portugal. The most recent research on this question suggests that he was born in La Rochelle, France. See Dorman, *Menasseh ben Israel*, 11–13; Herman Prins Salomon, "The Portuguese Background of Menasse Ben Israel's Parents as Revealed Through the Inquisitorial Archives at Lisbon," *Studia Rosenthalina* 17, no. 2 (1983): 107.

8. See Yosef Kaplan, *From Christianity to Judaism: The Story of Isaac Orobio de Castro*, trans. Raphael Loewe, ed. Albert H. Friedlander, Louis Jacobs, and Vivian Lipman (Oxford, 1989), 308–13.

9. Yoseph Kaplan has published a number of articles that examine this issue. See Yosef Kaplan, "An Alternative Path to Modernity: The Sephardi Jews of Amsterdam in Early Modern Times," in *Everything Connects: In Conference with Richard H. Popkin*, ed. James E. Force and David S. Katz (Leiden, 1999). Cf. Yosef Kaplan, "From Apostasy to Return to Judaism; the Portuguese Jews in Amsterdam," *Binah* 1 (1989a): 99–117; Yosef Kaplan, "Wayward New Christians and Stubborn New Jews; the Shaping of a Jewish Identity," *Jewish History* 8, nos. 1–2 (1994).

10. See Dorman, *Menasseh ben Israel*, 19.

11. See J. Faur, *In the Shadow of History: Jews and Conversos at the Dawn of Modernity* (Albany, 1992); Yovel, *Spinoza and Other Heretics: The Marrano of Reason* (Princeton, N.J. 1989).

12. On the acquisition of Jewish knowledge by conversos while still in the Iberian

penninsula, see Kaplan, *From Christianity to Judaism: The Story of Isaac Orobio de Castro;* Yosef Hayim Yerushalmi, *From Spanish Court to Italian Ghetto: Isaac Cardoso—A Study in Seventeenth-Century Marranism and Jewish Apologetics* (New York, 1971).

13. On da Costa's lengthy struggle with the Jewish community of Amsterdam, his "heresies," the bans he suffered, his dissimulating reconciliation, and his suicide in 1640, see the following recent studies: Henry Méchoulan, "L'anticlericalisme d'Uriel da Costa et de Spinoza face a l'orthodoxie," in *Aspects de l'anticlericalisme du Moyen Âge à nos jours*, ed. Jacques Marx and Robert Joly (Bruxelles, 1988); E. Rivkin, "Los cristianonuevos portugueses y la formacion del mundo moderno," in *Judíos, sefarditas, conversos: La expulsión de 1492 y sus consecuencias*, ed. Angel Alcalá (Valladolid, 1995). The treatise of da Costa is now availabe as Uriel da Costa, *"Examination of Pharisaic Traditions"; Supplemented by Semuel da Silva's "Treatise on the Immortality of the Soul,"* trans. H. P. Salomon and I. S. D. Sassoon (Leiden, 1993).

14. See Alexander Altmann, "Eternality of Punishment: A Theological Controversy within the Amsterdam Rabbinate in the Thirties of the Seventeenth Century," *Proceedings of the American Academy for Jewish Research* 40 (1973): 19.

15. See ibid., 20. Altmann here relies upon H. John McLachlan, *Socinianism in Seventeenth-Century England* (Oxford, 1951).

16. Altmann, "Eternality of Punishment: A Theological Controversy within the Amsterdam Rabbinate in the Thirties of the Seventeenth Century," 23.

17. See Robert Bonfil, "Halakhah, Kabbalah and Society: Some Insights into Rabbi Menahem Azariah da Fano's Inner World," in *Jewish Thought in the Seventeenth Century*, ed. Isadore Twersky and Bernard Septimus (Cambridge, Mass., 1987); Robert Bonfil, "Change in the Cultural Patterns of a Jewish Society in Crisis: Italian Jewry at the Close of the Sixteenth Century," *Jewish History* 3 no. 2 (1988): 11–30; Allison P. Coudert, *The Impact of the Kabbalah in the Seventeenth Century: The Life and Thought of Francis Mercury Van Helmot, 1614–1698* (Leiden, 1999).

18. Menaḥem Recanati was a late 13th–early 14th-century Italian Kabbalist, Menaḥem Ẓioni was a late 14th–early 15th-century kabbalist from Cologne, and Judah Ḥayyat lived from c. 1450 to 1510 in Spain and Italy.

19. See Joseph Dan, "Menasseh ben Israel's *Nishmat Ḥayyim* and the Concept of Evil in Seventeenth-Century Jewish Thought," in *Jewish Thought in the Seventeenth Century*, ed. Isadore Twersky and Bernard Septimus (Cambridge, 1987), 72–73. Cf. Joseph Dan, "The Doctrine of Evil and Demonology in the Book *Nishmat Ḥayyim* of R. Manasseh ben Israel" (in Hebrew), in *Studies in Aggadah and Jewish Folklore*, ed. Joseph Dan. and I. Ben-Ami (Jerusalem, 1983); Joseph Dan, "Menasseh ben Israel: Attitude Towards the Zohar and Lurianic Kabbalah," in *Menasseh ben Israel and His World*, ed. Yosef Kaplan, Henry Méchoulan, and Richard Popkin (Leiden, 1989).

20. Dan, "Menasseh ben Israel's *Nishmat Ḥayyim* and the Concept of Evil in Seventeenth-Century Jewish Thought," 75.

21. Moshe Idel, "Kabbalah, Platonism and *Prisca Theologia*: The Case of R. Menasseh ben Israel," in *Menasseh ben Israel and His World*, ed. Yosef Kaplan, Henry Méchoulan, and Richard Popkin (Leiden, 1989), 213 n. 36.

22. In addition to Idel's article on Menasseh, see Moshe Idel, "Kabbalah and

Ancient Theology in R. Isaac and Judah Abravanel" (in Hebrew), in *Filosophiat ha-Ahavah shel Yehudah Abarbanel* (The Philosophy of Love of Leone Ebreo), ed. M. Dorman and Z. Levy (Haifa, 1987); Moshe Idel, "Major Currents in Italian Kabbalah between 1560 and 1660," in *Essential Papers on Jewish Culture in Renaissance and Baroque Italy*, ed. David B. Ruderman (New York, 1992). See also James Bono, *The Word of God and the Languages of Man: Interpreting Nature in Early Modern Science and Medicine* (Madison, 1995); David B. Ruderman, "The Italian Renaissance and Jewish Thought," in *Renaissance Humanism: Foundation, Forms, and Legacy*, ed. A. Rabil, Jr. (Philadelphia, 1988); Charles Schmitt, "Perennial Philosophy from Agostino Steuco to Leibniz," *Journal of the History of Ideas* 27 (1966): 505–32.

23. Menasseh ben Israel, *Nishmat Ḥayyim* (Jerusalem, 1995), 47b. On the forty-two-lettered divine name, see Chapter 2, n. 94.

24. Ibid., 48b.

25. This work was published simultaneously in Latin as *Miqweh Israeli. Hoc est Spec Israelis.* On this work, see Henry Méchoulan and G. Nahon, eds., *Menasseh ben Israel: The Hope of Israel* (Oxford, 1987).

26. Nissim Yosha, "Between Theology and Anthropology: An Examination of Menasseh ben Israel's 'De la fragilidad humana y inclinacion del hombre al peccado' " (in Hebrew), *Tarbiẓ* 61, no. 2 (1992): 276–78. The first part of the *Conciliador* (1632) was also published in Spanish and Latin, whereas the subsequent sections appeared exclusively in Spanish.

27. Ben Israel, *Nishmat Ḥayyim*, 6.

28. Ibid., 7. In chapter 16 of Book One, Menasseh refers to his *De Resurrectione Mortuorum* as having been written in "*La'az*" (non-Hebrew) for the benefit of his people. Ben Israel, *Nishmat Ḥayyim*, 83b.

29. Ben Israel, *Nishmat Ḥayyim*, 10. He refers here to chapter 3 of the first discourse.

30. On predestination, see his comments on p. 7a; on original sin, see p. 22b; and regarding preadamitism, see p. 6b.

31. Ben Israel, *Nishmat Ḥayyim*, 6. Menasseh's employment of Gen. 23:11 also resonates with the theme of his work, taken as it is from the scene in which Abraham purchases the Cave of Makhpelah for the burial of Sarah. On the Cave of Makhpelah as the channel between the living and the dead, see Chapter 2, n. 11 above.

32. Menasseh frequently treats Plato and the Kabbalists together, writing of certain metaphysical views that they were "according to the Kabbalists and Plato." See, e.g., ibid., II 13, II 29.

33. Da Silva, in his treatise against Da Costa, stressed repeatedly the latter's Hebrew illiteracy. See Dorman, *Menasseh ben Israel*, 31. Cf. the pertinent comments in Henry Méchoulan, "Menasseh ben Israel and the World of the Non-Jew," in *Menasseh ben Israel and His World*, ed. Yosef Kaplan, Henry Méchoulan, and R. H. Popkin (Leiden, 1989).

34. The classic formulation, found in Mishnah *Avot* 2: 14.

35. Otis H. Green, *Spain and the Western Tradition*, 4 vols., vol. 3 (Madison, 1965), 180–81.

36. Ibid., vol. 3, 183.

37. Ben Israel, *Nishmat Ḥayyim*, 7.

38. Ibid., 72a.

39. Ibid., 72b.

40. An *apikorus* is defined by Menasseh as one who denies any of the following: the existence of God, prophecy, the possibility of man's knowledge of God, the prophecy of Moses, or God's knowledge of human affairs.

41. Ben Israel, *Nishmat Ḥayyim*, 73a.

42. Ibid., 157a.

43. Scholars from talmudic times to the present have debated which works were meant here. Judeo-Christians and their New Testament may be the reference; others suggest Gnostics.

44. The Islamic position regarding the relationship between magic and heresy was similar, with medieval jurists debating the question of whether heresy or malicious harm was the crime for which a magician was to be executed. See, e.g., Ibn Khaldun, *The Muqaddimah: An Introduction to History*, trans. Franz Rosenthal, 2nd ed., 3 vols., vol. 3 (Princeton, N.J., 1967), 159.

45. BT *Sanhedrin* 67b.

46. See, e.g., Chapter 3 above and the works cited there.

47. BT *Sanhedrin* 67b.

48. For a short summary of this topic, and relevant bibliography, see *Encyclopedia of the Renaissance*, s.v., "Jewish Magic and Divination."

49. See Dan, "Menasseh ben Israel's *Nishmat Ḥayyim* and the Concept of Evil in Seventeenth-Century Jewish Thought," 67; Idel, "Kabbalah, Platonism and *Prisca Theologia*: The Case of R. Menasseh ben Israel."

50. This work was published in tens of editions in the seventeenth century, beginning with the Louvain edition of 1599.

51. Stuart Clark, *Thinking with Demons: The Idea of Witchcraft in Early Modern Europe* (Oxford, 1997), 535.

52. Ben Israel, *Nishmat Ḥayyim*, 253. They may, nevertheless, still be permissible in the case of healing, as Menasseh discusses in III 25 (258ff.).

53. On sympathetic bleeding, see Keith Thomas, *Religion and the Decline of Magic*, (New York, 1971), 220, 578.

54. I know of no better treatment of the "natural" dimension of natural magic than Clark, *Thinking with Demons: The Idea of Witchcraft in Early Modern Europe*, 214–32.

55. Ben Israel, *Nishmat Ḥayyim*, 190.

56. Ibid., 275.

57. See *The Encyclopedia of Witchcraft and Demonology*, s.v. "Ligature." Robbins points out that Church canons and theologians beginning in the twelfth century stressed the Devil's role in effecting the ligature—with God's consent, of course. Cf. Thomas, *Religion and the Decline of Magic*, 437 n. 1.

58. See Ben Israel, *Nishmat Ḥayyim*, 266, 187, 256, and 240–42 (III 20). Cf. Clark, *Thinking with Demons: The Idea of Witchcraft in Early Modern Europe*, 166ff.

59. For a concise summary of the intellectual foundation of the witch-hunt, see Levack, *The Witch-Hunt in Early Modern Europe*, (New York, 1987), 25–62.

60. Ben Israel, *Nishmat Ḥayyim*, 236. The Zohar 3:43a described one who practiced demonic magic as removing himself from the "dominion" of the Lord, his Master, to the dominion of the demonic "Side of Impurity."

61. Ibid., 253 III 23.

62. See esp. Jeffrey Burton Russell, *Witchcraft in the Middle Ages* (Ithaca, 1972), 228–33, 41. For the Dutch writers in this tradition, see Marijke Gijswijt-Hofstra, "Six Centuries of Witchcraft in the Netherlands: Themes, Outlines, and Interpretations," in *Witchcraft in the Netherlands from the Fourteenth to the Twentieth Century*, ed. Marijke Gijswijt-Hofstra and Willem Frijhoff (Rotterdam, 1991), 19.

63. Menaḥem Ẓiyuni also endorsed the full European witch doctrine in his Torah commentary of 1430. See Joshua Trachtenberg, *Jewish Magic and Superstition: A Study in Folk Religion* (New York, 1939), 14.

64. The Hebrew transliteration is unclear, though "hex" would appear to be a reasonable understanding of its beginning. For lists of terms for witches and sorcerers in the documents of the early modern period, see Gijswijt-Hofstra, "Six Centuries of Witchcraft in the Netherlands: Themes, Outlines, and Interpretations," 14–15; Robbins, *The Encyclopedia of Witchcraft and Demonology*, s.v. "witch,"; Russell, *Witchcraft in the Middle Ages*, 15–16. Trachtenberg touches on the issue of the Hebrew transliteration of such terms in Trachtenberg, *Jewish Magic and Superstition: A Study in Folk Religion*, 38.

65. Ben Israel, *Nishmat Ḥayyim*, 232.

66. The first English edition of Scot's *Discovery of Witchcraft* appeared in 1584. The Dutch translation of Thomas Basson (*Ontdecking van Tovery*) appeared in Leyden in 1609 and in Beverwyck in 1638.

67. Ben Israel, *Nishmat Ḥayyim*, 232.

68. See Norman Cohn, *Europe's Inner Demons: An Enquiry Inspired by the Great Witch-Hunt*, (New York, 1975) 174, 234–37; H. C. Erik Midelfort, *Witch Hunting in Southwestern Germany, 1562–1684: The Social and Intellectual Foundations* (Stanford, 1972), 20–25.

69. Ben Israel, *Nishmat Ḥayyim*, 232.

70. Menasseh's rejoinder to the compassionate view of Weyer approximates the position of George Gifford, among others, whose *Discourse of the Subtle Practices of Devils by Witches and Sorcerers* appeared in London, 1587, as a response to Scot.

71. The meaning of the term *ov* was itself a recurrent topic in the exegetical literature. It was generally taken to mean "bottle" or "(subterranean) ghost." For a sense of the variety of contexts and definitions offered, see Francis Brown, S. R. Driver, Charles A. Briggs, Edward Robinson, and Wilhelm Gesenius, *A Hebrew and English Lexicon of the Old Testament, with an Appendix Containing the Biblical Aramaic* (Boston, 1906), s.v. "*ov*."

72. *Encyclopedia Judaica*, s.v. "The Nature of Man in the Bible." For a recent and more extensive treatment, see Aron Pinker, "Sheol," *Jewish Bible Quarterly* 23, no. 3 (1995): 168–79.

73. Ben Israel, *Nishmat Ḥayyim*, 31.

74. I am currently preparing a separate study of the exegetical history of this text, with particular emphasis on early modern reevaluations of its meaning.

75. A survey of these views can be found in Gedaliah Ibn Yaḥia, *Shalshelet ha-Kabbalah* (Venice, 1586), 198.

76. "A certain Sadducee said to R. Abbahu: You maintain that the souls of the righteous are hidden under the Throne of Glory: then how did the bone [practicing] necromancer bring up Samuel by means of his necromancy?—There it was within twelve months [of death], he replied. For it was taught: For a full [twelve months] the body is in existence and the soul ascends and descends; after twelve months the body ceases to exist and the soul ascends but descends nevermore" (BT *Shabbat* 152b–153a).

77. Ben Israel, *Nishmat Ḥayyim*, 33.

78. A view Menasseh identifies with the Jewish philosopher Joseph Albo, but one that was also held by many Christian sages, including Menasseh's younger contemporary, Balthasar Bekker (who occasionally cited Menasseh in his works).

79. Ben Israel, *Nishmat Ḥayyim*, 64.

80. On the meaning of *hekesh* in Jewish philosophical literature, Jacob Klatzkin, *Thesaurus Philosophicus (Otzar ha-munaḥim ha-philosophiim ve-etnologia philosophit)*, 4 vols., vol. 2 (Berlin, 1933), s.v. *"hekesh,"* 164.

81. The late R. Shlomo Carlebach told me this story.

82. Ben Israel, *Nishmat Ḥayyim*, 27.

83. See ibid., 13.

84. Ibid., 21.

85. See, e.g., " 'And the Righteous shall live by his faith' (Habakkuk 2, 4), and being that experience proves that the Righteous live no longer in this world than the wicked, we have judged that the scripture is speaking of the life of the World to Come" and " 'For the upright shall dwell in the land, and the innocent shall remain in it. But the wicked shall be cut off from the earth' (Proverbs 2, 21–22) yet experience proves the opposite: the wicked extends his evil and 'all the evil doers boast themselves.' Thus of the Land of the Living the scripture speaks." Ibid., 40, 43.

86. Ibid., 28–29. In this context, Menasseh asserts, "there was no need to elaborate upon the destiny of the soul which their own eyes had seen [at Sinai], for the most compelling proof of anything that can be made is 'that's it!' " 27.

87. Ibid., 187.

88. Ibid., 189.

89. Ibid., 236.

90. Joseph Solomon Delmedigo, *Maẓref le-Ḥokhmah*, 3rd ed. (Warsaw, 1890; repr. Jerusalem, n.d.), 69. I have used David Ruderman's translation from David B. Ruderman, *Jewish Thought and Scientific Discovery in Early Modern Europe* (New Haven, 1995), 142.

91. Ben Israel, *Nishmat Ḥayyim*, 234.

92. Menasseh accepts that demonic divination is still practiced wherever the descendents of Abraham's concubines live, though wherever Jews live ("Asia, Europe, and Egypt") these practices are extinct. See ibid., 234 (III 17).

93. Ibid., 204.

94. Eric Clapton, "Tears in Heaven." I consulted the rendition on *Unplugged*, Warner Brothers, 1992, track 4.

95. Ben Israel, *Nishmat Ḥayyim*, 204–5.

96. The phrase *towering edifice of authority* was used by Sydney Anglo to describe the intellectual consensus that placed the existence of demons beyond doubt for so many centuries. See Sydney Anglo, "Melancholia and Witchcraft: The Debate between Wier, Bodin, and Scot," in *Folie et déraison à la Renaissance* (Brussels, 1976). Many of the tropes we have been discussing are present in the work of Abraham Yagel, and are discussed in David B. Ruderman, *Kabbalah, Magic, and Science: The Cultural Universe of a Sixteenth-Century Jewish Physician* (Cambridge, 1988b). See 46–47 on Yagel's critique of Gersonides' denial of the demonic: "Therefore, you see that the intention of this philosopher is to deny that demons have any reality or that spiritual power can be diffused into the heavens and like phenomena, to all of which the senses testify that the opposite [is the case], given the reality of such occurrences that happen to us in every generation. . . . For the conclusions of Gersonides are philosophical; however the senses testify to the contrary of his words. If he actually had seen with his own eyes the incident we described that happened in Mantua, how could he falsify [the impressions based on] his senses and upon his imagination?" Ruderman, *Kabbalah, Magic, and Science: The Cultural Universe of a Sixteenth-Century Jewish Physician*, 46. Cf. Ruderman, *Jewish Thought and Scientific Discovery in Early Modern Europe*, 142–45.

97. First published as *On Credulity and Incredulity* in 1668, it was renamed for the second edition of 1672.

98. I consulted the third edition of 1689.

99. See Parsons, "Glanvill's Witch Book and Its Influence (Introduction to Joseph Glanvill's *Saducismus triumphatus*: or, Full and Plain Evidence Concerning Witches and Apparitions)."

100. Joseph Glanvill, *Saducismus triumphatus: or, Full and Plain Evidence Concerning Witches and Apparitions*, 3rd ed. (London, 1689; repr. Gainesville, 1966), 27. More's additions appeared initially as *Philosophical Considerations Touching Witches and Witchcraft* in 1666. The most recent scholarly treatment of the work may be found in Ian Bostridge, *Witchcraft and Its Transformations, c.1650–c.1750*, Oxford Historical Monographs (Oxford, 1997), 73–78.

101. See Sarah Zfatman-Biller, " 'Tale of an Exorcism in Koretz'—A New Stage in the Development of a Folk-Literary Genre" (in Hebrew), *Jerusalem Studies in Jewish Folklore* 2 (1982): 17–65.

102. An interesting precedent to Menasseh's marshaling of the demonic for its usefulness in demonstrating matters divine may be found in the literature of medieval German-Jewish Pietism. Joseph Dan has discussed the phenomenon in a series of closely related articles. See, for example Joseph Dan, "Demonological Stories from the Writings of R. Judah the Pious" (in Hebrew), *Tarbiẓ* 30 (1961), 277; Joseph Dan, "The Princes of Thumb and Cup" (in Hebrew), *Tarbiẓ* 32, no. 4 (1963): 359–69, reprinted in *Iyyunim Be-Sifrut Ḥasidei Ashkenaz* (Ramat Gan, 1975), 39; Joseph Dan, *The Secret Doctrine of the German Pietists* (in Hebrew) (Jerusalem, 1968), 95.

103. "Alan Charles Kors and Edward Peters, eds., *Witchcraft in Europe, 1100–1700: A Documentary Study* (Philadelphia, 1972), 299. Cited in Walter Stephens, "The Quest

for Satan: Witch-Hunting and Religious Doubt, 1400–1700," in *Stregoneria e streghe nell'Europa moderna: convegno internazionale di studi: Pisa, 24–26 marzo 1994*, ed. G. Bosco and P. Castelli (Pacini, 1996), 61.

104. Cited in Stephens, "The Quest for Satan: Witch-Hunting and Religious Doubt, 1400–1700," 61.

105. Ben Israel, *Nishmat Ḥayyim*, 237 (III 19). See also the opening of III 14, p. 225.

106. Ibid., 215 (III 19).

107. *Routledge Encyclopedia of Philosophy*, s.v. "Cambridge Platonism." In his assertion of the inadequacy of philosophical or logical demonstrations to provide certainty with regard to key theological issues, Menasseh could be considered something of a fideistic skeptic himself. On this variety of skepticism, see Richard H. Popkin, *The History of Scepticism from Erasmus to Spinoza*, rev. and expanded ed. (Berkeley and Los Angeles, 1979), 29ff.

108. Walter Stephens, "Tasso and the Witches," *Annali d'Italianistica* 12 (1994): 181–202.

109. See Kaplan, "Political Concepts in the World of the Portuguese Jews of Amsterdam during the Seventeenth Century: The Problem of Exclusion and the Boundaries of Self-Identity," in *Menessah ben Israel and His World*, ed. Yosef Kaplan, Henry Méchoulan, and R. H. Popkin (Leiden, 1989).

## *Appendix*

The translations of these *dybbuk* accounts are my own. Several appeared in an earlier version in Matthew Goldish, ed., *Studies in Spirit Possession in Jewish Culture* (Detroit, 2003).

1. Yehuda Ḥallewa, *Zafnat Pa'aneaḥ*, Ms. Dublin, Trinity College B. 5. 27 / Institue of Microfilmed Hebrew Manuscripts # 16958. 143b–45a.

2. Ibid.

3. Shimon Shtober, ed., *Sefer Divrei Yosef by Yosef ben Yitzhak Sambari* (Jerusalem, 1994), 319–24.

4. Ibid., 324–25. Parentheses indicate passages that appear in Menasseh ben Israel, *Nishmat Ḥayyim*, (Amsterdam, 1651), 111a–b. A Yiddish version appeared in *Ma-aseh Buch* (Basel, 1601). The Yiddish version differs from the Hebrew in a number of respects: the spirit identifies the sin of sodomy among the onlookers, the exchange between the sage and the spirit is omitted, Constantinople is not mentioned, and the spirit is successfully exorcised. See Moses Gaster, ed., *Maaseh Book*, vol. 1 (Philadelphia, 1934), 301–3.

5. *"Kitvei Shevaḥ Yakar u-Gedulat ha-Ari z"l,"* in *Ta'alumot Ḥokhmah*, ed. Joseph Delmedigo (Basel, 1628), 49b–50b.

6. Shtober, ed., *Sefer Divrei Yosef by Yosef ben Yitzhak Sambari*, 350–51; Ya'aqov Ẓemaḥ, *Ronu le-Ya'akov*, 164a.

7. Shlomo ben David Gabbai, ed., *Ma'aseh Nissim shel ha-Ari Z"L (Shivḥei ha-Ari)* (Constantinople, 1666), 17b–18b. There are only minor variations in the version

preserved in *Eleh Toldot Yiẓḥak*, which may be found in Meir Benayahu, *Toledot ha-Ari*, 253–56.

8. Gedalya ibn Yaḥia, *Shalshelet ha-Kabbalah* (Venice, 1586), 86b–87a.
9. Ẓemaḥ, *Ronu le-Ya'akov.*
10. Vital, *Sefer ha-Ḥezyonot*, 25–36.
11. I.e., it is forbidden to fast.
12. Vital, *Sha'ar ha-Gilgulim*, 77b–78a.

# *Bibliography*


Alexander, P. S. "Incantations and Books of Magic." In *Emil Schürer, History of the Jewish People in the Age of Jesus Christ*, edited by G. Vermes, F. Millar, M. Goodman and M. Black, 3:341–79. Edinburgh, 1986.

Altmann, Alexander. "Eternality of Punishment: A Theological Controversy within the Amsterdam Rabbinate in the Thirties of the Seventeenth Century." *Proceedings of the American Academy for Jewish Research* 40 (1973): 1–88.

Anglo, Sydney. "Melancholia and Witchcraft: The Debate between Wier, Bodin, and Scot." In *Folie et déraison à la Renaissance*, 209–28. Brussels, 1976.

Ashkenazi, Eliezer. *Ma'asei ha-Shem*. Venice, 1583.

Avivi, J. "The Works of R. Ḥayyim Vital in Lurianic Kabbalah" (in Hebrew). *Moriah* 10 (1981): 77–91.

Avizur, S. "Safed—Center of the Manufacture of Woven Woolens in the Fifteenth Century" (in Hebrew). *Sefunot* 6 (1962): 43–69.

Azikri, Elazar. *Sefer Ḥaredim*. Venice, 1601. Reprint, Jerusalem, 1990

Azulai, Avraham. *Ḥesed le-Avraham*. Jerusalem, [1996].

Bacharach, Naftali ben Jacob. *'Emek ha-Melekh*. Amsterdam, 1648.

Bacher, W. "La Legende de L'Exorcisme d'un Demon par Simon B. Yoḥai." *Revue des études juives* 35 (1897): 285–87.

Baer, Y. "The Messianic Movement in Spain in the Period of the Expulsion" (in Hebrew). *Ẓion* 5 (1930): 61–77.

Bar-Ilan, Meir. "Exorcism of Demons by Rabbis: On the Involvment of Talmudic Sages in Magic." (in Hebrew). *Da'at* 34 (1994): 17–31.

———. "Writing a Sefer Torah, Tefilin, and Mezuzah on Deer Skin" (in Hebrew). *Beit Mikrah* 30, no. 102 (1985): 375–81.

Baroja, Julio Caro. *The World of the Witches*. Translated by O. N. V. Glendinning. Chicago, 1964.

Beinart, Ḥaim. "Conversos of Chillón and Siruela and the Prophecies of Mari Gómez and Inés, the Daughter of Juan Esteban" (in Hebrew). *Ẓion* 48 (1983): 241–72.

———. "The Conversos of Halia and the Movement of the Prophetess Ines" (in Hebrew). *Ẓion* 53 (1988): 31–52.

———. "A Prophesying Movement in Cordova in 1499–1502" (in Hebrew). *Ẓion* (Y. Baer Memorial Volume), 44 (1980): 190–220.

———. "The Prophetess Inés and Her Movement in Her Hometown, Herrera" (in Hebrew). In *Studies in Jewish Mysticism, Philosophy, and Ethical Literature Presented to Isaiah Tishby on His Seventy-fifth Birthday*, 459–506. Jerusalem, 1986.

———. "The Prophetess Inés and Her Movement in Puebla de Alcocer and in Talarrubias" (in Hebrew). *Tarbiẓ* 51 (1982): 633–58.

———. "The Prophetess of Extremadura: Inés of Herrera del Duque." In *Women in the Inquisition: Spain and the New World*, edited by Mary Giles, 42–52. Baltimore, 1999.

Bell, Rudolph. *Holy Anorexia*. Chicago, 1985.

Benayahu, Meir. "The Book 'Shoshan Yesod ha-'Olam' by Rabbi Joseph Tirshom (MS Sassoon 290)" (in Hebrew). In *Temirin*, edited by Israel Weinstock, 187–269. Jerusalem, 1972.

———. "Devotional Practices of the Kabbalists of Safed in Meron" (in Hebrew). In *Sefer Ẓfat* (*Sefunot* 6), edited by Meir Benayahu and Y. Ben Zvi, 10–40. Jerusalem, 1962.

———. "R. Ḥayyim Vital in Jerusalem" (in Hebrew). *Sinai* 30 (1952): 65–75.

———. "Rabbi Israel Najara" (in Hebrew). *Asufot* 4 (1990): 203–84.

———. "The Tax Concession Enjoyed by the Scholars of Safed" (in Hebrew). In *Sefer Ẓfat* edited by Meir Benayahu and Y. Ben Zvi, 103–17. Jerusalem, 1963.

———. *Toledot ha-Ari* Studies and Texts. Jerusalem, 1967.

———. *Yosef Beḥiri: Maran Rabi Yosef Karo* (Joseph, My Chosen: Our Master Rabbi Joseph Karo). Jerusalem, 1991.

ben Israel, Menasseh. *Nishmat Ḥayyim*. Amsterdam, 1651.

———. *Nishmat Ḥayyim*. Jerusalem, 1995.

Ben-Shammai, Ḥaggai. "Transmigration of Souls in Tenth Century Jewish Thought in the Orient" (in Hebrew) *Sefunot*, n.s., 5 (1991): 117–36.

Bethencourt, Francisco. "Portugal: A Scrupulous Inquisition." In *Early Modern European Witchcraft: Centres and Peripheries*, edited by Bengt Ankarloo and Gustav Henningsen, 403–22. Oxford, 1990.

Betz, Hans Dieter. "Jewish Magic in the Greek Magical Papyri." In *Envisioning Magic*, edited by Peter Schäfer and Hans G. Kippenberg, 45–63. Leiden, 1997.

———, ed. *The Greek Magical Papyri in Translation, Including the Demotic Spells*. Chicago, 1986.

Bilinkoff, Jodi. "Charisma and Controversy: The Case of María de Santo Domingo." *Archivo Dominicano* 10 (1989): 55–66.

———. "A Spanish Prophetess and Her Patrons: The Case of María de Santo Domingo." *Sixteenth Century Journal* 23 (1992): 21–34.

Bilu, Yoram. "*Dybbuk* and *Maggid*: Two Cultural Patterns of Altered Consciousness in Judaism." *AJS Review*, 21, no. 2 (1996): 341–66.

———. "The Taming of the Deviants and Beyond: An Analysis of *Dibbuk* Possession and Exorcism in Judaism." In *The Psychoanalytic Study of Society*, edited by L. Bryce Boyer and Simon A. Grolnick, 1–32. Hillsdale, N.J., 1985.

Blau, L. *Das altjüdische Zauberwesen*. Budapest, 1898.

Boddy, Janice. "Spirit Possession Revisited: Beyond Instrumentality." *Annual Review of Anthropology* 23 (1994): 407–34.

———. *Wombs and Alien Spirits*. Madison, Wis., 1989.

Bodin, Jean. *De la Démonomanie des sorciers*. Paris, 1580.

———. *On the Demon-Mania of Witches.* Abr. ed. Translated by Randy A. Scott. Edited by Jonathan L. Pearl. Toronto, 1995.
Bonfil, Robert. "Change in the Cultural Patterns of a Jewish Society in Crisis: Italian Jewry at the Close of the Sixteenth Century." *Jewish History* 3, no. 2 (1988): 11–30.
———. "Halakhah, Kabbalah and Society: Some Insights into Rabbi Menahem Azariah da Fano's Inner World." In *Jewish Thought in the Seventeenth Century,* edited by Isadore Twersky and Bernard Septimus, 39–62. Cambridge, Mass., 1987.
———. *Jewish Life in Renaissance Italy.* Translated by Anthony Oldcorn. Berkeley and Los Angeles, 1994.
Bonner, C. "The Technique of Exorcism." *Harvard Theological Review* 36 (1943): 39–76.
Bono, James. *The Word of God and the Languages of Man: Interpreting Nature in Early Modern Science and Medicine.* Madison, Wis., 1995.
Bornstein, Daniel, and Roberto Rusconi, eds. *Women and Religion in Medieval and Renaissance Italy.* Translated by Margery J. Schneider: Chicago, 1996.
Bos, Gerrit. "Ḥayyim Vital's 'Practical Kabbalah and Alchemy': A Seventeenth Century Book of Secrets." *The Journal of Jewish Thought and Philosophy* 4 (1994): 55–112.
———. "Moshe Mizrachi on Popular Science in Seventeenth Century Syria-Palestine." *Jewish Studies Quarterly* 3 (1996): 250–79.
Bostridge, Ian. *Witchcraft and Its Transformations, c. 1650–c. 1750.* Oxford Historical Monographs. Oxford, 1997.
Bourguignon, Erika. *Possession.* San Francisco, 1976.
———. "World Distribution and Patterns of Possession States." In *Trance and Possession States,* edited by Raymond Prince, 3–34. Montreal, 1968.
Boxer, B. M. "Wonder-Working and the Rabbinic Tradition: The Case of Ḥanina ben Dosa." *Journal for the Study of Judaism,* 16 (1985): 42–92.
Briggs, Robin. *Witches and Neighbours: The Social and Cultural Context of European Witchcraft.* New York and London, 1996.
Burke, Peter. "Rituals of Healing in Early Modern Italy." In *The Historical Anthropology of Early Modern Italy: Essays on Perception and Communication,* 207–20. Cambridge, 1987.
Burnyeat, M., ed. *The Skeptical Tradition.* Berkeley and Los Angeles, 1983.
Bynum, Caroline Walker. "The Complexity of Symbols." In *Gender and Religion: On the Complexity of Symbols,* edited by Caroline Walker Bynum, Stevan Harrell, and Paula Richman, 1–22. Boston, 1986.
———. *Holy Feast and Holy Fast: The Religious Significance of Food to Medieval Women.* Berkeley and Los Angeles, 1987.
———. *Jesus as Mother: Studies in the Spirituality of the High Middle Ages.* Berkeley and Los Angeles, 1982.
———. "Religious Women in the Later Middle Ages." In *Christian Spirituality: High Middle Ages and Reformation,* edited by Jill Raitt, John Meyendorff, and Bernard McGinn, 121–39. New York, 1988.

Caciola, Nancy. "Discerning Spirits: Sanctity and Possession in the Later Middle Ages." Ph.D. diss., University of Michigan, 1994.

———. "Wraiths, Revenants, and Ritual in Medieval Culture." *Past and Present* 152 (1996): 3–45.

Castañega, Martin de. *Tratado de las supersticiones y hechicerías* (Treatise of superstitions and sorcieries). Logroño, 1529.

Certeau, Michel de. "Discourse Disturbed." In *The Writing of History*, 244–68. New York, 1988.

———. *The Mystic Fable: The Sixteenth and Seventeenth Centuries.* Translated by Michael B. Smith. Chicago, 1992.

———. *La Possession de Loudun.* Collection Archive Series, vol. 37. Paris, 1970.

Chajes, J. H. "Judgments Sweetened: Possession and Exorcism in Early Modern Jewish Culture." *Journal of Early Modern History*, 1, no. 2 (1997): 124–69.

———. "Spirit Possession and the Construction of Early Modern Jewish Religiosity." Ph.D. diss., Yale University, 1999.

Chajes, Z. H. "Demons, Witchcraft, Incantations, Dreams, and Planetary Influences, Medical Prescriptions, and Curative Methods in the Aggadah (Including also References to Additions in the Gemara by the Saboraim)." In *The Student's Guide Through the Talmud*, 233–44. London, 1952.

Christian, William A., Jr. *Apparitions in Late Medieval and Renaissance Spain.* Princeton, N.J., 1981.

Ciruelo, Pedro. *A Treatise Reproving all Superstitions and Forms of Witchcraft Very Necessary and Useful for all Good Christians Zealous for Their Salvation.* Translated by E. A. Maio and D'Orsay W. Pearson. Edited by D'Orsay W. Pearson. London, 1977.

Clark, Stuart. *Thinking with Demons: The Idea of Witchcraft in Early Modern Europe.* Oxford, 1997.

Coakley, J. W. "Female Saints and Male Confidants in Medieval Dominican Hagiography." Paper presented at the conference Images of Sainthood in Medieval and Renaissance Europe, Barnard College, New York, 1987.

Cohn, Norman. *Europe's Inner Demons: An Enquiry Inspired by the Great Witch-Hunt.* New York, 1975.

Coppenhagen, J. H. *Menasseh ben Israel: Manuel Dias Soeiro, 1604–1657: A Bibliography.* Jerusalem, 1990.

Cordovero, Moses. "*Drishot be-'Inyanei ha-Malakhim me-ha-RM"K.*" In *Malakhei 'Elyon*, edited by R. Margalioth, 64–114. Jerusalem, 1945. New edition, *Or Yakar* vol. 17, Jerusalem, 1989.

———. *Or Yakar.* Edited by Menachem Zev Ḥasida. Vol. 13. Jerusalem, 1985.

———. *Pardes Rimonim.* Munkacz, 1906. Reprint, Jerusalem, 1962.

———. "*Shemu'ah be-'Inyan ha-Gilgul.*" In *Or Yakar*, 79–80. Jerusalem, 1991.

———. *Tefillah le-Moshe.* 2 vols. Vol. 1. Przemysl, 1892.

Coudert, Allison P. *The Impact of the Kabbalah in the Seventeenth Century: The Life and Thought of Francis Mercury van Helmot, 1614–1698.* Leiden, 1999.

———. "The Myth of the Improved Status of Protestant Women: The Case of the Witchcraze." In *The Politics of Gender in Early Modern Europe*, edited by Jean R.

Brink, Allison P. Coudert and Maryanne C. Horowitz, 61–89. *Sixteenth Century Essays and Studies*, vol. 12. Kirksville, Mo., 1989.

Couliano, Ioan P. *Eros and Magic in the Renaissance.* Chicago, 1987.

da Costa, Uriel. *Examination of Pharisaic Traditions; Supplemented by Semuel da Silva's "Treatise on the Immortality of the Soul."* Translated by H. P. Salomon and I. S. D. Sassoon. Leiden, 1993.

Daiches, S. *Babylonian Oil Magic in the Talmud and in Later Jewish Literature.* London, 1913.

Dan, Joseph. "The Case of the Spirit and the She-Demon" (in Hebrew). *Ha-Sifrut* 18–19 (1974): 74–84.

———. "Demonological Stories from the Writings of R. Judah the Pious" (in Hebrew). *Tarbiẓ* 30 (1961): 273–89. Reprinted in I. G. Marcus, *Dat ve-Ḥevrah be-Mishnatam shel Ḥasidei Ashkenaz*, 165–181. Jerusalem, 1986.

———. "The Doctrine of Evil and Demonology in the Book *Nishmat Ḥayyim* of R. Manasseh ben Israel" (in Hebrew). In *Studies in Aggadah and Jewish Folklore*, edited by Joseph Dan and I. Ben-Ami, 263–74. Jerusalem, 1983.

———. "Hagiographic Literature: East and West" (in Hebrew). *Pe'amim* 26 (1986): 77–86.

———. "Menasseh ben Israel: Attitude Towards the Zohar and Lurianic Kabbalah." In *Menasseh ben Israel and His World*, edited by Yosef Kaplan, Henry Méchoulan, and Richard Popkin, 199–206. Leiden, 1989.

———. "Menasseh ben Israel's *Nishmat Ḥayyim* and the Concept of Evil in Seventeenth-Century Jewish Thought." In *Jewish Thought in the Seventeenth Century*, edited by Isadore Twersky and Bernard Septimus, 63–76. Cambridge, Mass., 1987.

———. "The Princes of Thumb and Cup" (in Hebrew). *Tarbiẓ* 32, no. 4 (1963): 359–69. Reprinted in *'Iyyunim Be-Sifrut Ḥasidei Ashkenaz*, 34–43. Ramat Gan, 1975.

———. "Rabbi Joseph Karo: Halakhist and Mystic" (in Hebrew). *Tarbiẓ* 33 (1964): 89–96.

———. *The Secret Doctrine of the German Pietists* (in Hebrew). Jerusalem, 1968.

———. "Towards the History of Hagiographical Literature" (in Hebrew). *Meḥkerei Yerushalayim be-Folklor Yehudi* 1 (1981): 82–100.

David, Abraham. "Demographic Changes in the Safed Jewish Community of the Sixteenth Century." In *Occident and Orient: A Tribute to the Memory of Alexander Scheiber*, edited by Robert Dan, 83–93. Leiden, 1988.

———. "Safed, foyer de retour au judaïsme de 'conversos' au XVIe siècle." *Revue des études juives* 146, no. 1/2 (1986): 63–83.

———. "The Spanish Exiles in the Holy Land." In *The Sephardi Legacy*, edited by Ḥaim Beinart, 77–108. Jerusalem, 1992.

———. *To Come to the Land: Immigration and Settlement in Sixteenth-Century Eretz-Israel.* Translated by Dena Ordan. Tuscaloosa, 1999.

Davis, Natalie Zemon. *Women on the Margins: Three Seventeenth-Century Lives.* Cambridge, Mass., 1995.

Deissmann, Adolf. *Light from the Ancient East: The New Testament Illustrated by Recently Discovered Texts of the Graeco-Roman World.* Translated by Lionel R. M. Strachan. London, 1927.

Delmedigo, Joseph Solomon. *Maẓref le-Ḥokhmah.* 3rd ed. Warsaw, 1890. Reprint, Jerusalem, n.d.).

de Vidas, Elijah. *Reshit Ḥokhmah ha-Shalem.* Edited by Chaim Waldman. 3 vols. Jerusalem, 1984.

Dols, Michael Walters, and Diana E. Immisch, eds. *Majnun: The Madman in Medieval Islamic Society.* Oxford, 1992.

Dorman, Menachem. *Menasseh ben Israel.* Ha-Kibbuẓ ha-Meuḥad, 1989.

Douglas, Mary. *Natural Symbols: Explorations in Cosmology.* London, 1970.

Eikelman, Dale. "The Islamic Attitude towards Possession States." In *Trance and Possession States*, edited by Raymond Prince, 189–92. Montreal, 1968.

Eire, Carlos M. N. *From Madrid to Purgatory: The Art and Craft of Dying in Sixteenth-Century Spain.* Cambridge, 1995.

Eklund, Ragnar. *Life between Death and Resurrection according to Islam.* Translated by Elsa Lundequist. Uppsala, 1941.

Elior, R. "The Doctrine of Transmigration in *Galya Raza.*" In *Essential Papers on Kabbalah*, edited by Lawrence Fine, 243–69. New York, 1995.

*Encyclopedia Judaica*, s.v. "Joseph Della Reina," "Sarfati (Ẓarefati, Sarfatti)."

*Encyclopedia of Islam, New Edition*, s.v., "Djinn," "Ifrit."

*Encyclopedia of Islam, New Edition*, s.v. "Rukya," "Shaytan."

*Encyclopedia of Religion*, s.v. "Exorcism," "Spirit Possession."

*Encyclopedia of the Renaissance*, s.v. "Jewish Magic and Divination."

Etkes, Immanuel. "The Role of Magic and *Ba'alei-Shem* in Ashkenazic Society in the Late Seventeenth and Early Eighteenth Centuries" (in Hebrew). *Ẓion*, 60, no. 1 (1995): 69–104.

Faierstein, Morris M., trans. *Jewish Mystical Autobiographies: Book of Visions and Book of Secrets.* New York, 1999.

Faur, J. *In the Shadow of History: Jews and Conversos at the Dawn of Modernity.* Albany, 1992.

Febvre, Lucien. *The Problem of Unbelief in the Sixteenth Century: The Religion of Rabelais.* Translated by Beatrice Gottlieb. Cambridge, Mass., 1982.

Fenton (Yanon), Paul B. (Yosef). "Sufi Influences upon Safedian Kabbalah" (in Hebrew). *Maḥanayim* 6 (1993): 170–79.

Ferber, Sarah. "The Demonic Possession of Marthe Brossier, France 1598–1600." In *No Gods Except Me: Orthodoxy and Religious Practice in Europe, 1200–1600*, edited by Charles Zika, 59–83. Melbourne, 1991.

Fine, Lawrence. "The Art of Metoposcopy: A Study in Isaac Luria's Charismatic Knowledge." *AJS Review* 11 (1986): 79–101.

———."The Contemplative Practice of *Yiḥudim* in Lurianic Kabbalah." In *Jewish Spirituality II: From the Sixteenth-Century Revival to the Present.* World Spirituality: An Encylopedic History of the Religious Quest. Edited by Arthur Green. 64–98. New York, 1987.

———. "Maggidic Revelation in the Teachings of Isaac Luria." In *Mystics, Philosophers and Politicians: Essays in Jewish Intellectual History in Honour of A. Altmann*, edited by J. Reinharz and D. Swetschinski, 141–57. Durham, N.C., 1982.

———. "Purifying the Body in the Name of the Soul: The Problem of the Body in Sixteenth-Century Kabbalah." In *People of the Body: Jews and Judaism from an Embodied Perspective*, edited by Howard Eilberg-Schwartz, 117–42. Albany, 1992.

———, ed. *Safed Spirituality: Rules of Mystical Piety, the Beginning of Wisdom.* New York, 1984.

Finucane, R. C. *Appearances of the Dead: A Cultural History of Ghosts.* London, 1982.

Firth, Raymond. *Tikopia Ritual and Belief.* London, 1967.

Fishbane, Michael. "The Imagination of Death in Jewish Spirituality." In *Death, Ecstasy and Other-Worldly Journeys*, edited by J. Collins and M. Fishbane, 183–208. Albany, 1995.

———. *The Kiss of God: Spiritual and Mystical Death in Judaism.* Seattle, 1993.

Fishman, T. "A Kabbalistic Perspective on Gender-Specific Commandments: On the Interplay of Symbols and Society." *AJS Review* 17 (1992): 199–245.

Flynn, Maureen. "Blasphemy and the Play of Anger in Sixteenth-Century Spain." *Past & Present* 149 (November 1995): 29–57.

Foucault, Michel. *The Order of Things: An Archaeology of the Human Sciences.* New York, 1970.

Frankfurter, David. "Narrating Power; The Theory and Practice of the Magical *Historiola* in Ritual Spells." In *Ancient Magic and Ritual Power*, edited by Marvin W. Meyer and Paul Allan Mirecki, 437–76. Leiden, 1995.

Franz, Adolf. *Die Kirchlichen Benediktionen im Mittelalter.* Freiburg im Breisgau, 1909.

Gabbai, Shlomo ben David, ed. *Ma'aseh Nissim shel ha-Ari Z"L (Shivḥei ha-Ari), Meirat 'Ainayim.* Constantinople, 1666.

Garb, Jonathan. "Power and Kavvanah in Kabbalah" (in Hebrew). Ph.D. diss., Hebrew University, 2000.

Gaster, Moses. *The Sword of Moses: An Ancient Book of Magic from a Unique Manuscript.* London, 1896.

———. "The Wisdom of the Chaldeans: An Old Hebrew Astrological Text." In *Studies and Texts*, 338–55. London, 1925–28.

———, ed. *Maaseh Book.* Vol. 1. Philadelphia, 1934.

Gijswijt-Hofstra, Marijke. "Six Centuries of Witchcraft in the Netherlands: Themes, Outlines, and Interpretations." In *Witchcraft in the Netherlands from the Fourteenth to the Twentieth Century*, edited by Marijke Gijswijt-Hofstra and Willem Frijhoff, 1–36. Rotterdam, 1991.

Giller, Pinchas. "Recovering the Sanctity of the Galilee: The Veneration of Sacred Relics in Classical Kabbalah." *Journal of Jewish Thought and Philosophy* 4 (1994): 147–69.

Gilligan, Carol. *In a Different Voice: Psychological Theory and Women's Development.* Cambridge, Mass., 1993.

Ginzburg, Carlo. *The Cheese and the Worms.* Translated by John and Anne Tedeschi. Baltimore, 1980.

———. *Ecstasies: Deciphering the Witches' Sabbath.* Translated by Raymond Rosenthal. New York, 1991.

———. *The Night Battles: Witchcraft and Agrarian Cults in the Sixteenth and Seventeenth Centuries.* Translated by John and Anne Tedeschi. Baltimore, 1983.

Glanvill, Joseph. *Saducismus Triumphatus: Or, Full and Plain Evidence Concerning Witches and Apparitions.* 3rd ed. London, 1689. Reprint, Gainesville, Fla., 1966.

Goddu, André. "The Failure of Exorcism in the Middle Ages." In *Soziale Ordnungen im Selbstverständnis des Mittelalters,* edited by A. Zimmermann, 540–57. Berlin, 1980.

Goldin, Judah. "The Magic of Magic and Superstition." *In Aspects of Religious Propaganda in Judaism and Early Christianity,* edited by Elizabeth Schussler Fiorenza, 115–47. Notre Dame, Ind., 1976.

———. "On Honi the Circle-Maker: A Demanding Prayer." *Harvard Theological Review* 56, no. 3 (1963): 233–37.

Goldziher, Ignaz. "Wasser als Dämonen abwehrendes Mittle." *Archiv für Religionswissenschaft* 13 (1910): 20–46.

Good, B. J. *Medicine, Rationality and Experience: An Anthropological Perspective.* Cambridge, 1994.

Goodman, Felicitas D. *Speaking in Tongues: A Cross-Cultural Study of Glossolalia.* Chicago, 1972.

Gordon, Bruce, and Peter Marshall. *The Place of the Dead in Late Medieval and Early Modern Europe.* Cambridge, 2000.

Gottlieb, Efraim. "The *Gilgul* Controversy in Candia in the Fifteenth Century" (in Hebrew). In *Meḥarim be-Sifrut ha-Kabbalah,* edited by Joseph Hacker, 370–96. Tel Aviv, 1976.

Green, Arthur. "Bride, Spouse, Daughter: Images of the Feminine in Classical Jewish Sources." In *On Being a Jewish Feminist: A Reader,* edited by S. Heschel, 248–60. New York: Schocken Books, 1983.

Green, Otis H. *Spain and the Western Tradition.* 4 vols. Vol. 3. Madison: University of Wisconsin Press, 1965.

Guarnieri, Romana. "Nec Domina Nec Ancilla, Sed Socia: Three Cases of Spiritual Guidance Between the Sixteenth and Seventeenth Centuries." In *Women and Men in Spiritual Culture, XIV–XVII Centuries: A Meeting of South and North,* edited by Elisja Schulte van Kessel, 92–147. The Hague, 1986.

Hacker, Joseph. "Jewish Society in Salonica and Its Environs in the Fifteenth and Sixteenth Centuries: A Chapter in the History of Jewish Society in the Ottoman Empire and Its Relation to the Authorities." Ph.D. diss., Hebrew University, 1978.

———. "The Payment of *Djizya* by Scholars in Palestine in the Sixteenth Century" (in Hebrew). In *Shalem: Studies in the History of the Jews in Ereẓ-Israel,* edited by Joseph Hacker, 63–117. Jerusalem, 1984.

———. "The Relationship and Immigration of Spanish Jews to the Land of Israel" (in Hebrew). *Katedra* 36 (1985): 3–34.

———. "Romaniyot Jews in Sixteenth-Century Safed: A Chapter in the History of Support for the Jews of *Ereẓ Yisrael* by Communities in the Ottoman Empire" (in Hebrew). In *Shalem: Studies in the History of the Jews in Ereẓ-Israel,* edited by Joseph Hacker, 133–50. Jerusalem, 2002.

Hall, David D. "A World of Wonders: The Mentality of the Supernatural in Seventeenth-Century New England." In *Seventeenth-Century New England,* edited by David D. Hall and David Grayson Allen. Charlottesville, 1984.

Hallamish, Moshe, ed. *A Kabbalistic Commentary of Yoseph ben Shalom Ashkenazi.* Jerusalem, 1985.
Hamilton, Alastair. *Heresy and Mysticism in Sixteenth-Century Spain: The Alumbrados.* Toronto, 1992.
Hammawi, Abraham. *Davek me-Aḥ.* Livorno, 1875.
Hanlon, Gregory, and Geoffrey Snow. "Exorcisms et cosmologie tridentine: trois cas agenais en 1619." *Revue de la Bibliothèque Nationale* 28 (1988): 12–27.
Harley, David. "Explaining Salem: Calvinist Psychology and the Diagnosis of Possession." *American Historical Review* 101, no. 2 (1996): 307–30.
Harrari, Yuval. *Ḥarba de-Moshe.* Jerusalem, 1997.
———. "Magic, Witchcraft and Adjurations: Methodological Reflections Toward a Renewed Definition of Ancient Jewish Magic" (in Hebrew). *Da'at* 48 (2002): 33–56.
Harris, C. "Possession Hysteria in a Kenyan Tribe." *American Anthropologist* 59, no. 6 (1957): 1046–66.
Hellner, Melila. "Transmigration of Souls in the Kabbalistic Writings of R. David ibn Zimra" (in Hebrew). *Pe'amim* 43 (1990): 16–50.
Hill, Christopher. *The World Turned Upside Down.* London, 1972.
Hiriki, Emanuel. *Mishnat Ḥasidim.* Amsterdam, 1727.
Homza, Lu Ann. *Religious Authority in the Spanish Renaissance.* Baltimore, 2000.
Horowitz, Elliott. "The Eve of the Circumcision: A Chapter in the History of Jewish Nightlife." *Journal of Social History* 23 (1989): 45–69.
———. "The Way We Were: 'Jewish Life in the Middle Ages'." *Jewish History* 1, no. 1 (1986): 75–90.
Huxley, Aldous. *The Devils of Loudun.* London, 1952.
Ibn Yaḥia, Gedalia. *Shalshelet ha-Kabbalah.* Venice, 1586.
Idel, Moshe. "Gazing at the Head in Ashkenazi Hasidism." *Journal of Jewish Thought and Philosophy* 6, no. 2 (1997): 265–300.
———. *Hasidism: Between Ecstasy and Magic.* Albany, N.Y., 1995.
———. "Investigations in the Methodology of the Author of *Sefer ha-Meshiv*" (in Hebrew). *Sefunot* 2, no. 17 (1983a): 185–266.
———. "Jewish Magic from the Renaissance Period to Early Hasidism." In *Religion, Science, and Magic, in Concert and in Conflict,* edited by Jacob Neusner, Ernest S. Frerichs, and Paul Virgil McCracken Flesher, 82–117. Oxford, 1989.
———. "Kabbalah and Ancient Theology in R. Isaac and Judah Abravanel" (in Hebrew). In *Filosophiat ha-Ahavah shel Yehudah Abarbanel* (The Philosophy of Love of Leone Ebreo), edited by M. Dorman and Z. Levy. Haifa, 1987.
———. *Kabbalah: New Perspectives.* New Haven, Conn., 1988.
———. "Kabbalah, Platonism and *Prisca Theologia*: The Case of R. Menasseh ben Israel." In *Menasseh ben Israel and His World,* edited by Yosef Kaplan, Henry Méchoulan, and Richard Popkin, 207–19. Leiden, 1989.
———. "Major Currents in Italian Kabbalah between 1560 and 1660." In *Essential Papers on Jewish Culture in Renaissance and Baroque Italy,* edited by David B. Ruderman, 345–72. New York, 1992.
———. "The Meaning of '*Ta'amei ha-Ofot ha-Temaim*' of Rabbi David ben Yehuda

he-Ḥasid" (in Hebrew). In *'Alei Shefer: Studies in the Literature of Jewish Thought Presented to Rabbi Dr. Alexandre Safran*, edited by Moshe Hallamish, 11–27. Ramat Gan, 1990.

———. *Messianic Mystics.* New Haven, Conn., 1999.

———. "On Mobility, Individuals and Groups: Prolegomenon for a Sociological Approach to Sixteenth-Century Kabbalah." *Kabbalah: Journal for the Study of Jewish Mystical Texts* 3 (1998): 145–73.

———. "R. Yehudah Ḥallewa and His *Zafnat Pa'aneaḥ*" (in Hebrew). *Shalem: Studies in the History of the Jews in Ereẓ-Israel* 4 (1984): 119–48.

———. "We Have No Kabbalistic Tradition on This." In *Rabbi Moses Nahmanides (Ramban): Explorations in His Religious and Literary Virtuosity*, edited by Isadore Twersky, 51–73. Cambridge, Mass., 1983.

Jacobs, Louis. "Eating as an Act of Worship in Hassidic Thought." In *Studies in Jewish Religious and Intellectual History Presented to Alexander Altmann on The Occasion of His Seventieth Birthday*, edited by Siegfried Stein and Raphael Loewe, 157–66. University, Ala, 1979.

Janowitz, Naomi. *Magic in the Roman World: Pagans, Jews and Christians.* London, 2001.

Kagan, Richard L. "Politics, Prophecy, and the Inquisition in Late Sixteenth-Century Spain." In *Cultural Encounters: The Impact of the Inquisition in Spain and the New World*, edited by Mary Elizabeth Perry and Anne J. Cruz, 105–24. Berkeley and Los Angeles, 1991.

Kallus, Menachem. "Pneumatic Mystical Possession and the Eschatology of the Soul in the Lurianic Qabbalah." In *Spirit Possession in Jewish Culture*, edited by M. Goldish, 159–85. Detroit, 2003.

Kanarfogel, Ephraim. *Peering Through the Lattices: Mystical, Magical, and Pietistic Dimensions in the Tosafist Period.* Detroit, 1999.

Kapferer, Bruce. *A Celebration of Demons: Exorcism and the Aesthetics of Healing in Sri Lanka.* Bloomington, Ind., 1983.

Kaplan, Yosef. "An Alternative Path to Modernity: The Sephardi Jews of Amsterdam in Early Modern Times." In *Everything Connects: In Conference with Richard H. Popkin*, edited by James E. Force and David S. Katz, 213–40. Leiden, 1999.

———. "From Apostasy to Return to Judaism; the Portuguese Jews in Amsterdam." *Binah* 1 (1989): 99–117.

———. *From Christianity to Judaism: The Story of Isaac Orobio de Castro.* Translated by Raphael Loewe. Edited by Albert H. Friedlander, Louis Jacobs, and Vivian D. Lipman. Oxford, 1986.

———. "Political Concepts in the World of the Portuguese Jews of Amsterdam during the Seventeenth Century: The Problem of Exclusion and the Boundaries of Self-Identity." In *Menasseh ben Israel and His World*, edited by Yosef Kaplan, Henry Méchoulan, and R. H. Popkin, 45–62. Leiden, 1989.

———. "Wayward New Christians and Stubborn New Jews; the Shaping of a Jewish Identity." *Jewish History* 8, no. 1–2 (1994): 27–41.

Kaplan, Yosef, Henry Méchoulan, and R. H. Popkin, eds. *Menasseh ben Israel and His World.* Leiden, 1989.

Karo, Joseph. *Maggid Mesharim*. Amsterdam, 1708.

———. *Maggid Mesharim*. Edited by Yehiel Avraham Bar Lev. Petaḥ Tikwah, 1990.

Katz, Jacob. "The Ordination Controversy between R. Jacob Berab and R. Levi b. Ḥabib" (in Hebrew). *Ẓion* 16 (1951): 28–45.

Kelly, Henry Ansgar. *The Devil, Demonology, and Witchcraft: The Development of Christian Beliefs in Evil Spirits*. Rev. ed. Garden City, N.Y., 1974.

Kieckhefer, Richard. *Forbidden Rites: A Necromancer's Manual of the Fifteenth Century*. University Park, Pa., 1998.

———. "The Holy and the Unholy: Sainthood, Witchcraft, and Magic in Late Medieval Europe." *Journal of Medieval and Renaissance Studies* 24, no. 3 (1994): 355–85.

———. *Magic in the Middle Ages*. Cambridge, 1990.

Kimmelman, Reuven. "An Introduction to '*Lekha Dodi*' and '*Kabbalat Shabbat*' " (in Hebrew). *Meḥkerei Yerushalayim be-Maḥshevet Yisrael* (Semoneta Memorial Volume), 14 (1998): 393–454.

"*Kitvei Shevaḥ Yakar u-Gedulat ha-Ari z"l*." In *Ta'alumot Ḥokhmah*, edited by Joseph Delmedigo, 49b–50b. Basle, 1628.

Klaits, Joseph. *Servants of Satan: The Age of the Witch Hunts*. Bloomington, 1985.

Klaniczay, Gábor. "Hungary: The Accusations and the Universe of Popular Magic." In *Early Modern European Witchcraft: Centres and Peripheries*, edited by Bengt Ankarloo and Gustav Henningsen, 219–55. Oxford, 1990.

Knox, W. L. "Jewish Liturgical Exorcism." *Harvard Theological Review* 31, no. 3 (1938): 191–203.

Kors, Alan Charles. *Atheism in France, 1650–1729*. Vol. 1, *The Orthodox Sources of Disbelief*. Princeton N.J., 1990.

Kors, Alan Charles, and Edward Peters, eds. *Witchcraft in Europe, 1100–1700: A Documentary Study*. Philadelphia, 1972.

Kotansky, Roy. "Greek Exorcistic Amulets." In *Ancient Magic and Ritual Power*, edited by Marvin Meyer and Paul Mirecki, *Religions in the Graeco-Roman World*, 243–77. Leiden, 1995.

Kramer, Heinrich, and James Sprenger. *The Malleus Maleficarum*. Edited by Montague Summers. New York, 1971.

Kriss, Rudolf, and Hubert Kriss-Heinrich. *Amulette, Zauberformeln und Beschwörungen*. Volksglaube im Bereich des Islam. Wiesbaden, 1962.

Kushnir-Oron, Michal, ed. *Sha'ar ha-Razim le-R. Todros ben Yosef ha-Levi Abulafia*. Jerusalem, 1989.

Lamdan, Ruth. *'Am Bifnei 'Aẓman* (A Separate People: Jewish Women in Palestine, Syria, and Egypt in the Sixteenth Century). Tel Aviv, 1996.

———. "Child Marriage in Jewish Society in the Eastern Mediterranean during the Sixteenth Century." *Mediterranean Historical Review* 11 (1996): 37–59.

———. "Deviations from Norms of Moral Behavior in the Jewish Society of Eretz Israel and Egypt in the Sixteenth Century" (in Hebrew). In *Sexuality and the Family in History*, edited by Israel Bartal and Isaiah Gafni, 119–30. Jerusalem, 1998.

Langermann, Y. T. "Maimonides' Repudiation of Astrology." *Maimonidean Studies*, 2 (1991): 123–58.

Lea, H. C. *Materials Toward a History of Witchcraft.* Edited by Arthur C. Howland. 3 vols. Philadelphia, 1939.

Le Goff, Jacques. *The Birth of Purgatory.* Translated by Arthur Goldhammer. Chicago, 1984.

Lesses, Rebecca M. "The Adjuration of the Prince of the Presence: Performative Utterance in a Jewish Ritual." In *Ancient Magic and Ritual Power,* edited by Marvin Meyer and Paul Mirecki, 185–206. Leiden, 1995.

Levack, Brian P. *The Witch-Hunt in Early Modern Europe.* New York, 1987.

Lévi-Strauss, C. "Symbolic Efficacity." In *Structural Anthropology,* ch. 10. New York, 1963.

Lewis, Bernard. *Notes and Documents from the Turkish Archives: A Contribution to the History of the Jews in the Ottoman Empire.* Jerusalem, 1952.

Lewis, I. M. *Ecstatic Religion: A Study of Shamanism and Spirit Possession.* Harmondsworth, 1971.

———. *Ecstatic Religion: A Study of Shamanism and Spirit Possession.* 2nd ed. London, 1989.

———. *Religion in Context: Cults and Charisma.* Cambridge, 1986.

———. "Spirit Possession and Deprivation Cults." *Man* 1 (1966): 307–29. Reprinted in *Witchcraft Confessions and Accusations,* edited by Mary Douglas, 311–33. London, 1970.

———. "A Structural Approach to Witchcraft and Spirit-Possession." In *Witchcraft Confessions and Accusations,* edited by Mary Douglas, 293–309. London, 1970.

Lieberman, Saul. "On Sins and Their Punishments." In *Texts and Studies,* 29–56. New York, 1974.

———. "Some Aspects of After Life in Early Rabbinic Literature." In *Texts and Studies,* 235–72. New York, 1974.

Liebes, Yehuda. "How the Zohar Was Written" (in Hebrew). *Meḥkerei Yerushalayim be-Maḥshevet Yisrael: Sefer ha-Zohar ve-Doro* 8 (1989): 1–72.

———. "Two Fawns of a Doe: The Secret Homily of the AR"I Delivered before His Death" (in Hebrew). In *Meḥkerei Yerushalayim be-Maḥshevet Yisrael,* edited by Rachel Elior and Yehudah Liebes, *Kabbalat ha-Ari,* 113–69. Jerusalem, 1992.

———. "New Directions in the Study of Kabbalah" (in Hebrew). *Pe'amim* 50 (1992b): 150–70.

———. "Perakim be-Milon ha-Zohar" (Chapters of a Zohar Dictionary). Ph.D. diss., Hebrew University, 1977.

———. "Towards a Study of the Author of '*Emek ha-Melekh:* His Personality, Writings, and Kabbalah" (in Hebrew). *Jerusalem Studies in Jewish Thought* 11 (1993): 101–37.

Luria, Solomon. *She'elot u'Teshuvot Maharshal.* Jerusalem, 1969.

*Ma'aseh Buch.* Basel, 1601.

MacDonald, Michael. *Mystical Bedlam: Madness, Anxiety, and Healing in Seventeenth-Century England.* Cambridge, 1981.

Mack, Phyllis. *Visionary Women: Ecstatic Prophecy in Seventeenth-Century England.* Berkeley and Los Angeles, 1992.

Maclean, I. *The Renaissance Notion of Woman.* Cambridge, 1980.

Mandrou, Robert. *Magistrats et sorciers en France au XVII^e siècle: Une analyse de psychologie historique.* Paris, 1968.
Marcus, Ivan G. *Rituals of Childhood: Jewish Culture and Acculturation in the Middle Ages.* New Haven, Conn., 1996.
Margalioth, Reuben. *Malakhei 'Elyon.* Jerusalem, 1945.
———, ed. *Sefer Ḥasidim.* Jerusalem, 1957.
Margaliyot, Mordechai, ed. *Sefer ha-Razim.* Jerusalem, 1966.
May, L. Carlyle. "A Survey of Glossolalia and Related Phenomena in Non-Christian Religions." *American Anthropologist* 58 (1956): 75, 77, 83–86.
McKendrick, Geraldine, and Angus MacKay. "Visionaries and Affective Spirituality during the First Half of the Sixteenth Century." In *Cultural Encounters: The Impact of the Inquisition in Spain and the New World,* edited by Mary Elizabeth Perry and Anne J. Cruz, 93–104. Berkeley and Los Angeles, 1991.
Méchoulan, Henry. "L'anticlericalisme d'Uriel da Costa et de Spinoza face a l'orthodoxie." In *Aspects de l'anticlericalisme du Moyen Âge à nos jours,* edited by Jacques Marx and Robert Joly, 57–71. Brussels, 1988.
———. "Menasseh ben Israel" (in Hebrew). In *Moreshet Sepharad: The Sephardi Legacy,* edited by Haim Beinart, 315–35. Jerusalem, 1992.
———. "Menasseh ben Israel and the World of the Non-Jew." In *Menasseh ben Israel and His World,* edited by Yosef Kaplan, Henry Méchoulan, and R. H. Popkin, 83–97. Leiden, 1989.
Méchoulan, Henry, and G. Nahon, eds. *Menasseh ben Israel: The Hope of Israel.* Oxford, 1987.
Menghi, Girolamo. *Compendio dell'arte essorcistica.* Bologna, 1580.
Meroz, Ronit. "Faithful Transmission versus Innovation: Luria and His Disciples." In *Gershom Scholem's Major Trends in Jewish Mysticism 50 Years After: Proceedings of the Sixth International Conference on the History of Jewish Mysticism,* edited by Peter Schäfer and Joseph Dan, 257–74. Tübingen, 1993.
———. "From the Compilation of Ephraim Penzieri: The Ari's Homily in Jerusalem and the Intentions for Eating" (in Hebrew). In *Meḥkerei Yerushalayim be-Maḥshevet Yisrael,* edited by Rachel Elior and Yehudah Liebes, *Kabbalat ha-Ari,* 211–57. Jerusalem, 1992.
Midelfort, H. C. Erik. "Catholic and Lutheran Reactions to Demon Possession in the Late Seventeenth Century: Two Case Histories." *Daphnis* 15 (1986): 623–48.
———. "The Devil and the German People: Reflections on the Popularity of Demon Possession in Sixteenth-Century Germany." In *Religion and Culture in the Renaissance and Reformation.* Vol. 11 of *Sixteenth Century Essays and Studies,* edited by Steven Ozment, 99–119. Kirksville, Mo., 1989.
———. *Witch Hunting in Southwestern Germany, 1562–1684: The Social and Intellectual Foundations.* Stanford, Calif. 1972.
Milikowsky, Chaim. "Gehinnom and 'Sinners of Israel' in the Light of *Seder 'Olam*" (in Hebrew). *Tarbiẓ* 55, no. 3 (1986): 311–44.
Miller, Patricia Cox. "In Praise of Nonsense." In *Classical Mediterranean Spirituality,* edited by A. H. Armstrong, 481–505. London, 1986.
Modena, Leoen. *The Autobiography of a Seventeenth-Century Venetian Rabbi: Leon*

*Modena's Life of Judah*, edited and translated by Mark R. Cohen. Princeton, N.J., 1988.

Modena, Yehudah Arieh. "Ben David." In *Ta'am Zekainim*, edited by Eliezer Ashkenazi, 61–64. Frankfurt am Main, 1854.

Monter, E. W. *Witchcraft in France and Switzerland.* Ithaca, N.Y., 1976.

Morgan, Michael A., ed. *Sefer ha-Razim* (Book of the Mysteries). Chico, Calif., 1983.

Muir, Edward. *Ritual in Early Modern Europe, New Approaches to European History.* 11. Cambridge, 1997.

Nadel, S. "A Study of Shamanism in the Nuba Hills." In *Reader in Comparative Religion: An Anthropological Approach*, edited by William Armand Lessa and Evon Zartman Vogt, 464–79. Evanston, Ill., 1958.

Naveh, Joseph. *'Al Ḥeres ve-Gomeh* (On Pottery and Papyrus). Jerusalem, 1992.

Naveh, Joseph, and Shaul Shaked. *Amulets and Magic Bowls: Aramaic Incantations of Late Antiquity.* 2nd corrected ed. Jerusalem, 1987.

———. *Magic Spells and Forumulae: Aramaic Incantations of Late Antiquity.* Jerusalem, 1993.

Neusner, Jacob. *The Wonder Working Lawyers of Babylonia.* Lanham, Md., 1987.

*New Catholic Encyclopedia*, "Exorcist: In the Church."

Nigal, Gedalyah. *Sippurei Dybbuk be-Sifrut Yisrael* (Dybbuk Stories in Jewish Literature). 2nd ed. Jerusalem, 1994.

Nitzan, Bilha. "Hymns from Qumran 'to Frighten and to Terrify' Evil Ghosts" (in Hebrew). *Tarbiẓ* 55, no. 1 (1985): 19–46.

O'Neil, Mary Rose. "Discerning Superstition: Popular Errors and Orthodox Response in Late Sixteenth Century Italy." Ph.D. diss., Stanford University, 1981.

———. "*Sacerdote ovvero strione*: Ecclesiastical and Superstitious Remedies in Sixteenth-Century Italy." In *Understanding Popular Culture: Europe from the Middle Ages to the Nineteenth Century*, edited by Steven Kaplan, 53–83. Berlin, 1984.

Oesterreich, T. K. *Possession Demoniacal and Other—Among Primitive Races in Antiquity, the Middle Ages and Modern Times.* New York, 1930.

Origen. *Contra Celsum.* Translated by Henry Chadwick. Cambridge, 1965.

Oron, Michal. "The Doctrine of the Soul and Reincarnation in Thirteenth-Century Kabbalah" (in Hebrew). In *Meḥkarim be-Hagut Yehudit* (Studies in Jewish thought), edited by S. O. Heller-Wilensky and Moshe Idel, 277–89. Jerusalem, 1989.

———. "Dream, Vision and Reality in Ḥayyim Vital's *Sefer ha-Ḥezyonot*" (in Hebrew). *Meḥkerei Yerushalayim be-Maḥshevet Yisrael* 10 (1992): 299–309.

Ortega, María Helena Sánchez. "Sorcery and Eroticism in Love Magic." In *Cultural Encounters: The Impact of the Inquisition in Spain and the New World*, edited by Mary Elizabeth Perry and Anne J. Cruz, 58–92. Berkeley and Los Angeles, 1991.

Pachter, Mordechai. "The Eulogy of R. Samuel Uzeda upon the Death of the ARI" (in Hebrew). In *From Safed's Hidden Treasures: Studies and Texts Concerning the History of Safed and Its Sages in the Sixteenth Century*, 39–68. Jerusalem, 1994.

———. *Milei de-Shemaya by R. Elazar Azikri.* Tel Aviv, 1991.

———. "The Parting Sermon of R. Shlomo Alkabetz in Salonika" (in Hebrew). In

*From Safed's Hidden Treasures: Studies and Texts Concerning the History of Safed and its Sages in the Sixteenth Century*, 17–38. Jerusalem, 1994.

———. " 'Terrible Vision' by R. Moses Alsheikh" (in Hebrew). In *From Safed's Hidden Treasures: Studies and Texts Concerning the History of Safed and its Sages in the Sixteenth Century*, 69–117. Jerusalem, 1994.

Parsons, C. O. "Glanvill's Witch Book and Its Influence (Introduction to Joseph Glanvill's *Saducismus triumphatus*: or, Full and Plain Evidence Concerning Witches and Apparitions)," 7-23. Gainesville, Fla., 1966.

Patai, R. "Exorcism and Xenoglossia among the Safed Kabbalists." *Journal of American Folklore* 91 (1978): 823–35.

Pearl, Jonathan L. " 'A School for Rebel Soul': Politics and Demonic Possession in France." *Historical Reflections* 16, no. 2/3 (1989): 286–306.

Peretz, Eliyahu. *Ma'alot ha-Zohar: Mafteaḥ Shemot ha-Sefirot.* Jerusalem, 1987.

Perfet, R. Isaac ben Sheshet. *She'elot u'Teshuvot ha-RIVaSh.* Constantinople, 1547.

Perry, Mary Elizabeth. *Gender and Disorder in Early Modern Seville.* Princeton, N.J., 1990.

Philips, Abu Ameenah Bilal. "Exorcism in Islam." Ph.D. diss., University of Wales, 1993.

Pines, S. "Le *sefer ha-Tamar* et les *Maggidim* des Kabbalistes." In *Hommage à Georges Vajda—Études d'histoire et de pensée juives*, edited by Gérard Nahon and Charles Touati, 333–63. Louvain, 1980.

———. "Shi'ite Terms and Conceptions in Judah Halevi's *Kuzari*" (in Hebrew). *Jerusalem Studies in Arabic and Islam* 2 (1989): 245–46.

Polidoro, Valerio. "Practica exorcistarum ad daemones et maleficia de Christi fidelibus pellendom." In *Thesaurus Exorcismorum [Cologne, 1626]*. Padua, 1582.

Popkin, Richard H. *The History of Scepticism from Erasmus to Spinoza.* Rev. and expanded ed. Berkeley and Los Angeles, 1979.

Pressel, Esther. "Disturbances in the Apostolic Church: A Trance-based Upheaval in Yucatan." In *Trance, Healing, and Hallucination: Three Field Studies in Religious Experience.* New York, 1974.

Purkiss, Diane. *The Witch in History: Early Modern and Twentieth-Century Representations.* London, 1996.

Rapoport-Albert, Ada. "On the Position of Women in Sabbatianism" (in Hebrew). In *The Sabbatian Movement and Its Aftermath: Messianism, Sabbatianism and Frankism*, edited by Rachel Elior, Jerusalem Studies in Jewish Thought, Volume 16, 143–327. Jerusalem, 2001.

Rivkin, E. "Los cristianonuevos portugueses y la formacion del mundo moderno." In *Judíos, sefarditas, conversos: La expulsión de 1492 y sus consecuencias*, edited by Angel Alcalá, 408–19. Valladolid, Spain, 1995.

Robbins, R. H. *The Encyclopedia of Witchcraft and Demonology.* New York, 1959.

Rohrbacher-Sticker, Claudia. "From Sense to Nonsense, from Incantation Prayer to Magical Spell." *Jewish Studies Quarterly* 3, no. 1 (1996): 24–46.

Roper, Lyndal. *Oedipus and the Devil: Witchcraft, Sexuality and Religion in Early Modern Europe.* London, 1994.

Rosenberg, Shalom. "Emunat Ḥakhamim." In *Jewish Thought in the Seventeenth*

*Century*, Harvard Judaic Texts and Studies, edited by Isadore Twersky and Bernard Septimus, 285–341. Cambridge, Mass., 1987.

Rosman, Moshe. *Founder of Hasidism: A Quest for the Historical Ba'al Shem Tov*. Berkeley and Los Angeles, 1996.

Roth, Cecil. *A Life of Menasseh ben Israel*. Philadelphia, 1945.

———. "The Religion of the Marranos." In *A History of the Marranos*, 168–94. New York, 1992.

Ruderman, David B. "The Italian Renaissance and Jewish Thought." In *Renaissance Humanism: Foundation, Forms, and Legacy*, edited by A. Rabil, Jr., 382–433. Philadelphia, 1988.

———. *Jewish Thought and Scientific Discovery in Early Modern Europe*. New Haven, Conn., 1995.

———. *Kabbalah, Magic, and Science: The Cultural Universe of a Sixteenth-Century Jewish Physician*. Cambridge, Mass., 1988.

———. "The Language of Science as the Language of Faith: An Aspect of Italian Jewish Thought in the Seventeenth and Eighteenth Centuries." In Shlomo Simonshon, *Studies on the History of the Jews in the Middle Ages and Renaissance Period*, Jubilee Volume, Harvard Judaic Texts and Studies, 177–89. Tel Aviv, 1993.

———, ed. *A Valley of Vision: The Heavenly Journey of Abraham ben Hananiah Yagel*. Philadelphia, 1990.

Ruggiero, Guido. *Binding Passions: Tales of Magic, Marriage, and Power at the End of the Renaissance*. Oxford, 1993.

Russell, Jeffrey Burton. *Witchcraft in the Middle Ages*. Ithaca, N.Y., 1972.

"R. Yehudah be'Rabi Kalonymus me'Shapira." In *Yeḥusei Tenaim ve-Amoraim*, edited by Y. L. Hakohen Maimon, 438. Jerusalem, 1962.

Sack, Bracha. *Be-Sha'arei ha-Kabbalah shel Rabbi Moshe Cordovero*. Beersheba, 1995.

———. "Some Remarks on Rabbi Moses Cordovero's *'Shemu'ah be-'Inyan ha-Gilgul'*." In *Perspectives on Jewish Thought and Mysticism—Proceedings of the International Conference Held by the Institute of Jewish Studies, University College, London, 1994*, 277–87. Amsterdam, 1998.

Sánchez Lora, José Luis. *Mujeres, conventos y formas de la religiosidad barroca*. Madrid, 1988.

Schäfer, Peter. "Jewish Magic Literature in Late Antiquity and Early Middle Ages." *Journal of Jewish Studies* 41 (1990): 75–91.

Schechter, S. "Safed in the Sixteenth Century: A City of Legists and Mystics." In *Studies in Judaism*, 2nd ser., 202–328. Philadelphia, 1908.

Schiffman, L. H. "A Forty-two Letter Divine Name in the Aramaic Magic Bowls." *Bulletin of the Institute for Jewish Studies* 1 (1973): 97–102.

Schmitt, Jean-Claude. *Ghosts in the Middle Ages: The Living and the Dead in Medieval Society*. Translated by Teresa Lavender Fagan. Chicago, 1998.

Scholem, Gershom. "A Document by the Disciples of Isaac Luria" (in Hebrew). *Ẓion*, n.s., 5 (1940): 113–60.

———. "Gilgul: The Transmigration of Souls." In *On the Mystical Shape of the Godhead*, edited by Jonathan Chipman, 197–250. New York, 1991.

———. " '*Golem*' and '*Dibbuk*' in the Hebrew Lexicon" (in Hebrew). *Leshonenu* 6 (1934): 40–41.

———. *Kabbalah.* New York, 1974.

———. *Kitvei Yad be-Kabbalah.* Edited by B. Joel. Vol. 1, *Kitvei ha-Yad Ha-'Ivriim: Ha-Nimẓaim be-Vait ha-Sefarim ha-Leumi ve-ha-Universitai be-Yerushalayim.* Jerusalem, 1930.

———. "The *Maggid* of R. Yosef Taitazak [Taytaczack] and the Revelations Attributed to Him" (in Hebrew). In *Sefunoth* (The Book of Greek Jewry—1), edited by Meir Benayahu, 69–112. Jerusalem, 1971–78.

———. *Major Trends in Jewish Mysticism.* 3rd rev. ed. New York, 1961.

———. *Meḥkerei Shabtaut* (Researches in Sabbateanism). Edited by Yehudah Liebes. Jerusalem, 1991.

———. "New Sources on R. Joseph Ashkenazi, the 'Tanna' of Safed" (in Hebrew). *Tarbiẓ* 28 (1958–59): 61–62.

———. "On the Biography and Literary Activity of the Kabbalist R. Jacob Ẓemaḥ" (in Hebrew). *Qiryat Sefer* 26 (1950): 185–94.

———. *Origins of the Kabbalah.* Translated by Allan Arkush. Philadelphia and Princeton, N.J., 1987.

———. "The Paradisic Garb of Souls and the Origin of the Concept of *Ḥaluka de-Rabbanan*" (in Hebrew). *Tarbiẓ* 24 (1955): 290–306.

———. *Sabbatai Sevi, the Mystical Messiah, 1626–1676.* Rev. and aug. translation of the Hebrew ed. Bollingen Series. Translated by R. J. Zwi Werblowsky. Princeton, N.J., 1973.

———. *"Sidrei de-Shimushei Raba." Tarbiẓ* 16 (1945): 196–209.

———. "Towards the Study of Transmigration in Thirteenth-Century Kabbalah" (in Hebrew). *Tarbiẓ* 16 (1944): 135–50.

Schrire, T. *Hebrew Amulets: Their Decipherment and Interpretation.* London, 1966.

Schwartz, Dov. "The Critique of the Doctrine of Transmigration in the Middle Ages" (in Hebrew). *Maḥanayim*, n.s., 6 (1994): 104–13.

Seng, Yvonne J. "Invisible Women: Residents of Early Sixteenth-Century Istanbul." In *Women in the Medieval Islamic World: Power, Patronage, and Piety*, edited by Gavin Hambly, 241–68. New York, 1998.

Sered, Susan Starr. *Priestess, Mother, Sacred Sister: Religions Dominated by Women.* Oxford, 1994.

Shoshan, Boaz. *Popular Culture in Medieval Cairo.* Cambridge Studies in Islamic Civilization. Edited by David Morgan. Cambridge, 1993.

Shtober, Shimon, ed. *Sefer Divrei Yosef by Yosef ben Yitzhak Sambari.* Jerusalem, 1994.

Sigal, Pierre-Andre. "La possession démoniaque das la région de Florence au XVe siècle d'après les miracles de Saint Jean Gualbert." In *Histoire et société: Mélanges offerts à Georges Duby.* Aix-en-Provence, 1992.

Simon, Marcel. *Verus Israel: A Study of the Relations between Christians and Jews in the Roman Empire (135–425).* Translated by H. McKeating. Oxford, 1986.

Sluhovsky, Moshe. "A Divine Apparition or Demonic Possession? Female Agency and Church Authority in Demonic Possession in Sixteenth-Century France." *Sixteenth Century Journal* 27, no. 4 (1995): 1036–52.

Smith, Jonathan Z. *Map Is Not Territory: Studies in the History of Religions.* Leiden, 1978.

Smith, Morton. *Jesus the Magician.* New York, 1978.

Soergel, Phillip M. *Wondrous in His Saints: Counter-Reformation Propaganda in Bavaria.* Berkeley and London, 1993.

Sperber, Daniel. "Some Rabbinic Themes in Magical Papyri." *Journal for the Study of Judaism* 16 (1985): 93–103, esp. 95–99.

Spiro, M. E. *Burmese Supernaturalism.* Englewood Cliffs, N.J., 1967.

Staehlin, Carlos María. *Apariciones.* Madrid, 1954.

Stephens, Walter. "The Quest for Satan: Witch-Hunting and Religious Doubt, 1400–1700." In *Stregoneria e streghe nell'Europa moderna: Convegno internazionale di studi: Pisa, 24–26 marzo 1994,* edited by G. Bosco and P. Castelli. Pacini, 1996.

———. "Tasso and the Witches." *Annali d'Italianistica* 12 (1994): 181–202.

Stow, Kenneth R. *Theater of Acculturation: The Roman Ghetto in the Sixteenth Century.* Seattle, 2001.

Swartz, Michael D. *Scholastic Magic: Ritual and Revelation in Early Jewish Mysticism.* Princeton, N.J., 1997.

Tallan, Cheryl. "Medieval Jewish Widows: Their Control of Resources." *Jewish History* 5, no. 1 (1990): 63–74.

Tamar, David. "Gleanings Regarding *Sefer ha-Ḥezyonot*" (in Hebrew). *Sinai* 46, no. 91 (1982): 92–96.

———. "The Greatness and Wisdom of Rabbi Haim Vital" (in Hebrew). In *Jubile Volume in Honor of Moreinu Hagaon Rabbi Joseph B. Soloveitchik,* edited by Shaul Israeli, Norman Lamm, and Yitzchak Raphael, 1297–1311. Jerusalem and New York, 1984.

———. "On the Book *Toledot ha-Ari*" (in Hebrew). In *Meḥkarim be-Toledot ha-Yehudim be-Ereẓ Yisrael u'be-Italia* (Studies in the History of the Jews in the Land of Israel and in Italy), 166–93. Jerusalem, 1986.

———. "On the Confraternities of Safed" (in Hebrew). In *Meḥkarim be-Toledot ha-Yehudim be-Ereẓ Yisrael u'be-Italia* (Studies in the History of the Jews in the Land of Israel and in Italy). Jerusalem, 1986.

Tambiah, Stanley. *Magic, Science, Religion, and the Scope of Rationality.* Cambridge, 1990.

———. "The Magical Power of Words." In *Culture, Thought, and Social Action: An Anthropological Perspective.* Cambridge, Mass.: Harvard University Press, 1985.

Temkin, Owsei. *The Falling Sickness.* 2nd ed. Baltimore, 1971.

Thomas, Keith. *Religion and the Decline of Magic.* New York, 1971.

Thompson, R. Campbell. *Semitic Magic: Its Origins and Development.* London, 1908.

Thorndike, Lynn. *A History of Magic and Experimental Science.* 8 vols. Vol. 8. New York, 1923–58.

Tirshom, Joseph. *Shoshan Yesod ha-'Olam,* Sassoon 290. Institute of Microfilmed Hebrew Manuscripts, #39891.

Tishby, Isaiah. *Torat ha-Ra ve-ha-Kelipah be-Kabbalat ha-Ari.* New ed. Jerusalem, 1984.

Tishby, Isaiah, and Yeruham Fishel Lachower. *The Wisdom of the Zohar: An Anthology of Texts.* Translated by David Goldstein. Oxford, 1989.

Tomlinson, Gary. *Music in Renaissance Magic: Toward a Historiography of Others.* Chicago, 1993.

Trachtenberg, Joshua. *Jewish Magic and Superstition: A Study in Folk Religion.* New York, 1939.

Twelftree, Graham H. *Jesus the Exorcist: A Contribution to the Study of the Historical Jesus.* Tübingen, 1993.

Urbach, Yakov. "On the Matter of the 42–Lettered Name" (in Hebrew). *Maḥanayim* 6 (1993): 238–40.

van den Berg, Jan. "Menasseh ben Israel, Henry More, and Johannes Hoornbeeck on the Pre-existence of the Soul." In *Menasseh ben Israel and His World,* edited by Yosef Kaplan, Henry Méchoulan, and Richard Popkin, 98–116. Leiden, 1989.

Veltri, Giuseppe. "The 'Other' Physicians; the Amorites of the Rabbis and the Magi of Pliny." *Korot* 13 (1998–99): 37–54.

Verman, Mark, and Shulamit H. Adler. "Path Jumping in the Jewish Magical Tradition." *Jewish Studies Quarterly* 1 (1993–94): 131–48.

Versnel, H. S. "Some Reflections on the Relationship Magic-Religion." *Numen* 38 (1991): 177–97.

Vital, Ḥayyim. *Adam Yashar.* Jerusalem, 1994.

———. *Eẓ Ḥayyim.* 15 vols. Vol. 2, *Kitvei Rabbenu ha-ARI ZT"L.* Jerusalem, 1988.

———. *Likkutei Torah.* Edited by Yehuda Zvi Brandwein. 15 vols. *Kitvei Rabbenu ha-ARI ZT"L.* Jerusalem, 1988.

———. *Sefer ha-Gilgulim.* Przemysl, 1875. Reprinted as *Torat ha-Gilgul,* vol. 1. Jerusalem, 1982.

———. *Sefer ha-Goralot* (Book of Lots). Jerusalem, 1997.

———. *Sefer ha-Ḥezyonot,* Cambridge-Trinity College F 12 43. Cambridge, Eighteenth Century Institute of Microfilmed Hebrew Manuscripts, # 12228.

———. *Sefer ha-Ḥezyonot.* Edited by A. Z. Aescoly. Jerusalem, 1954.

———. *Sefer Pri Eẓ Ḥayyim.* Edited by Yehuda Zvi Brandwein. 15 vols. Vols. 13–14, *Kitvei Rabbenu ha-ARI ZT"L.* Jerusalem, 1988.

———. *Sha'arei Kedusha.* Jerusalem, 1985.

———. *Sha'ar ha-Gilgulim.* Jerusalem, 1863.

———. *Sha'ar ha-Gilgulim.* Edited by Yehuda Zvi Brandwein. 15 vols. Vol. 10. *Kitvei Rabbenu ha-ARI ZT"L.* Jerusalem, 1988.

———. *Sha'ar ha-Gilgulim* Radomsk ed. Przemysl, 1875.

———. *Sha'ar ha-Yiḥudim.* Koretz, 1783.

———. *Sha'ar Ruaḥ ha-Kodesh.* Edited by Yehuda Zvi Brandwein. 15 vols. Vol. 10, *Kitvei Rabbenu ha-ARI ZT"L.* Jerusalem, 1988.

Volpato, Antonio. "Tra sante profetesse e santi dottori: Caterina da Siena." In *Women and Men in Spiritual Culture, Fourteenth–Sixteenth Centuries: A Meeting of South and North,* edited by Elisja Schulte van Kessel, 149–61. The Hague, 1986.

Walker, Anita M., and Edmund H. Dickerman. " 'A Woman under the Influence': A Case of Alleged Possession in Sixteenth-Century France." *Sixteenth Century Journal* 22 (1991): 535–54.

Walker, D. P. *Unclean Spirits: Possession and Exorcism in France and England in the Late Sixteenth and Early Seventeenth Centuries.* Philadelphia, 1981.

Wear, Andrew. "Medicine in Early Modern Europe, 1500–1700." In *The Western Medical Tradition: 800 B.C.–1800 A.D.*, edited by Lawrence I. Conrad, Michael Neve, Vivian Nutton, Roy Porter, and Andrew Wear, 215–361. Cambridge, 1995.

Weber, Alison. "Between Ecstasy and Exorcism: Religious Negotiation in Sixteenth-Century Spain." *Journal of Medieval and Renaissance Studies* 23, no. 2 (1993): 221–34.

Weber, Henri. "L'Exorcisme à la fin du seizième siècle, instrument de la Contre Réforme et spectacle baroque." *Nouvelle Revue du seizième siècle* 1 (1983): 79–101.

Weissler, Chava. *Voices of the Matriarchs: Listening to the Prayers of Early Modern Jewish Women.* Boston, 1998.

Werblowsky, R. J. Zwi. *Joseph Karo: Lawyer and Mystic.* 2nd ed. Philadephia, 1977.

Wilson, P. J. "Status Ambiguity and Spirit Possession." *Man*, n.s., 2, no. 3 (1967): 366–78.

Wolfson, Elliot R. *Circle in the Square: Studies in the Use of Gender in Kabbalistic Symbolism.* Albany, N.Y., 1995.

———. "Weeping, Death, and Spiritual Ascent in Sixteenth-Century Jewish Mysticism." In *Death, Ecstasy and Other-Worldly Journeys*, edited by J. Collins and M. Fishbane, 209–47. Albany, N.Y., 1995.

———. "Woman—The Feminine as Other in Theosophic Kabbalah: Some Philosophical Observations on the Divine Androgyne." In *The Other in Jewish Thought and History: Constructions of Jewish Culture and Identity*, edited by Laurence J. Silberstein and Robert L. Cohn, 166–204. New York, 1994.

Yaari, A. *Ha-Defus ha-'Ivri be-Arẓot ha-Mizraḥ* (Hebrew printing in the East). 2 vols. Vol. 1. Jerusalem, 1936.

Yasif, Eli. *Sippur ha-'Am ha-'Ivri.* Jerusalem and Beersheba, 1994.

Yerushalmi, Yosef Hayim. *From Spanish Court to Italian Ghetto: Isaac Cardoso—A Study in Seventeenth-Century Marranism and Jewish Apologetics.* New York, 1971.

Yosha, Nissim. "Between Theology and Anthropology: An Examination of Menasseh ben Israel's 'De la fragilidad humana y inclinacion del hombre al peccado' " (in Hebrew). *Tarbiẓ* 61, no. 2 (1992): 273–95.

Yovel, Yirmiyahu. *Spinoza and Other Heretics: The Marrano of Reason.* Princeton N.J., 1989.

Yuval, Israel. "Revenge and Curse, Blood and Libel." (in Hebrew). *Ẓion* no. 58 (1993): 33–90.

Zacuto, Moshe. *Iggerot ha-Remez.* Livorno, 1780.

———. *Sefer ha-Shemot* (MS facimile). Jerusalem, 1987.

Zacuto, Moshe, and Abraham Alnakar. *Shorshei ha-Shemot.* 2 vols. Vol. 1. Jerusalem, 1995.

Zafrani, Haïm. *Kabbale, vie mystique et magie.* Paris, 1986.

Zarri, Gabriella. "Living Saints: A Typology of Female Sanctity in the Early Sixteenth Century." In *Women and Religion in Medieval and Renaissance Italy*, edited by Daniel Bornstein and Roberto Rusconi and translated by Margery J. Schneider, 219–303. Chicago, 1996.

Zbinden, Ernst. *Die Djinn des Islam und der altorientalische geisterglaube.* Bern, 1953.

Ẓemaḥ, Ya'aqov. *Meshivat Nafesh*, London Montefiore Library 342. Institute of Microfilmed Hebrew Manuscripts # 05286. Cf. other seventeenth century mauscripts: Oxford, Bodleian Ms. opp. 121. Institute of Microfilmed Hebrew Manuscripts # 18799, Moscow, Russian State Library Ms. Günzburg 696. Institute of Microfilmed Hebrew Manuscripts # 47870.

———. *Ronu le-Ya'akov*, Ms. Bodleian 1870. Institute of Microfilmed Hebrew Manuscripts # 18805. Cf. Ms. Cincinnati 544. Institute of Hebrew Microfilmed Manuscripts # 19469, Ms. Machon Ben-Zvi 203 Institute for Microfilmed Hebrew Manuscripts # 26559.

Zfatman-Biller, Sara. " 'Tale of an Exorcism in Koretz'—A New Stage in the Development of a Folk-Literary Genre" (in Hebrew). *Jerusalem Studies in Jewish Folklore* 2 (1982): 17–65.

Zilfi, Madeline C., ed. *Women in the Ottoman Empire: Middle Eastern Women in the Early Modern Era.* Leiden, 1997.

Zimmels, H. J. *Magicians, Theologicans, and Doctors: Studies in Folk-Medicine and Folk-Lore as Reflected in Rabbinical Responsa (Twelfth–Nineteenth Centuries).* New York, 1952.

Zimra, David ibn. *She'elot u'Teshuvot RaDBaZ.* New York, 1967.

Zwemer, Samuel M. "The Familiar Spirit or *Qarina.*" In *Studies in Popular Islam: A Collection of Papers Dealing with the Superstitions and Beliefs of the Common People*, 53–68. London and New York, 1939.

———. *The Influence of Animism on Islam: An Account of Popular Superstitions.* London, 1920.

# Index

Levack, Brian, 129
Lévi-Strauss, Claude, 82
Lewis, I. M., 116
ligature, 128, 134, 238 n.57
Luria, Isaac (AR"I): AR"I as acronym for, 190 n.52; Bin Nun exorcism, 46–47; exorcism of water, 23–24; and holy *'ibburim*, 24–25, 28; legacy of and *Shoshan Yesod ha-'Olam*, 65–66; Lurianic exorcism, afterlife of, 85–95; and *maggid* possession, 29; and narratives of spirit possession, 45–56; and possessed widow of Safed, 47–54, 202 n.70; and possessed woman of Safed, 71–75; reform of exorcism techniques, 57, 83–85, 91–92; in Safed, 34; on transmigration, 22–23; Vital and, 21, 22–23, 32, 48, 49, 84, 107–8, 203 n.75, 215 n.94; *yiḥud* exorcism techniques, 21, 71–85. *See also* exorcism rituals and techniques

*Ma'aseh Buch* (Story Book), 36
*Ma'asei ha-Shem* (Deeds of the Lord) (Ashkenazi), 3, 11, 36, 186 n.6
*Macanthropos*, 25
Mack, Phyllis, 112, 234 n.99
*maggidism*, 28–29
*Maggid Mesharim* (Angel of Righteousness) (Karo), 28, 29, 48–49, 227 n.28
magic: and ancient exorcism rituals, 61–62, 64–65; ben Israel's *Nishmat Ḥayyim* and, 127–28, 132; and Christian demonological healing, 92–93; Christian use of Hebrew magical names, 61–62, 64–65; early Christian superstitions regarding, 64–65; heresy and, 127–28, 132, 238 n.44; Islamic demonology and, 238 n.44; Jewish exorcism and magical recidivism, 95–96; kabbalistic techniques for binding souls, 14–16; Karo's pragmatic view of, 94, 223 n.167; Lurianic exorcism and, 77–79, 84–85, 91–92, 218 n.125; *maggidic* possession pursued through, 28–29; magical manuscripts, 4, 64; medieval Jewish magical bowls, 66; post-Lurianic adoption of, 91–95; Psalms, use of, 66, 68–69, 76, 210 n.45; *Shoshan Yesod ha-'Olam* as pivotal text, 65–66; sympathetic magical sensibility, 77–79; Zacuto's pragmatic approach to healing and, 91–95. See also *Greek Magical Papyri* (*PGM*)
"The Magical Power of Words" (Tambiah), 76
magnets, 134
Maharshal (Solomon Luria), 93–94, 222 n.165
Maimonides, 94, 95, 222 n.165
*Malleus Maleficarum* (Kramer and Sprenger), 92
Mather, Cotton, 212 n.65
*Maẓref la-Ḥokhmah* (Delmedigo), 134
*mazzikim* (destructive spirits), 11, 12–13
McKay, Angus, 184 n.37
McKendrick, Geraldine, 184 n.37
medieval Jewish exorcism rituals and techniques (pre-Lurianic), 65–70; adjuration of spirits, 66–68; amulets to prevent repossession, 70, 90; as broad-spectrum remedies, 66–67; capture of demon in a glass flask, 67–68; Falcon case, 69–70, 90, 212 n.65; forcing spirit to speak, 68; fumigations, 69–70; goals of spirit's rectification, 69, 70; Karo's Safed exorcism, 68–69, 212 nn.56–57; magical bowls, 66; medieval Christian parallels, 3–4; names of demons, 67–68; and negotiation with spirit, 70; and penitential ceremonies, 70; physical manipulation of victim's body, 70, 212 n.65; Psalms and, 66, 210 n.45; rabbinic confrontation with possession, 3, 182 n.11; recitation of prayers, 68–69, 212 nn.56–57; theatrical elements of public exorcism, 68, 211 n.53; and Tirshom's *Shoshan Yesod ha-'Olam*, 65–68
*Megillat Aḥima'az* (Klar, ed.), 182 n.12
Meir, Menachem ben, of Speyer, 208 n.24
Menghi, Girolamo, 89–90
mental illness, 88–89, 220 n.139
*Meshivat Nafesh* (Restoration of the Soul) (Ẓemaḥ), 35
mezuzahs, 54, 63, 205 n.98
Midelfort, H. C. E., 6, 39, 43, 55, 112, 232 n.78
*Millei di-Shemaya* (Azikri), 227 n.28
Mira (Jewish woman mystic), 102, 228 n.33
*Mishna Rosh ha-Shanah*, 82
*Mishnat Ḥasidim* (Teaching of the Pious) (Ḥiriki), 79
monastic communities, Christian, 1–2
Montaigne, Michel de, 40, 199 n.40
More, Henry, 119, 132–33, 136, 137, 138

Naḥman, Moshe bar (Ramban), 12, 15
Najara, Israel, 110–12
names: in ancient exorcism rituals, 61–62, 64–65; backward/forward order, 72–73, 76,

88, 212 n.57; in Christian exorcism rituals, 61–62, 64–65, 82; of demons/spirits, 63, 67–68, 74, 81, 82; Hebrew, 61–62, 64–65, 73–74, 208 n.24; and Lurianic *yiḥudim* techniques, 72–74, 76, 81, 82, 84, 88, 219 n.132; magic and, 61–62, 64–65; medieval Jewish exorcism rituals, 67–68; and numerical value of Safed, 34, 195 nn.9–10
Naveh, Joseph, 64
necromancy, 14–15, 20–22, 108–9, 230 n.62
*nefesh* (vital soul), 16, 18–20, 189 n.48
*neshamah* (*spiritus*, rational soul), 16, 20
New Testament, 59
Nigal, Gedalyah, 119
*Nishmat Ḥayyim* (Soul of Life) (ben Israel): alignment of Jewish and Christian traditions, 129; attack on atheism by demonstration of the demonic, 119, 125–26, 137–38; authoritative tradition as way of knowing, 133, 134; characterization of the work, 119–20, 122–26, 136–38, 139; converso context and cultural attitudes, 121, 123, 124, 125; and demonic divination, 135, 240 n.92; demonological hermeneutics of, 126–33, 138; epistemology of direct experience and arguments against heresy, 133–38; and Falcon case, 36, 39, 200 nn. 42, 45; *Gan Eden* and Gehinnom, 127, 132; heresy and magic conflated, 127–28, 132; on heresy and necessity of doctrinal fidelity, 126–28, 129, 132; intended audience, 123–25; kabbalah and, 121, 122–23; logical demonstration as way of knowing, 133; magic, demonization of, 127–29, 132; Menasseh's rhetoric of direct experience, 134; and new genre of "polemical demonology," 119–20, 125–26, 136–38, 139; non-Jewish sources, 122, 124–25, 134–35; other contemporary works, 136–37, 138, 241 n.102; and plain sense of scripture, 131–32, 240 n.78; and Platonism, 122, 125, 132, 237 n.32; possession stories as proof for the immortality of the soul, 135–38; witch doctrine and, 128–30, 132, 239 n.66; the "Witch of Endor" and biblical hermeneutics, 130–32

Oesterreich, T. K., 229 n.46
Origen, 62, 208 n.29

Pachter, Mordechai, 199 n.31, 205 n.104
Parsons, C. O., 136–37
Patai, R., 200 n.49
*Perek Ḥelek* (rabbinic text), 126–27
Perfet, Isaac ben Sheshet, 69, 182 n.19
*PGM*. See *Greek Magical Papyri* (*PGM*)
Pines, Shlomo, 7–8
*Pirkei de-Rabbi Eliezer*, 11
Piso, Ḥakham, and Anav, the Oracle of Damascus, 105–6, 108–12; Abulafia and, 108–10, 112; criticism of Najara, 110–12; message to Vital, 105; possession of Anav, 105, 109
Plato, 11, 125, 237 n.32
Platonism, 122, 125, 132, 237 n.32
Polidoro, Valerio, 90
possession, genealogy of, 11–31; Ashkenazi's natural explanation, 11–12; candidates for souls of wicked dead, 11–12; Christian suppression of possession by dead, 13, 30; Cordovero and the evil *'ibbur*, 16–18; Cordovero and living contact with the dead, 18–20; and the evil *'ibbur*, 16–18, 22–23; and Garments of Light, 19–20, 189 n.44; ghosts and possessing spirits, 4, 11–14; *gilgul* and possession, 24–28; Ḥallewa's stories and Safed atmosphere, 25–27; and Jewish expulsion from Spain, 30–31, 195 n.104; Jewish view of possession by dead as a possibility, 13–14, 187 n.14; late medieval Christian Spanish views, 29–30; *maggidism* pursued as positive possession, 28–29; and methods of bringing about possession by holy *'ibburim*, 24–25; possession as form of prophecy, 30, 194 n.102; practices/techniques for living contact with the dead, 14–16, 18–22; Spanish antecedents, 17–31; Spanish necromantic techniques, 20–22; terminological fluidity, 12–13; transmigration theories, 22–24
possession narratives in sixteenth-century Safed, 35–56; accounts of failed exorcisms, 43–44; the Luria cases, 45–56; mystical women in Vital's *Sefer ha-Ḥezyonot*, 101–15, 117; and popular skepticism, 40, 53, 54–55; provenance of early narratives, 35–36, 198 n.23; and Safed's special religious environment, 33–35, 55–56, 205 n.104; sexual transgression and, 41–42, 44–45, 47, 50, 54–55, 202 n.60. *See also* Christian possession accounts; possession phenomenon
possession phenomenon: academic study of,

popular accounts of, 49–50, 54, 203 n.77; Vital's role in, 48–50, 52, 53–54, 202 n.72, 205 n.96. *See also* woman of Safed
Wilson, P. J., 116
Winston, William, 69
witchcraft doctrine: ben Israel's *Nishmat Ḥayyim* and, 128–30, 132, 239 n.66; and classic Jewish sources, 182 n.20; critiques of, 129–30, 239 n.66; and demonic pacts, 128–29, 130; and embodied female spirituality, 5; and Jewish spirit possession, 4–6
*The Witch in History* (Purkiss), 8–9
"Witch of Endor," 130–32
Wolfson, Elliot R., 226 n.22
woman of Safed, 71–75, 155–58. *See also* widow of Safed
women's religiosity and spirit possession, 27–28, 97–118, 140; Aberlin, Rachel, and Vital, 113–15, 117, 118, 232 nn. 83, 86, 233 n.90; academic study of, 5, 97–98, 115–17; Anav, the Oracle of Damascus, 104–13, 160–77; characteristics of Christian women's religiosity, 97–98; comparative perspectives, 97–98; denial of, in Jewish historiography, 99–100, 226 nn. 20, 22, 227 n.24; divinatory skills and, 102, 228 n.31; Francesa Sarah of Safed, 102–4, 118; functionalist presumptions of social/psychological motivations, 5, 115–17; identifying sources of inspiration, 98; Inés, 99, 113; Mira, 102, 228 n.33; and participation in textual culture, 101, 227 n.25; and religious culture of Safed, 117–18, 234 nn.102–3; and Sabbatian movement, 118, 140; Soñadora, 101–2; texts of possession narratives, 150–54, 155–58, 160–80; Vital's descriptions of women, 101; and Vital's *Sefer ha-Ḥezyonot*, 101–15, 117; volition in, 5, 117, 234 n.99; Weiser, Esther, 85–87, 177–80; widow of Safed, 45, 47–55, 150–54; witchcraft and embodied female spirituality, 5, 102; woman of Safed, 71–75, 155–58

xenoglossia, 89, 90, 200 n.49

Yagel, Abraham, 13
Yaḥia, Gedalia ibn, 3, 36, 37, 81, 86, 198 n.23
*yiḥudim*, 21. *See also* exorcism rituals and techniques
Yizḥaki, Solomon (Rashi), 13, 186 n.10
Yohai, Shimon bar, 33, 60
Yosha, Nissim, 123
young man of Safed, 44–45, 47, 149–50, 242 n.4

Zacuto, Moshe: on characteristics of possession, 28, 88–89; letter of, 85, 87–89, 90–92, 95, 219 n.131; and natural mental illness and possession, 88–89; reconstruing of Lurianic exorcism by, 90–95
*Ẓafnat Pa'aneaḥ* (Exposer of Mysteries) (Ḥallewa), 25–26, 35, 36
Ẓarfati, Joseph: family name of, 199 n.40; and Sambari's account of Falcon case, 39–41
Ẓarfati, Samuel, 40–42, 52, 200 n.42
Zarri, Gabriella, 97
Ẓemaḥ, Jacob (Ya'aqov), 35, 66, 105
Zimra, David ibn, 94
Zohar: Cordovero's commentary on, 18–20, 190 n.50; and notion of *'ibbur*, 16

# *Acknowledgments*

I would like to thank the many scholars at Yale University, the University of Michigan, and the Hebrew University whose inspiration and encouragement kept me on the path: Paula Hyman, Geoffrey Parker, Todd Endelman, Marvin Becker, Moshe Rosman, Warren Zev Harvey, and Carlos Eire. Moshe Idel has been my teacher, advisor, and academic ally since I began auditing his graduate seminars in 1990 while playing hooky from yeshiva. Since my return to Israel in 1995, his generosity of spirit has been enriching in a variety of ways, including hours of conversation, reams of typescripts, and support at key times and places. David Ruderman saw to it that throughout these years, I have never wanted for guidance. I have benefited immeasurably from his wisdom, innovative scholarship, wealth of ideas, and boundless enthusiasm. His careful consideration of my written work provided the pruning necessary for clarity and precision, while encouraging creativity and intellectual risk taking.

I am grateful to a number of foundations for their generous support. During my four years of graduate study in New Haven, I was privileged to be a Wexner Graduate Fellow. Just when I thought the well had run dry, I was fortunate enough to receive a Fulbright Doctoral Fellowship that took my family and me back to Jerusalem. I should also like to thank the National Foundation for Jewish Culture and the Memorial Foundation for Jewish Culture, from which I received the Mark Uveeler Special Doctoral Scholarship. I was also a recipient of an Interuniversity Fellowship (1997–98) and, from the Hebrew University, the Horace W. Goldsmith Distinguished Scholar Award and the Rose and Andrew Miller Memorial Scholarship. Finally, despite all this bounty, without the assistance of my mother- and father-in-law, Karin and the late Professor Emanuel Fenz, life with a growing family would have been a lot more austere. My deepest gratitude to them for their support and inspiration.

Since returning to Israel, I have enjoyed three primary workplaces: the National and University Library at Givat Ram (and its Scholem Library in particular), the Shalom Hartman Institute, where I was privileged to be a fellow in the Institute for Advanced Jewish Studies for a number of years, and the University of Haifa, where I now work. In each setting I have had the good fortune to meet outstanding scholars and to make good friends. Special thanks are due to Dr. Esther Liebes of the Scholem Library, to Rabbi Dr. David Hartman of the Hartman Institute, and to Professor Kenneth Stow and my other wonderful colleagues at Haifa for inviting me up and making me feel immediately at home.

A few readers made it possible for me to improve this manuscript in a substantial manner. Special thanks to Professor Edward Peters and to my friend Dr. Moshe Sluhovsky for their particularly constructive comments.

I bless my mother with many more joyous years of good health, and thank her for always accepting—and even appreciating—my life choices. I am also grateful to my brothers Richard and David for their unwavering love. As at my wedding and the births of my children, the absence of my father *z"l* at this moment is sorely felt. If there is one reason why I have become a scholar of Jewish culture, it may be my father's magical ability to have connected me to the great Chajes rabbis in our family's past. While I will never approach their scholarly achievements, I continue our family tradition of living in—and between—multiple worlds.

If my father's inspiration was largely responsible for getting me on the path of Jewish life and learning, my rebbe, R. Shlomo Carlebach *zt"l*, relit my flame when it was precariously low. He continues to be an inspiration and to infuse my life with meaning through my memories of him and, no less, through the *chevre*, my closest friends. Knowing winks to Josh and Orli Lauffer, Micha and Naama Odenheimer, Menachem and Batya Kallus, Ya'akov and Chava Sack, Steve and Andrea Peskoff, the other Thursday nighters, and good friends back in the States. Among the latter, special thanks for love and support to David and Jane Blumenstein, Ruth Fagen and Jeff Bocarsly, Lisa Epstein, and Marc Epstein.

My children, Ketoret Shalva (11), Levana Meira (9), Yoel Shlomo (7), and Nehora Sherei Leah (4), have probably seen quite a bit more of their father than most children do nowadays, so I won't apologize to them here for bearing the cost of my scholarship. On the contrary, my scholarship must bear the cost of my insatiable love of them. My wife, Hadas, and I have also managed to pursue our love affair since late 1985 despite the pressures of work and children, and if I needn't apologize, I must thank her for everything. My love for her is sweeter than honey and stronger than death.